THREE
VIEWS
ON

THE RAPTURE
PRETRIBULATION, PREWRATH, OR POSTTRIBULATION

Books in the Counterpoints Series

Church Life

Bible and Theology

SECOND EDITION WITH
NEW CONTRIBUTORS

THREE
VIEWS
ON

THE RAPTURE
PRETRIBULATION, PREWRATH, OR POSTTRIBULATION

Pretribulation Rapture: Craig Blaising

Prewrath Rapture: Alan Hultberg

Posttribulation Rapture: Douglas Moo

Stanley N. Gundry, series editor
Alan Hultberg, general editor

COUNTERPOINTS
► BIBLE & THEOLOGY ◄

ZONDERVAN®

ZONDERVAN.com/
AUTHORTRACKER
follow your favorite authors

ZONDERVAN

Three Views on the Rapture
Copyright © 2010 by Alan Hultberg, Craig Blaising, and Douglas Moo
Copyright © 1984, 1996 by Zondervan

This title is also available as a Zondervan ebook. Visit www.zondervan.com/ebooks.

This title is also available in a Zondervan audio edition. Visit www.zondervan.fm.

Requests for information should be addressed to:

Zondervan, *Grand Rapids, Michigan 49530*

Library of Congress Cataloging-in-Publication Data

Hultberg, Alan, 1962-
        Three views on the Rapture : pretribulation, prewrath, posttribulation Rapture / Alan Hultberg,
    [also] general editor, Craig Blaising, Douglas Moo.
        p. cm. — (Counterpoints)
        Rev. ed. of: Three views on the Rapture / Gleason L. Archer, Jr. et al. c1996.
        Includes bibliographical references and index.
        ISBN 978-0-310-27720-0 (softcover)
        1. Rapture (Christian eschatology) 2. Tribulation (Christian eschatology) I. Blaising, Craig A. II.
    Moo, Douglas J. III. Three views on the Rapture. IV. Title.
    BT887.R37 2010
    236'.9 — dc22   2010019272

Cover design: *Tammy Johnson*
Cover photography: *Visuals Unlimited / Masterfile*
Interior design: *Matthew VanZomeren*

Printed in the United States of America

QG 09-18-15

11 12 13 14 15 /QG/ 23 22 21 20 19 18 17 16 15 14 13 12 11 10 9 8 7 6 5 4 3 2

CONTENTS ████████████████████

LIST OF ABBREVIATIONS

AB	Anchor Bible
ABD	*Anchor Bible Dictionary.* Edited by D. N. Freedman. 6 vols. New York, 1992.
AnBib	Analecta biblica
ApocAb	*Apocalypse of Abraham*
BAGD	Bauer, W., W. F. Arndt, F. W. Gingrich, and F. W. Danker. *Greek-English Lexicon of the New Testament and Other Early Christian Literature.* 2nd ed. Chicago, 1979.
BDAG	Bauer, W., F. W. Danker, W. F. Arndt, and F. W. Gingrich. *Greek-English Lexicon of the New Testament and Other Early Christian Literature.* 3rd ed. Chicago, 1999.
BDF	Blass, F., A. Debrunner, and R. W. Funk. *A Greek Grammar of the New Testament and Other Early Christian Literature.* Chicago, 1961.
BECNT	Baker Exegetical Commentary on the New Testament
BNTC	Black's New Testament Commentary
BSac	*Bibliotheca sacra*
CBQMS	Catholic Biblical Quarterly Monograph Series
CGTC	Cambridge Greek Testament Commentary
CNT	Commentaire du Nouveau Testament
ConBNT	Coniectanea biblica: New Testament Series
EBC	Expositor's Bible Commentary
ESV	English Standard Version
ET	English Translation
ET	*Evangelische Theologie*
ExpTim	*Expository Times*
FOTL	Forms of the Old Testament Literature
GTJ	*Grace Theological Journal*
HKNT	Handkommentar zum Neuen Testament
HNT	Handbuch zum Neuen Testament
HNTC	Harper's New Testament Commentaries

HUCA	*Hebrew Union College Annual*
ICC	International Critical Commentary
IVPNTC	InterVarsity Press New Testament Commentary
JBL	*Journal of Biblical Literature*
JETS	*Journal of the Evangelical Theological Society*
JSNT	*Journal for the Study of the New Testament*
JSNTSS	Journal for the Study of the New Testament: Supplement Series
JSOT	*Journal for the Study of the Old Testament*
KBANT	Kommentare und Beiträge zum Alten und Neuen Testament
KJV	King James Version
LSJ	Liddell, H. G., R. Scott, H. S. Jones, *A Greek-English Lexicon*, 9th ed. with revised supplement. Oxford, 1996.
LXX	Septuagint
MNTC	Moffatt New Testament Commentary
MT	Masoretic Text
NAC	New American Commentary
NASB	New American Standard Bible
NCB	New Century Bible
NCBC	New Cambridge Bible Commentary
NET	New English Translation (NET Bible)
NICNT	New International Commentary on the New Testament
NIDNTT	*New International Dictionary of New Testament Theology*. Edited by Colin Brown. 4 vols. Grand Rapids, 1975–85.
NIGTC	New International Greek Testament Commentary
NIV	New International Version
NIVAC	New International Version Application Commentary
NLT	New Living Translation
NovTSup	Novum Testamentum Supplements
NSBT	New Studies in Biblical Theology
NTAbh	Neutestamentliche Abhandlungen
NTS	*New Testament Studies*
NTTS	New Testament Tools and Studies

PNTC	Pillar New Testament Commentary
SJT	*Scottish Journal of Theology*
SNTSMS	Society for New Testament Studies Monograph Series
SP	Sacra pagina
TNIV	Today's New International Version
TNTC	Tyndale New Testament Commentaries
TOTC	Tyndale Old Testament Commentaries
TUGAL	Texte und Untersuchungen zur Geschichte der altchristlichen Literatur
WBC	Word Biblical Commentary
WTJ	*Westminster Theological Journal*
ZAW	*Zeitschrift für die altestamentliche Wissenschaft*

INTRODUCTION

ALAN HULTBERG

This is a book debating the timing of the rapture. The *rapture* is a theological term that refers to the "catching up" of the church to meet the Lord in the air in association with his return and with the resurrection of believers. The term comes from the Latin verb *rapio* ("I seize," "I [violently] carry off"), which is the Vulgate's equivalent of the root Greek verb *harpazō* ("I seize," "I snatch away") that Paul uses in 1 Thessalonians 4:17, the primary text that teaches this concept. In this passage, Paul writes:

> According to the Lord's word, we tell you that we who are still alive, who are left till the coming of the Lord, will certainly not precede those who have fallen asleep. For the Lord himself will come down from heaven, with a loud command, with the voice of the archangel and with the trumpet call of God, and the dead in Christ will rise first. After that, we who are still alive and are left will be caught up (*harpagēsometha*) together with them in the clouds to meet the Lord in the air. And so we will be with the Lord forever. (1 Thess. 4:15–17)

Though 1 Thessalonians 4:17 is the only verse in Scripture that explicitly teaches the rapture, two other passages have been deemed to teach it more or less implicitly. In John 14:2, Jesus tells his disciples that, despite his soon departure, he is going to his Father's house to prepare a place for them. He then adds in verse 3, "And if I go and prepare a place for you, I will come back and take you to be with me that you also may be where I am." Here, Jesus' "taking" his disciples to be with him at his second coming is surely equivalent to Paul's rapture teaching in 1 Thessalonians 4. Similarly, 1 Corinthians 15:51–52, while not explicitly mentioning the rapture, notes the change from mortality to immortality that will overcome living believers "in a flash, in the twinkling of an eye, at the last trumpet. For the trumpet will sound, the dead will be raised imperishable, and we will be changed." It is the association of this instantaneous change to immortality with the resurrection of the dead in Christ that ties the event to the rapture of 1 Thessalonians 4. Still other passages have been considered relevant to a discussion of the rapture, including, for example, Matthew 24:31; 2 Thessalonians 1:10; and Revelation 14:14–16, but these are contested, and the main doctrine is established on the former three.

The Question of the Timing of the Rapture

Modern debate concerning the rapture has not so much to do with its reality[1] as with its timing. This is especially true among modern premillennialists, those who hold that, in accordance with a literal reading of Revelation 20:1–6, Jesus will establish a temporary earthly kingdom (the "millennium," from *mille anni*, Latin for "one thousand years") following his second coming.[2] According to the usual premillennial eschatology,[3] which is based on a futurist reading of Daniel, the Olivet Discourse (Matt. 24–25, pars.), Paul (especially the Thessalonian correspondence), and Revelation, the final seven years of this age, the so-called "seventieth week of Daniel" (Dan. 9:24–27; cf. 12:1–13), will be dominated by the ultimate, satanically inspired, imperial opponent of God and his people, the Antichrist. The final seven years will begin when the Antichrist makes a covenant with Israel (Dan. 9:27). Three and one-half years after making this covenant, however, he will

---

1. But see N. T. Wright, *The Resurrection of the Son of God*, Christian Origins and the Question of God, vol. 3 (Minneapolis: Fortress, 2003), 215. Both Tertullian (*The Soul* 55; *Against Marcion* 3.25; 5.20) and Origen (*First Principles* 2.11.5) argue that the rapture proves that God redeems the body for a heavenly destiny, indicating that some in the early centuries of the church thought otherwise, but the discussion seems to take the reality of the rapture for granted.

2. The other major eschatological systems are amillennialism, which understands the reign of Christ in Revelation 20:1–6 to be spiritual and heavenly and to have begun at his ascension in the first century AD and concluded at his second coming, and postmillennialism, which understands the millennium to be a long, final period of time before the second coming in which the fully Christianized world will be governed according to the dictates of Jesus and be concluded when Christ returns in glory. Amillennialists and postmillennialists often do not anticipate a future tribulation under an Antichrist, understanding the Scriptures that speak of this period as either fulfilled in the destruction of Jerusalem in AD 70 or in the general persecutions of the church in the current age.

3. The eschatology outlined here and the texts cited for each element are not intended to prejudge the question that will be debated in this book. Many modern premillennialists, including contributors to this volume, will want to nuance this outline or even reject it outright, but in general it fairly represents the traditional futurist eschatology of premillennialists.

INTRODUCTION • Alan Hultberg • 13

desecrate the Jerusalem temple by setting up the "abomination of desolation" (Dan. 9:27; 11:31; 12:11; Matt. 24:15; Mark 13:14), which Paul apparently interprets as his taking his seat in the temple and proclaiming himself to be God (2 Thess. 2:3–4; cf. Dan. 11:36; Rev. 13:8, 11–15). Thereafter, the Antichrist will severely persecute God's people for a final three and one-half years (Dan. 12:1, 11; cf. 7:25; Matt. 24:15–22; Mark 13:14–20; Rev. 11:7; 12:1–6; 12:13–13:8), at the end of which Christ will return, destroy the Antichrist and his followers, and establish his earthly kingdom (Dan. 7:13–14, 21–27; Matt. 24:29–31; Mark 13:24–27; 2 Thess. 2:8–12; Rev. 19:11–20:6; cf. 1 Thess. 1:5–11; 2 Thess. 1:6–10).

In particular, the debate centers around whether the rapture will occur before, during, or after this final seven-year period. Because the modern circles in which this debate developed often referred to these final seven years as "the tribulation," the sides of the debate have been labeled *pretribulationism, midtribulationism*, and *posttribulationism*. Pretribulationists hold that the rapture will occur before the final seven-year period; midtribulationists hold that it will occur during the final period, sometime soon after the abomination of desolation; and posttribulationists hold that it will occur at the very end of the final seven years.[4] Frequently, midtribulationists and posttribulationists deny that the entire seventieth week can properly be called the tribulation, since in Daniel and the Olivet Discourse that language focuses on the period of persecution following the abomination of desolation. Thus some midtribulationists have preferred the language of "mid-seventieth-week rapture" to refer to their position, though posttribulationists remain posttribulationists no matter when the tribulation begins.

A dividing issue between mid- and posttribulationists on the one hand and pretribulationists on the other is whether the church will experience persecution under the Antichrist. Mid- and posttribulationists hold that it will; pretribulationists that it will not since it will have been raptured before the Antichrist begins his reign of terror. More recently, midtribulationism has been supplanted by "prewrath rapturism," which posits, like midtribulationism, that the rapture occurs after

---

4. Another view, "partial rapturism," understood the rapture to occur before the tribulation but posited that only a portion of the church, watchful believers, would be "raptured." The rest would go through the tribulation.

the abomination of desolation and before the end of Daniel's seventieth week, but which emphasizes the association of the rapture not with the middle of the week, as in midtribulationism, but with the beginning of the outpouring of God's wrath on the unbelieving world some time during the last half of the week. In this book, the debate will be carried on by representatives of the pretribulational, posttribulational, and prewrath rapture views.

In addition to the basic issue of the timing of the rapture, the related issue of the nature of Christ's return separates pre- and midtribulationism from posttribulationism. In the former two, the second coming, or parousia (from Gk. *parousia*, "coming, presence"), is a two-stage event, beginning with the rapture (Christ's coming for his church) and culminating with his return to earth (his coming in vengeance and glory; in older literature often referred to as his coming "with" his church). No such distinction is possible (or required) in posttribulationism; Christ's coming for his church is equivalent to his return to earth. In this view, the church is caught up to meet the returning Lord in the air and to return immediately with him to the earth in glory. The debate about the timing of the rapture, then, besides considering direct evidence of the timing and evidence concerning the relation of the church to the Antichrist, also considers evidence of a two-stage second coming. Evidence for a two-stage coming counts for pre- or midtribulationism; evidence against a two-stage coming counts for posttribulationism.

The debate regarding the timing of the rapture developed especially during the nineteenth and twentieth centuries among British and American evangelicals after a resurgence of interest in futurist eschatology.[5] The earliest Christian writings we possess after the New Testament indicate no real question in the first three centuries of the church regarding the timing of the rapture. The basic futurist (and premillen-

---

5. On the history of the modern debate regarding the timing of the rapture, see Richard R. Reiter, "A History of the Development of the Rapture Positions," in *The Rapture: Pre-, Mid-, or Post-Tribulational*, by Gleason L. Archer Jr. (gen. ed.), Paul D. Feinberg, Douglas Moo, and Richard Reiter (Grand Rapids: Zondervan, 1984), 11–44; and J. Barton Payne, *The Imminent Appearing of Christ* (Grand Rapids: Eerdmans, 1962), 30–42. For earlier periods, see ibid., 11–29; George Eldon Ladd, *The Blessed Hope: A Biblical Study of the Second Advent and the Rapture* (Grand Rapids: Eerdmans, 1956), 19–46; Robert H. Gundry, *The Church and the Tribulation: A Biblical Examination of Posttribulationism* (Grand Rapids: Zondervan, 1973), 172–88.

nial) eschatology appears to have been taken for granted by most,[6] and the rapture, when it was discussed at all, was assumed to be contemporaneous with the return of Christ to earth to establish his kingdom; that is, to be posttribulational.[7] At the very least, where they speak of it, the ante-Nicene fathers consistently maintained that the church would witness the abomination of desolation and experience persecution under the Antichrist.[8] As time went on, due to certain philosophical, religious, and political factors, premillennialism fell out of favor among most theologians, as did a futurist reading of the texts upon which the "classic" premillennial eschatology was built.[9]

From the Middle Ages to the opening of the nineteenth century, other eschatological opinions were ascendant, including especially amillennialism (the teaching that Christ's kingdom is spiritual and contemporaneous with the church age) and historicism (the teaching that Daniel and Revelation are prophecies about the history of the church, usually denying a future Antichrist and tribulation),[10] though postmillennialism (the teaching that the kingdom of Christ would be realized when the church Christianized the world sometime before the return of Christ) became popular toward the end of this period. The issue of the timing of the rapture was a nonquestion in these traditions.

---

6. See, e.g., Papias (in Irenaeus, *Against Heresies* 5.33.3); Justin, *Dialogue with Trypho* 110; Irenaeus, *Against Heresies* 5.25–26, 35; Hippolytus, *Treatise on Christ and Antichrist* 60–67. Cf. Tertullian, *Against Marcion* 3.25. Justin, *Dialogue with Trypho* 80, however, famously acknowledges the existence of orthodox nonpremillennialists in his day; cf. Irenaeus, *Against Heresies* 5.31–32.1. For a focused study on ante-Nicene nonpremillennialism, see Charles E. Hill, *Regnum Caelorum: Patterns of Millennial Thought in Early Christianity*, 2nd ed. (Grand Rapids: Eerdmans, 2001).

7. E.g., Tertullian, *On the Resurrection of the Flesh* 24–25, 41; Methodius, *The Banquet of the Ten Virgins* 6.4.

8. *Didache* 16; *Ep. Barn.* 4.9–14; Justin, *Dialogue with Trypho* 110; Irenaeus, *Against Heresies* 5.25–26, 35; Tertullian, *On the Resurrection of the Flesh*, 25, 41; *Apostolic Constitutions* 7.2.32; Hippolytus, *Treatise on Christ and Antichrist* 60–61; Commodianus, *Instruction* 44; Victorinus, *Commentary on Revelation*; Methodius, *The Banquet of the Ten Virgins* 6.4.

9. For a brief overview of the decline of futurist premillennialism after Augustine, see Ladd, *Blessed Hope*, 31–34; Payne, *Imminent Appearing*, 19–30; Ian S. Rennie, "Nineteenth-Century Roots of Contemporary Prophetic Interpretation," in *Dreams, Visions, and Oracles: The Layman's Guide to Biblical Prophecy*, ed. Carl Edwin Armerding and W. Ward Gasque (Grand Rapids: Baker, 1977), 43–44.

10. A notable exception was the Jesuit Ribera and other Catholic counter-reformationists who followed him. In opposition to Protestant historicism, which identified the papacy with the Antichrist, Ribera argued in his commentary on Revelation for a future, personal Antichrist who would persecute the church before the return of Christ. See Ladd, *Blessed Hope*, 37–38; Payne, *Imminent Appearing*, 30.

By the beginning of the nineteenth century, however, premillennialism enjoyed a resurgence, and with it a futurist reading of Daniel and Revelation.[11]

Impetus for this resurgence was gained at prophetic conferences first in England and later in the United States, most important for our survey being those at Albury Park and Powerscourt House in the British Isles in the early 1800s and at Niagra, Ontario, and later Long Island, New York, in the later 1800s and early 1900s. It was at Albury Park and Powerscourt in the 1830s that Church of Scotland pastor Edward Irving and Brethren leader John Darby began to teach a pretribulational "secret" rapture[12] over against the predominant posttribulational position.[13] As a result of several preaching tours in the United States conducted by Darby from 1859 to 1874, Darby's theological views, and in particular his futurist prophetic views, including pretribulationism, became widely adopted there. By the late 1800s, at the Niagra Bible Conferences, pretribulationism and posttribulationism competed for dominance among American premillennialists, and by 1920 it was pretribulationism that had essentially won the day.[14]

While advocates for posttribulationism (and midtribulationism, a minority position) were productive in the middle decades of the twentieth century, it was not until the publication in 1956 of *The Blessed Hope* by George Eldon Ladd that posttribulationism began to make a comeback, solidified especially by Robert H. Gundry's more exegetical

---

11. Prior to and during the early resurgence of the popularity of premillennialism, what premillennialists there were, were generally historicist in their understanding of the prophecies of Daniel and Revelation.

12. Darby also taught at this time other tenets of what came to be known as "dispensationalism," including especially the distinction between the church and Israel in God's economy, which "historic" posttribulational premillennialists rejected. On the origins of modern pretribulationism, see Ladd, *Blessed Hope*, 40–44; Payne, *Imminent Appearing*, 31–34; Gundry, *Church and Tribulation*, 185–88; Rennie, "Roots," 46–57; Dave MacPherson, *The Unbelievable Pre-Trib Origin* (Kansas City: Heart of America Bible Society, 1973)—the first of several books of his on the issue—but cf. Rennie, "Roots," 51–52. Although recent dispensationalists have rightly argued there is no necessary connection between dispensationalism and pretribulationism (e.g., Gundry, cited approvingly by Paul D. Feinberg, "The Case for the Pretribulation Rapture Position," in Archer, Feinberg, Moo, and Reiter, *The Rapture*, 48–49), it nevertheless remains the case that pretribulationism has been primarily a position of dispensationalists since its inception.

13. Darby was opposed especially by Brethren scholar Samuel Tregelles, *The Hope of Christ's Second Coming: How Is It Taught in Scripture? And Why?* (London/Plymouth: n.p., 1864).

14. For a detailed study of this period, see Reiter, "History," 11–30.

work, *The Church and the Tribulation*, published in 1973.[15] By 1980 the playing field had, to a degree, leveled, resulting in a formal debate at the 1981 annual conference of the Evangelical Free Church in America. Here, three members of the faculty of the EFCA seminary, Trinity Evangelical Divinity School, each an advocate of one of the three positions, argued the cases for and against pre-, mid-, and posttribulationism. Their debate was published in 1984 as *The Rapture: Pre-, Mid-, or Post-Tribulational?* The present book is an attempt to bring *The Rapture* up to date.

In *The Rapture: Pre-, Mid-, or Post-Tribulational?* pretribulationism was argued by Paul D. Feinberg. Feinberg's case consisted of four main theses. First, Feinberg argued that the Bible promises the church exemption from the divine wrath that will be poured out during Daniel's seventieth week, and that since the period of divine wrath includes the entire week, the church must be protected during the entire week. Second, he argued that, more specifically, Revelation 3:10 promises that the exemption from divine wrath includes exemption from the actual period of time in which the wrath is poured out — that is, Revelation 3:10 promises removal from the earth prior to Daniel's seventieth week. Third, Feinberg contended that the biblical requirement of "nonglorified" believers entering the millennial kingdom necessitates an interval of time between the rapture and the return of Christ to earth to establish his kingdom. A posttribulational rapture allows no such time, and a midtribulational rapture allows insufficient time. Only a pretribulation rapture, in his opinion, is sufficient for this requirement. And, fourth, Feinberg contended that a comparison of rapture and second advent passages in the New Testament demonstrates a distinction in kind between the two events. In some cases, significant omissions demonstrate the difference; in others, important contradictions do so.

---

15. Ladd was countered especially by John F. Walvoord, a leading pretribulationist, in *The Rapture Question* (Findlay, Ohio: Dunham, 1957) and in *The Blessed Hope and the Tribulation: A Historical and Biblical Study of Posttribulationism* (Grand Rapids: Zondervan, 1976), 40–59. The classic defense of posttribulationism (and critique of pretribulationism) was produced earlier by Alexander Reese, *The Approaching Advent of Christ: An Examination of the Teaching of J. N. Darby and His Followers* (London/Edinburgh: Marshall, Morgan and Scott, 1937). Gundry was countered especially by John A. Sproule, *In Defense of Pretribulationism* (Winona Lake, Ind.: BMH, 1980), and John F. Walvoord in *The Blessed Hope*, 60–69.

The midtribulation proponent in the book, Gleason L. Archer Jr., seems generally to have accepted these theses in essence, though he disagreed with Feinberg that the divine wrath would be executed during the entire seven-year period of Daniel's seventieth week, maintaining instead that the structure of Revelation indicates that God's wrath will be poured out only in the second half of the week, while the church will experience the wrath of the Antichrist during the first half. On the other hand, the proponent of posttribulationism, Douglas Moo, took issue with the entirety of Feinberg's argument. He considered Feinberg's exegesis flawed with regard to the timing of the outpouring of God's wrath, the nature of the exemption from wrath promised to the church, and the distinction between rapture and second advent texts. Additionally, Moo argued against any theological necessity of the church being removed from the earth in order to be protected from the machinations of the Antichrist and the wrath of God, since, on the one hand, God has allowed his people in the past both to experience tribulation and at times experience divine protection in the midst of an outpouring of divine wrath, and on the other will manifestly do so even under the pretribulational schema for the "tribulation saints."

Moo's own case for posttribulationism rested on some of these foregoing assertions and was pursued through five basic lines of inquiry. He asked first whether there is any necessary theological reason the church cannot be present during the final period of God's wrath; second, whether the language for Christ's second advent in Scripture demands a distinction between the rapture and the return to earth; third, whether "clear" rapture texts (John 14:1–4; 1 Cor. 15:51–55; 1 Thess. 4:13–18) indicate the timing of the rapture; fourth, whether other related texts (1 Thess. 5:1–11; 2 Thess. 1:5–7; Matt. 24:1–31; various passages in Revelation) imply the timing of the rapture; and fifth, whether the concept of imminence in Scripture demands an "any-moment" rapture. In the case of the first, second, and fifth questions, Moo answered in the negative. On the third and fourth questions, however, Moo argued that careful exegesis of most of the "clear" and related rapture texts indicates a posttribulational rapture, since in various ways they either relate the church to the coming of Christ in wrath or to the time of the vindication of Israel, both of which he understands as posttribulational. His argument is concluded by a comparison of the eschatological events presented in the major parousia texts of the New Testament, demonstrating their similarity and relatedness and allowing each, then, to attest to a posttribulational rapture.

Both Feinberg and Archer, to one degree or another, reject Moo's equation of texts, suggesting instead that a close reading of especially 1 Thessalonians 4–5 and Revelation 3:10 shows that what Moo conflates into a single event ought to be separated into multiple events. They argue that, on the one hand, a two-stage parousia consisting of the rapture to escape God's wrath followed some time later by the return of Christ, and, on the other, multiple resurrections, better account for these passages. Feinberg further argues that Moo has overlooked elements of the Olivet Discourse that focus that passage on Israel rather than the church, so that the Pauline and Johannine texts that Moo relates to the Olivet Discourse to argue posttribulationism are irrelevant to the discussion.

Archer, for his part, made the alleged shortcomings of both pretribulationism and posttribulationism the cornerstone of his case for midtribulationism. He sought to show that neither pretribulationism nor posttribulationism is able to account for all the data and suggested that midtribulationism was left as an appropriately mediating position. Thus, he argued, posttribulationists cannot account for a first-century attitude of expectation, the sequence of events in 1 Thessalonians 4–5, the fact that the church will not experience God's wrath, the fact that the saints will return with Christ in Revelation 19:12, and the fact that "nonglorified" believers will enter the millennium. On the other hand, pretribulationists cannot account for the signs that are said to precede the rapture, not least the abomination of desolation. Only midtribulationism can account for both sets of facts. Archer also attempted a second, more positive argument for his position, but it is more difficult to follow, since he does not explicitly draw out its implications. First, he argued that the emphasis on the final three and one-half years of Antichrist activity in Daniel and Revelation indicates a significant shift in the Antichrist's focus after the abomination of desolation, presumably implying that the rapture's occurrence at that juncture best accounts for the shift. Second, he argued that Revelation 14:14–16 is a picture of the rapture that is followed by the return of Christ with his saints in Revelation 19:12. Based on his response to Feinberg, it seems he understood from the structure of Revelation that the wrath of God in Revelation 16–18 intervenes between the two events, thus making the rapture separate in time from the glorious return.

Neither Feinberg nor Moo found Archer's case compelling. Both argued that he had not established any connection between the rapture and the middle of the seventieth week, and neither found his arguments against their own positions decisive. Feinberg claimed that in his argument against pretribulationism, Archer confused second coming texts, which speak of preceding signs, and rapture texts, which do not. He further asserted that the New Testament expectancy of a first-century return of Christ is far more compatible with an "any-moment," that is, pretribulational, rapture than a rapture preceded by signs as required by both mid- and posttribulationism. Moo, while generally agreeing with Archer's case against pretribulationism, denied that any of the texts cited by Archer against posttribulationism were compelling. None clearly implied the significant temporal gap between the rapture and the second coming that Archer required; each could equally be read as posttribulational. Beyond that, Archer's application of Matthew 24 to the church in his argument against pretribulationism undermines his own case, since not only is the church warned of events in the middle of the week but also of events occurring in the second half of the "week," after the church would supposedly have been raptured.

The give and take format of *The Rapture*, though not producing a clear "winner," was helpful in defining the terms of the debate. Certain issues once deemed important, such as the theological necessity or lack thereof of the absence of the church from the tribulation and the significance of individual New Testament "second coming" terms, were either conceded as indecisive or achieved a stalemate in the debate. Two sorts of questions, however, did emerge from its pages as central. First were questions dealing with the church and God's wrath: When does divine wrath begin in relation to Daniel's seventieth week? What does it mean for the church to be exempt from divine wrath? Is there any exegetical basis for separating the rapture of the church from the return of Christ to earth by a period of divine wrath? Second were questions dealing with the relationship of eschatological "signs" to the church. These can be broadly summarized by asking about the nature of the Olivet Discourse and its relation to other parousia texts of the New

Testament. Is the Olivet Discourse to be understood as giving signs to the church of the coming of Christ? How do the signs in the Olivet Discourse relate especially to Paul's argument in the Thessalonian epistles and perhaps to the Revelation to John? Clearly other, more focused exegetical questions will assume importance as one attempts to answer these. The debate, however, seemed to shift from the theological and lexical to the more purely exegetical.

Rise of the Prewrath View

Though no "winner" clearly emerged from the debate in *The Rapture*, a clear "loser" did. While Archer's impulse to integrate what he saw as the strengths of pretribulationism and posttribulationism was relatively tenable, his attempt to tie the rapture to the very middle of Daniel's seventieth week failed for lack of evidence.[16] Such failure on the part of midtribulationism has led to a refinement of the basic position called "prewrath" rapturism.[17] Like midtribulationists, prewrath rapture proponents seek to integrate the primary thesis of pretribulationists, that the church will be raptured before the outpouring of God's wrath associated with the return of Christ, and the major thesis of posttribulationism, that the church will witness the abomination of desolation and experience persecution by the Antichrist.[18] Prewrath rapturism differs from midtribulationism in understanding the church to be persecuted by the Antichrist in the tribulation that follows the abomination of desolation and in understanding the wrath of God, equated with the biblical concept of the day of the Lord, to begin sometime in the midst of the second half of Daniel's seventieth week.

---

16. Attempts by other midtribulationists were similarly considered unsuccessful. J. Oliver Buswell (*A Systematic Theology of the Christian Religion*, vol. 2 [Grand Rapids: Zondervan, 1963], 390) linked the rapture to the resurrection of the two witnesses of Revelation 11:1–13, which he understood to occur three and one-half days after the abomination of desolation. His argument, however, never gained traction among scholars.

17. Major proponents of a prewrath rapture do not consider their position to be a refinement of midtribulationism, but in maintaining the basic inclination to integrate the strengths of pre- and posttribulationism, it can be so considered. See Robert Van Kampen, *The Rapture Question Answered: Plain and Simple* (Grand Rapids: Revell, 1997), 42.

18. Archer's scheme had the church experience Antichrist persecution during the first half of Daniel's seventieth week and be raptured shortly after the abomination of desolation. Buswell is closer to prewrath rapturism in that he has the church experience a brief, intense period of persecution (the great tribulation) after the abomination of desolation and be raptured immediately after it, when Jesus comes in wrath. Cf. Harold J. Ockenga, *The Church in God: Expository Values in Thessalonians* (Westwood, N.J.: Revell, 1956), 259, who also intimates a prewrath understanding.

The two earliest public proponents of the prewrath view were Robert Van Kampen, a Christian businessman and church leader, who had developed the position in the 1970s, and Marvin Rosenthal, now director of Zion's Hope, a Christian mission, whom Van Kampen had persuaded of the position in the late 1980s. The view was first published in 1990 in *The Pre-wrath Rapture of the Church* by Rosenthal.[19] This was followed up by the 1992 publication of *The Sign* by Van Kampen. Since then numerous other books and publications have appeared both supporting and critiquing the position.[20]

Rosenthal's argument for a prewrath rapture can be taken as representative. He posits two major theses: that the day of the Lord, the day of God's wrath, begins sometime during the last half of Daniel's seventieth week, immediately following the cosmic disturbances of Matthew 24:28–29 and Revelation 6:12–14, and that the rapture will occur immediately prior to the day of the Lord. In support of his first thesis, Rosenthal cites Matthew 24:22, 29–31 in combination with Revelation 6:12–17 and 8:1–11:15. He argues that these passages, which depend on Old Testament imagery for the day of the Lord, make the day of God's wrath (Rev. 6:17), summarized in the seventh seal and corresponding trumpet judgments, begin after a shortened tribulation period, a period that, according to Daniel 12:1 and Matthew 24:15–21, begins after the abomination of desolation. Corroborating evidence is found in the coming of "Elijah" in Revelation 11:3 (cf. Mal. 4:5), the trumpet sequence in Revelation 8:8–11:19 (as representative of Joel 2:1), and the sequence of events in 2 Thessalonians 2:1–4. In support of the second thesis, Rosenthal cites Luke 17:26–27, which compares the day of the Son of Man to the judgment of the antediluvian world, the latter of which began "on the day" Noah was rescued, thus implying that God's wrath begins to be poured out on the very day the church is raptured. Corresponding evidence is found in Revelation 7, where the church is pictured as raptured prior to the trumpet judgments; Mat-

---

19. Marvin J. Rosenthal, *The Pre-wrath Rapture of the Church: A New Understanding of the Rapture, the Tribulation, and the Second Coming* (Nashville: Nelson, 1990).

20. See especially, pro, H. L. Nigro, *Before God's Wrath: The Bible's Answer to the Timing of the Rapture*, rev. and exp. (Lancaster, Pa.: Strong Tower, 2004); and, contra, Paul S. Karleen, *The Pre-wrath Rapture of the Church: Is It Biblical?* (Langhorne, Pa.: BF Press, 1991); and Renald E. Showers, *The Pre-wrath Rapture View: An Examination and Critique* (Grand Rapids: Kregel, 2001).

thew 24:29–31; 1 Corinthians 15:51–52; 1 Thessalonians 4:16–17, in which the church is raptured at the cosmic disturbances and angelic trumpet that signals the day of wrath; Matthew 13:37–40; 24:14; 28:20, which indicate that the church age ends prior to the outpouring of God's wrath; and 1 Thessalonians 5:9, which promises the church deliverance from the coming wrath. In addition, Rosenthal spends a chapter rebutting arguments for a pretribulational rapture.[21]

Rosenthal's argument, then, while adopting the basic framework of midtribulationism, removes the problematic attachment of the rapture to the exact middle of Daniel's seventieth week found in that position. Instead, it allows the rapture to float free of specific events associated with the week. The rapture occurs in association with the onset of God's wrath on earth sometime in the last half of the seventieth week, signaled by the cosmic disturbances of Matthew 24:29 and Revelation 6:12–14. Responses to Rosenthal and Van Kampen, which have primarily come from pretribulationists, have thus focused especially on the exegesis establishing the relationship of the tribulation and time of God's wrath (or day of the Lord) to one another and to Daniel's seventieth week. A point of particular contention, which surfaced in the older debates but gains impetus with the emergence of the prewrath view, is whether the wrath of God in Revelation begins with the opening of the first seal (Rev. 6:1–2) or with the seventh (Rev. 8:1–5), the first seal usually being associated with the beginning of the seventieth week and the seventh with some point within the week. Similarly, the prewrath view has brought to heightened prominence the question of whether there is any depiction of the rapture in Revelation, especially whether the innumerable multitude in Revelation 7:9–17 represents the raptured church (taken to heaven from the great tribulation, or persecution, prior to the outpouring of God's wrath in Revelation 8–11; 16).

How This Book Will Work

This book seeks to further the debate begun by Archer, Feinberg, and Moo and advanced by Rosenthal. It will proceed as the former *Rapture* had, with primary essays arguing for a pretribulation, a prewrath,

---

21. Van Kampen's argument has similar elements but is much broader and somewhat more speculative than Rosenthal's.

and a posttribulation rapture, followed by responses from the advocates of the opposing positions. The original author of each essay will then present a rejoinder to the responses to his essay. A concluding chapter will summarize the debate and make suggestions for further study. It is hoped that readers will find this approach helpful as they consider the positions and search the Scriptures for themselves.

Though the issue of the timing of the rapture is not central to the Christian faith, it *is* an element of Scripture and of a well-informed eschatology. It also touches on the doctrine of the church and on issues of normative Christian experience, as will be seen in the chapters that follow. It is thus not an inconsequential doctrine but one that the church at large needs continually to wrestle with. We pray that this book will be of some small service to the church in that worthy endeavor.

A CASE FOR THE PRETRIBULATION RAPTURE

CRAIG BLAISING

Mention the word *rapture* these days and you will most likely get one of two responses. Some will have no clue what you are talking about. The word is a religious, theological term, and it is unfamiliar because, in an era of increasing secularism, theological knowledge and its technical vocabulary have greatly diminished in public discourse. Even the non-technical sense of the word *rapture*, meaning something like an ecstatic joy, a meaning that derives from the technical, theological use, has all but disappeared from common usage.

On the other hand, for many the word *rapture* is a key term whose very mention brings to mind a whole set of eschatological notions, ideas, terms, and images that have to do with the rescue of God's people from troubling times coming upon the earth. A person may not know much of the technical theological vocabulary for this eschatology. But if they are familiar with these ideas at all, they most likely do know the word *rapture*, and many of those who do know it will also know the word "tribulation," which speaks of the troubling times that form the context of the Lord's coming. In fact, in popular evangelical discourse, the ideas of rapture and tribulation are so closely associated that they are like two sides of a coin — the one always goes with the other.

The position being argued in this essay — that of pretribulation-ism — is a particular way of understanding the relationship of the rapture to the tribulation, a way that is quite popular in contemporary evangelical thought. Pretribulationism is the view that the rapture, the "catching up" of resurrected and translated believers to meet the coming

Christ in the air and be with him forever, precedes the tribulation, the time of trouble and judgment. At the climax of the tribulation, Christ will visibly descend to the earth with his saints to begin his millennial reign. In this view, the rapture is *pretribulational* because it takes place *before* the *tribulation*.

Most likely, people did not think much about the relationship of the rapture to the tribulation prior to the popularization of pretribulationism. The reason for this is that through much of the history of Christian thought, the second coming of Christ has been treated as if it is a singular event. At the appointed time, Christ will suddenly descend to earth in visible form. After that the final judgment will take place and then the commencement of eternal destinies. In fact, through much of the history of the church, these eschatological events of the second coming tended to be thought of as the transition between time and eternity, a transition that would take place suddenly and definitely as time came to an end.

This simple view of eschatology was challenged by modern premillennialism, which proposed a more complex understanding of end-time events. Premillennialism predicted a one-thousand-year reign of Christ on earth between the second coming and the eternal state. Such a reign divided both the eschatological judgment and the resurrection of the dead into phases separated in time. Furthermore, modern premillennialism brought a renewed interest in the "tribulational" conditions of the second coming. Whereas medieval theology had equated the tribulation either with the early history or the long, ongoing history of the church, modern premillennialism became a forum for the consideration and testing of a futurist view of the tribulation, seeing it as a future time of trouble that would lead to and be the context for the second coming of Christ.

Working out the interpretation of biblical eschatology into a temporal sequence involving a future tribulation and a future millennium has consistently been affirmed by premillennialists as proper to a historical, grammatical, literary reading of the biblical text. But it raises a number of problems that were glossed over by earlier medieval hermeneutics. In the working out of these problems, aiming at a consistent interpretation, some premillennialists in the early nineteenth century proposed the interpretation of the pretribulational rapture.

In what follows, I will present what I believe to be the argument for pretribulationism. This argument is an interpretation of the relationship of the rapture to the day of the Lord as presented by the apostle Paul in his letters to the Thessalonians, understood in the greater canonical context of the teaching of Jesus and the Old Testament prophets. Before concluding, we will also consider implications from the book of Revelation and the way in which pretribulationism harmonizes some aspects of premillennialism. At the end, I will comment on the relationship of pretribulationism to dispensational thought.

The Rapture and the Day of the Lord

We begin with the text that most clearly designates the rapture, 1 Thessalonians 4:13–18. In the first chapter of this letter, Paul describes the Thessalonian Christians as waiting for the Lord to come from heaven and deliver them from the wrath to come (1:10). Apprehension had apparently arisen concerning believers who die before his coming. They will not be lost, Paul assures his readers; when the Lord comes, he will raise them from the dead. How that will happen is described in 4:16: "For the Lord himself will come down from heaven, with a loud command, with the voice of the archangel and with the trumpet call of God, and the dead in Christ will rise first.

After resurrecting the dead in Christ, the Lord will then "snatch up" living believers together with them to meet him "on the clouds," and "in the air." After that, we who are still alive and are left will be caught up together with them in the clouds to meet the Lord in the air. And so we will be with the Lord forever (4:17). The Greek verb *harpagēsometha*, translated "caught up" in 1 Thessalonians 4:17, is more vividly rendered "snatched up" (NET note), correctly indicating a sudden, forceful removal of the whole lot of resurrected and living believers up to the presence of the Lord.[1] This is the same verb that is used in Acts 8:39 to describe how the Spirit of the Lord "snatched away" (NET; Gk., *hērpasen*) Philip after the baptism of the Ethiopian eunuch.[2] In the Vulgate, *harpagēsometha* is translated *rapiemur*, from *rapio*, and it is from that word that the English word *rapture* is derived. Accordingly, 1 Thessalonians 4:17 would be correctly rendered "Then we who are alive, who are left, will be *raptured* together with them."

---

1. BAGD, s.v. *harpazō*: "snatch, seize, i.e., take suddenly and vehemently, or take away … (2b) in such a way that no resistance is offered" (109).

2. Other uses of *harpazō* to describe being caught up into heaven can be found in 2 Cor. 12:2, 4, and Rev. 12:5.

The immediate purpose of the rapture in 1 Thessalonians 4:17 is to meet the Lord in the air. The phrase "to meet the Lord," *eis apantēsin tou kyriou*, as many have pointed out, was used of a welcoming delegation coming out of a city to receive and accompany an arriving dignitary.[3] The assembling of the saints around the coming Lord surely carries this connotation, but with certain differences. First, it is not actually a delegation that meets him but the whole company of saints, those previously dead now resurrected and those alive at his coming. Second, they do not "go out" to meet him at their own discretion, but they are "snatched up" by the Lord, who has descended apparently for this very purpose of rapturing them. Third, the text says nothing about their accompanying him on the completion of his descent; rather, Paul concludes his description of the event with the assembly in heaven, encouraged by the fact that "we will always be with the Lord" (NET).[4] In other words, while the notions of greeting and accompanying an arriving dignitary are not absent from the image being conveyed here, there is another image at work complicating and dominating the overall picture. This other image is that of a rescue. The Lord rescues dead saints from death (this is further developed in 1 Corinthians 15), and with them he snatches up living saints, who were described in 1:10 as waiting for him to come from heaven and deliver them from the wrath to come.[5] He raptures them to deliver them from a coming wrath. Once the wrath is completed, we may assume on the basis of the other image

---

3. Many have argued this point. For a recent discussion of the metaphor, see Gene L. Green, *The Letters to the Thessalonians*, PNTC (Grand Rapids: Eerdmans, 2002), 226–28.

4. Wanamaker believes that a return to the earth is not in the teaching of this text. "Apart from the possible connotation that *apantēsin* might have for a return to earth, the rest of the imagery (the clouds and being caught up to the Lord) are indicative of an assumption to heaven of the people who belong to Christ. That Paul adds his own definitive statement concerning the significance of this meeting in the clause *kai houtōs pantote sun kuriō esometha* ('and thus we will always be with the Lord') suggests that both dead and living Christians will return to heaven with the Lord, not only to enjoy continuous fellowship with him, but also, in terms of 1:10, to be saved from the coming wrath of God" (Charles A. Wanamaker, *The Epistles to the Thessalonians*, NIGTC [Grand Rapids: Eerdmans, 1990], 175). Bruce also expresses his reservations on an immediate return in F. F. Bruce, *1 and 2 Thessalonians*, WBC (Nashville: Nelson, 1982), 103.

5. We do not need to develop here the idea of the transformation, or translation, that will be granted to the living at the point of the rapture. For this, one can turn to 1 Cor. 15:50–57; Phil. 3:20–21; and 2 Cor. 5:4–5. The first two texts have marked similarities to 1 Thess. 1:10 and 4:15–16, both being set at the time of the Lord's coming, and together with the last express the joyful hope of being changed into immortality.

that the whole assembly would then accompany him in the completion of his expected return.

In 1 Thessalonians 5, Paul turns to the matter of how believers should live in light of the coming "day of the Lord." The day of the Lord is a well-known theme in the Old Testament Prophets indicating a climactic outpouring of divine wrath. Israel was warned about a coming day of the Lord that manifested itself in the destruction of the northern kingdom in 721 BC.[6] The Babylonian invasion and destruction of the southern kingdom involving eventually the siege and overthrow of Jerusalem and the destruction of the temple in 586 BC were prophesied as a day of the Lord.[7] However, many prophecies spoke of the later destructions that would come upon these invaders and other nations complicit with them as being days of the Lord, God visiting his wrath upon them for their wickedness and hostility toward the people of God.[8] Some of these prophecies contain predictions that are global in scope.[9] They resonate with yet another group of day of the Lord prophecies that are mostly postexilic and foresee a yet future day of judgment coming against the whole world for its evil and sin.[10]

These days of the Lord are similar in description, with literary features that are oftentimes repeated. They are days of darkness, dread, and gloom. The earth and the heavens are shaken. People are gripped in terror as destruction and death come upon them. They are days of battle and slaughter—a sacrifice to appease the wrath of God. The repetition of such elements among the days of the Lord forms a literary type, and this type carries forward into the predictions of an ultimate day in which God's wrath is yet to be poured out. That day will be a time in which the Lord once again gathers the nations into war, but it will be the Lord who will fight against them. Fear and terror will seize them, the earth will be shaken, the heavens will be darkened, and death will overtake them. The proud and arrogant will be humbled, the wicked will be consumed, and both idols and idolaters will be destroyed. But

---

6. See Hos. 1:4–5; Amos 2:13–16; 3:14; 5:18, 20; 8:1–9:10.

7. See, e.g., Isa. 22:1–14; Ezek. 7:1–27; Zeph. 1:1–3:8.

8. See Isa. 13:1–22; 34:1–17; Jer. 46:1–12; Ezek. 30:1–19; Obad. 1–21; Nah. 1:1–3:19.

9. See, e.g., Isa. 13:11.

10. See, e.g., Isa. 2:12–21; 24:1–23; Joel 2:30–3:16; Zech. 12:1–13:9; 14:1–15; Mal. 3:1–4; 4:1–6.

the Lord will be a refuge for his people. He will save them, sanctify them, and bring them into the rich blessings of his kingdom. The Old Testament in fact ends on just this note, with Malachi's prophecy of the coming day of the Lord, which will bring judgment to the wicked and deliverance to the righteous (Mal 4:1–6).

The New Testament picks up this theme with both John the Baptist and Jesus addressing the coming judgment and the salvation that God will provide.[11] Although the Gospels do not per se use the phrase "day of the Lord," the expression reappears in the Epistles, often altered to reflect the New Testament understanding that Jesus is the Lord who comes on that day to execute divine judgment and deliver the righteous.[12]

In this sense, Paul references the day of the Lord in 1 Thessalonians 5 after talking about the coming of the Lord to rapture the saints who have been waiting for him to deliver them from the coming wrath. The day of the Lord is the broader eschatological event that connects these themes. And it is in consideration of both of these themes that Paul proceeds to make his parenetic point.

Paul reminds the Thessalonians that the day of the Lord will arrive suddenly and unexpectedly, coming "like a thief in the night" (1 Thess. 5:2). The point of the metaphor was made by Jesus, who, after using it, said, "If the owner of the house had known at what time of night the thief was coming, he would have kept watch and would not have let his house be broken into" (Matt. 24:43). Just as one has no idea when a thief will come, so one does not know when the day of the Lord will begin. Its sudden arrival will surprise people (5:4), who will have no clue from conditions that prevailed before its onset. In fact, those conditions will be exactly opposite that of the day of the Lord itself ("peace and safety" versus "sudden destruction," 5:3).

---

11. See, e.g., John the Baptist's message in Matt. 3:7–12 (Luke 3:7–17).

12. So, e.g., 1 Cor. 1:7–8 speaks of the Corinthians waiting for the revealing of our Lord Jesus Christ, "who will sustain you to the end, guiltless in *the day of our Lord Jesus Christ*" (ESV, emphasis added). In 2 Tim. 4:8, Paul speaks of "the crown of righteousness, which the Lord, the righteous judge, will award to me on that Day, and not only to me but also to all who have loved his appearing" (ESV; cf. also 4:1, which speaks of the appearing of Christ Jesus "who is to judge the living and the dead" [ESV]). Second Peter also thematically connects questions about the coming of Jesus to the coming of "the day of the Lord" (3:10) or "day of God" (3:12), just as Paul connects questions about the coming of the day of the Lord to the theme of "the coming of our Lord Jesus Christ" in 2 Thess. 2:1–2.

Paul's next point is that although the day of the Lord will arrive suddenly, the effect of its arrival will be completely different for those who belong to Christ and those who do not. Paul makes this point by a careful distinction between second and third person plural pronouns: "While *people* are saying, "Peace and safety," destruction will come on *them* suddenly ... and *they* will not escape. But *you*, brothers, are not in darkness so that this day should surprise *you* like a thief" (1 Thess. 5:3–4, emphasis added). The verb *katalabē* ("overtake"; see NET) conveys the idea of seizure with hostile intent.[13] Paul's point is that the onset of the day is the onset of destruction on "them," as if they were seized by an enemy intent on doing them harm. But its sudden arrival will not bring destruction on "you," for "they" belong to the darkness, but "you" belong to the light (5:5). Paul follows this immediately with his parenetic point that those who belong to the light should live in the light, that is, in the day with "daytime" not "nighttime" behavior. But, for our purposes here, it is important to note that he comes back around to the point of the different effect the arrival of the day of the Lord will have on those who belong to Christ. "For," he says, in 5:9–10, "God has not destined us for wrath, but to obtain salvation through our Lord Jesus Christ, who died for us so that whether we are awake or asleep we might live with him" (ESV). The day of the Lord is a day of divine wrath. The destruction of the day of the Lord that suddenly comes upon "them" (5:3) is none other than the "wrath to come" (1:10 ESV). However, those who are waiting for the Lord expect to be delivered from this wrath (1:10; cf. Rom. 5:9, which has in mind the day of wrath [Rom 2:5]). They belong to the day and have the "hope of salvation" (5:8), a salvation that will be given to them "through our Lord Jesus Christ" (5:9).

What is this salvation that is given to believers at the beginning of the day of the Lord in contrast to the wrath that comes upon unbelievers? The answer is made clear by the phrase "so that whether we are awake or asleep we might live with him" (ESV). This takes us back to 4:14–17 where Christ descends from heaven and snatches up to himself all who belong to him, raising those who are dead and gathering those who are alive together with them, the phrase "so that ... we might

---

13. BAGD, s.v. katalambanō, 412–13.

live with him" paralleling "so we will always be with the Lord" (ESV) and the conclusion, "Therefore encourage one another," being an exact restatement of the conclusion of 4:18. In other words, Christ will save those who belong to him by means of the rapture.[14] Those who don't belong to him will be overtaken, seized by the destruction and wrath of that day. The two concepts, being snatched up by the Lord on the one hand and being seized by the destruction of that day on the other, form a conceptual parallel of initiatory experiences reinforcing the understanding that the day of the Lord is a decisive divine act of deliverance and judgment from its outset.

The day of the Lord comes, then, suddenly. Those who belong to Christ know that it is coming, but they do not know when. Those who do not belong to Christ not only do not know when it is coming; they are not even aware that it is in fact coming. But when it begins — that is the important point, its onset, its beginning — a separation occurs in the experience of all people. For those who belong to Christ, that sudden beginning of the day of the Lord is the sudden rapture, with resurrection (for those who sleep) or translation (for those who are awake) to meet the descended Lord on the clouds and in the air, delivered thereby from the ensuing wrath of the day of the Lord. For those who do not belong to Christ, the sudden onset of that day is the experience of being suddenly seized by wrath and judgment.

The Day of the Lord and the Tribulation

So far, what we have seen in 1 Thessalonians 4:13 – 5:10 is a pre – or inaugural day of the Lord's rapture. But is this the same thing as a pretribulational rapture? Should we understand the day of the Lord here to be coextensive with or identical to the seventieth week of Daniel, which pretribulationists understand by the term *tribulation*?

---

14. Green notes that the terminology in 1 Thess. 5:10 connects with 4:15–17 and, on this basis, connects the salvation in 5:9 to the rapture in 4:16–17: "This final salvation is now described in v. 10 as living *together with him*. As in 4:16–17, the theology of v. 10 has to do with the resurrection of the dead and the catching away of the living and the dead 'to be with the Lord forever'" (Green, *Thessalonians*, 244). See also Wanamaker, *Thessalonians*, 188–89. For the argument that "awake" and "sleep" refer to life and death rather than moral alertness or lack thereof (as in 5:5–7), see the arguments of Wanamaker, 188–89, and Bruce, *Thessalonians*, 114–15.

The Seventieth Week of Daniel

The book of Daniel gives a set of narratives mostly in relation to Daniel himself regarding his service to Babylonian and Persian kings. A key feature is the set of dreams or visions in which God reveals to Daniel a sequence of empires that will be brought to an end by the establishment of the kingdom of God. These dreams or visions have parallel features that indicate a common projected sequence even though some visions may only focus on aspects of it.[15] Most important, these visions describe by means of typology and prediction a future time of wrath in which a powerful king along with his kingdom will be destroyed by God and in whose place God will establish his own kingdom forever.[16]

The structure of this future time of wrath, or time of the end, 'et qēts, is a projected pattern that is typed from the sequence of kingdoms given in the visions of Daniel 2, 7, 8, 9, and 10–12. Daniel 7 juxtaposes a vision of God's throne room and the coming of one like a Son of Man on the clouds with a vision of an arrogant, wicked world ruler associated with the last of the sequential kingdoms. The latter is destroyed by divine decree, and kingdom authority is given to the Son of Man and the saints of the Most High. Daniel 9 presents a vision of "seventy sevens" decreed for Jerusalem and the people of Israel, sixty-nine of which span the time from a decree to rebuild the city to the cutting off of the Messiah. The last

---

15. Collins notes the parallelism of the visions even though he denies that they have any eschatological bearing beyond the second century BC: "All the visions are concerned with essentially the same events — the persecution of the Jews by Antiochus Epiphanes. The final revelation [Dan. 10–12] is the most detailed but in no way supersedes those that go before it. Rather, the different visions look at the same events from different angles. Taken together they provide a more fully rounded picture than any one of them alone." John J. Collins, *Daniel: With an Introduction to Apocalyptic Literature*, FOTL 20 (Grand Rapids: Eerdmans, 1984), 32–33, cf. 103. See also the discussion on the parallels between the visions in Joyce G. Baldwin, *Daniel: An Introduction and Commentary*, TOTC 21 (Downers Grove, Ill.: InterVarsity, 1978), 59–63, 161–62; Leon Wood, *A Commentary on Daniel* (Grand Rapids: Zondervan, 1973), 177–79, 206, 222–24, 264; and the extended discussion in C. F. Keil and F. Delitzsch, *Ezekiel, Daniel*, A Commentary on the Old Testament, trans. J. Martin and M. G. Easton (Edinburgh: T & T Clark, 1866–91), 9:654–79.

16. On the wrath as an extended time, see Collins, *Daniel: With an Introduction to Apocalyptic Literature*, 95; and John J. Collins, *Daniel*, Hermeneia (Minneapolis: Fortress, 1993), 338–39: "In the present context, the 'wrath' is not just a day of reckoning but a period of history.... The most immediate parallel to v. 19 is found below at v. 23, which refers to the latter time of the gentile kingdoms 'when their sins are complete.'... The 'wrath' has become a quasi-technical term for the tribulation caused by these kingdoms, especially in its latter phase." On the eschatological, as opposed to historical, bearing of the phrase "time of the end"('et qēts), see Wood's comments in *Daniel*, 222–24, 303–6; and Keil and Delitzsch, *Ezekiel, Daniel*, 699–702.

seven extends from a covenant made by a coming prince to "the decreed end." However, in the middle of the seven, the same one perpetrates an abomination in the temple, causing the sacrifices to cease. The character type presented here is the same as that given in Daniel 7 and in Daniel 8 (although notably, the character type is projected from different points in the kingdom sequence in those visions; Daniel 9 is parallel to Daniel 7 in the kingdom sequence, whereas Daniel 8 parallels Daniel 10–12). Stopping the sacrifices in Daniel 9:27 is a repeat feature from Daniel 8. The half-seven links with "time, times and half a time" of Daniel 7:25, while "the decreed end" links all the visions together.

In Daniel 10–12, Daniel receives the final vision that repeats the pattern once more, adding several features in the process. From our standpoint in later history, it is quite clear that the first half of this vision was fulfilled by military conflicts in the Hellenistic period, between Seleucid and Ptolemaic kings. Especially prominent in the vision is a character who was undoubtedly Antiochus Epiphanes (as was also the case in the first part of the vision in Daniel 8). A lengthy character description is given along with comments on how he would come to power and conduct his campaigns. Attention is also brought to bear on his act of desecrating the temple—the perpetration of an abomination of desolation that caused the sacrifices to cease. However, in Daniel 11:36 another description of character is given that appears to be typed from that just given for Antiochus Epiphanes.[17] It is this verse (11:36) that Paul quotes in 2 Thessalonians 3 as referring to the Man of Lawlessness who is yet to come.

After the typological shift from near future to far future, we are once again told that this pertains to "the time of the end," and that it persists "until the indignation is accomplished" (Dan. 11:36, 40; 12:4, 9, 13 ESV). Note that the whole basic pattern is repeated in the shift from type to antitype. We are told once again about an abomination that makes desolate, that caused the regular sacrifices to cease, and of a time period of 1,290 days (roughly equivalent to three and a half years)

---

17. Collins notes that vv. 36–37 do not continue in chronological sequence but recapitulate the king's behavior during persecution (Collins, *Daniel*, Hermeneia, 386). However, this literary feature is best interpreted not as a recapitulation but as a typological projection, as in 8:19–26. A recapitulation would be unnecessary and awkward stylistically. In addition, in spite of the similarities in description (necessary for the type) there are differences between this description and what is known of Antiochus that signal the type-antitype distinction. See Keil and Delitzsch, *Ezekiel, Daniel*, 802–3, and Wood, *Daniel*, 304–5.

extending from that point (12:11), which seems to be the same as "time, times and half a time" just a few verses earlier (12:7). New features include the involvement of Michael (12:1), "a time of trouble, such as never has been since there was a nation till that time" (12:1 ESV), a deliverance of the elect of Daniel's people, and a resurrection of both the righteous and unrighteous dead (12:1–3).

The picture of the "time of the end" in Daniel is built up and reinforced by repetition and overlapping elements placed into a common structure that has an identifiable chronology and basic narrative sequence. Generally, it is the time of the end, the time of wrath (8:17, 19; 11:36, 40; 12:7, 9). Specifically, it is "one seven"—a seven-year period, with special attention on the time from the middle of this seven-year period to the end (9:27), a duration also specified as "time, times and half a time" (7:25; 12:7), 1,290 days (12:11), and "later in the time of wrath" (8:19). A powerful political figure will appear on the earth, inaugurating the seven-year time of the end with a covenant made with "many." However, he attains (or seizes) greater power in the second half of this time (7:24–25), which begins with an abomination that desolates the temple and causes the regular sacrifice to cease (9:27; 12:11) and ushers in a time of great stress (great tribulation) not seen before (12:1). By action of this one, it will be a time of warfare, blasphemy, deception, and persecution of the saints (7:8, 11, 20–22, 24–25; 8:9–14, 23–25; 9:27; 11:20–35, 36–45) until he and his kingdom are destroyed by God (2:34–35; 7:9–11, 26; 8:25; 9:27; 11:45). The people of God will be delivered (12:1, 7), and God will then set up a kingdom over the whole earth (2:35, 44), which will be specifically given to "one like a son of man," whom Daniel saw "coming with the clouds of heaven" (7:13–14). Apparently through him the kingdom is also given to "the saints of the Most High" (7:22, 27).

The Olivet Discourse

The integration of Daniel's time of the end with the coming day of the Lord takes place in the teaching of Jesus and is carried on in the letters of Paul and in the book of Revelation. In the teaching of Jesus, the integration is most clearly seen in the Olivet Discourse presented in Matthew 24:1–51; Mark 13:1–37; and Luke 21:5–36 (cf. Luke 17:22–37). Consequently, we turn now to examine this discourse. We will follow primarily Matthew's account, making reference to Mark and Luke for a fuller canonical picture.[18]

The Synoptics present this discourse in response to questions posed by Jesus' disciples — questions that were provoked in their minds by his prophecy that the temple in Jerusalem would be completely destroyed (Matt. 24:1–2: "Truly, I say to you, there will not be left here one stone upon another, that will not be thrown down"; cf. Mark 13:1–2; Luke 21:5–6). Matthew, in fact, juxtaposes this prophecy with Jesus' lament over Jerusalem, in which he also prophesied, "Look, your house is left to you desolate" (Matt. 23:38). The questions posed by the disciples are:

"Tell us, when will this happen, and what will be the sign of your coming and of the end of the age?" (Matt. 24:3)	"Tell us, when will these things happen? And what will be the sign that they are all about to be fulfilled?" (Mark 13:4)	"Teacher, when will these things happen? And what will be the sign that they are about to take place?" (Luke 21:7)

Much of the hermeneutical discussion regarding these questions and the discourse that follows tends to fall in one of three main camps: those who see the discourse as thoroughly eschatological, those who see it as thoroughly historical (this is the preterist view, seeing the discourse as wholly focused on the events of AD 70), and those who see it as somehow dealing with both historical and eschatological matters.

---

18. The approach followed here is canonical, harmonizing the synoptic contributions even though making primary reference to Matthew. The reason for the primarily Matthean focus is because Matthew gives the longest version of the Olivet Discourse. Matthew also renders the disciples' second question more explicit in relation to the parousia. Most of the more recent structural studies relating the division of the Olivet Discourse to the disciples' questions have come from treatments of Matthew's account. It may be easier to see this in Matthew because the longer version provides more material for the second major division, making the contrast with the first major division more apparent. The reticence to harmonize the synoptic accounts seems at least in part to be tied to assumptions that the differences are to be accounted for referentially—for example, that the Lukan account deals exclusively with the near future destruction of AD 70, whereas Matthew or Mark may deal with the church age or with the future parousia. As will be seen, the patterned typological interpretation of the Olivet Discourse advocated here allows for the first-century referents in Jesus' narrated sequence while forming a typed pattern that has eschatological bearing. This also helps to explain why the Lukan account, for example, seen by many as focusing especially on the events of AD 70, nevertheless has clear day of the Lord eschatological features. The typological approach taken here allows us to recognize the common features of the synoptic accounts and draw them together into a canonical synthesis.

We cannot review the different positions here.[19] For the purpose of this discussion, I will advocate the third position—that both historical and eschatological matters are in view. Clearly, the disciples had in mind Jesus' prediction of the destruction of the temple then standing when they asked, "When will these things happen?" And they certainly included within their intent the glorious coming of Jesus and his kingdom, as we can see by Matthew's specification of the second question. However, different views prevail among those who would agree that both historical and eschatological events are in view.

Some believe that Jesus' answer first sets forth conditions that will prevail throughout the church age, conditions that should not be interpreted as end-time events. This view holds that this portion of the discourse describes conditions that form the setting of the mission of the church, given the Lord's statement that "this gospel of the kingdom will be preached in the whole world as a testimony to all nations, and then the end will come" (Matt. 24:14).[20] Surely, persecutions as well as general disasters have been the experience of the world and of the church since the days of the apostles. This view would then argue that the discourse goes on to speak of the future coming of Christ as a separate event that will take place suddenly and catastrophically after the mission of the church is finished.[21]

A number of recent studies focusing on the structural relationship of the disciples' two questions to the discourse proper have argued that the Olivet Discourse concerns two events: the destruction that was about to take place in AD 70 and the parousia of the end times. The general disasters and persecutions, it is said, are particularly descriptive of first-century

---

19. For surveys of the various approaches, see D. A. Carson, "Matthew," in *Matthew, Mark, Luke*, EBC, ed. Frank E. Gaebelein, 12 vols. (Grand Rapids: Zondervan, 1984), 8:488–95; W. D. Davies and D. C. Allison, *The Gospel according to Saint Matthew*, ICC, 3 vols. (London: T & T Clark, 1997), 3:328–33; Donald Hagner, *Matthew 14–28*, WBC 33b (Nashville: Nelson, 1995), 685. Also see the helpful overview given by David L. Turner, "The Structure and Sequence of Matthew 24:1–41: Interaction with Evangelical Treatments," *GTJ* 10 (1989): 3–27.

20. The completion of the worldwide evangelistic task has been defined by many in the modern era as making a verbal witness present to every language group. This goal is consistent with the mandate of the Great Commission (Matt. 28:18–20). However, to see it as a condition for the return of the Lord essentially nullifies the unknown any-moment quality of the parousia, for it effectively ties the timing of the parousia to the modern accomplishment of these goals.

21. For examples of this approach among recent commentaries, see the works by Carson and Davies and Allison noted above. Also see Craig L. Blomberg, *Matthew*, NAC (Nashville: Broadman, 1992), 353–64.

conditions. Even the mission of the gospel to the whole world described in 24:14, it is claimed, was completed prior to AD 70. In short, this view argues that in the Olivet Discourse, Jesus proceeds to distinguish the two events of the temple destruction and his coming. The first part of the discourse, Matthew 24:4–35, speaks to the destruction of AD 70. The second section, Matthew 24:36–25:46, speaks to the parousia.[22]

Both of these views have much to contribute to the understanding of the Olivet Discourse; however, both appear to be deficient in crucial points. The second view above fails to do justice not just to the coming of Christ described in 24:29–31, but to the way that the coming is a preoccupation throughout the first section of the discourse.[23] It ignores the many eschatological features of this section in its attempt to emphasize the applicability of the language to the first-century situation.[24]

The first view above renders the discourse somewhat confused by an apparent rambling sequence that starts with a specific agenda to discuss the temple's destruction, begins instead with general remarks about the church age, abruptly returns to the intended agenda with the abomination of desolation, and then rockets forward to the topic of the parousia. The "great distress" that follows the abomination of desolation is turned into the long history of the church and "immediately after" the distress of those days is rendered meaningless, a vague reference to some time in the future.[25]

---

22. See, e.g., R. T. France, *The Gospel of Matthew*, NICNT (Grand Rapids: Eerdmans, 2007), 889–967. This work repeats and updates France's previously published views on this subject. Also see David E. Garland, *Reading Matthew: A Literary and Theological Commentary on the First Gospel* (New York: Crossroad, 1995), 234–45; Alistair Wilson, *When Will These Things Happen? A Study of Jesus as Judge in Matthew 21–25* (Carlisle, Cumbria: Paternoster, 2004), 109–74, 224–47; and Jeffrey A. Gibbs, *Jerusalem and Parousia: Jesus' Eschatological Discourse in Matthew's Gospel* (St. Louis, Mo.: Concordia, 2000), 167–222.

23. It is the Lord himself who raises the topic of his coming in the setting of the discourse — see Matt. 23:38–39. The warnings against those who claim to come in his name keep the topic at the forefront (24:4, 11, 23, 26) as well as his description of the manner of his coming in 24:27. The disciples pair the parousia and the end in their question (24:3), and Jesus speaks of the end coming in 24:14, invoking the connection. In all of these ways, the coming persists as a featured topic throughout the first part of the discourse.

24. This is seen especially in the citations and allusions to Daniel through this section. See Davies and Allison, *Matthew*, 3:332. The Daniel structure and day of the Lord features of this part of the Olivet Discourse will be developed in what follows.

25. Hagner writes: "It is very difficult to believe that the words 'immediately after the tribulation of those days' refer only to something general in the indeterminate future. Rather than something vague, the words seem to require a specific antecedent (note the definite article *tēn* and the demonstrative pronoun *ekeinōn*). The only specific item in the preceding context that could correspond to '*the* suffering of *those* days' is the desecration of the temple

Both of these approaches fail to observe the literary and thematic connections between the Olivet Discourse and the two Old Testament eschatological events of the day of the Lord and Daniel's time of the end. Recent studies on the structure of the Olivet Discourse in relation to the disciples' questions are helpful but fall short because of an apparent assumption that remarks concerning the temple destruction have nothing to do with the parousia. In many of these studies, the transition in the discourse is not just from the question of the sign to the question of when (or vice versa), but a transition of topic or event from the AD 70 near-future event to the parousia far-future event.[26]

The problem here is a failure to appreciate fully the Lord's remark in 24:36 that he himself did not know the day or the hour. Aside from the interesting christological question that this raises, the point has to be fully appreciated that at the time this discourse was given, Jesus, by his own admission, does not know whether the AD 70 destruction and the parousia will be one and the same or two different events. He certainly knew that the temple and the city would be destroyed in that generation. He himself is the prophet who predicts it. He of course knew that a temple desecration and an embattled Jerusalem are both features of Old Testament end-time predictions, that is, features of the day of the Lord and Daniel's time of the end. In fact, it is the contention of this essay that he himself deliberately invokes these patterns in his narrative sequence. However, his warning that the time of the parousia is *unknown*, even to himself, must have cautioned the disciples that the *foreknown* impending destruction of that temple and city in that generation might not be the parousia itself.[27] In fact, the parables illustrating

---

referred to in v. 15" (Hagner, *Matthew 14–28*, 712). Hagner believes, however, that Matthew got confused at this point and misunderstood the Lord's teaching on imminency, but his literary grammatical observation on Matt. 24:29 stands nevertheless. The additional point that needs to be added is the typology being set up by the Lord in relation to the uncertainty about the parousia (24:36). If the Father chooses to delay, then that temple desolation projects as a type to a future temple desolation that fulfills the grammatical literary pattern proposed here.

26. See n. 21 above.

27. The unknown time of the parousia is emphasized again in Acts 1:6–7 where Jesus responds to the disciples' question as to whether their current time would be the time of the restoration of the kingdom. He tells them, "It is not for you to know times or seasons that the Father has fixed by his own authority" (ESV). As in Matthew 24:36, the time determination is attributed to the Father. Peter makes reference to this after the ascension in his second Jerusalem sermon, when he says that Christ must remain in heaven "until the time for restoring all the things about which God spoke by the mouth of his holy prophets long ago" (Acts 3:21 ESV).

the uncertainty of the parousia contain hints that it might be delayed longer than anyone thinks (Matt. 24:48, 50; 25:19). Nevertheless, it still remained possible at the time of the discourse that the impending judgment on Jerusalem could have been the parousia.

The point of this study is that in the first part of the Olivet Discourse (Matt. 24:4–35), Jesus gives a pattern that includes the sign of the Son of Man coming on the clouds of heaven. This pattern has as its structure Daniel's time of the end, and it carries the descriptive features of the day of the Lord. It is, in fact, this integrated day of the Lord, time of the end pattern that constitutes the contribution of the Olivet Discourse to the development of biblical eschatology. This whole pattern is the parousia. However, just as was the case in the Old Testament, it is possible for a type of the eschatological day of the Lord to appear in history in advance of the antitype. Jesus alerts his disciples to this possibility in the parable of the fig tree when he distinguishes between "all these things" of the pattern up to the sign of the Son of Man ("when you see *all these things*, you know that he is near"; 24:33 NIV alternate reading, emphasis added) and the sign itself, and then tells them that "all these things" (understood now as all the things up to the sign of the Son of Man) will come upon that generation. If it had been the day chosen by the Father, the sign of the Son of Man would have followed the distress of those days and the entire sequence would have been the eschatological day of the Lord, the parousia of the Son of Man. But the possibility existed for a type/antitype division, with the type fulfilling the prophesied destruction of that temple and the city of that time, and in keeping with the purpose of a type, foreshadowing the greater fulfillment of the parousia yet to come—a greater fulfillment, that is, of the entire pattern, not just a part.[28]

---

28. As has already been noted, this explains why there are first-century features in the pattern. What is being said here is similar to the observations of G. B. Caird on the language of biblical eschatology. See G. B. Caird, *The Language and Imagery of the Bible* (Philadelphia: Westminster, 1980), 243–71. He writes: "The prophets looked to the future with bifocal vision. With their near sight they foresaw imminent historical events which would be brought about by familiar human causes; for example, disaster was near for Babylon because Yahweh was stirring up the Medes against them (Isa. 13:17). With their long sight they saw the day of the Lord; and it was in the nature of the prophetic experience that they were able to adjust their focus so as to impose the one image on the other and produce a synthetic picture" (258). This "prophetic camera technique," as Caird labels it (259), is what we see in Old Testament day of the Lord prophecies, in Daniel's visions of coming desolation, and in the Olivet Discourse—near future and far future event descriptions superimposed upon each other in synthetic fashion. When the near future event comes to pass, the same language that references

We now turn to the two questions. The first question expresses an overall concern: When will these things be? The second question expresses a more specific concern with respect to "these things," asking, as Mark tells us, about the sign indicating when all these things will be accomplished. Matthew renders this as a question about the sign of "your coming and of the end of the age." Putting the synoptic accounts together, it is clear that the second question has to do with the sign that all predicted eschatological events would be completed, including the parousia and the end of the age.

The discourse itself divides structurally into two parts, with the structural change occurring at Matthew 24:36 (Mark 13:32).[29] The first part, in Matthew 24:4–35 (Mark 13:5–31; Luke 21:8–33), presents a movement, a narrative sequence that has a beginning (*archē*, 24:8) and an end (*telos*, 24:6, 13, 14). The movement is marked by the repetitive use of "then" (*tote*) and culminates in the appearing of the sign of the Son of Man in heaven. The narrative sequence ends with this sign, and the discourse immediately moves to a teaching point in 24:32–35, which functions as a conclusion or postscript. This is the parable of the fig tree: "When you see all these things, you know that he is near" (NIV alternate reading). Here we find the prediction that the generation at that time would see "all these things" in the pattern that came near to the point of his appearing.

---

it connects it typologically to the far future referent. In the case of the Olivet Discourse, the narrative structure which is itself a synthesis of the prophetic patterns—the day of the Lord and Daniel's time of the end—references both the AD 70 destruction and the future parousia with language that may be wholly applicable to one, wholly applicable to another, or equally applicable to both at the same time, and is appreciated in its dual reference by what Caird calls "the paratactical Hebrew mind" (267).

29. The structural change at this point, dividing the Olivet Discourse into two parts, is observed by many, including France, Davies and Allison, Blomberg, Garland, Wilson, and Gibbs in n. 22 above. Hagner sees the second division beginning with 24:37 (Hagner, *Matthew 14–28*, 717–19.). The corresponding material in Luke is much briefer but is separated from the rest by Marshall and Bock and an "application." See I. Howard Marshall, *The Gospel of Luke*, NIGTC (Grand Rapids: Eerdmans, 1978), 781–82; and Darrell L. Bock, *Luke*, vol. 2, BECNT (Grand Rapids: Baker, 1996), 1658, 1693. Of the recent commentators on Mark, Evans notes T. W. Manson's division of the Markan version of the Olivet Discourse into two parts with the hinge at 13:32 and believes it has merit but does not give it the significance observed by the Matthean commentators (Craig A. Evans, *Mark 8:27–16:20*, WBC 34b [Nashville: Nelson, 2001], 340). See T. W. Manson, *The Teaching of Jesus: Studies of Its Form and Content* (1931; repr. London: Cambridge University Press, 1967), 262. Of course, France draws the point of a structural division at 13:32 in his commentary on Mark. See R. T. France, *The Gospel of Mark*, NIGTC (Grand Rapids: Eerdmans, 2002), 541–43. France cites P. Carrington as one who earlier observed this structural division. See P. Carrington, *According to Mark* (Cambridge: University Press, 1960), 293–94, 298.

The second part of the discourse begins in Matthew 24:36. The mood and content abruptly changes.[30] The point of this portion of the discourse, made over and over with various illustrations, is that no one knows the day or the hour. This continues until Matthew 25:31–46, where the judgment of the sheep and goats functions as the conclusion to this section.

The suggestion of many that the two parts of the discourse be related to the two questions seems reasonable.[31] However, there is not agreement as to whether the questions neatly divide between the two sections of the discourse and, if they do, which questions go with which part.[32] The proposal given here is that the question about the sign goes with the part of the discourse that focuses on the sign—the sign of the Son of Man. The question *when* is a more general question and is related to that part of the discourse having to do with the complex event as a whole. Thus the questions relate to the discourse chiastically: Jesus answers the questions (a) when will these things happen and (b) what will be the sign in reverse order, addressing first (b) the sign of his coming and of the end of the age—that is, the sign when *all* eschatological events will be completed, and then addressing (a) the overall question of when.

What Will Be the Sign?

I wish to make two primary observations regarding Jesus' narrative in response to the disciples' question concerning "the sign." One is that the narrative has basically the same structure and many of the major features of Daniel's "time of the end." The second observation is that the

---

30. The contrast in mood and content is commented on at length by Gibbs, *Jerusalem and Parousia*, 170–74.

31. Garland, *Reading Matthew*, 235: "The key to the structure of this discourse is the disciples' double question in 24:3." See also Gibbs, *Jerusalem and Parousia*, 174; Blomberg, *Matthew*, 353; France, *Matthew*, 899.

32. Hagner, for example, thinks that Jesus does not answer the first question, so that the whole discourse is directed to the second question (Hagner, *Matthew 14–28*, 688). Nolland connects the word "sign" in the second question to the use in 24:30, but he is not clear on the structural nature of these questions. See John Nolland, *The Gospel of Matthew*, NIGTC (Grand Rapids: Eerdmans, 2005), 983. Many follow France in relating the first question to the first part of the discourse and the second question to the second part of the discourse. However, the guiding principle seems to be the desire to divide the discourse into near-future and far-future prophecies. Since the first question entails the destruction of the temple then standing and the first part of the discourse includes first-century events, they are thereby related. However, this ignores the connection between the second question and the first part of the Olivet Discourse by means of the word *sign* as well as the way the second part of the Olivet Discourse provides a clear answer to the first question, *when* (answer: no one knows).

entire narrative sequence is presented, by means of intertextual descriptive references, as the day of the Lord.

First, the fact that the sequence carries the structure of Daniel's time of the end is not difficult to see. The discourse begins with a future destruction of the temple as a primary concern. Whereas many day of the Lord prophecies speak of Jerusalem, Daniel explicitly focuses on the temple and its future desolation and destruction. Both Matthew and Mark refer to a desecration of the temple with Daniel's phrase "the abomination of desolation," while in Matthew, Jesus cites Daniel explicitly by name. The abomination of desolation is placed climactically in the middle of his narrative sequence similarly to the way it functions in Daniel's "time of the end." Jesus then quotes from Daniel 12:1 and speaks of "great tribulation" (24:21 ESV) occurring from the time of the abomination of desolation to the end. Daniel 12:7, 11 marks the time from the abomination of desolation to the end as "time, times, and half a time" or 1,290 days. This is the same structure as that in Daniel 9:26–27 where the abomination of desolation is set up in the middle of a seven-year period—the middle, that is, of Daniel's seventieth week.[33]

In conjunction with this, we should note that this part of the discourse in both Matthew and Mark is (from the beginning of the narrative sequence to the appearing of the sign of the Son of Man) structured by means of an inclusio—a warning about false christs. This warning appears both at the beginning and at the end of the narrative sequence just before the sign of the Son of Man. Matthew, however, repeats the warning a third time midway between the two ends of the inclusio, emphasizing the point that the predominant concern throughout this whole time (even more perhaps than famine, war, and persecution) is false christs. Although Mark omits this middle reference to false christs, he does use the masculine participle *hestēkota* with the neuter abomination of desolation (in contrast to Matthew, who maintains proper subject-verb agreement), indicating that the desecration is linked to the presence of the perpetrator himself in the temple.[34] The abomination of

---

33. On allusions to Daniel in the Olivet Discourse, see Davies and Allison, *Matthew*, 3:332.

34. Hengel gives an extended discussion of the personification of the abomination in Mark 13:14, demonstrating that the event "has not taken place." His linkage of the verse to 2 Thess. 2:3–4 is convincing. See Martin Hengel, *Studies in the Gospel of Mark*, trans. John Bowden (Minneapolis: Fortress, 1985), 16–20. Evans provides an overview of attempts to identify the

desolation functions as a climax, a turning point, not just in the experience of trouble per se, but in the danger represented by a false christ.

Except for the absence of temporal markers (such as one seven; time, times, half a time; 1,290 days), the structure is precisely that of Daniel's seventieth week—the appearance of Antichrist (several false christs) with the attending phenomena of war and persecution, the turning point of the abomination of desolation perpetrated by a "false christ," which takes the whole tenor of the times to high stress and which anticipates the destruction of this one at the conclusion of the typed pattern.

The conclusion to the narrative is the coming of the Son of Man on the clouds of heaven. Jesus quotes Daniel 7:13 with the change from "one like a son of man" to "Son of Man." This is the sign in contrast to the deception offered by false christs, the sign of his coming and of the end of the age, the sign that all these things will be completed. The sign of the Son of Man occurs at the end of the typed pattern, at the point where in Daniel the arrogant world ruler is destroyed and the kingdom is given to the Son of Man and the saints of the Most High.

Having observed the Danielic structure of the narrative portion of the Olivet Discourse, the second observation I wish to make about this portion of the discourse is that the whole complex of events that constitutes this narrative sequence is presented in the "day of the Lord" description. The conclusion I will draw from this is that the whole complex of events, including its Danielic narrative movement, is thereby meant to be taken as the day of the Lord.

Jesus begins the discourse with reference to what is sometimes called "messianic woes."[35] Matthew and Mark list these as war, famine, and earthquakes, features that are common elements in day of the Lord descriptions.[36] The Lukan account adds to these features the phenomena of pestilences, terrors, and great signs from heaven. The "great signs from heaven" are repeated at the end of the discourse as "signs in the sun, moon and stars" (21:11, 25).[37] The terror in this early part is also

---

personal reference and also concludes, "The prophecy itself has not been fulfilled" (Evans, *Mark 8:27–16:20*, 320 [see the extended discussion in 317–20]).

35. See, e.g., Carson, "Matthew," 498.

36. "Much of the language of these verses again reflects standard apocalyptic imagery" (Hagner, *Matthew 14–28*, 691).

37. The parallel between these descriptions is noted by Bock, *Luke*, 2:1668. Both Marshall and Bock note that these descriptions are common in Old Testament prophecy (Marshall,

repeated at the end by the description of "people fainting with fear and with foreboding of what is coming on the world" (21:26 ESV). The literary repetition of these elements draws them together thematically, but the statement after the first set of descriptions that "the end will not be at once" (21:9 ESV; Matthew [24:6] and Mark [13:7] have "the end is not yet" [ESV]) allows for the eschatological narrative structure, inserted between these descriptive elements, to unfold.[38] That narrative structure thus takes place in the setting of these conditions—conditions that are typical features of the day of the Lord.

Most interesting is Jesus' description of these early phenomena (Matt. 24:5–7; Mark 13:6–8) as "the beginning of birth pains" (Gk., *archēōdinōn*).[39] While the metaphor of labor is used in various biblical texts to describe divine judgment, the *onset* of labor is particularly used in Isaiah 13:8 to describe the coming of the day of the Lord. Features from the Isaiah 13 prophecy of the day of the Lord reappear at the end

---

Luke, 765; Bock, *Luke*, 2:1667). Marshall, however, asserts that "such phenomena are *not* apocalyptic signs of the end" (766). Bock also states that "the chaos itself is not, however, a sign of the end" (2:1668). However, this seems to reflect different ways of understanding the "end," as Bock sees the events connected in an extended sequence.

38. On Luke 21:9 indicating an extended eschatological event, see Bock, *Luke*, 2:1666.

39. The problem in interpretation is how to relate "the beginning of birth pains" to "the end is not yet." Hagner notes correctly that the point being made is that there will be "an extended period of travail" (Hagner, *Matthew 14–28*, 691). This is consistent with the imagery of labor and with the integration of Daniel's time of the end structure. However, Blomberg seems to take "the end is not yet" as dismissive, as if Jesus is saying that none of these things has anything to do with "the end." That leads him to suggest that Jesus might be warning his disciples against "false labor" or suggesting to them that the beginning of labor is something indeterminate (Blomberg, *Matthew*, 354). Contra Blomberg, Jesus is not warning against these phenomena as "false signs" (353) but against false christs. The sign of his coming will appear only at the end of a pattern he is outlining as the "time of the end," namely, after the great distress that follows the abomination of desolation. His only point at this part of the discourse is that the appearance of these cosmic phenomena per se are not to be taken as validation for the claims of a false christ—claims that the Christ has already appeared. Many, like Blomberg, have argued that Jesus is here predicting the interadvent age, and some have correlated the reference to birth pains to Paul's use of the labor metaphor in Rom. 8:22–23 (see, e.g., Carson, "Matthew," 498). However, it is not by any means clear that the meaning is the same in both places. Romans 8 speaks of the creation in travail anticipating immortality. In the Olivet Discourse, as in Isa. 13:8, the labor travail is the beginning of the day of wrath. We may reason that these are related theologically, but that does not mean the image has the same literary use in both places. Undoubtedly, at least one purpose in such a linkage is to validate an interpretation of the Olivet Discourse in which the first part equals the long interadvent age (see also Davies and Allison, *Matthew*, 3:331, 340–41). Even though many of these phenomena are seen in the interadvent age, just as some of these phenomena have characterized postfall human conditions generally, this does not preclude a special formation and concentration of the phenomena in a future day of the Lord. The general occurrence of earthquakes, anxiety, and military battles in Old Testament times did not preclude the occurrence of a day of the Lord with these very features. Neither do the occurrence of these things in the interadvent age preclude a yet future day of the Lord.

of the narrative just before Jesus speaks of the sign of the Son of Man. Quoting from Isaiah 13:10, Jesus says, "The sun will be darkened, and the moon will not give its light; the stars will fall from the sky" (Matt. 24:29). Between these references to Isaiah 13:8 and 13:10 unfolds the eschatological narrative with its Danielic structure.

Other day of the Lord descriptions that are woven into the narrative structure include the siege of Jerusalem by armies and ensuing battle (Luke 21:20, 24).[40] This picks up the general reference to war in the early part of the discourse (Luke 21:9–10) and focuses it on Jerusalem, just as in many day of the Lord prophecies.[41] The proverbial statement about bodies and vultures (Matt. 24:28, cf. Luke 17:37) is in keeping with the battlefield imagery. The feature of increased darkness referenced in Isaiah 13:10 reappears in Matthew 24:22 and Mark 13:20 as the shortening of days. Darkness is a feature of many day of the Lord predictions and goes together with the shaking of the heavens and the onset of battle. Luke's reference to the coming of wrath (Luke 21:23) is likewise consistent with the theme. Finally, the trumpet call associated with the coming Son of Man appears to be taken from Joel 2, which also conveys the imagery of the shaking and darkening of the heavens and the coming of battle. Significantly, it is the Lord who comes and issues his call in Joel; it is he before whom the trumpet is blown. By clothing the Danielic Son of Man imagery with this day of the Lord imagery

---

40. Bock argues that the language in Luke, as opposed to Matthew and Mark, definitively speaks of the "fall of Jerusalem in AD 70 rather than the end," but he believes that Luke views the near future destruction as "a preview, but with less intensity, of what the end will be like ... a typological picture of what the consummation will be like—except that at the consummation, the nation Israel will be rescued as the O.T. promised" (Bock, *Luke*, 2:1675–76; see also his summary on 1696). The typological function of the discourse is the same point that is being argued in this essay. However, I would emphasize more strongly the Old Testament day of the Lord as a thematic context for the battle imagery. As for the structured parallel of Luke 21:20 with Matthew 24:15 and Mark 13:14, Desmond Ford has provided a helpful suggestion that the abomination of desolation may be best thought of as a complex event that results in the temple desecration. This would connect Luke's reference to armies to the abomination mentioned by the other Synoptics. See Desmond Ford, *The Abomination of Desolation in Biblical Eschatology* (Washington D.C.: University Press of America, 1979), 163.

41. Wright has drawn attention to the connection between the day of the Lord battle imagery and the setting of the discourse on the Mount of Olives, arguing for an intended allusion to Zechariah 14 (N. T. Wright, *Jesus and the Victory of God* [Minneapolis: Fortress, 1996], 344–45). He goes on to observe numerous day of the Lord and Danielic parallels but argues for a preterist interpretation. He seems to be misled by the assumption (by the main tradition of amillennialism and the "consistent eschatology" of Albert Schweitzer) that the parousia brings about the end of time. Since the discourse doesn't speak of the end of time, in his view it doesn't speak of the parousia (339–68).

from Joel and Isaiah, a further point about the identity of the Son of Man is achieved.

The point being made here is that there is a deliberate intertextual weaving of day of the Lord imagery into Daniel's time of the end structure. This is not just a feature at the end of the Olivet Discourse; it appears throughout the discourse with a heavy occurrence of the imagery at the beginning and the end. Day of the Lord imagery lends itself to this, because typically day of the Lord prophecies are filled with descriptive terminology. Day of the Lord predictions do not usually present a sequential structure except perhaps the structural sequence of a siege and battle. The one other exception to this is the labor metaphor that appears in Isaiah 13 and at the beginning of the Olivet Discourse. Labor consists of a sequence of contractions and pains that culminates in a birth—an appearance of someone previously hidden now openly revealed. The imagery of the beginning of labor pains at the beginning of the discourse connects to the appearance of the Son of Man at the end of the sequence, giving a coherence to the whole structure that operates in tandem with Daniel's time of the end structure. In the teaching of Jesus, the typologies of the day of the Lord and Daniel's time of the end have been integrated.

Concluding this first part of the Olivet Discourse is the parable of the fig tree. All the events of the narrative sequence indicate that he is near, just as buds on a tree indicate that summer is near.[42] But the sign of his coming is none of these things in and of themselves—the sign of his coming is the sign of the Son of Man in the sky. This distinction allows for the possibility that the entire pattern up to this point may be fulfilled as a type, a type which in fact did befall that generation to which Jesus and his disciples belonged.

When Will These Things Be?

Having spoken to the unfolding pattern of the time of the end / day of the Lord—a pattern of events that constitutes the parousia when it

---

42. A popular interpretation of the fig tree parable is that the fig tree is a metaphor for the nation Israel and that the blossoming of the fig tree is the reappearance of Israel as a nation on the world scene (which took place in 1948). The indication that this is not the Lord's intent in these words comes by considering the parallel passage in Luke 21:29, where he says, "Look at the fig tree, and all the trees" (ESV). The addition of "and all the trees" indicates that this is not a metaphor about Israel. It is a botanical metaphor about the interconnection and movement of the day of the Lord pattern.

includes the sign of the Son of Man—Jesus, beginning in Matthew
24:36 [Mark 13:32; Luke 21:34], addresses the more general question,
the disciples' first question, as to when these things will be. The lesson
of the fig tree was that "when you see all these things, you know that
he is near, at the very gates" (24:33 ESV). But the question remains,
when will all these things be—the whole pattern, including his appearing? The shift in topic is noted in Matthew and Mark by the structural
marker "But concerning" (*peri de*), the temporal reference, "that day or
that hour," and the didactic point, "no one knows" (*oudeis oiden*; Matt.
24:36; Mark 13:32 ESV).[43] Mark follows this introductory comment
with a more general reference to "the time," saying, "you do not know
(*ouk oidate*) when the time will come" (*pote ho kairos estin*; v. 33). The
phrasing is almost an exact parallel to the phrasing of the disciples'
first question in 13:4, "when will these things be ...?" (*pote tauta estai*;
ESV).[44] Luke presents the temporal reference at this point in the discourse as simply "that day" which is coming. Most commentators are
agreed that "that day or that hour" is not a reference to the temporal
positioning of the coming of the Son of Man within the event sequence
of the time of the end presented in the earlier portion of the discourse.
It is not a reinterpretation of what has just been given in 24:33–34.[45]
Rather, "that day or that hour" looks at the day of the Lord itself—in a
singular, comprehensive way.[46] And this fits with Mark's more general
reference to "that time" (13:33) or Luke's "that day" (21:34).

Unlike the pattern that unfolds within the day of the Lord (in which
the Son of Man's coming on the clouds follows the distress caused by
the abomination of desolation), the day of the Lord itself—as a comprehensive whole—will set into history without warning, without signs
by which one can approximate its coming. "No one knows," the Lord
says, "but only the Father"—recalling Zechariah's comment that the
day of the Lord is "a unique day, which is known to the LORD" (14:7

---

43. The significance of *peri de* for the "hinge" at this part of the discourse is developed by
Gibbs, *Jerusalem and Parousia*, 172. See also France's *Mark*, 541, and his *Matthew*, 936.

44. Hagner, *Matthew 14–28*, 716.

45. Wilson, *When Will These Things Happen?* 224–26.

46. So Wilson, ibid., 224–25: "It is clear that reference is being made to the 'Day of the
Lord.'" Davies and Allison, *Matthew*, 3:378: "'That day' is the Old Testament's 'Day of the
Lord,' which in the New Testament is the *parousia*; and 'that hour' is a further specification
that is effectively synonymous." Cf. Blomberg, *Matthew*, 365; and France, *Matthew*, 939.

ESV; Zechariah is referring in context to "a day [that] is coming for the LORD," 14:1).[47]

Note also that the coming of "that day," "the time," or "that day or hour," is further referenced in Matthew as "the coming of the Son of Man" (*hē parousia tou huiou tou anthrōpou*) (24:37, 39), with follow-up references to "your Lord is coming" (24:42 ESV), "the Son of Man is coming" (24:44 ESV), and "when the Son of Man comes" (25:31 ESV), as well as illustrations from parables to a master of servants coming ("when he comes," 24:46 ESV; "will come on a day," 24:50; or "came," 25:19 ESV) or a bridegroom coming ("the bridegroom came," 25:10 ESV). Mark, in this portion of the discourse, speaks of the Son of Man coming only by parabolic reference (13:34–37), and Luke speaks only of the coming of "that day" (21:34). References to the coming of the Son of Man are not inconsistent with the point that this part of the discourse focuses on the coming of the day of the Lord as an entire event. The day of the Lord was understood to be "the day of his coming" (Mal. 3:2). On the day of the Lord, the Lord will rise "to terrify the earth" whose inhabitants will flee "from before the terror of the LORD, and from the splendor of his majesty" (Isa. 2:19, 21 ESV). The coming of the day of the Lord is the coming of "the LORD and the weapons of his indignation" (Isa. 13:5–6 ESV). The prevailing imagery is that of a military campaign dispensing destruction and death until the campaign is finished (see in addition to the aforementioned references Joel 2:1, 11; Mic. 1:3-4; 2:4; Nah. 1:2–8; Hab. 3:2–15; Zech. 14:3, 5, 12–14). The point is that the entire day of the Lord is a coming of the Lord in judgment. All of its destructive elements—for however long their duration or however extensive their reach—are poured out by the God who has "come" enacting this judgment. This is true whether or not the Lord makes an "appearance" in or at the end of the day. The historical "days of the Lord" did not involve a theophany even though they were "days" on which the Lord came in judgment. The theophany at the end of the day of the Lord in Zechariah 14 climaxes an extended event in which he has come in judgment—the point being that the coming does not just take place at the end of an extended disaster which is merely its prelude. Following the imagery of a military campaign, the entire

47. Hagner, *Matthew 14–28*, 716.

campaign, whether the devastation of the countryside or the siege and battle for the city—however long these last—is due to the coming of a general and his army who are perpetrating it. His coming is not merely his triumphal entry into the defeated city at the end of the campaign. His coming is the whole destructive event that completes itself when the city is defeated and he then makes his entry into it.

Accordingly, what is being said here is that the coming of the Son of Man in Matthew 24:36–25:46 is entirely the same thing as the coming of the day of the Lord itself. The Son of Man will visibly appear at the climax of this day, but the whole day is the day of his coming.

The imagery of labor and birth, used in the first part of the Olivet Discourse, is particularly suitable for this notion of an *extended* coming. The day of the Lord sequence sets in to human experience as the onset of labor, and it is characterized as a coming of God (cf. Isa. 13:5–8). Here, in the Olivet Discourse, the labor process culminates in the visible appearing of the Son of Man. Accordingly, what is being said here is that in this second part of the Olivet Discourse, Jesus is making reference to the day of the Lord as a whole—as an entire complex event. The day of the Lord is the day of his coming, and consequently, the reference to the day of the Lord and to the coming of the Son of Man amount to the same thing. When Jesus refers to the parousia of the Son of Man in Matthew 24:37, 39, he is not simply and merely referring to the appearing of the Son of Man in the sky as in 24:30. Rather, he is referring to the entire travail of his coming that culminates in his appearing.

With this in mind, we can understand why in the Olivet Discourse Jesus speaks on the one hand of signs and on the other of no signs. He speaks of "his coming" or the coming of "that day" as a surprise, occurring suddenly without any preceding signs. Yet he speaks of the sign of his appearing on the clouds of heaven as taking place after the abomination of desolation, which itself occurs in a context of false christs, wars, and earthly and heavenly disturbances—all day of the Lord or time of the end features. All the signs are in the day of the Lord. They are signs leading up to his appearance at the end of this coming. The day of the Lord taken as a whole—the day of his coming in judgment and which culminates in his appearance—sets in to history without warning, without signs. Once the day of the Lord begins, a pattern of events ensues that renders his appearing near—near because the beginning of the day of the Lord is the beginning of his coming, and once his coming in judgment begins, his appearing is near in accordance with the well-known pattern that has been revealed about that coming.

So, to conclude our observations on the Olivet Discourse: Jesus does speak of destructive events coming upon Jerusalem and especially the temple, a prophecy that his disciples link to his prophecies about his coming as the Son of Man to execute judgment and establish his kingdom. In answer to their question about the sign for all these things, he gives an eschatological pattern formed by integrating the labor imagery and descriptive features of the prophetic day of the Lord with Daniel's time of the end. That patterned judgment would fall upon that generation at least up to the sign of his appearing. The sign of his coming, the sign of the end, the sign that all the eschatological events are being fulfilled would occur *within this kind of pattern* after a time of distress caused by an abomination of desolation in the temple. But whether the events of AD 70 would be the complete pattern including the sign of the Son of Man—in other words, whether the judgment that would come upon Jerusalem in that generation would be the eschatological day of the Lord in which the Son of Man comes—was unknown. Whether we would have a type-antitype division or a complete singular fulfillment was unknown. And if we did have a type application of the pattern in advance of the complete fulfillment (and we did), then the time between the type and the antitype is unknown. The whole complex will set in unexpectedly into history. Undoubtedly, it was the Lord's intent to say that the pattern of those events would begin without prior signs in the experience of that generation—the appearance of false christs, cosmic and terrestrial disturbances, and persecution leading up to a siege of the city (Luke) and desolation of the temple (Matthew and Mark). But looking at it after AD 70, one could see that it was not the will of the Father that *that* judgment pattern be the coming of the Son of Man. Consequently, the pattern projects into the future to be repeated in full in the Son of Man's coming, in his execution of judgment, and in his bringing to final fulfillment the eschatological kingdom of God. And, when it comes—when he comes—it will begin suddenly and unexpectedly in the experience of people on the earth.

With respect to the argument for pretribulationism, we can say that the Olivet Discourse presents an enhanced notion of the day of the Lord—enhanced by the integration of Daniel's time of the end structure. This Danielic enhanced day of the Lord is what pretribulationists call the tribulation, and it is to this that Paul refers in 1 Thessalonians 5 when he speaks of the coming of the day of the Lord.

Pauline Pretribulationism

We return now to 1 Thessalonians 5, where Paul asserts a deliverance of believers from God's wrath at the onset of the day of the Lord—a deliverance which in context is the rapture. The question is, is this the same thing as a pretribulational rapture? The point to be made here is that it is. And this can be seen by the way Paul's understanding of the day of the Lord and its coming is dependent on Jesus' teaching in the Olivet Discourse.

The dependence of Paul in 1 Thessalonians 5 on the Olivet Discourse is widely recognized due to the many verbal and thematic connections between these texts in a composition that is clearly referencing a received tradition.[48] The Thessalonians already knew something about the coming of the day of the Lord. Paul reminds them of what they know by means of key illustrations and summary teachings that derive from the Olivet Discourse, all except one of which come from the second part of the Olivet Discourse, the part that looks at the eschatological pattern as a whole and answers the disciples' first question: "When will these things be?" The day of the Lord will come "like a thief in the night" (5:2; cf. Matt. 24:43), as a "surprise" (5:4; cf. Matt. 24:43–44, 50), as "sudden destruction," "while people are saying, 'There is "peace and security"'"(5:3; cf. Matt. 24:37–41, 50–51; Mark 13:36; Luke 17:26–37; 21:34) in light of which they are admonished to "keep awake" and "be sober" (5:6, 8; cf. Matt. 24:42, 44; 25:13; Mark 13:33, 35, 37; Luke 21:34, 36). Although Jesus in the Olivet Discourse did not use the term "day of the Lord," we have already seen that it is

---

48. See David Wenham, *The Rediscovery of Jesus' Eschatological Discourse* (Sheffield: Sheffield University Press, 1984), 176–80, 295–96. See also, Davies and Allison, *Matthew*, 3:385; Blomberg, *Matthew*, 367; France, *Matthew*, 942; Bruce, *Thessalonians*, 108–9; and Robert Thomas, "1 Thessalonians," in *Ephesians–Philemon*, EBC, 12 vols. (Grand Rapids: Zondervan, 1978), 11:282–83.

clear that in this second part of the Olivet Discourse it is in fact the coming day of the Lord that he has in mind. And we have seen that this day of the Lord is the eschatological pattern that he presents in the first part of the Olivet Discourse, a pattern that begins and ends with day of the Lord descriptive features taken from the Old Testament prophets. Paul, by quoting from the second part of the Olivet Discourse, indicates that he is deriving his understanding of the coming day of the Lord from that given by Jesus.[49] This is the day of the Lord integrated with Daniel's time of the end structure given in the first part of the Olivet Discourse. By connecting his term, "day of the Lord," to that taught by Jesus, Paul evidently intends the same integrated event—that is, the day of the Lord structured as the seventieth week of Daniel.

Even more significantly, if there was any doubt about a connection in Paul's mind between the day of the Lord spoken of by Jesus in the second half of the Olivet Discourse and that integrated pattern in the first half of the Olivet Discourse, Paul puts that doubt to rest by reaching back into that first part of the Olivet Discourse and retrieving the metaphor that characterizes the beginning of the pattern—the metaphor of the beginning of labor (5:3; cf. Matt. 24:8; Mark 13:8)—to further elaborate the sudden onset of the day which is the theme of the second part of the Olivet Discourse. Thus Paul himself connects both parts of the Olivet Discourse—the whole pattern of part 1 is the event spoken of in part 2—and indicates that the proper theme of both is the day of the Lord.

To say it again, Jesus has integrated Daniel's time of the end, seventieth week structure with the prophetic concept of the day of the Lord. It is to this that Paul refers in 1 Thessalonians 5 when he speaks of the day of the Lord. Furthermore, Paul focuses on the coming, the onset, the beginning of the day of the Lord by drawing upon Jesus' own teaching about the onset of the day as a whole in the second part of the Olivet Discourse and by referencing the beginning of the day of the Lord with Jesus' own description of that beginning in the first part of

---

49. Green, speaking about the thief metaphor, writes, "This assertion finds its roots in the teaching of Jesus about his coming (Matt. 23:43–44; Luke 12:39–40) and was then incorporated into the instruction given to the church about the end (2 Pet. 3:10; Rev. 3:3; 16:15)" (Green, *Thessalonians*, 232). Wanamaker writes, "Paul has used the traditional eschatological and apocalyptic images, perhaps all of them already part of the Jesus tradition, for his own parenetic ends" (*Thessalonians*, 180).

the Olivet Discourse. In other words, Paul is speaking of the seven-year tribulation — the seventieth week of Daniel — when he speaks of the day of the Lord in 1 Thessalonians 5. And he is speaking of the onset, the beginning of this tribulation as coming suddenly, without warning, like a thief, at which time those who belong to Christ will be raptured to be forever with the Lord while destruction overtakes the rest.

The question naturally arises at this point about Paul's discussion of these matters in 2 Thessalonians. Does his discussion of the coming of Christ in that letter confirm or contradict what we have seen in 1 Thessalonians?

In 2 Thessalonians 2:1, Paul turns once again to the topic of "the coming (*tēs parousias*) of our Lord Jesus Christ and our being gathered together (*episynagōgēs*) to him" (ESV).[50] It seems reasonable to understand "our being gathered together to him" as the rapture. In his earlier letter, Paul had described the rapture as an event in which we who are left alive until the coming (*eis tēn parousian*; 1 Thess. 4:15) would be "caught up together with them (*syn autois*) . . . so we will always be with the Lord" (*syn kyriō*; v. 17).

Both verbally and conceptually, the rapture as an occasion of being gathered together to the Lord is linked to the parousia. Because Paul posted these as linked topics, one naturally expects the ensuing treatment to address them. However, Paul proceeds immediately to the matter of a false rumor concerning the day of the Lord. This should not be surprising, however, since as we have seen in the preceding discussion of both 1 Thessalonians 4–5 and the Olivet Discourse, the expression *parousia* is not used merely of the visible descent but of the day of the Lord as a whole, of which the visible descent is the culmination. In what follows, Paul sketches a similar pattern to that given by the Lord in the Olivet Discourse, which conveys the key elements of Daniel's seventieth week; but in doing so, he draws out the explicit meaning of the personification of the abomination of desolation given in Mark 13:14. The sequential pattern that Paul gives begins with an "apostasy" and the revelation of a "man of lawlessness," who is described by means of a citation from Daniel 11:36 (note the intentional intertextuality with

---

50. Most of the commentators are agreed on this: Bruce, *Thessalonians*, 163; Green, *Thessalonians*, 302; Wanamaker, *Thessalonians*, 238; Thomas, *2 Thessalonians*, 318.

Daniel and the Olivet Discourse, especially the Markan version of the Olivet Discourse.[51] The blasphemous self-exaltation that character-izes the Man of Lawlessness leads him to an act in the temple of self-deification—this temple blasphemy corresponding to and apparently interpreting the abomination of desolation in Daniel's seventieth week and in the Olivet Discourse.[52] The sequence of events is marked by false signs and deception, which the Lord had warned about, and it is finally brought to an end by the *appearance* of the Lord's coming (*tē epiphaneia tēs parousias autou* [2 Thess. 2:8]—which corresponds to the Lord's words in Matthew 24:30, "then will *appear [phanēsetai]* ... the sign of the Son of Man").

All this is very interesting to us as further revelation on the tribu-lation sequence—especially as it contributes to the developing New Testament doctrine of the Antichrist and his activity in the midtribu-lational abomination of desolation. However, the question does arise as to how Paul intended this brief sketch of the tribulational pattern to answer the false rumor that the day of the Lord had already arrived. The problem in following Paul's argument is the ellipsis in 2:3–4. Paul clearly begins to enumerate a sequential pattern—first comes the "apostasy" and the revelation of the Man of Lawlessness, the one who will blasphemously exalt himself as God in the temple—but after men-tioning the Man of Lawlessness, he breaks from his sentence to exhort them to remember what he taught them. Perhaps if the Thessalonians had had poorer memories, they would have requested Paul to write them a third letter reviewing the whole of his eschatology. Apparently, however, they did recall his teaching and were presumably helped by his remarks in this letter to dismiss the false rumor that the day of the

51. Hengel, *Studies in Mark*, 18–20.

52. Green provides a helpful overview of the hermeneutical discussion surrounding the identity and activity of the Man of Lawlessness, including the intertextual connections to Daniel, the Olivet Discourse, and other references. The suggestion he gives, however, that the temple is not likely the Jerusalem temple on the supposition that events in Jerusalem were too remote and not of interest to this audience seems shortsighted. Obviously, the Thessalonians were greatly interested in the Jerusalem event of the death and resurrection of Jesus, and they were very much interested in knowing about his return. There is no reason to think that the Lord's slaying of an antichrist, self-deified in the Jerusalem temple, as part of a sequence of events that would involve their resurrection and translation would not have been a topic of interest to them. Green, *Thessalonians*, 308–13. In contrast to Green, see the discussion by Ernest Best, *A Commentary on the First and Second Epistles to the Thessalonians* (New York: Harper and Row, 1972), 286–87.

Lord had begun. But the ellipsis is a problem for modern-day interpreters. Translators invariably attempt to fill the ellipsis and usually do so with something like, "that day will not come." Paul is then thought to be arguing that the day of the Lord will not come until *after* certain eschatological events, in this case the "apostasy" and the revelation of the Man of Lawlessness.[53] Whatever the apostasy refers to, the activity of the Man of Lawlessness presented here actually belongs to the integrated day of the Lord / time of the end pattern taught by the Lord and recalled by Paul, not something that precedes it. The coming of the day of the Lord in both the Olivet Discourse and in 1 Thessalonians 5 is without signs, without warning. It comes suddenly and unexpectedly, as a surprise. No one knows when it is coming. Without something in the text to indicate otherwise, we are compelled to fill the ellipsis with something that accords with this canonical and, for Paul's readers, traditional understanding (something that Paul himself apparently expected, as he directs them in 2:15 to "hold to the traditions that you were taught by us ... by our letter" [ESV]). Consequently, it would be better to surmise something like, "For that day would not be here unless there was first the apostasy" (2:3).[54]

---

53. Note the view of Best and Wanamaker that the apostasy and the Man of Lawlessness are not to be taken as sequential elements but rather together, suggesting that the appearing of both of these elements, not one after the other, is in view (Best, *Thessalonians*, 281; Wanamaker, *Thessalonians*, 243–44).

54. This view taken here rehabilitates a suggestion made by Giblin (Charles Giblin, *The Threat to Faith: An Exegetical and Theological Re-examination of 2 Thessalonians 2* [Rome: Pontifical Biblical Institute, 1967], 122–39) without affirming the main point of his argument. The problem in the text is that the apodosis is unstated. Contrary to the traditionally suggested complement, one has to remember that "Paul did *not say* what he is alleged [traditionally] to have had in mind" (128). It is just as possible that Paul intended, as Giblin noted, something like "the Day of the Lord will not have arrived." The problem with Giblin's view, however, is his denial that Paul sees the issue as a matter of "clock-and-calendar time," and that Paul was trying to communicate to the Thessalonians that the day of the Lord "is neither simply present *nor* simply future." This is at the heart of Giblin's contention that Paul was more concerned for qualitative aspects of the day of the Lord. This view has been rightly criticized by Best (*Thessalonians*, 280–81), who has been followed in this by Wanamaker (*Thessalonians*, 243–44) and Green (*Thessalonians*, 306–7). However, the rejection of Giblin's qualitative as opposed to calendrical interpretation of the problem does not in itself rule out the suggested alternative solution to the missing apodosis—an alternative that can also be seen as answering the temporal concern. At this point, the interpreter makes a choice influenced by a broader, contextual understanding of the subject matter. The view chosen here fits with what we have seen as a developed notion of the day of the Lord as a complex event *containing* the elements Paul is highlighting and the tradition extending from the Olivet Discourse to 1 Thessalonians 5 that the day of the Lord *begins without signs*.

Of course, it would have been simpler for this debate about the rapture's relationship to the tribulation if Paul had made the obvious point that the rapture had not yet taken place.[55] The fact that Paul begins to itemize tribulational events has seemed to some to favor a mid- or posttribulational view. However, this is neither necessarily nor even probably so. It is not necessary, because the itemization of unseen tribulational events is a legitimate way to discount the rumor regardless of the rapture's relationship to the tribulation. Furthermore, is it really the case that Paul says nothing about the rapture in his response?

The topic posted at the outset of 2 Thessalonians 2 was the parousia and "our being gathered to him." If we are right in assuming that this refers to the rapture, then one naturally expects it to be addressed in the text that follows. Keeping in mind that Paul expected his readers to supply information from their earlier instruction on these things, the portion of his letter that seems to take up this part of the dual topic is 2:13–15.[56] Here we find the contrast between "you" and "them." In contrast to "them" whose destiny is to be condemned and to perish (2:10–12; cf. 1:7–9, esp. "destruction," *olethros*, used here in 1:9 and in 1 Thess. 5:3), "God chose you to be saved" (*heilato hymas ... eis sōtērian*). We have here a clear parallel to 1 Thessalonians 5:9, "For God did not appoint us (*etheto hēmas*) to suffer wrath but to receive salvation" (*eis ... sōtērias*).[57] In 1 Thessalonians 5 this language of "salvation" for "you" as opposed to "destruction" for "them" refers to the separation that takes place at the *onset*, the beginning of the day of the Lord, with the "salvation" taking place by means of the rapture described in 4:13–17. Significantly, Paul concludes his remarks on "the parousia and our being gathered to him" by referring them explicitly to "the tradition that you were taught by us, either by our spoken word or by our letter." In other

---

55. E. Schuyler English made an interesting suggestion (E. Schuyler English, *Re-Thinking the Rapture* [Traveler's Rest, S.C.: Southern Bible Book House, 1954], 69–71) that *hē apostasia*, literally meaning "departure," was actually a reference to the rapture. However, *apostasia* consistently means a "moral departure," not a spatial departure. The view has rightly been rejected. Thomas, a dispensationalist, does not even mention it (Thomas, *2 Thessalonians*, 321–22). See Bruce on various suggestions for *apostasia* (*Thessalonians*, 166–67).

56. Wanamaker, *Thessalonians*, 264–65.

57. Bruce, *Thessalonians*, 264–65; Green, *Thessalonians*, 326, 328. Wanamaker notes the additional connection with 1 Thessalonians 5:9 by means of the word *peripoiēsis* (*Thessalonians*, 267). On the many similarities in thought between this section and 1 Thessalonians, see Best, *Thessalonians*, 310–22.

words, he refers them back to the earlier letter where the rapture's relationship to the day of the Lord is made clear.[58] Thus, Paul refutes the
false rumor that the day of the Lord has already come by first pointing
out that the early elements of the day of the Lord, that is, the tribulation sequence, have not occurred, and second, by reminding them of his
earlier teaching that at the beginning of the day of the Lord they are
destined for a raptured deliverance—which also has not occurred. The
intended result of this teaching, stated in 2 Thessalonians 2:16–17, is to
leave them at the same point as 1 Thessalonians 4:18, to be comforted
in the hope of this coming salvation.

Pretribulationism and the Book of Revelation

The book of Revelation offers the most extended treatment of the
theme of the tribulation found anywhere in the Bible. The integrated
synthesis of the day of the Lord and Daniel's time of the end that the
Lord sketched out for his disciples in the Olivet Discourse and which
Paul drew upon and partially elaborated in his Thessalonian correspondence is re-presented here in a grand synthesis of biblical prophecies,
types, and images rich in intertextual resonance. This prophetic synthesis dominates the book, beginning in the fourth chapter (after John's
commissioning and his transmission of the seven letters, which occupies
chapters 1–3) and extending to the final exhortations in chapter 22.
Both of the two main divisions of this long section present the synthesis
of which we have been speaking.[59] The first portion, beginning in chapter 4 and running to the conclusion of chapter 11, integrated Daniel's
heavenly throne and Son of Man vision (Dan. 7:9–14) with judgment
features that are typical of day of the Lord predictions. The second
portion, beginning in chapter 12 and running through chapter 22, also
integrates Daniel's time of the end narrative and chronology with day

---

58. Some, such as Wanamaker, have argued that 2 Thessalonians preceded 1 Thessalonians. If this were so, the prior letter in 2 Thess. 2:15 would be unknown to us. However, this
would not change the fact that the salvation at the onset of the day of the Lord was part of the
tradition received by the Thessalonians (1 Thess. 5:1–2, 9). If Wanamaker's suggestion were
correct, then we might see 1 Thessalonians 4:13–5:10 as clearing up any ambiguity remaining for 2 Thessalonians. However, most do not follow Wanamaker's view of the order of the
letters, and I am not arguing for it in this essay.

59. On the structure of Revelation, see Christopher R. Smith, "The Structure of the Book
of Revelation in Light of Apocalyptic Literary Conventions," *Novum Testamentum* 36 (1994):
373–93.

of the Lord features. And both sections are filled with intertextual allusions and citations to many other biblical texts. A full accounting and exposition is obviously not possible in this essay. However, some remarks are necessary regarding the extent of this integration, particularly the question of whether the beginning of the tribulation, as presented by the book of Revelation, is correctly identified as the day of the Lord. The focus of this consideration is on Revelation 6, in which the Lamb begins to break the seals on the seven-sealed book. It is common among pretribulationists to see these events as beginning the tribulation.

As the seals are being broken, John sees calamities breaking out upon the earth. Here we have the famous four horsemen of the Apocalypse, each introduced in tandem with the breaking of a seal: a conqueror, war, famine, and death. With the breaking of the fifth seal is a scene of martyred souls, and then with the breaking of the sixth seal, John sees great heavenly and earthly disturbances—a great earthquake, the eclipsing of the sun and moon, the stars falling, and all humankind fleeing to the mountain rocks and caves to hide from "him who is seated on the throne, and from the wrath of the Lamb, for the great day of their wrath has come, and who can stand?" (6:16–17 ESV).

There is no doubt that what John is seeing in the sixth-seal scene is the day of the Lord. The imagery parallels that found in a group of day of the Lord texts: Isaiah 2:19–21; 13:9–10, 13; Joel 2:10–11, 30–31; 3:15; and the explicit reference to "the great day of their wrath" is unmistakable. The question is whether this seal-breaking series presents the day of the Lord as occurring subsequent to the tribulational events of the first five seal visions or whether all of these events are meant to be taken as the day of the Lord.

Three considerations support the latter view—the view that all the tribulation events envisioned in Revelation 6 should be identified with the day of the Lord. The first is the parallel between the elements of John's seal visions and the early elements of Jesus' Olivet Discourse.[60]

---

60. Mounce writes, "It should be noted that although the form of John's vision is related to Zechariah, the subject matter corresponds to the eschatological discourse of Jesus in the synoptic gospels" (Robert Mounce, *The Book of Revelation*, NICNT [Grand Rapids: Zondervan, 1977], 152–53). For an overview of the synoptic parallels, see R. H. Charles, *A Critical and Exegetical Commentary on the Revelation of St. John*, vol. 1, ICC (Edinburgh: T & T Clark, 1920), 158–60. Also, on the synoptic and Old Testament background, see G. K. Beale, *The Book of Revelation*, NIGTC (Grand Rapids: Eerdmans, 1999), 372–74.

The parallel is striking. War, famine, and martyrdom are highlighted by Jesus in each of the synoptic accounts. The first vision—the conqueror—appears related to Jesus' first warning in the Olivet Discourse, that of false christs—a warning that in turn is linked to the Danielic prediction of an imperialistic, militaristic, and arrogant figure who will appear at the beginning of the time of the end.[61] This is the Antichrist figure who will perpetrate the abomination of desolation in the middle of the tribulation and whom the Lord will destroy at its end. His character and activity are further developed in subsequent chapters of Revelation. Earlier in this essay, I argued that the elements listed in the early part of the Olivet Discourse should be taken as day of the Lord features, and that the whole of the Olivet Discourse presents a narrative pattern in which the day of the Lord and Daniel's time of the end are thoroughly integrated. The obvious parallel between the beginning of the tribulation in John's seals vision and the elements beginning the narrative in Jesus' Olivet Discourse would favor taking the early Revelation 6 features as day of the Lord characteristics as well.

The second consideration has to do with the way the day of the Lord is said to begin in the second part of the Olivet Discourse and, as we have seen, in Paul's teaching as well. The day of the Lord will begin suddenly, without any warning, in a time of relative peace and security. The corresponding point in John's Revelation 6 visions would be the breaking of the first seal. No conditions, no signs, are presented as leading up to this event. It simply happens. But when it happens, the other elements follow—war, famine, death, and persecution leading to martyrdom. They are features of the day of the Lord, not of the setting in which it begins.

The third consideration is related to the grammatical/literary description of the day of the Lord's "coming" in Revelation 6. What

---

61. There is, of course, a number of interpretations for this figure. For a summary of views, see Stephen S. Smalley, *The Revelation to John* (Downers Grove, Ill.: InterVarsity, 2005), 148–51. Smalley rejects the identification with the Antichrist "because," he says, "it breaks the sequence of otherwise impersonal causes which are mentioned during this scene" (150). He agrees with Mounce that the figure is a reference to "military conquest in general" (151; cf. Mounce, *Revelation*, 154). However, he notes that a majority of modern commentators view the rider as "a militaristic figure" (150). Support for a personal reference may be drawn from the Olivet Discourse, which forms a parallel to this text. In the Olivet Discourse, "false Christs" are not general, impersonal forces, even though they are listed with a group of "impersonal causes." Perhaps it is best to put the two together in the sense that the initial appearance of the Antichrist does provoke general conditions of war according to the typology given in Daniel.

is not usually observed is the connection between *ēlthen hē hēmera* in 6:17 and the use of *erchomai* earlier in the chapter. In the visions that correspond to the breaking of the first four seals, John hears each of the four living creatures calling "Come!" (*erchou*). In response we see the appearance of these elements, which we have already recognized as being features of the day of the Lord. A summons such as we see here in Revelation 6:1–8 is typical in Old Testament day of the Lord prophecies. See, for example, the summons by which the day of the Lord is introduced in Isaiah 13:2–4. In response to the summons, "they come ... the LORD and the weapons of his indignation" (13:5 ESV), and "Behold, the day of the LORD comes" (13:9 ESV). Likewise, in Joel 3:9 the summons "Let them come up" (ESV) and in 3:11, "Hasten and come" (ESV), bring on the day of the Lord. The summons is issued to participants of the day of the Lord, which by virtue of their arrival constitute the coming of the day itself. In Revelation 6:17 the expression "the day ... has come" is an acknowledgment by all people in the context of the heavenly and earthly disturbances of 6:12–14 and the flight to the mountains and caves in 6:15–16. However, within the literary structure of this unit—the breaking of the seven seals—the "has come" (*ēlthen*) in the sixth vision is an acknowledgment of the results of the summons to come (*erchou*), which is repeated four times at the beginning of the series. The summons "come" calls forth elements of the day of the Lord. The declaration "has come" looks back over all these elements and acknowledges what has in fact come to be.[62]

The next and obvious question (for the purposes of this book) concerns the relationship of the rapture to the tribulation in the book of Revelation. The problem we have in answering this question is that, as in the Olivet Discourse, there is no *explicit* mention of the rapture in the book of Revelation. This silence per se favors none of the tribulational positions presented in this book. All one can conclude is that an explicit discussion of the topic of the rapture was not in keeping with the purposes of the book or the purpose of the Lord in revealing these

---

62. Few of the recent commentaries discuss the use of *erchomai* in 6:17, much less its literary connection to the first part of the chapter. Thomas is correct to note that the aorist indicative *ēlthen* refers "to a previous arrival of wrath, not something that is about to take place." He suggests that although the day of wrath extends back to the breaking of the extended seals, it is not recognized as such until its progression makes the change in times undeniable (Robert Thomas, *Revelation, an Exegetical Commentary* [Chicago: Moody, 1992], 1:457–58).

visions. A pretribulational position will have to rely on Paul's teaching of a pre–day of the Lord rapture in 1 Thessalonians 4:13–5:10, the tribulational understanding of the day of the Lord by means of (1) Jesus' own integration of day of the Lord features with Daniel's time of the end structure and (2) Paul's own access of this integrated understanding in 1 and 2 Thessalonians, and the application of this understanding to the tribulation / day of the Lord scenario in the book of Revelation, building up a canonical answer to the rapture-tribulation relationship.

Although there is no explicit reference to the rapture in the book of Revelation, there does seem to be an implicit reference in the letters to the seven churches, the portion of the book that precedes the visionary exposition of the tribulation. In the letter to the church at Philippi, we find Jesus' promise (Rev. 3:10–11): "Since you have kept my command to endure patiently, I will also keep you from the hour of trial that is going to come upon the whole world to test those who live on the earth. I am coming soon."

Much has been written about this promise in relation to the rapture.[63] One point of agreement is that "the hour of trial that is coming on the whole world to try those who dwell on the earth" is the future tribulation.[64] The "hour of trial" does not refer to a sixty-minute period, but is an accepted general reference to a coming time of trial, as is the case in the Olivet Discourse when Jesus refers to "the day or the hour." This time of trial is further explicated by the universal extent — the whole world, those who dwell on the earth — which excludes the idea

---

63. This passage has frequently been cited in pretribulational writings; however, much of the recent literature has come in response to Robert Gundry, *The Church and the Tribulation* (Grand Rapids: Zondervan, 1973). Gundry's views were similar to the interpretation of Schuyler Brown, "The Hour of Trial, Rev. 3:10," *JBL* 85 (1966): 308–14; and that of George Eldon Ladd, *A Commentary on the Revelation of John* (Grand Rapids: Eerdmans, 1972), 62. A major response to Gundry was published by Jeffrey L. Townsend, "The Rapture in Revelation 3:10," *BSac* 137 (1980): 252–66. See also David G. Winfrey, "The Great Tribulation: Kept 'Out Of' or 'Through?'" *GTJ* 3 (1982): 3–18; Thomas R. Edgar, "Robert H. Gundry and Revelation 3:10," *GTJ* 3 (1982): 19–49; and Thomas, *Revelation*, 1:283–90. Paul Feinberg's essay, "The Case for the Pretribulational Rapture Position," in Richard Reiter, Paul D. Feinberg, Gleason L. Archer, and Douglas J. Moo, *The Rapture: Pre-, Mid-, or Post-Tribulational* (Grand Rapids: Zondervan, 1984), 47–86, the forerunner to this book, devotes considerable attention to Revelation 3:10 and is dependent on Townsend. In fact, all three contributors discuss Revelation 3:10 in their essays or response articles.

64. Preterists, obviously, would not agree, but the majority would favor seeing the day of the Lord here. See e.g., Grant Osborne, *Revelation*, BECNT (Grand Rapids: Baker, 2002), 192–94; also Beale, *Revelation*, 289–92.

of a merely local trial. These descriptions are repeated later in the book of Revelation, clearly linking this "hour of trial" to the tribulation envisioned in the greater part of the book.[65]

The major point of disagreement has to do with the interpretation of the promise, "I will keep you from the hour of testing." Pretribulationists have repeatedly argued that this means being kept away from the time of the tribulation, and they have seen this as a promise of the pretribulational rapture. Obviously, a pretribulational rapture would in fact be a way of keeping some — those who are raptured — away from the time of the tribulation. A number of posttribulationists, however, have argued that the promise in Revelation 3:10 means being *protected through* the time of the tribulation. This view depends on a "dynamic" interpretation of the preposition *ek* and a particular comparison with John 17:15, where the same verb *tēreō* is used in combination with *ek* for Jesus' prayer, "that you *tērēsēs autous ek* the evil one."[66] The weakness of this comparison for the posttribulational argument has been noted by several scholars.[67] It is likelier that in John 17:15 Jesus was asking that the Father "keep them away from" the Evil One than "keep them through" the Evil One. The failure of the typical posttribulational interpretation in both passages is the failure to appreciate fully the object of the verbal phrase. In John 17:15 Jesus is asking that the disciples be kept from, preserved from, a personal being, the Evil One. Jesus' qualification of his request — "I do not ask that you take them out of the world" (ESV) — simply excludes (from this particular prayer) one possible option for "keeping them away from" this Evil One, a "keeping away," which could take place either in or out of the world. Jesus clarifies his request by eliminating a possible interpretation of his words.

As pretribulationists have often pointed out, in Revelation 3:10 the object of the verbal phrase is not the Evil One but "the hour of trial." The promise is that they will be kept from the time of testing, and on the basis of John 17:15, we may consider that "removal from the world" is one of the possible ways this promise might be fulfilled. How else

---

65. See Rev. 6:10; 8:13; 11:10; 12:12; 13:8, 12, 14; 17:2, 8.
66. See Gundry, *The Church and the Tribulation*; and Beale, *Revelation*, 290–91.
67. See the works by Townsend, Edgar, Winfrey, and Thomas in n. 63 above.

might it be fulfilled? Why not consider how it was actually fulfilled for the Philadelphian recipients of this letter? It is certainly *not* true that they were *kept through* the tribulation, for they died before the tribulation came. They were *kept from* the time of the tribulation by being *kept away from* it. The typical posttribulational interpretation is thus precluded from *possibility* by the actual fulfillment of these words to their original recipients.[68]

Of course, this raises the question as to whether the promise in Revelation 3:10 has anything to do with the rapture's relationship to the tribulation. Maybe not. On the other hand, since we have raised the question of different *possible* ways the promise, worded in this way, might have been fulfilled, we may consider the possibility that a pretribulational rapture *could have* fulfilled these words. Like the actual fulfillment, and unlike the typical posttribulational proposal, it would have involved *removal from the time of trial*. Furthermore, this removal would have taken place by means of removal from the earth, one of the possible means by which "keep away from" could be fulfilled, as seen in John 17:15, and as experienced by the Philadelphians by virtue of their physical death prior to the time of the day of the Lord.

The point is that the actual fulfillment of this promise to the original recipients solves the question as to whether *tēreō ek* meant "keep away from" or "keep through." It meant "keep away from." And once that has been established, we can ask what the possible ways are in which such a promise might be fulfilled. A pretribulational rapture, though, as it turned out, not the actual fulfillment for the Philadelphians, would have been a possibility. A posttribulational rapture would not have been.

---

68. Amazingly, neither side in this debate has considered this point, including the recent commentaries on Revelation. Aune, discussing the debate between pre- and posttribulationists, notes, "unfortunately, both sides of the debate have ignored the fact that the promise made here pertains to Philadelphian Christians" (David E. Aune, *Revelation 1–5*, WBC 52a [Nashville: Nelson, 1997], 240). However, he proceeds from this observation to infer a local protection only. John Walvoord, however, has acknowledged that the death of the Philadelphians must be seen as the immediate fulfillment of the promise in Rev. 3:10 so that the bearing of the promise on the future tribulation is typological—a typology that supports pretribulationism: "If the Rapture had occurred in the lifetime of the Philadelphian church, they would have been kept from the Great Tribulation by the Rapture. However, they died before this event took place" (John F. Walvoord, *Major Bible Prophecies* [Grand Rapids: Zondervan, 1991], 278).

Before we leave Revelation 3:10, we should note that in the pretribulational view being advanced in this essay, the Philadelphian Christians, who were kept from the time of tribulation by death, will in fact be raised from the dead at the beginning of the tribulation when it comes. And they will be raptured to be with the Lord along with living believers who altogether are delivered from the wrath to come. Thus, even though they died, they will be raised from the dead, so that their death prior to the time of the tribulation will not finally be the way they will have been kept from the time of the tribulation. When the tribulation comes, their state will be changed. They will no longer be dead, but raised. And, in that resurrection state, they will be kept from the time of the tribulation by being caught up, or raptured, to be with the Lord.

Coherence of Pretribulational Eschatology

So far we have focused on the biblical teaching on the parousia and tribulation in relation to the rapture taught by Paul in 1 Thessalonians 4–5. But in the conclusion of this essay, I would like to address two harmonization matters that pretribulationism helps to resolve. One we have already addressed in part — the matter of two different orientations to the parousia on the part of redeemed peoples. The other has to do with two different entries into the kingdom, related to two modes of kingdom life.

The two orientations to the parousia are most easily seen in the Olivet Discourse. On the one hand, there is the orientation described in the second part of the discourse, in which one does not know the day or the hour, for the Son of Man is coming at an unexpected time. This is the same orientation given to the disciples in Acts 1, where the Lord tells them, "It is not for you to know times or seasons that the Father has fixed by his own authority" (v. 7 ESV). As noted earlier in this essay, Paul draws upon the second part of the Olivet Discourse when he tells the church that the day of the Lord will come suddenly, like a thief.

The other orientation is that given in the first part of the Olivet Discourse and summarized in the illustration of the fig tree: "when you see all these things, you know that he is near" (Matt. 24:33 ESV). This is the orientation of watching the signs as the tribulational pattern unfolds.

Pretribulationism offers an eschatological pattern that fully respects both of these orientations—both expressions of hope in the Lord's coming. Prior to the beginning of the day of the Lord/parousia, all those who belong to Christ are in the position described in the second part of the Olivet Discourse; 1 Thessalonians 1:10; 4:13–5:10; and Acts 1:7. There are no signs that clearly indicate whether the Lord's coming will be sooner or later. That coming could happen at any time. At any time, the Lord may descend from heaven and take them up to himself to form the company that he will bring with him when he concludes the day of the Lord.

On the other hand, even though the day of the Lord is an expression of divine wrath and an exercise of divine judgment, there will be those who repent, who heed the warnings (Rev. 14:9–11), and who in spite of a growing intense persecution, overcome the Beast and the Devil by their testimony and the blood of the Lamb because they "loved not their lives even unto death" (Rev. 12:11 ESV). They form the company who will be received by the Lord into the kingdom at the end of the day of the Lord, when he descends to the earth and begins his reign. Through the tribulation period, they are in the position described in the first part of the Olivet Discourse and in the book of Revelation. They will see the developing main feature of the day of the Lord—the revelation of the Antichrist and the abomination of desolation—that the church prior to the tribulation will not (2 Thessalonians 2). They will see the signs and know when he—that is, when his appearing (or as Paul says, the appearing of his parousia)—is near.

These two orientations are different and manifest two different forms of "imminency." The imminence of the rapture is due to the lack of any signs by which its proximity may be determined. It may be near or far. The time is unknown. It will occur unexpectedly. It could happen at any moment for those who will form the company that Christ will bring with him when he descends to the earth at the end of the day of the Lord to begin his millennial reign. This is the imminency that pretribulationism has traditionally advocated when describing the rapture.

The imminence of the "appearing of his coming"—which is his descent to earth to begin his millennial reign—is related to the revealed structure of the tribulation and the signs that mark passage from its beginning to its end. Those who come to faith during this time and look for the coming of the Lord know that he is near when they see "all these things." His coming will become imminent in the sense that it is known to be near as the revealed seven-year tribulation structure concludes. They will "lift up their head, for their redemption draws near." Both posttribulationism and prewrath rapture views confuse these two forms of imminency, essentially replacing the imminency of the parousia (which is the imminency of the day of the Lord as a whole) with the imminency of the appearing of his coming.[69]

The second harmonization matter has to do with how entrance into the kingdom is related to two modes of kingdom life—one mortal and one immortal.[70] This duality does not apply to the final everlasting kingdom, for the final abolition of physical death, and consequently physical mortality, occurs at the point of transition from the millennial phase to the final kingdom. But the conditions of human immortality begin to appear in advance of the final kingdom. Already now, Christ is the firstfruits from the dead, manifesting in himself the glorified human immortality that will characterize life in the future kingdom. At the rapture, Paul teaches, Christ will bestow this immortality on the saints either by resurrection from the dead or by translation. Revelation 20 also teaches that at the beginning of the millennium, the dead in Christ will be raised and will reign with him for a thousand years. The immortal glorified saints, whether by resurrection or translation, inherit the kingdom with Christ and constitute a vast resurrected human population in accordance with kingdom prophecies.

However, the millennium also fulfills a number of prophecies that predict mortal kingdom conditions—with actual or possible death, biological multiplication, and other features that indicate a continuity with mortal life as we know it now. This expanding mortal life will grow to become a large population in the millennial kingdom.

---

69. The imminency of the rapture has also traditionally been related to passages expressing Christian hope in terms of the coming of Christ for the church without any reference to a preceding time of trouble—passages such as John 14:1–3; 1 Cor. 15:51–55; Phil. 3:20–21; Titus 2:11–14; and 1 John 3:1–3; as well as the passages we have looked at in 1 Thess. 1:10; 4:13–5:10. For a classical discussion of the pretribulational view of imminency, see John F. Walvoord, *The Rapture Question* (Grand Rapids: Zondervan, 1957), 75–82.

70. See the discussion by Feinberg, "Case for the Pretribulational Rapture," 72–79.

Entrance into the millennial kingdom takes place with a view toward these modes of kingdom life. Obviously, some will have to enter as mortals if mortal kingdom conditions are going to be fulfilled. The entrance of immortals, is, as we already know, by resurrection or translation.[71]

The problem is how to account for the kingdom entry of mortals and immortals within the parameters of the biblical texts. What are those parameters? First, whenever the rapture takes place, it will result in the translation of *all believers alive at that time* into immortality (1 Cor. 15—we will all be changed; 1 Thess. 4—those who are alive, who are left—both passages indicating *all living believers*). Second, when the judgment takes place to determine who among the mortals will enter the kingdom, *only mortal believers will enter* (Matt. 25:31–46). The problem is, of course, that the more proximate the rapture is to the judgment of mortals, the fewer if any believers there will be to be admitted as mortals into the kingdom. Posttribulationism obviously has the greatest difficulty with this problem. Prewrath and midtribulational views allow more time for a believing remnant to develop, albeit during the time of the greatest distress and deception. Pretribulationism resolves the problem better than the others not only by its expectation of the maximum time differential for the believing mortal remnant to develop—the full tribulational period of seven years—but also because it more reasonably places the post-rapture conversion/revival in the first half of the tribulation, prior to the greatest distress and greater deception.

Dispensationalism and the Pretribulational Rapture

As is well known, the doctrine of the pretribulational rapture has been a key feature of dispensationalism. The argument given in this essay, however, is not particularly dispensational. The argument presented here is an interpretation of the relationship of the rapture to the day of the Lord in Paul's first letter to the Thessalonians, drawing out

---

71. Not all of those who come to faith in the post-rapture revival survive the persecutions of the tribulation period. Revelation 6:9–11 speaks of martyrs at that time, and Revelation 7:9–17 portrays them as a great multitude from every tribe, tongue, and nation. These martyrs will be raised from the dead after Christ's descent to earth (Rev. 20:4–6) and will enter the kingdom as immortals.

the tribulational meaning of the day of the Lord by means of a context established through clear intertextual connections. Hopefully, this is an argument that will prove helpful to dispensationalists and nondispensationalists alike. However, dispensationalists have typically brought other considerations to bear in their argument for a pretribulational rapture, considerations that contribute to the meaning and purpose of the rapture and its role in the unfolding plan of God as that has been understood by dispensational theology.

Traditionally, dispensationalists have seen the tribulation as a period of dispensational change—from the dispensation of the church to that of the millennial kingdom. This dispensational change also marked a shift of focus in the purpose of God, from the church to Israel, or as classical dispensationalists put it more generally, from the heavenly people to the earthly people. In much of this thinking, the pretribulational rapture was a systemic feature of dispensational theology tied directly to ecclesiology—that is, to the identity of the church as a unique and separate redeemed people in the plan of God. As a "heavenly people," the church was distinct from redeemed "earthly people," meaning primarily Israel. The church, as a previously unrevealed heavenly program, comes into existence as a parenthesis within the earthly program of God's purpose for Israel. This parenthesis must be closed for the earthly program to resume. The closure of that parenthesis is the pretribulational rapture. By means of the rapture—signless, sudden, mysterious, like the church itself in the plan of God—the heavenly people would be removed from the earth to heaven. Daniel's chronology of the seventy sevens, having been interrupted by the church, would resume. The seventieth week—the seven-year tribulation—would commence, and God would begin again to prepare an earthly people for the fulfillment of the earthly promises.

Many of the classical dispensational arguments for the rapture take into account this dispensational view of the church as a unique heavenly people. For example, *the church by definition* cannot be present when Daniel's "earthly" chronology resumes. The church cannot suffer "wrath," because it cannot by definition be present in the time of tribulation wrath. It is not just the existing church at the time of the rapture that is taken up; it is the church as a program in the plan of God that is consummated. Consequently, the promise in 1 Thessalonians 5:9, "for God has not destined us for wrath" (ESV) was used to argue that God has determined that the church per se will not be present during the tribulation period. Since the baptism of the Holy Spirit is the distinguishing mark of identity for the church, this meant that the baptizing work of the Holy Spirit ceases with the rapture. It logically follows, then, that those who come to faith during the tribulation period are not part of the church as the church is defined universally to be those united to Christ by the baptism of the Holy Spirit. This is why dispensational arguments have typically stressed the observation that the word *church* does not appear in the book of Revelation after chapter 3. In accordance with this, dispensationalists have typically identified the restrainer in 2:6–7 as the Holy Spirit in his mode of indwelling the church—that is, in his church-forming work of baptizing believers into Christ. The removal of the restrainer would be the removal of the church. And finally, the dispensational view of the church has often been combined with a church-age view of the letters to the seven churches, with the Philadelphian church representing the true church being removed from the earth at the time of the rapture.

This church-program view of the rapture has in turn conditioned arguments formulated against pretribulationism—arguing, for example, that pretribulationism must be wrong because the presence of believers in the post-Revelation 3 tribulation scenario indicates the church must be present, or arguing that pretribulationism is wrong because the restrainer cannot be clearly identified as the Holy Spirit in his baptizing ministry.

The reader who wishes to pursue classical or semiclassical dispensational arguments for pretribulationism is directed to various publications in which they are set forth.[72] Many of these works present strong

---

72. The following are just some of the works one might consider. A classic in dispensational eschatology is J. Dwight Pentecost, *Things to Come* (Grand Rapids: Zondervan, 1958). The many writings of John F. Walvoord bear on the subject, including *The Rapture Question*, which has already been mentioned. See also his trilogy, *Israel in Prophecy*, *The Church in Prophecy*, and *The Nations in Prophecy* (Grand Rapids: Zondervan, 1962, 1964, and 1967). Walvoord published a study of the different types of posttribulationism in his work *The Blessed Hope and the Tribulation* (Grand Rapids: Zondervan, 1976), and later in his life, *Major Bible Prophecies*, which has already been mentioned, and *The Prophecy Knowledge Handbook* (Wheaton: Victor, 1990). Another classic is Charles Ryrie's *The Basis of the Premillennial Faith* (Neptune, N.J.: Loizeaux, 1953). See also Ryrie's *What You Should Know about the Rapture* (Chicago: Moody, 1981). Finally, two essays in particular are recommended. One, as already noted, is the essay by Paul Feinberg, "The Case for the Pretribulation Rapture Position," in *The Rapture*, 47–86.

arguments for pretribulationism, and the reader is encouraged to consider these presentations. However, one needs to be aware of the ecclesiological dimension of the argument in these works and be prepared to pursue the matter in that direction.

Not all dispensationalists follow the classical model in distinguishing Israel and the church as two eternally separate redeemed people groups. Progressive dispensationalists distinguish Israel and the church administratively (organizationally), constitutionally (ethnic versus multiethnic), politically, historically, and typically—both revealing aspects or dimensions of the coming kingdom: multinational (including Israel and gentile nations) and united together in Christ by the Holy Spirit (testified to by the church in the present dispensation). But since they do not see the church as a uniquely separate redeemed people group, they typically do not argue that the pretribulational rapture is the programmatic separation of the church for the purpose of forming another group of the redeemed.[73] For progressive dispensationalists, the rapture occurs at the beginning of the tribulation because God wills it so, as revealed by Paul in his Thessalonian correspondence, not because it is necessary to separate the program of the church.

However, having arrived at this point, the argument having been made on exegetical grounds and distinguished from earlier programmatic arguments, I feel some obligation to suggest at least what larger eschatological meaning a pretribulational rapture might carry. Of course, as has been pointed out, the rapture will be a bestowal of grace on all who hope or have hoped in Christ—the deliverance from the day of wrath and bestowal of glory. It constitutes a sign of the sure and certain triumph of God's salvation in contrast to the judgment

Another is the article by Zane Hodges, "The Rapture in 1 Thessalonians 5:1–11," in *Walvoord: A Tribute*, ed. Donald K. Campbell (Chicago: Moody, 1982), 67–79.

73. For an overview of progressive dispensationalism, including a review of the historical development of dispensationalism, see Craig A. Blaising and Darrell L. Bock, *Progressive Dispensationalism* (Wheaton: Victor, 1993), as well as the earlier work *Dispensationalism, Israel and the Church*, ed. Craig A. Blaising and Darrell L. Bock (Grand Rapids: Zondervan, 1992). One should also note the work of Robert L. Saucy, *The Case for Progressive Dispensationalism* (Grand Rapids: Zondervan, 1993). A well-known work on dispensationalism is Charles Ryrie, *Dispensationalism Today* (Chicago: Moody, 1965). This was revised and expanded and published in 1995 under the title *Dispensationalism*. It offers a critique of progressive dispensationalism. For a comparison of views, see Herbert W. Bateman IV, *Three Central Issues in Contemporary Dispensationalism: A Comparison of Traditional and Progressive Views* (Grand Rapids: Kregel, 1999).

that is about to be poured out, a pattern that will be played out again in the unfolding events as the righteous are kept from the judgment that falls on the lost (cf. the sheep and goats judgment and the translation of mortal believers at the end of the millennium in contrast to the judgment of hell). Many pretribulationists have pointed out the prophetic events that take place between the rapture and the appearance at the end of the tribulation, when the saints will come with Christ in glory. These include the judgment seat of Christ and the marriage supper of the Lamb, which presumably do not take place instantaneously. During the time of the tribulation, the raptured saints prepare to appear with Christ in his glorious descent. But we also may consider the impact of the fact of the rapture on those who will come to faith during the tribulation. We know that grace is extended during the tribulation period. The book of Revelation extends comfort and encouragement to those undergoing trial by consideration of Christ's resurrection and power to extend resurrection life to those he will. A pretribulational rapture would be a manifestation of Christ's ability to extend resurrection power and grant immortality—a sign that would strengthen those who will come to faith in the midst of the severest time of trouble and deception—to those who wash their robes in the blood of the Lamb and make them white (Rev. 7:14), those who will conquer by the blood of the Lamb and by their testimony and who will love not their lives unto death (Rev. 12:11), those who are called upon to endure to the end (Rev. 14:12) and who will likewise be granted immortality either sooner (at the beginning of the millennium by resurrection, Rev. 20:4, 6) or later (at the end of the millennium by translation, Rev. 21:4).

Conclusion

My task in this essay has been to set forth the argument for pretribulationism. This is not the only argument that could be given, and the reader is reminded of references to other works on the subject given above. However, I hope that it is evident that there are biblical reasons for taking a pretribulational view of the rapture.

All of us in this volume have the advantage of following a previous publication on this subject that has been widely used with much benefit in evangelical institutions. The reader may want to consult the fine essay by my predecessor in the work, Paul Feinberg, for a different approach to the same subject.

Of course, each of us as contributors to this volume disagree about the relationship of the rapture to the tribulation. But the reader should be reminded that there is so much on which we do agree. Christ is coming again. He is coming to rule on the earth. There will be a resurrection of the dead in Christ and a translation of those who are alive at his coming. And we will reign with him, not just for a millennium, but forever. There is so much more that each of us could list that we affirm together. We have a living hope in the resurrection of Christ from the dead and a secure inheritance kept for us in heaven, coming with him when he comes (1 Peter 1:3−4).

Peter also reminds us that the prophets who prophesied about Christ's coming "searched and inquired carefully" not only as to who the Messiah would be, but also concerning the time of prophetic events (1 Peter 1:10−12). Their work was not simply for themselves, but for others who would follow.

We are not prophets, just servants of Christ, trying to be faithful in understanding the Scripture, searching and inquiring carefully to understand the time of his coming in relation to the time of tribulation. All this work related to the timing of prophetic events will be useful if through it we and those who come after us, if the Lord tarries, actually grow thereby into a better understanding of God's Word and a more reliable knowledge of the hope that we have in Christ. One way to do that is to put these views on the table and seriously consider and critique them in the light of Scripture. I have full confidence and the highest esteem for my colleagues in this endeavor and look forward to this exercise of searching the Scriptures together. I think I can speak for all of us in saying that our desire for you the reader is to join us in this endeavor, to take these essays, and like the Bereans of old, examine the Scriptures with us to see if these things are so (Acts 17:11). Our desire, even more than wanting our readers to gain a better understanding of the Scriptures, is that as properly working parts of the body, we may all grow up in every way—in faith, hope, and love—into him who is the head, into Christ (Eph. 4:15−16).

ALAN HULTBERG

Dr. Blaising argues a provocative, new case for the pretribulation rapture. I find myself in agreement with many parts of his essay, but ultimately I am not persuaded by his argument. In particular, I agree with Blaising's first major thesis, that in 1 and 2 Thessalonians Paul promises that the church will be raptured at the outset of the day of the Lord prior to (and to save them from) the outpouring of God's wrath. I do not agree, however, with his second major thesis, that the day of the Lord is coextensive with Daniel's seventieth week. He attempts to demonstrate this latter point by showing (1) that Daniel presents a typological pattern of a seven-year period of wrath at the "time of the end," (2) that the Olivet Discourse (especially Matthew 24) integrates features of the day of the Lord and Daniel's seven-year "time of the end," and (3) that the use of the Olivet Discourse in the Thessalonian epistles and the book of Revelation confirms this interpretation of Matthew. Blaising also makes some ancillary points regarding the coherence of pretribulational theology—namely, that a pretribulation rapture makes better sense than other views of both the two modes of orientation to the parousia and the two modes of entrance into the kingdom found in Scripture, and of the function of the rapture in giving hope to believers during the tribulation. I will focus the bulk of my response on Blaising's primary argument but would like briefly to address these latter points here.

With regard to the two modes of entrance into the kingdom and the giving of hope to tribulation saints, Blaising argues that a pretribulation rapture best allows both mortal and immortal believers to enter the millennial kingdom and gives greatest assurance to tribulation saints that God can and will deliver them from the terrors of the tribulation. But I can see no substantive advantage to the pretribulation view over the prewrath in these matters. First, though pretribulationism grants slightly more time and initially better conditions for believers to be saved after the rapture, the advantage is only a matter of a few years. Certainly both views allow for mortal believers at the end of the tribulation. Second, there is no reason why tribulation saints would be more encouraged by a pretribulation rapture of the church than a prewrath rapture; both equally demonstrate the commitment of God to save his people.

With regard to the two modes of orientation to the parousia found in Scripture, a few observations are in order. First, while I agree that pretribulationism coheres somewhat more easily than the other views with the general biblical data, this observation carries little weight in and of itself as long as the other views can also be supported by the biblical texts. For if the argument for pretribulationism fails on other grounds, then the fitness of the modes of orientation with the pretribulation rapture is irrelevant. The biblical data remain but must be dealt with differently, and this is precisely what prewrath and posttribulation advocates do. Second, it is simply not the case that for the arrival of something to be unknowable or unexpected, signs cannot precede that arrival. The timing can be unknowable as long as the length of time between the signs and the start of the event is unknown ("I'll be coming sometime after 3:00"), and it can be unexpected as long one does not take proper notice of the signs ("You're here already? I wasn't paying attention to the clock!"). There is nothing in the biblical data that undermines either of these conditions in relation to a prewrath rapture.

Furthermore, I contend in my primary essay that the exhortations in the New Testament (especially in the Olivet Discourse) about both the unknowable timing of the parousia and the observance of signs prior to it are given to the church, making the "fit" between the pretribulation rapture and the biblical data more complicated than might at first appear. Blaising's own argument on Matthew 24:36 supports this point. According to Blaising, Jesus tells his disciples that they would see events in the first century that could possibly signify his parousia, since they correspond to events of the end as outlined in the Old Testament, though Jesus admits that he does not know whether those first-century events would prove to be the actual end-time events of his return. But this makes the "unknowability" of the parousia in Matthew 24 not an absolute "unknowability" but only an admission of Jesus' ignorance of the timing of his coming in broad relation to world history. He knows the type of events that will precede it, just not which manifestation of those events will prove ultimate. Also, Jesus indicates that if his parousia was to happen in the first century, his first-century disciples would have witnessed the signs of his parousia, including the abomination of desolation. But if first-century Christians could possibly witness the eschatological signs of the parousia, then Christians of any century can. I will say more about this last point below; for now it is sufficient to note that Blaising's arguments from theological coherence are neither exclusively helpful to pretribulationism nor perhaps fully coherent with his own argument. We turn our attention, then, to the major elements of that argument.

Daniel

To make his case, Blaising must show that the wrathful day of the Lord is coextensive with Daniel's seventieth week. His argument rests on three lines of evidence. The first comes from the book of Daniel, where Blaising claims that the "time of the end" (and its type in the Antiochene persecution) is a structured pattern that encompasses the entire seventieth week and apparently includes in temporal order the appearance of an Antichrist, wars, persecution, an abomination of desolation, unprecedented tribulation, and the coming of the Son of Man. He also seems to imply that the seventieth week/"time of the end" is a period of divine wrath. The evidence in Daniel, however, does not easily comport with these claims.

Language regarding the "time of the end"[74] is used in three contexts in Daniel (8:15–19; 11:20–44; and 12:4–13). But associating the language with a particular set of events is difficult. Daniel 12:4–13 provides no real help. In 12:4–13 the "time of the end" is that time until which Daniel's prophecy will be sealed, presumably some point before its total fulfillment, since during the period of persecution those with insight will be able to understand the prophecy (12:10). The wonders

---

74. The language includes "time of the end" ('ēṭ qēṣ, Dan. 8:17; 11:35, 40; 12:4; 12:9), "appointed time/end" (mô'ēd, mô'ēd qēṣ, Dan. 8:19; 11:27, 29, 35), and "end [of days]" (qēṣ, qēṣ hayyāmîn (Dan. 12:13,)).

prophesied will end with the resurrection (12:2–3; cf. 12:6), which occurs at "the end of the days" (12:13), so that here "the time of the end" may merely be a general reference to the last days, though a reference to a specific period of time within the last days is not out of the question. In Daniel 8:15–19, "the time of the end" and "the appointed time of the end" refer to the end of the period prophesied in Daniel 8, that is, the career of Antiochus IV at the "end" of the Persian and Greek domination of the eastern Mediterranean as revealed in the vision.[75] This is made clear by 8:23, which begins a focus on Antiochus with the words "In the latter part of their reign." Daniel 11:20–35 refers to this same Antiochene era, but here "the appointed time" (11:27, 29) has especially to do with the period when Antiochus "rages (zā'am) against the holy covenant" (11:30). "The time of the end" mentioned in 11:35 seems also to refer to this period, but the reference is not entirely straightforward. As many note, Daniel 11:36–12:3 hardly speaks of Antiochus but appears instead to jump to the events of the very end of the age (cf. 12:1–3), shifting from Antiochus, the type, in 11:29–34, to Antichrist, the antitype, in 11:36–40. Like 11:29–34, the period described in 11:36–12:3 is also designated a "time of wrath" (za'am, 11:36) and "the time of the end" (11:40), so that the statement in 11:35 that "[the time of the end] will still come at the appointed time" may be intended not to close the prophecy of Antiochus but to link "the end" of the Antiochus prophecy to its antitype in Antichrist persecution.

The "time of the end," then, is not a simple concept in Daniel. Initially it refers generally to the final portion of the prophetic period under consideration, whether of the vision of the ram and the goat or of the Gentile domination of Judah that began in Daniel's day and will continue to the end of this age. More specifically, however, "the time of the end" focuses on the careers of the last kings of these visions, and especially on their careers as persecutors of the Jews. Daniel 8:23–26 thus interprets the Antiochene persecution of 8:9–14, with a focus on the abomination of desolation and the events following from it. This "time of the end" occurs in "the latter part of the period the wrath" (b^e'ah^arît hazzā'am, 8:19); that is, either at the latter part of the career

75. So, e.g., Joyce G. Baldwin, *Daniel: An Introduction and Commentary*, TOTC 21 (Downers Grove, Ill.: InterVarsity, 1978), 59.

of Antiochus or the latter part of the Persian-Greek domination of
the ancient Near East, the whole being designated as "the [period of]
wrath" (*hazzā'am*). Daniel 11:20–44 specifies this focus more precisely.
After reviewing the initial career of Antiochus in verses 20–27a, the
reader is told in 27b that "an end will still come at the appointed time."
Verses 29–34 then focus on this "appointed time" (v. 29) as the time
after Antiochus's Roman humiliation, during which he "rages" against
the covenant, setting up the abomination of desolation, removing the
regular sacrifice, and persecuting faithful Jews. Verses 36–44 pick up
at this parallel stage in the career of the Antichrist, when he magnifies
himself above all gods during a period of "wrath" (11:36) and of unprecedented distress (12:1) for the Jews. Though Daniel 9:24–27 does not
mention "the time of the end" or "the period of wrath," the relationship of Daniel 8:9–14; 11:29–35; and 11:36–12:3 is clearly meant to
correspond to the latter half of the seventieth "week," since it is that
portion of the week that follows the establishment of the abomination
of desolation (9:27). Thus, though both "the time of the end" and "the
[period of] wrath" can possibly refer to the entire career of Antiochus/
Antichrist, they more specifically refer to the terror of their final three
and one-half years. It is much too facile, then, to refer to "the time of the
end" as a structured pattern in Daniel encompassing the entire seventieth "week." The pattern Daniel focuses on is the period of persecution
and ultimate deliverance following the abomination of desolation.

This leads to a second observation: the "wrath" that occurs at "the
time of the end" is not the wrath of God against sinners, but the wrath
of the Gentile kings against God and his people. Daniel's only use
of the verb *zā'am* ("to rage against, be indignant against, curse") is in
11:30, where it describes Antiochus's hostility to the covenant. This
implies that the equivalent periods of *za'am* referred to in 8:19 and 11:36
are periods of imperial opposition to God's people. Those who contend
that the wrath there is God's indignation against sin generally argue
from the use of *z'm* elsewhere in the Old Testament and from the claim
that in Daniel Gentile domination is overall a result of Israel's sin. But
while it is true that Daniel presents God as ultimately in control of the
rise and fall of the Israel-dominating kingdoms and that the Babylonian
captivity has covenantal overtones, one is hard pressed to find evidence
that specifically links the Antiochene and Antichrist persecutions to

God's indignation over Israel's sins. When Daniel does speak of wrath against the people, it is explicitly imperial wrath, and when he portrays the function of God as judge in the prophecies, it is God as judge of the imperial desolator (7:9–11; cf. 8:25; 9:27; 11:45–12:1).[76]

Blaising's claims about the evidence in Daniel, then, do not hold up. "The time of the end" is not presented in Daniel as a period of divine wrath, nor can "the time of the end" easily be identified with the entirety of the seventieth week. In fact, it much more readily focuses on only the last half of the week.

The Olivet Discourse

The linchpin of Blaising's argument is that in the Olivet Discourse Jesus distinguishes between his coming in judgment in the day of the Lord and his glorious appearing at the end of that period. The former begins unexpectedly and incorporates the events of the entire seventieth week of Daniel; the latter happens after the observable abomination of desolation. More specifically, Blaising seeks to show that the events of Matthew 24:4–35 are patterned on the structure of Daniel's "time of the end," that the description of the events in this section is infused with day of the Lord language, and that when Jesus speaks of his unknown coming in Matthew 24:36–25:30, he is speaking of the entire day of the Lord complex of Matthew 24:4–35.

The Use of Daniel in the Olivet Discourse

In arguing that the events of Matthew 24:4–35 are patterned on the structure of Daniel's "time of the end," Blaising makes two observations. First, Matthew 24:4–35 is presented as a narrative sequence with an explicit beginning (v. 8) and end (vv. 6, 13, 14) and marked by a series of "thens" (vv. 9, 14, 16, 23 [ESV], 30 [ESV]). Second, the sequence has a Danielic character, beginning with the appearance of false christs (Antichrist) and attendant wars and persecution, having

---

76. Counterevidence might be found in Daniel 8:12, but the transgression there is almost certainly that of Antiochus and not the Jewish people. Cf. the *happeša' šōmēm* of v. 13 (cf. Dan. 9:27; 11:31; 12:11) and the parallel passage to Dan. 8:12 in 11:31. See Martin Pröbstle, "Truth and Terror: A Text-Oriented Analysis of Dan. 8:9–14," vol. 1 (Ph.D. diss., Andrews University, 2006), 243–309. Cf. John J. Collins, *Daniel*, Hermeneia (Minneapolis: Fortress, 1993), 335; Baldwin, *Daniel*, 157–58; John E. Goldingay, *Daniel*, WBC 30 (Dallas: Word, 1989), 197; *Peshitta*, Vulgate, KJV, and the Tanakh translations.

a reference to the abomination of desolation at its middle, and ending with the coming of the Son of Man. This sequence, he claims, follows that of "the time of the end" he had outlined earlier.

A few responses to these claims are in order. First, I have already argued that the very idea of any significant Danielic "time of the end" sequence that precedes the abomination of desolation is questionable. Thus, proposed references to typical "first-half" events in the Olivet Discourse are prima facie dubious (further, see below).

Second, while it is true that Jesus envisions a sequence of events that begins with, among other things, a period of false christs, wars, and persecutions, and that ends with his glorious return, Matthew 24:4–31 is not structured as a simple sequence. Rather, verses 4–14 outline general phenomena that explicitly do not signal the end, while in contrast, verses 15–31 follow a sequence from the abomination of desolation to the coming of the Son of Man. The general phenomena will certainly occur first, but it is not until the Danielic abomination of desolation that the final series of events will be set in motion. Thus verses 4–14 are marked not by sequential language but by general parataxis[77] and, more important, by the disavowal that these events are events of the end (24:6, 14). The point of equating the events of verses 4–14 with the beginning of labor pains (v. 8) is not to make them part of "the end" but to distinguish them from it.[78] A contrast is signaled in verse 15, however, by an adversative or transitional *oun*, "however."[79] Thereafter clear sequential material predominates. Thus, while a sequence is outlined in Matthew 24:4–31, it is not the straightforward sequence Blaising requires.

Third, it is not clear that anything prior to the explicit Danielic allusions in verses 15–31 is intended to refer to a Danielic sequence at all. Blaising cites Davies and Allison[80] in support, but the only two

---

77. On the use of *tote* in vv. 9 and 10, see among others Michael J. Wilkins, *Matthew*, NIVAC (Grand Rapids: Zondervan, 2004), 774.

78. So, e.g., see D. A. Carson, "Matthew," in *Matthew, Mark, Luke*, EBC, ed. Frank E. Gaebelein, 12 vols. (Grand Rapids: Zondervan, 1984), 8:498; Donald A. Hagner, *Matthew 14–28*, WBC 33B (Dallas: Word, 1995), 689–92; Craig L. Blomberg, *Matthew*, NAC 22 (Nashville: Broadman, 1992), 353–54; Craig S. Keener, *A Commentary on the Gospel of Matthew* (Grand Rapids: Eerdmans, 1999), 566–67; Wilkins, *Matthew*, 772–74.

79. Cf. *de* ("but") in Mark 13:14.

80. W. D. Davies and Dale C. Allison Jr., *A Critical and Exegetical Commentary on the Gospel according to Saint Matthew*, vol. 3, ICC (Edinburgh: T & T Clark, 1997), 332.

allusions to Daniel that they propose can be found in verses 4–14 are rumors of wars (v. 6) and persecution of the saints (vv. 9–10[81]), neither of which has much to commend it. "Rumors of wars" supposedly alludes to the "war" of Daniel 9:26 and the "rumors" of Daniel 11:44, but "war" is hardly unique to Daniel, even war in Jerusalem; and Daniel 11:44 refers to "reports from the east" that the Antichrist will respond to, not "rumors of war" that the disciples will hear about and respond to in fear. Furthermore, nothing in the further description of these wars in Matthew 24:7 alludes to Daniel. Similarly, the description of persecution in Matthew 24:9–10 has nothing especially Danielic about it, either thematically or verbally, except the use of the term "tribulation" (*thlipsis*), but even this is explicitly distinguished from the Danielic tribulation (*thlipsis*) in verse 21. And since nothing else in Matthew 24:4–14 is even remotely Danielic, it thus seems very unlikely that Jesus intends the general phenomena there to indicate the beginning of a Danielic "time of the end" sequence, even if such a sequence could be established for the first half of Daniel's seventieth week. Rather, the Danielic sequence begins with its explicit mention in verse 15.

The Day of the Lord in the Olivet Discourse

Blaising is on firmer ground when he argues that all of Matthew 24:4–35 is about the day of the Lord. The strength of his case rests on the proposed allusion to Isaiah 13:8 in the phrase "the beginning of birth pains" (Matt. 24:8), so that Matthew 24:4–31 is framed by allusions to Isaiah 13 (cf. Isa. 13:10; Matt. 24:31), intentionally subsuming the section under the Isaian day of the Lord. Still, I do not think that Blaising makes his case. For while I am inclined to accept the allusion to Isaiah 13:8 and even to agree that the phenomena of Matthew 24:4–14 (famines, earthquakes, wars, persecutions) are intended to signal general eschatological conditions, these observations are mediated by the function of verses 4–14 generally and verse 8 specifically in the discourse. As stated above, verse 8 marks an intentional distinction between the general "eschatological" events of verses 4–14 and "the end" mentioned in verses 6 and 14. They are thus not *the* labor pains of the day of the Lord but the *beginning* of labor pains. The significant events would

81. Ibid, "9–11 [*sic*]."

begin with the Danielic abomination of desolation (v. 15), after the gospel had been preached to the whole world (v. 14). In fact, that the gospel must be preached to the whole world before the end would come at least implies that the general "eschatological" events of verses 4–14 would be typical of the church age. This is a regular perspective in the New Testament, that the "last days" began with the first coming of Christ and associated events, and even that the first-century persecution of the church was a manifestation of the eschatological judgment of God. Blaising is no doubt correct to recognize that the labor mentioned in verse 8 comes to its conclusion in the glorious appearing of Christ in verse 30, but neither that observation nor the allusion to Isaiah 13:8 more specifically means that the final, eschatological day of the Lord began in the first century, far less that it will begin some time in the future with the general phenomena of Matthew 24:4–14. Rather, like the explicit allusions to Daniel in verses 15, 21, and 30, which highlight the significant events of the "end," the explicit allusion to Isaiah 13:10 in verse 29 highlights the onset of the eschatological day of the Lord.

Blaising contends that such a view cannot account for the professed ignorance of Jesus regarding the timing of these things in Matthew 24:36, especially since in verses 33–34 Jesus distinguishes between the presaging events the disciples would see and the culminating event of his parousia. But I fail to see the point. It makes no difference whether the significant typological events are those of verses 4–28 or verses 15–28; in either case Jesus may not know whether their first-century manifestation will prove to be the eschatological manifestation. Either set of events signals that "it" — that is, the day of the Lord, the parousia of Jesus of verses 29–31 — is near.

The Day of the Lord as the Extended Coming of Christ

Blaising also claims that when Jesus speaks of his unknown coming in Matthew 24:36–25:30, he is speaking of the entire day of the Lord complex of Matthew 24:4–31. This claim allows Blaising to distinguish the glorious appearing in 24:29–31, which is preceded by signs, from the coming mentioned in 24:36–25:30 (namely, the entire complex of events in 24:4–31), which presumably is not. In response, first, as I noted in my opening remarks, this point is incompatible with

Blaising's earlier argument about the Olivet Discourse. Though earlier Blaising maintained that Jesus expects the disciples to experience the phenomena of 24:4–28, even if they prove to belong to the eschatological day of the Lord, his exegesis of 24:36–25:30 suggests that the disciples should not expect to see any of those things should they so prove. It is not clear to me how he can maintain both positions. Second, while I agree with Blaising that Jesus is speaking about the day of the Lord when he refers in 24:36 to "that day," there is no good reason to distinguish the parousia that encompasses that day (vv. 37 and 39) from the explicit reference to the parousia in 24:30–31, especially given the flow of the discussion of Jesus' parousia from verses 3 to 35. The parousia of 24:30–31 *is* the parousia of 24:36–39. It is only a supposed necessary dichotomy between signs and "unknowability" that drives Blaising to deny this and thus to try to establish that all of 24:4–31 is the day of the Lord/parousia to which verse 36 refers. But I have shown above that this latter attempt falls short, and I have argued earlier that the former supposition is false. So, while I agree on other grounds with Blaising that the day of the Lord/parousia is a complex of events that begins with the rapture and concludes with the glorious appearing of Christ, this point is not established in the Olivet Discourse.

2 Thessalonians

Other sections of Blaising's argument depend on his conclusion regarding the Olivet Discourse. Since that conclusion is doubtful, the rest of his argument is doubtful as well. Thus, with regard to the day of the Lord in 1 Thessalonians 5, Blaising is correct to identify the rapture as that which rescues believers from God's wrath at the outset and to recognize Paul's dependence on the tradition behind the Olivet Discourse for his day of the Lord material. But Blaising is off target when he proposes that Paul integrates the day of the Lord with the entire seventieth week of Daniel in dependence on the Olivet Discourse, since, as I have shown, Jesus (at least as represented by Matthew) does not in fact make that integration. The only support that Blaising offers is Paul's use of the labor metaphor in 1 Thessalonians 5:3. He argues that since Paul is dependent on the day of the Lord as outlined in the Olivet Discourse, and since the day of the Lord in the Olivet Discourse begins with the labor pains of Matthew 24:4–14, then Paul must also understand the day to begin with the phenomena of Matthew 24:4–14. However, I have shown that the mention of the labor pains in Matthew 24:8 is explicitly to distinguish the general difficulties of 24:4–14 from the significant "eschatological" events of the second half of Daniel's seventieth week. The day of the Lord in that general sense probably begins with the dawn of the Christian era. But this is not how Paul uses the metaphor, as is clear from the fact that he picks up none of the other language of Matthew 24:4–14. Rather, Paul focuses the metaphor on the suddenness and ferocity of the wrath to be experienced by unbelievers in the day of the Lord. He thus seems to use the metaphor more like the original intention of Isaiah 13:8; he is not thinking of the general beginning of labor pains of Matthew 24:8 but the specific onset of the agonizing wrath at the outset of the parousia (Matt. 24:29–31; cf. Luke 21:25–27). This is confirmed by 2 Thessalonians 2:1–15, where Paul more explicitly expects the day of the Lord to begin after the abomination of desolation.

I have already argued this point extensively in my main essay, but I would like to respond to Blaising's counterargument. Blaising contends, on the basis of his interpretation of the Olivet Discourse, that the crucial missing words in 2 Thessalonians 2:3 ("for [something will not happen], unless the rebellion [NASB "apostasy"] comes first") should be "that day would not be here" or "will not have arrived" rather than "that day will not come." But I cannot see how this supports Blaising's position. For if the abomination of desolation occurs in the middle of the day of the Lord, as Blaising contends, the day could certainly be present without the abomination of desolation having had occurred. Paul's evidence that the day could not be present (2:2) would be no evidence at all. This is compounded by the fact that Paul says, "Unless the apostasy comes *first*," suggesting, in greater conformity to Paul's proffered evidence, that the apostasy and abomination of desolation *precede* the day of the Lord or initiate it. And though it is true that Paul could explain the nonpresence of a day that begins with the rapture by referring to the absence of events that will occur in it long after the rapture, there seem to be no good reasons why he would, particularly when he focuses so much attention, nine verses, on these "unseen tribulational events" and particularly if the issue at hand is the missing rapture. At the very least, Blaising needs to give an explanation for this. Blaising notes, and I agree with him, that Paul does bring the rapture back into the discussion in 2 Thessalonians 2:13–15, but this observation does nothing to mitigate the difficulty of accounting for Paul's reasoning in 2:3–12 under the pretribulation view. At best, then, 2 Thessalonians 2 is extremely difficult to understand from a pretribulation rapture perspective, but even likelier, it undermines that perspective, and with it Blaising's reading of the Olivet Discourse, entirely.

Revelation

Blaising also relies on his exegesis of the Olivet Discourse when he considers the evidence of Revelation, especially because he sees no explicit mention of the rapture in Revelation. In particular, he believes Revelation 6 corroborates his understanding that the day of the Lord begins with the phenomena of Matthew 24:4–14. He argues (1) that the opening of the first six seals of the seven-sealed scroll (Rev. 6:1–17) follow the phenomena of Matthew 24:4–29; (2) that since in Matthew 24:36–25:30 and 1 Thessalonians 5:2–3 the day of Lord begins suddenly and unexpectedly, the day of the Lord must begin with the first seal of Revelation 6, the only seal whose effect is compatible with suddenness and unexpectedness; and (3) that the use of *ēlthen* ("came," "has come") in Revelation 6:17 (seal 6) recalls the day of the Lord summonses of Revelation 6:1–8 (the first four seals) and implies that by the sixth seal people recognize that they have been in the day of the Lord.

I agree with Blaising's first observation, that the six seals of Revelation 6 consciously parallel the phenomena detailed in the Olivet Discourse. This is a common observation among commentators. But despite Blaising's other two points, that John intends this correspondence to reflect an understanding of the Olivet Discourse tradition that begins the day of the Lord with the first seal is highly questionable. First, while it is true that, given a temporal sequence in the seals, suddenness and unexpectedness can most easily be applied to the first seal, two facts call into question the value of such an observation. On the one hand, even on Blaising's reckoning, the earth dwellers do not recognize the arrival of the day of the Lord until the cosmic portents of the sixth seal. This suggests that the phenomena of seals 1–5 did not appear abnormal to them, and in fact, false messiahs, wars, famines, and so on hardly are abnormal; they have been occurring since at least the first century AD. Thus the appearance of false christs, or even a "messianic" imperial figure, cannot be considered sudden or unexpected, and John does not portray it as such. The suddenness of the day of the Lord explicitly appears in the sixth seal. On the other hand, it is doubtful that either Jesus in Matthew 24:37–39 or Paul in 1 Thessalonians 5:2–3 mean that the world will be entirely peaceful when the day of the Lord dawns. The analogies they use only indicate that life will be essentially normal when the day dawns, not that there will be no wars or famines or false messiahs at the time. Beyond this, it is probable that Paul relies on such passages as Jeremiah 6:14; 8:11; and Ezekiel 13:10 for the unbelievers' cry of "peace and safety" immediately before the day of the Lord. But in these passages the people and their leaders say "peace, peace" to maintain the delusion that everything is all right when in fact "there is no peace." Thus, the biblical notion of suddenness and unexpectedness at the coming of the day of the Lord is quite compatible with the sixth seal, where John puts it.

Blaising, however, attempts to show that the explicit recognition of the arrival of the day of the Lord in the sixth seal refers back to seals 1–5. But while I agree with him that the summons of Isaiah 13:1–6 bears thematic correspondence to the summoned "warriors" of the first four seals (Blaising's evidence from Joel is much less compelling), and that this can suggest that John begins the day of the Lord with those seals, the crucial question really concerns the meaning of *ēlthen* ("came," "has come") in the sixth seal (Rev. 6:17), and here the evidence is decisively against Blaising. Blaising claims that *ēlthen* in Revelation 6:17 is intended to recall the same verb used in the summonses of the first four seals ("Come!" *erchou*; Rev. 6:1, 3, 5, 7) and to indicate recognition by the earth dwellers that the events effected by the first five seals were part of the day of the Lord. But, on the one hand, *erchesthai* is a common verb in Revelation, used thirty-six times with relative uniformity throughout the book, so that with no other clear connection between its use in seal 6 and seals 1–4, there is no good reason to posit one. On the other hand, *ēlthen* is used three other times in Revelation in expressions similar to its use 6:17, each with the meaning "has now arrived" or "is now about to begin" (Rev. 14:7, 15; 19:7). As I argue in my main essay and in my response to Moo, it is clear from the narrative development of the seals and trumpets vision that this is the intended meaning of *ēlthen* in 6:17. Thus the sequence of a prayer for vengeance with an exhortation to patience (seal 5), followed by an announcement of the arrival of the day of wrath (seal 6), followed by a forestalling of the implementing of wrath until certain conditions were met (chap. 7), followed by a response to the prayer for vengeance by an outpouring of wrath (seal 7, trumpets), and concluded with a statement that the wrath and vindication had now been completed (trumpet 7), makes it certain that *ēlthen* in 6:17 is forward referring and not backward.

Revelation 6, then, gives no credence to the notion that the day of the Lord begins with the phenomena of Matthew 24:4–14. The day of the Lord begins in Revelation 6 in the same place it began in Matthew 24, with the explicit day of the Lord events of the sixth seal, the events of the parousia of the Son of Man in Matthew 24:29–31. And what is especially significant about this observation, as I argue in my main essay, is that within the sequence of the seals and trumpets outlined above, the interlude of chapter 7 apparently depicts the rapture. This is true despite Blaising's generally acceptable observation that there is no explicit mention of the rapture in Revelation. It is thus noteworthy that of the two groups singled out in chapter 7 for protection from the impending day of wrath, one, the 144,000, remains protected on earth, while the other, the innumerable multitude of the church is protected by their sudden appearance in heaven. Chapters 14 and 15 relate a similar scene. Prior to the outpouring of wrath in the grape harvest (Rev. 14:17–20), resulting in the bowls of wrath (Rev. 15:1, 5–16:21), one like a son of man comes on a cloud (cf. Dan. 7:13; Rev. 1:7, 13) and makes his own harvest, apparently resulting in the appearance of the victors over the Beast in heaven (Rev. 15:2–4). Both of these scenes correspond to the parousia of Matthew 24:29–31. If these are rapture scenes, and I believe I have given considerable proof in my primary essay that they are, they serve to confirm my reading of Paul and Matthew over-against Blaising's — that is, that the parousia, with its attendant rapture and outpouring of wrath on the earth, occurs after the abomination of desolation and in concert with the cosmic signs of the day of the Lord.

Conclusion

Dr. Blaising's argument for a pretribulation rapture rests primarily on a supposed integration of the entirety of the seventieth week of Daniel with the day of the Lord in the Olivet Discourse. Because the church will be raptured before the day of the Lord, the church will necessarily be raptured before the beginning of the seventieth "week." Blaising tries to show this integration within the Olivet Discourse itself and within the use that Paul makes of the Olivet Discourse in 1 Thessalonians 5 and that John makes of it in Revelation 6. I have tried to show that in none of these cases can that integration be maintained. On the one hand, there is no seventieth-week structure in Daniel that can be integrated with day of the Lord items, beyond a focus on the last half of the "week," the half initiated by the abomination of desolation and characterized by the wrath of Antichrist against the Jews. Thus we find no good evidence that Daniel material appears in the Olivet Discourse until its explicit mention with the abomination of desolation in Matthew 24:15. On the other hand, the evidence that the day of the Lord begins in Matthew, Paul, and John with the phenomena of Matthew 24:4–14 is far from compelling. The use of Isaiah 13:8 in Matthew 24:8 is explicitly intended to dissociate the phenomena of Matthew 24:4–14 from the significant events of verses 15–31, and the entire tenor of the Discourse, from the disciples' question to the parables of the end, focuses the day of the Lord/parousia on Matthew 24:29–31. In Paul the labor metaphor of 1 Thessalonians 5:3 is used quite differently than in Matthew 24:8, and the clear meaning of 2 Thessalonians 2:3 is that the day of the Lord and attendant rapture will not begin until after the abomination of desolation. Finally, in Revelation, the use of *ēlthen* in the book and the narrative development from the fifth seal through the seventh trumpet show that the day of the Lord arrives with the opening of the sixth seal, which corresponds to the parousia of Matthew 24:29–31. In fact, Revelation appears to place the rapture at precisely this point, arguing forcefully against a pretribulation rapture and for a prewrath rapture. I believe these counterarguments are decisive. I commend Dr. Blaising for a thoughtful and vigorous defense of the pretribulation rapture, but in the end, I remain unpersuaded.

DOUGLAS MOO

I am very grateful for the opportunity, after a quarter of a century, to engage once more in debate over the relationship between the time of the final tribulation and the rapture of believers. I am grateful for two reasons in particular. First, I enjoy the opportunity to clarify my own views and interpretation of important passages that is afforded by the back-and-forth format of this volume. We all learn best in vigorous dialogue with proponents who hold different views than our own. Craig Blaising and Alan Hultberg have given me a lot to think about. Second, I welcome the opportunity to engage in debate on this matter with viewpoints that have developed in some significant ways over the last twenty-five years. In the first edition of this book, my late colleague Paul Feinberg represented very well the mainstream pretribulation perspective of that time—a perspective tied to classic dispensational theology. Since then the so-called "progressive dispensational" view has arisen and gained considerable popularity. Blaising defends pretribulationism from within this paradigm—a paradigm that I find, on the whole, has a much better exegetical basis than traditional dispensationalism. Similarly, I find the prewrath view defended by Hultberg to be an interesting and, in most ways, better-based view than the midtribulational view defended in the first edition by another late colleague, Gleason Archer. Perhaps, then, I should not really be grateful at all, for Blaising and Hultberg have made my task of arguing for a posttribulational rapture even more difficult. Nevertheless, after a quarter of a century, I still find this way of putting the various pieces of the biblical "puzzle" of end-time events together to be the best option. To be sure, careful readers who compare my essays in this volume with the original volume will detect some differences in the way I interpret particular texts and in the overall context within which I am viewing these matters. But the position I am defending is substantially the same.

If my basic opinion on this matter has remained the same, so has my perspective on it. The issue debated in this volume should be seen by all sides as a relatively minor matter. No significant doctrine of the church is affected. No text is interpreted so differently that its general theological and practical teaching is obscured. I think my fellow authors agree that the very reason a volume such as this is needed is because the Scriptures are not clear about the timing of the rapture. Any view — including certainly my own — involves an attempt to construct an overall picture from disparate and at times apparently contradictory pieces of evidence. We need to add a strong dose of humility to our defense of these views.

In response to Blaising's defense of the pretribulational rapture, I would point readers first of all to my own basic essay. I deal there with most of the exegetical and theological issues that Blaising raises in more detail than I can here. Nevertheless, I offer the following as a summary of some of the questions that I have about Blaising's argument.

Blaising's basic argument is easily summarized. (1) Paul teaches in 1 Thessalonians 4–5 that the rapture will take the form of a "rescue operation" from the impending wrath of God associated with the day of the Lord. (2) The day of the Lord is equivalent to the seventieth week of Daniel (Dan. 9:25–27), and thus to the final tribulation. (3) Therefore the rapture is pretribulational. Blaising supports his second key point about the equivalence of the day of the Lord and the final tribulation by arguing that the Olivet Discourse mixes day of the Lord allusions with references to Daniel's eschatological sequence. By his allusions to the Olivet Discourse, Paul shows that he also refers to the final tribulation when he predicts that believers will be rescued before the day of the Lord begins. Blaising finds a similar situation in the book of Revelation and concludes by noting that the pretribulational rapture position succeeds in solving several tensions within the New Testament. Blaising's argument is solidly grounded in careful exegetical work and is logically clear. But at the end of the day, I do not find the argument compelling, and I will explain why below, dealing with Blaising's points in the same order that he presents them. Briefly, however, let me say at the outset that our basic disagreement is over the day of the Lord. Blaising argues that the "day" is extended over the "seven years" of Daniel's seventieth week and includes the final tribulation. I contend that the "day" follows the final tribulation.

1 Thessalonians 4 – 5

As I have noted, Blaising's basic point is that 1 Thessalonians 4–5 teaches a "pre–or inaugural day of the Lord rapture." And since this day of the Lord is equivalent to the final tribulation, the rapture must be pretribulational. In fact, Blaising argues, the rapture is presented in this passage as the means by which believers are rescued from God's wrath, which is poured out on the day of the Lord. Hultberg makes a similar argument, and in order to conserve space, I will deal with the argument in my response to his essay. Suffice it to say here that I am not convinced that salvation from God's wrath takes the form of rapture in this context.

Blaising argues that a basic separation between believers and unbelievers is taught in this passage. And he is right. As he points out, the shift from "people"/"them" in 5:2–3 to "you" in verse 4 is emphatic. Blaising argues, further, that this passage teaches that the separation between believers and unbelievers occurs at the "onset" of the day of Lord. This point is important for his argument, as we have seen, because he wants to locate the rapture at the very beginning of the day of the Lord, which he identifies with the final tribulation. The text does, indeed, suggest that the coming of the day of the Lord will affect believers and unbelievers in different ways. Unbelievers are unprepared, so it comes upon them like "a thief in the night"—as a surprise. Like the scoffers in 2 Peter 3, unbelievers convince themselves that things will always go on as they do now—they can live their lives without any worry about judgment. But believers know better, and so the day of the Lord, while it will also come upon them, will not "surprise" them "like a thief" (v. 4). The difference between these two groups is not whether they experience the day of the Lord but *how* they experience it. Blaising suggests that the separation between believers and unbelievers has to do with rescue from the wrath of that day versus being left to experience it. But this is not what Paul is saying. Moreover, Blaising's focus on the "onset" of the day of the Lord in this passage appears to be, at least, an overemphasis. There is nothing in this text to suggest any "duration" to the day of the Lord, as if we could distinguish between its "onset" and its continuing unfolding. Blaising's reason for suggesting a drawn-out day of the Lord in 1 Thessalonians 5 comes from other texts. To these we now turn.

The Seventieth Week of Daniel and the Final Tribulation

As I noted above, Blaising's main argument for a pretribulational rapture is that the day of the Lord in 1 Thessalonians 5 must be equivalent to the seventieth week of Daniel and thus to the final tribulation. The key middle term in this argument is the seventieth week of Daniel. For Blaising's argument to work, he must show (1) that the seventieth week of Daniel is equivalent to the final tribulation, and (2) that the seventieth week of Daniel is equivalent to the day of the Lord. Only by doing so can he claim that Paul's day of the Lord language must refer to the final tribulation. My argument in this section will take up each of these points. I contend that the first point is unproven and that the second is not clear.

Curiously, Blaising provides little argument for his crucial first point — that the seventieth week of Daniel is equivalent to the final tribulation. He notes that pretribulationists understand this equivalence to be the case. But this is to assume what one must prove. Blaising also suggests this equivalence by arguing that the "seventieth week" is equivalent to other passages in Daniel. Daniel's prophecies, Blaising correctly notes, are about "the time of the end" (8:17, 19; 11:36, 40; 12:4, 9), a time of "wrath" (8:19; 11:36), and prominently feature the rise and career of a political figure who oppresses the people of God for a period of "time, times and half a time" (Dan. 7:25). This figure is particularly associated in Daniel with a desecration of the temple, and the period of oppression he initiates comes to an end when God himself intervenes to take his sovereignty away and bestow it on the saints. Blaising suggests that this sequence of events is equivalent to the seventieth week of Daniel and refers to the final tribulation. But I am not so sure of this interpretation.

First, the time of tribulation in Daniel appears to be focused on the second half of Daniel's week, when the "ruler to come" violates his covenant agreement and desecrates the temple (9:26–27; see also 7:25, cited above). Blaising never explains why the Danielic pattern, taken up in the Olivet Discourse, does not logically entail mid- rather than pretribulationism. More important, as I note in my main essay, Blaising's assumption about the meaning of the seventieth "seven" of Daniel can hardly be accepted without careful argument. The seventy "sevens" passage of Daniel 9:25–27 is difficult to interpret and has given rise to an extraordinary variety of interpretations. I have neither the time nor the competence to look at the text in any detail. But I want to suggest two reasons for questioning the identification of the seventieth "seven" of Daniel and associated prophecies with the final tribulation.

First, we must remember that Daniel's claim to be predicting "the time of the end" does not mean that his prophecies can only be fulfilled at the end of history. Indeed, as Blaising and most interpreters agree, Daniel clearly has in view the events of the Maccabean period. I think those who insist that Daniel, in typical prophetic fashion, is also predicting ultimate "eschatological" events are certainly correct. But it is not at all easy to sort out which prophecies are fulfilled in the Maccabean period, which ones are fulfilled in the ultimate eschatological scenario, and which may be fulfilled, to some degree, in both periods. My key point here, however, is that there is no good reason to confine "the time of the end" that Daniel has in view to the very end of human history. As I argue in my essay, "eschatology" includes, from the New Testament perspective, everything from Christ's first coming to and including his second coming and subsequent events. The events of the "time of the end" to which Daniel refers could, then, include events from the time of Christ and from early Christian history as well as from the end of the Christian era. This being the case, the "seventieth seven" of Daniel may be (and I think probably is) a reference to the entire period of eschatological culmination, beginning with Christ's first coming. There is certainly nothing in Daniel 9:25–27 to suggest a "gap" of two millennia or more between the sixty-ninth and seventieth "sevens"—and the burden of proof would seem to fall on those who posit such a gap (as Blaising appears to do).

Second, the New Testament use of Daniel confirms this view of Daniel's prophecies. Paul's use of Danielic language to describe the "man of lawlessness" in 2 Thessalonians 2 makes clear that Daniel's prediction about a great oppressor of the people of God finds its ultimate fulfillment in *the* Antichrist of the final tribulation. But the New Testament also warns us that "many antichrists" will arise before this climactic Antichrist (1 John 2:18). The oppressor and his desecration of the temple could well, then, have preliminary fulfillments. Indeed, as we shall see, Blaising concedes that this may be the case. But more important for our point are other allusions to Daniel in the New Testament. The most obvious references to Daniel 9:27 occur in the several references to a roughly three-and-a-half-year time period in Revelation. They are as follows:

> Gentiles trample on the Holy City for "forty-two months" (11:2).
> The "two witnesses" prophesy for 1,260 days (11:3).
> People gaze on the bodies of the two witnesses for three and a half days (11:9).
> The two witnesses are revived by the breath of life from God after three and a half days (11:11).
> A woman is taken care of by God in the wilderness for 1,260 days (12:6).
> A woman is protected from the dragon hurled down from heaven for "time, times and half a time" (12:14).
> The Beast is given authority for forty-two months (13:5).

That these refer to one (probably the second) half of the seventieth "seven" of Daniel is clear—and the allusions here, along with the reference to a similar period of time in Daniel, is why many interpreters think that the final tribulation should be confined only to the second half of Daniel's seventieth week. But to what period of time do these texts in Revelation refer? Those who think that Revelation 6–16 describes the final tribulation have a ready answer. But this is another assumption that we cannot make. For myself, I doubt that these Revelation references all refer to the final tribulation period; some of them, probably most of them, seem to me to refer more naturally to the church age more broadly conceived.[82] Even more important, however, are New Testament texts that appear to locate the eternal kingdom to be brought in through the Son of Man at the first coming of Christ. Among many texts that we could cite, note, for example, Jesus' claim in Matthew 28:18: "All authority in heaven and on earth has been given

---

82. A comparison between the commentaries on Revelation of Grant Osborne and Greg Beale is instructive here. Osborne takes all these texts to refer to the final period of redemptive history (Grant Osborne, *Revelation* [BECNT; Grand Rapids: Baker, 2002], 417–18, 463–64, 498–99). Beale, on the other hand, thinks that they all refer to the age of the church, the "three and a half" year period bounded by Christ's death on the front end and his return in glory at the back end (G. K. Beale, *The Book of Revelation: A Commentary on the Greek Text*, NIGTC [Grand Rapids: Eerdmans, 1999], 565–67, 646–47, 694–95).

to me," which appears to be at least an initial fulfillment of Daniel 7:14, and the prediction in Luke 1:33 that Jesus' kingdom "will never end," another apparent allusion to Daniel's predictions of the eternal kingdom that will succeed the kingdoms of this world. Many, indeed, think that New Testament references to the Son of Man "coming on the clouds of heaven" (Dan. 7:13) refer not to the coming *down* to earth of Christ at the end of history but to his *coming* up, into the presence of God, at the time of his ascension.[83] I doubt this, however. And, in general, I think it is clear that the New Testament sees the consummation of Daniel's prophecies about an eternal kingdom as coming only with Christ's second advent. But the kingdom, of course, is even now inaugurated, and Daniel's kingdom prophecies are therefore even now finding initial fulfillment.

For these reasons, I question whether we can equate the seventieth week of Daniel with the final tribulation, as Blaising suggests. And this undercuts his crucial claim that the association of the day of the Lord with Daniel's seventieth week in the Olivet Discourse means that the day of the Lord is equivalent to the final tribulation.

The Day of the Lord and the Olivet Discourse

The space that Blaising devotes to the Olivet Discourse indicates the importance of this text for his argument. For it is here, he argues, that Daniel's prophetic sequence (which, as we have seen, Blaising identifies with the final tribulation) is mixed with day of the Lord language to indicate that the day of the Lord is coextensive with the final tribulation. Blaising's interpretation of the Olivet Discourse is well informed and has a number of very attractive features. But I am finally unconvinced of two key points that he argues: that day of the Lord language in the Olivet Discourse shows that Jesus is referring (at least by way of an "antitype") to the final tribulation; and that the shift in focus in Matthew 24:36 and parallels signals a shift from the posttribulational parousia to the parousia conceived as a sequence of events.

---

83. See, e.g., R. T. France, *The Gospel of Mark: A Commentary on the Greek Text*, NIGTC (Grand Rapids: Eerdmans, 2002), 609–10 (on Mark 14:62), who notes a considerable shift of opinion from the traditional view that the text denotes a "coming" of the Son of Man to earth to the view that it refers to the "coming" of the Son of Man into the presence of God.

Blaising is correct to note that imagery often associated with the day of the Lord is scattered throughout the Olivet Discourse. There is some justification for claiming, then, that the Olivet Discourse describes what the Old Testament called the "day of the Lord." Must this not, then, indicate that the Olivet Discourse has in view the final period of human history? Not necessarily. The key point here again is to take with full seriousness the inaugurated eschatology of the New Testament. As I argue in my main essay, the New Testament claims quite clearly that Jesus' death and resurrection have inaugurated the "last days" envisaged by the Old Testament prophets. "Day of the Lord" language in the New Testament (for a complete list, see my main essay) is, to be sure, usually used for the climactic consummation of the last days when Christ returns to save his people and judge his enemies. But "day of the Lord" language is also applied to the current stage of salvation history. Paul quotes Isaiah 49:8 and then applies it to his own day: "For he says, 'In the time of my favor I heard you, and in the day of salvation I helped you.' I tell you, now is the time of God's favor, now is the day of salvation" (2 Cor. 6:2). Similarly, James applies a prophecy about the day of the Lord from Amos (9:11) to the inclusion of Gentiles in the early Christian church (Acts 15:14–18). Jesus' death and resurrection mark the first installment in God's "day of the Lord" program. The "day of the Lord" language in the Olivet Discourse need not, then, indicate that a final period of time at the end of history is in view. The discourse may, as I think, cover the whole sweep of salvation history between Jesus' first coming and his second.

I have made the case for this broader interpretation of the discourse in my main essay. Blaising is unpersuaded of this view of the discourse, claiming that it involves a "rambling sequence" that starts with a specific agenda to discuss the temple's destruction, moves from that to general remarks about the church age, then returns to the key issue of the temple and finally "rockets forward" to the time of the parousia. I can only say that I find this to be an unfair caricature of the sequence that I argue for in my essay. But more important is an assumption that Blaising makes here: that a move from the temple destruction to parousia is to "rocket forward." This language appears to assume what Blaising elsewhere rightly denies: that Jesus knew, as he taught the discourse, that there would be a substantial amount of time between the temple destruction and his parousia. On the whole, I find Blaising's own interpretation of the basic outline of the discourse to be less likely than my own. He divides the discourse into two basic parts. The first part, Matthew 24:4–35, presents a narrative sequence of events, climaxed with Christ's second coming. He argues that this sequence has a typical quality. Up until the "sign of the Son of Man," the events predicted by Jesus could (and indeed did) occur within the lifetime of the disciples. Because it climaxes the narrative sequence, the "coming" of Jesus in this part of the discourse refers to his return to earth at the end of history. This first part of the discourse then answers the disciples' second question in 24:3: "What will be the sign of your coming and of the end of the age?" The first question—"When will this happen?"—is answered in the second part of the discourse, Matthew 24:36–25:46. In these verses, the focus is on the uncertainty of the time of Jesus' parousia. Because of this uncertainty, in contrast to the "predictability" of the parousia in 24:4–35, Jesus must here be referring in this second part of the discourse not to return in glory at the end of history per se, but to the whole complex of end events. By making this distinction, Blaising can "have his cake and eat it too." He can recognize (as interpreters must, I think) that Jesus has in view the events of AD 70 and that the "coming" of Matthew 24:29–35 is posttribulational. But he can also preserve a pretribulational rapture by arguing that the second half of the discourse encourages believers to be ready for a "coming" that includes the entire seventieth week of Daniel, the final tribulation. Why do I not find this interpretation convincing?

A shift in the discourse at verse 36 can be granted. But what must be questioned is whether, as Blaising thinks, the shift signals a different focus in the key word *parousia*. Jesus' "coming" is the climax of the first part of the discourse (v. 30). In the second part of the discourse, Jesus then appears to refer back to this "coming" with the noun *parousia* (24:37, 39), the same noun that refers to Jesus' coming in the first part of the discourse (v. 27; cf. v. 3). Yet Blaising argues that the referent of the word changes. But the text does not support such a change. When Jesus refers to "that day or hour" in verse 36, he may (as Blaising thinks) have some allusion to the "day of the Lord." But it cannot be the main referent, or the imagery would make no sense: just try plugging "that day of the Lord or hour" into the verse. As the commentators universally note, the "day or hour" that is uncertain must refer to the time of the parousia that Jesus has just been talking about.[84] A different, or wider, reference cannot be established without clear indication to that effect. To be sure, Blaising thinks that the context provides just such an indication, arguing that the parousia of 24:4–35 is preceded by signs whereas the parousia of 24:36–25:46 comes upon people unexpectedly. The presence of these two kinds of texts throughout the New Testament admittedly constitutes a difficulty, and pretribulationists have often argued that the chronological distinction between Jesus' "coming" for the church (rapture) and his "coming" in judgment at the end of the tribulation solves the problem. Blaising's interpretation is a form of this argument; indeed, in my view, a superior form of this argument. But the problem, as I have noted, is to find any reason to make a distinction between the parousia in verses 4–35 and the parousia in 24:36–25:46. Indeed, as I have argued in my main essay, I can find no basis for a distinction in the referent of the word *parousia* (in its technical sense) anywhere in the New Testament. In the Olivet Discourse, then, references to Jesus' "coming" all go back to the critical text, Matthew 24:29–35 — where the "coming" is a posttribulational event.

A second problem with Blaising's interpretation is the way he relates the parts of the discourse to the questions in 24:3. Blaising's claim that Jesus answers the question "When will this happen?" in the second part of the discourse runs afoul of the fact that the "this" in this question refers to the destruction of the temple (see v. 2). It is only in the first part of the discourse (see v. 15) that there is any reference to the temple; so it is here that Jesus is answering this question. This makes it likelier that Jesus answers the two questions in verse 3 in order, explaining first that the temple would be destroyed and great tribulation would begin within the lifetime of the disciples (vv. 4–28). It is in verses 29–35, which focus on Jesus' "coming," that Jesus answers the second question. The second part of the discourse (Matt. 24:36ff.–25:46) consists of a series of exhortations based on this scenario. As I argue in my main

---

84. E.g., France, *Matthew*, 936–37; Donald A. Hagner, *Matthew 14–28*, WBC 33B (Dallas: Word, 1995), 716; John Nolland, *Matthew: A Commentary on the Greek Text*, NIGTC (Grand Rapids, 2005), 991; W. D. Davies and Dale C. Allison, *Matthew 19–28: A Critical and Exegetical Commentary on the Gospel according to Matthew*, ICC (Edinburgh: T &T Clark, 2004), 378; Craig L. Blomberg, *Matthew*, NAC 22 (Nashville: Broadman, 1992), 365; and David L. Turner, *Matthew*, BECNT (Grand Rapids: Baker, 2008), 588.

essay, then, the first part of Jesus' narrative description (vv. 4–28) refers to the tribulation that characterizes the entire age of the church now that Messiah has come and the kingdom is pressing into history. It is "after that" tribulation (v. 29) that Jesus will return in glory to gather his saints (v. 31).

I also question whether Blaising's interpretation is ultimately successful in dealing with a key problem for pretribulationism in the Olivet Discourse. As I note in my main essay, and as Hultberg argues at length in his, Jesus addresses his disciples as representatives of the church in the discourse. Blaising does not explicitly contest this. But if this is so, then Jesus appears to assume that Christians are those who need to be warned about coming events (24:4–14), who will see the "abomination of desolation" (v. 15), and who will experience the great tribulation (vv. 18–21). I may admit, for the sake of argument, Blaising's claim that this sequence has typical significance and could be repeated in history. But he provides no reason to think that the final "antitypical" sequence, involving the final tribulation and climaxed in the return of Christ in glory, will impact any different audience than the "typical" manifestations of the sequence earlier in history.

Back to the Thessalonian Letters

Having established to his own satisfaction the equation "day of the Lord" = final tribulation period, Blaising then returns to 1 Thessalonians 5. The many parallels between this passage and the Olivet Discourse reveal that the day of the Lord in the former passage must be coextensive with the extended parousia of Matthew 24:4–35—including, of course, the final tribulation. I admit the parallels, but I do not admit the conclusion. The parallels Blaising cites are mainly with the second part of the Olivet Discourse. But only if we buy into Blaising's unusual view of the discourse do the parallels prove what Blaising wants them to. The parallel expressions to which Blaising refers in the Olivet Discourse all have to do with the parousia ("day of the Lord" or similar expressions [e.g., "that day"] do not occur in the discourse [see above for Matt. 24:36]). What the parallels establish is that Paul views the day of the Lord in 1 Thessalonians 5 as parallel to the parousia (which in any case is suggested by 4:15–16). I readily grant that. But does Paul's "day of the Lord" include an extended period of time, including the final tribulation? I have already contested Blaising's claim that the parousia refers to an extended period of time in the Olivet Discourse. And there is no reason in the Thessalonian letters to think this is the case either.

In 2 Thessalonians 1:5–10 Paul teaches that God will "give relief" to the suffering believers in Thessalonica when "the Lord Jesus is revealed from heaven in blazing fire with his powerful angels." At this same time, God will punish their persecutors with "everlasting destruction." The imagery in this passage points to Jesus' return at the very end of history—after the "tribulation," which, of course, the Thessalonians are already suffering. The same scenario is suggested by 2 Thessalonians 2:3, where Paul seeks to calm the Thessalonians by reminding them that certain tribulational events—the "rebellion" and the revelation of the "man of lawlessness"—must occur before the day of the Lord comes. Blaising denies that this is what this text teaches by noting that this conclusion depends on a conjecture in the text. In the Greek text of this verse, we have an "if" clause with no explicit "then" clause: "if the rebellion does not occur and the man of lawlessness is not revealed...." We wait in vain for the other shoe to drop. Everyone agrees that Paul's elliptical Greek must be filled in with something from the context. Almost all the commentators argue that we should fill the verse in with the immediately preceding language: "the day of the Lord will not come." Blaising, however, argues that we should translate "that day would not be here." He argues for this translation out of a concern for canonical integrity. He notes that the day of the Lord elsewhere in the New Testament is presented as arriving without any prior signs. Therefore Paul cannot here be claiming that signs will precede the day of the Lord. The rebellion and the revelation of the Man of Lawlessness must be components of the day of the Lord, not precedents to it. But Blaising is on shaky ground here. First, his own rendering hardly accomplishes what he wants it to do. As long as the "first" is included (as it must be, since it represents the Greek), a sequence appears to be intended—whether we render the phrase "that day will not come" or "that day is not here." Second, his rendering finds very little support in the literature.[85] All the major English transla-

---

85. The only serious support for Blaising's reading comes from the idiosyncratic book by Charles Giblin, *The Threat to Faith: An Exegetical and Theological Re-examination of 2 Thessalonians 2*, Analecta Biblica 31 (Rome: Pontifical Biblical Institute, 1967), 122–39. Blaising

tions have something equivalent to TNIV's "that day will not come," and this tradition of translation should only be departed from with the clearest evidence.

As I argue in my main essay, then, there are very good reasons to conclude that the "day of the Lord" in the New Testament refers to the climax of human history, a climax that follows the tribulation of this church age (including the final tribulation): the rapture and resurrection of believers and the judgment of unbelievers.[86]

Since Hultberg's argument depends considerably on the interpretation of the book of Revelation, I will deal with that book in my response to him. But Blaising makes one argument from Revelation that I need to deal with here. Blaising and Hultberg agree that the syntax of the famous promise in Revelation 3:10 cannot determine whether Jesus' promise is that he will keep the Philadelphia Christians out of the "time of trial" (that is, rapture them before it begins) or that he will protect them during it. But Blaising does claim that history makes a posttribulational interpretation impossible, since the Philadelphia Christians were, in fact, not preserved intact during the final tribulation but were kept from it by death. Of course, the fact that this promise is directed to first-century Christians leads some interpreters to think that the "time of trial" here is a past historical persecution, in which case the verse has no relevance for the rapture question. But most interpreters think that the text does at least include the final tribulation. For this verse is similar to other texts throughout Revelation that have in view a tribulation that culminates in Christ's return in glory. Nevertheless, Blaising's suggestion that the Philadelphia Christians were saved from this tribulation by dying before it came does not sit well in this context. Christ appears to promise deliverance from the time of trial on the basis of the Philadelphia Christians' faithfulness to God's Word (v. 10a). Death (which, of course, all people experience) would be an unusual way for God to honor this promise. But the bigger problem with Blaising's argument about 3:10 is a failure to appreciate the way the first-century audience

---

distances himself from Giblin's overall interpretation, but it is hard to see how Giblin's translation can be accepted without the larger package of his interpretation.

86. Note in this regard that Peter's quotation from Joel in Acts 2 clearly indicates that some of the cosmological disturbances referred to in the Olivet Discourse (Matt. 24:29) occur "before the coming of the great and glorious day of the Lord" (Acts 2:17–20).

of Revelation is functioning in the letter. As I argue in my main essay, John addresses his contemporary Christians as if they might be the last generation in history. Because Jesus' first coming initiated the "time of the end," Daniel's predicted "time of tribulation" has already begun; and the Philadelphia Christians are threatened by it. It also seems to me that the hermeneutical approach that Blaising follows here creates problems for other New Testament eschatological passages. For instance, Paul speaks as if he and the Thessalonians will experience the rapture ("we who are still alive" [1 Thess. 4:17]) and that the Thessalonians will be delivered from their distress when the Lord appears in glory (2 Thess. 1:5–10). Surely in all these texts first-century Christians are being addressed as representative of believers throughout history, some of whom will live to see the events of the end of history.

CRAIG BLAISING

I very much appreciate Alan Hultberg's and Doug Moo's responses to my essay. I am also grateful to Zondervan for including in the volume the opportunity of a rejoinder. I find the dialogue created by this format helpful, and I trust the reader will as well.

A point-by-point response is not possible given the limited space allowed for a rejoinder. The reader should note that many of the issues raised by Hultberg and Moo have been addressed in my responses to their essays. What remains, however, can be summarized under five headings.

Inaugurated Eschatology and Typological Fulfillment

Moo and Hultberg appeal to inaugurated eschatology to argue that various features in the Olivet Discourse and Revelation are fulfilled in the history of the church, not in a future tribulation. However, this is a category mistake. Inaugurated eschatology affirms both present and future fulfillment. Inaugural fulfillment does not preclude but rather confirms and guarantees fulfillment in the future.

The inauguration of kingdom promises in the present guarantees their complete fulfillment in the future. Jesus has already risen from the dead, but we do not on that account deny our future resurrection. Both Paul and John say that the spirit of Antichrist (or lawlessness) is presently in the world, but both expect an Antichrist to come in the future. The point is that even if one agrees that tribulation prophecies have inaugural manifestations, that in no way precludes their future fulfillment. Rather, following the logic of inaugurated (as opposed to realized) eschatology, we would expect a more complete fulfillment in the future of what we see partially in the present. The future fulfillment would also include any order or pattern interrelating the elements of those prophecies. Furthermore, nothing precludes an earlier occurrence of that pattern as an integral type within (or at the beginning of) the inaugural period. The question is merely whether we have evidence that such has been or will be the case. I argue that we do have such evidence of a type-antitype correspondence between late first-century and future tribulation events. In addition, the pattern has been typed earlier in prophetic history as well. The repetition of this pattern is significant and bears on our understanding of how biblical prophecy will be finally and completely fulfilled. The interpreter must pay attention to this typological fulfillment in addition to inaugural features that characterize the interadvent age.

The Integrity of the Seventieth Week Structure in Daniel

Moo and Hultberg question the integrity of the seventieth week as a unified eschatological period. But they ignore or miss several features. First, in Daniel 9:26–27, the seventieth seven is positioned and treated separately from the preceding sixty-nine sevens. Second, it is linked to the destruction of the city and the temple. (The preceding sixty-nine sevens are specifically associated with the rebuilding of the city.) Third, it is the only "seven" that is described with a plot structure—a structure that unifies it even while dividing it into two halves. Fourth, the primary character of that plot structure, a coming prince, is active through the entire seven-year pattern. In fact, the two halves of the narrative are defined with respect to his activity. Fifth, the second half of the seventieth week is presented as an escalation within the plot structure, not as a wholly separate narrative. Sixth, in the book of Daniel, the seventieth week draws together the antitypes of the other visions and contextualizes them in a time after the cutting off of the Messiah. The introduction of the Antichrist in the first half of the week corresponds to the rise of the "little horn" in Daniel 7 and the typological rise of Antiochus in Daniel 8 and 11. The repeated attention given to the second half of the week in other visions reinforces by literary effect the notion of escalation in the Daniel 9 description.

Hultberg complains about my use of the label "time of the end" to refer to the entire seventieth week. However, I do not agree that the label is restricted in Daniel 8, 11, and 12 to the second half of that week. Those passages speak of both the rise of the Antichrist type and of his temple desecration, thereby referencing both halves of the week. Furthermore, the repeated use of "end" in Daniel 9:26–27, especially the final phrase, "the decreed end," provides a literary link to Daniel 11–12 where references to "end" and "what is decreed" are clustered with references to "the time of the end" (11:35, 36, 40, 45; 12:4, 7, 9, 13). So, I think I am justified in using the label as I do. But more important than the label is the fact that the seventieth week pattern is carried over and applied in the New Testament.

The Integrity of the Seventieth-Week Structure in the Olivet Discourse

In response to Moo's and Hultberg's attempt to extricate the seventieth week structure from the Olivet Discourse, I note the following. First, the Olivet Discourse is given the same setting as the seventieth week in Daniel 9:26—the destruction of the city and the temple (cf. Matt. 23:37–24:3). It seems to me that one reason Moo has trouble with the integrity of the pattern is because he fails to grasp that the prophecy is focused on Israel, Jerusalem, and the temple. This focus links the various typological fulfillments to the antitype, the pattern projecting to a future judgment with Jerusalem and a temple as its setting. What most likely underlies the dissipation of the prophecy into the history of the church is a supersessionist or replacement theology. But that is a topic for another forum.

The setting must be kept in mind when addressing the structure of the discourse. Moo's criticism of how I handle the disciples' two questions fails to take into account the Lukan and Markan versions where the subject of both questions is "this" or "these things" (*tauta*, Mark 13:4; Luke 21:7). Matthew's nuance of the second question should be interpreted within the synoptic context. Rather than contrasting a parousia and a temple destruction, Jesus is presenting one pattern capable of type-antitype double fulfillment. The sign of complete or antitype fulfillment is the actual appearing of the Son of Man. Absent that sign in the first-century destruction, we are projected forward to a future antitype, involving a future temple destruction, the timing of which is unknown. Accordingly, the structured response to the disciple's questions most likely divides on the topics of "when" and "sign." It cannot divide, as Moo suggests, on the subject of *tauta*, or "this" (a temple destruction).

Second, with regard to the integrity of the seventieth week, Moo and Hultberg fail to note the structural feature of "false christs." False christs appear at the beginning and end of the Olivet Discourse pattern (and in Matthew with a middle reference as well) so as to form an inclusio on the entire period. The entire pattern (not just its second half) concerns the activity of false christs just as in Daniel 9:27 the entire seventieth week (not just the second half) concerns the activity of an Antichrist.

Third, Hultberg's attempt to discount the structural significance of *tote* ("then"), linking the two halves of the discourse as a sequential narrative, seems weak to me. He acknowledges the sequential force of *tote* in Matthew 24:15–31 but disputes it in 24:4–14. However, of the three uses of *tote* in 24:4–14, one (v. 14) is undoubtedly sequential, and one (v. 10) is most likely sequential (the falling away and betrayal most likely provoked by the persecution). The remaining *tote* stands at the beginning of the sequence.[87]

Fourth, Moo tries to insert a long interadvent age between the abomination of desolation and the appearing of Christ on the basis of the Lord's ignorance of the interval. But the Lord connects the two events with the phrase "immediately after the tribulation of those days" (v. 29). The construction *eutheōs de meta tēn thlipsin tōn hēmerōn ekeinōn* is quite specific. But it is reduced to incoherence by Moo's interpretation. There is simply no room here for a long interadvent age, even one of which the Lord was ignorant at the time. It is better to understand this as a connected pattern that will apply to his actual coming.

Parousia, Day of the Lord, and the Olivet Discourse

Hultberg's criticism of my interpretation of the Olivet Discourse as a day of the Lord prophecy is weak for several reasons. First, he fails to recognize that the phenomena of famines, earthquakes, and wars (in the first half of the Olivet Discourse pattern) are features belonging to day of the Lord typology. Second, he fails to take into account the development of the day of the Lord, especially in postexilic prophecy,

---

87. A sequential usage of *tote* is typical of Matthew generally. Accordingly, a similar usage here is not surprising. See F. Blass and A. Debrunner, *A Greek Grammar of the New Testament and Other Early Christian Literature*, trans. R. Funk (Chicago: University of Chicago Press), 240.

into a two-stage event, with a military attack on Jerusalem as the dividing point (cf. the Lukan version of the Olivet Discourse). Third, more consideration should be given to the labor metaphor than what Hultberg allows. If Matthew 24:8 is an intentional use of a day of the Lord image, then its force is not simply dismissive but informative. The application of "beginning" and "end" to the metaphor develops a potential within the imagery (since labor is a process that begins and ends), a potential that is appropriate to the later development of the day of the Lord theme and its integration with Daniel's seventieth week.

Moo and Hultberg both complain that my interpretation of the Olivet Discourse requires two meanings of *parousia* within the same context, one narrow (e.g., Matt. 24:27) and one broad (e.g., Matt. 24:37). But I believe this is justified within the Olivet Discourse itself. First, in the second part of the discourse, Luke and Mark substitute "the day" or "the time" for Matthew's "coming of the Son of Man" (Matt. 24:36–37, 39; Mark 13:33; Luke 21:34). This is similar to the way the coming of the day of the Lord is functionally interchangeable with the coming of the Lord in some texts (see, e.g., Mal. 3:1–2). In other words, it is already the case in biblical theology that the coming can be thought of in both broad (more extended) and narrow senses. The synoptic parallels indicate that the coming in the second part of the discourse should be viewed in the broader sense. Second, the labor metaphor adds to the conceptuality by providing an image that is immediately recognizable: a baby's "coming" can reference either the entire labor process or the specific appearance at its end. The use of the labor metaphor to cover the entire sequence of the Olivet Discourse prepares the reader for the broader meaning of "coming." When *parousia* is used within the sequence, as it is in Matthew 24:27, it has the narrower meaning—the appearance at the end of the labor process. But *parousia* in 24:36 properly refers to the broader notion of the whole labor, a conclusion confirmed by the synoptic parallels.

Recognizing these two related senses helps resolve the tension between the *parousia* settings of Matthew 24:32–35, a coming with signs, and Matthew 24:36ff., a coming without signs. Hultberg tries to reconcile the two with the illustration of someone not paying attention to the clock—possibly being distracted by routine matters, and then being "surprised" by a previously scheduled but forgotten meeting. But this is hardly applicable to a timed tribulation sequence that is intensifying into the greatest threat the earth has ever known. Such are not conditions in which watching saints get distracted by routine matters.

Revelation

Briefly, I did not say that in Revelation 3:10 the Lord *promised* death to the Philadelphians, but rather that death was the way he *fulfilled* the promise to them. Likewise, he has thus fulfilled it to every generation of believers since then, and this clarifies the intent of the promise to keep believers *from* not *through* the tribulation.

A CASE FOR THE PREWRATH RAPTURE

ALAN HULTBERG

The prewrath rapture position rests on two major theses: that the church will enter the last half of Daniel's seventieth week[1] and that between the rapture of the church and the return of Christ to earth will be a significant period of extraordinary divine wrath.[2] If these two theses are demonstrated, then of necessity the rapture can neither be pretribulational, a position that requires that the rapture occur before the middle of Daniel's seventieth week (though that usually argues for a rapture before the beginning of that week) nor posttribulational (in the classic sense), a position that requires no significant period of time intervening between the rapture and the return of Christ to earth. It seems to me, however, that absolute demonstration of these points is close to impossible, since much of the evidence is patient of multiple interpretations. I will thus seek in this essay to demonstrate the prob-

---

1. I assume the following in this essay: (1) that Daniel's seventieth "week" represents the final seven years of world history, (2) that the final kingdom in Daniel is Rome, and (3) that Daniel presents Rome's domination of the Jews as having both a historical (first-century AD) and an eschatological (end of history) manifestation. See Stephen R. Miller, *Daniel*, NAC 18 (Nashville: Broadman & Holman, 1994), 267–73; Gleason L. Archer Jr., "Daniel," in *Daniel–Minor Prophets*, EBC (Grand Rapids: Zondervan, 1985), 7:116–19. Cf. Joyce G. Baldwin, *Daniel: An Introduction and Commentary*, TOTC 21 (Downers Grove, Ill.: Inter-Varsity, 1978), 171, 177–78. The Olivet Discourse, the Thessalonian correspondence, and the Apocalypse all seem to rely on these assumptions, as will be shown below.

2. A number of other theses regarding eschatology are maintained by one or more proponents of the prewrath rapture, including, for example, the significance of the 1,290 and 1,335 days mentioned in Dan. 12:10–11 and the identity of the restrainer in 2 Thessalonians 2. These are sometimes disputed by critics, and in many cases I believe the critique to be justified. But the basic prewrath position does not stand or fall on these theses, and I will not consider them in what follows.

ability of the prewrath rapture; that is, that the most probable reading of the evidence serves to support the two major theses of this position.[3] My argument will proceed by demonstrating these theses in turn. First, I will show that the church will enter the last half of Daniel's seventieth "week"; then I will show that the church will be raptured before the end of that week, prior to the outpouring of God's wrath. We begin, then, with evidence for the first thesis.

The Church Will Enter the Second Half of Daniel's Seventieth Week

Three passages in Scripture are especially important in demonstrating that the church will enter the last half of Daniel's seventieth week: the Olivet Discourse, 2 Thessalonians 2, and Revelation. In the Olivet Discourse, Jesus seems to indicate that his disciples would see both the Danielic abomination of desolation and the subsequent tribulation (Matt. 24:15–22; Mark 13:14–20) immediately prior to his parousia. Paul appears to expect the former in 2 Thessalonians 2, and John appears to expect at least the latter in Revelation 2, 7, 13, and 17. In what follows, I will attempt to show that in each of these cases the author does in fact expect the church to see the abomination of desolation or to experience the Danielic tribulation and thus to enter the last half of Daniel's seventieth week. If any of my arguments prove successful, then this part of the case for a prewrath rapture will have been made. The case, of course, is considerably strengthened if all the arguments prove successful. We will begin with a consideration of the Olivet Discourse.

---

3. Such an argument is usually attacked in at least one of two ways. First, it is frequently suggested that providing alternative interpretations of key texts undermines the probability of the argument. This is a red herring. The question in all exegesis is, which is the best interpretation? And the best interpretation is not overthrown or made less probable merely because competing interpretations exist. Second, it is sometimes argued that such a case is necessarily weak because it builds inference upon inference, one uncertainty on another (see, e.g., Paul S. Karleen, *The Pre-wrath Rapture of the Church: Is It Biblical?* [Langhorne, Pa.: BF Press, 1991]). This is only true if, on the one hand, the inferences are not the most probable, and, if, on the other, one inference actually depends upon other weak inferences. My case will not depend for the most part on this kind of linking of inferences but on an accumulation of relatively independent strands of highly probable evidence. There is nothing necessarily weak about such a case. Finally, it is valid to test the probability of interpretations by comparison with other related texts. On the supposition that the biblical authors will not contradict one another, the thesis that best harmonizes the greatest number of the most probable interpretations of the various texts is the best thesis, and an interpretation can be made more probable if it fits with that harmonization. This is a valid case of building inference upon inference.

Matthew 24

The Olivet Discourse is a response by Jesus to his disciples' question concerning the end of the age (Matt. 24:3).[4] Their question was elicited by Jesus' prediction of the destruction of the Jewish temple, and their assumption seems to have been that the destruction of the temple was an eschatological event.[5] Jesus' response is designed in part to distinguish the first-century destruction of the temple from the end of the age when the Son of Man comes.[6] Thus Jesus notes that the disciples will see certain catastrophic events surrounding the destruction of the temple[7] but that explicitly do not signal the end (Matt. 24:5–13; see esp. v. 6). These, Jesus says, are merely the beginning of birth pains (Matt. 24:8). The primary sign of the end will be "'the abomination that causes desolation' spoken of through the prophet Daniel"

---

4. For simplicity's sake, and because I will later consider Matthew's perspective on the audience of the Olivet Discourse, I will talk here about the Olivet Discourse in its Matthean form. The basic analysis holds true for the Markan version and, for the most part, the Lukan, though Luke places a greater emphasis on first-century events. For a reconstruction of the tradition behind the New Testament, see David Wenham, *The Rediscovery of Jesus' Eschatological Discourse*, Gospel Perspectives 4 (Sheffield: JSOT, 1984).

5. This assumption probably comes from Dan. 9:26–27, which predicts the destruction of Jerusalem and the temple by "the people of the ruler who will come," the final opponent of God and his people. First-century Jews recognized the Romans as the people of the ruler to come. See Baldwin, *Daniel*, 174–75; Craig S. Keener, *A Commentary on the Gospel of Matthew* (Grand Rapids: Eerdmans, 1999), 561–62.

6. There is considerable debate as to the relationship of the first-century destruction of Jerusalem to the Danielic tribulation and the return of Christ. For an older but still useful overview, see D. A. Carson, "Matthew," in *Matthew, Mark, Luke*, EBC, ed. Frank E. Gaebelein, 12 vols. (Grand Rapids: Zondervan, 1984), 8:491–95. The two best alternatives are the following: (1) Jesus was claiming that the destruction of Jerusalem was the Danielic abomination of desolation and that the subsequent Danielic tribulation is a characterization of the persecution of God's people since then, one that will continue until the second coming (see, e.g., Craig L. Blomberg, *Matthew*, NAC 22 [Nashville: Broadman and Holman, 1992], 355–57). On this scenario, the abomination of desolation is not a sign of the end or is so only in the sense that the last days began with the destruction of Jerusalem but will not end till the coming of the Son of Man. This view requires that Daniel's relatively precise three and one-half years is symbolic. (2) Jesus is claiming that the destruction of the temple is like, and even prophetically related to, the abomination of desolation and tribulation, but that the two are not to be equated. Though the destruction of Jerusalem is a significant eschatological event, and even if the interadvent age is characterized by tribulation, the coming of the Son of Man will nevertheless be immediately preceded by the abomination of desolation and three-and-one-half-year tribulation as outlined in Daniel (see, e.g., David Hill, *The Gospel of Matthew* [Grand Rapids: Eerdmans, 1972]). The hyperbolic language of Matt. 24:21–22 supports this reading, as do the "immediately" of v. 29 and Paul's anticipation of an actual Antichrist figure and his very specific understanding of the abomination of desolation in 2 Thessalonians 2.

7. Note v. 6, "You are about to hear ..." (*mellēsete ... akouein*).

(v. 15),[8] which will initiate the great Danielic tribulation (v. 21; cf. Dan. 12:1). This tribulation will end when the "sign of the Son of Man" will appear in the sky and the angels will gather his elect from the four winds (Matt. 24:29–31). Though the disciples would see a proleptic fulfillment of these events in the destruction of Jerusalem,[9] the end of the age and the coming of the Son of Man were yet future. The disciples are thus addressed as both primary witnesses of these tribulational events and as representatives of the final generation.

The context of the Olivet Discourse is thoroughly Jewish, and this has led most pretribulationists to deny that the church is in view in this chapter, especially as the "elect" of the final generation who are gathered at the end of the age and who are addressed representatively in the warnings to the disciples. So, for example, Renald Showers points to (1) the Jewish referents in the Old Testament allusions in the discourse, (2) the Jewish environment of the discourse and its warnings, and (3) the fact that Gentiles aren't explicitly addressed as a topic till Matthew 25 as proof that Jesus addresses the Olivet Discourse to his disciples as Jews.[10] John Walvoord adds that the nature of the disciples' question, a question that assumes Jewish kingdom hopes, points to the Jewish nature of Jesus' discourse.[11] None of those assertions are objectionable. The disciples do not view themselves, nor are they treated by Jesus in Matthew, as anything other than faithful Jews who are beginning the community of the Messiah. It is not surprising then that the question and response recorded in the Olivet Discourse have such a Jewish character. But neither do they show that the church is not in view in the Olivet Discourse, unless one begins with the assumption of a radical discontinuity between the church and Israel. This assumption, however, is very unlikely.

---

8. A major shift is indicated by *oun* ("therefore"; NIV "so") in verse 15 (*de*, "but," in Mark 13:14). See BDAG, 736–37, where *oun* can indicate a transition to something new or even adversative to what precedes. Cf. Wenham, *Rediscovery*, 177; W. D. Davies and Dale C. Allison, *A Critical and Exegetical Commentary on the Gospel according to Saint Matthew*, ICC (Edinburgh: T & T Clark, 1997), 3:326, 345.

9. Note the "you" of vv. 15, 23, 25, 26, the injunctions in vv. 32–35, and the parallels in Luke 21.

10. Renald E. Showers, *The Pre-wrath Rapture View: An Examination and Critique* (Grand Rapids: Kregel, 2001), 124–29.

11. John F. Walvoord, *The Blessed Hope and the Tribulation* (Grand Rapids: Zondervan, 1976), 87.

Space does not permit a full discussion of this topic;[12] it will suffice for our purposes to show that for Matthew the church is viewed as in some sense the inheritor of the Jewish kingdom, with the destruction of Jerusalem playing a significant role in the transition, and that the disciples form the core of the new messianic community.[13] That Matthew has such a view can be seen in the following lines of evidence.

1. *Israel comes to its fulfillment in Jesus as Messiah.* Quite apart from the clear motif in Matthew that as the promised Messiah Jesus brings the Old Testament to its fulfillment (summed up in Matthew 5:17 and seen in the numerous fulfillment quotations but attested in several other ways throughout the gospel), many scholars have noted that Matthew portrays Jesus as fulfilling the role of Israel itself.[14] Thus, for example, in the early chapters of Matthew, Jesus, like eschatological Israel, is visited by Gentiles bearing gold and frankincense (Matt. 2:11; cf. Isa. 60:1–6); like Israel is called as God's son out of Egypt (Matt. 2:13–14; Hos. 11:1; cf. Ex. 4:22–23), and, like Israel, successfully endures temptation in the wilderness through filial obedience to the law (Matt. 4:1–11; Deut. 6–8; see esp. 8:1–5).[15] Later he is presented as both the Suffering Servant (Matt. 8:17; 12:17–21; 20:28) and the Son of Man, both corporate "messianic" figures representing Israel.[16] Thus for Matthew, to belong to Israel one must belong to the Messiah, Jesus.

2. *Jesus founds a new community centered in the twelve apostles.* Matthew is well known for explicitly presenting Jesus as founding a new community, the *ekklēsia* (16:18; 18:17). The language comes from the Greek translation of the Old Testament *āhal [yiśrāēl]* or "congregation

---

12. The exegetical and theological questions are voluminous. My own perspective is a form of progressive dispensationalism. For a general introduction, see Craig Blaising and Darrell L. Bock, eds., *Dispensationalism, Israel, and the Church: The Search for Definition* (Grand Rapids: Zondervan, 1992); idem, *Progressive Dispensationalism: An Up-to-Date Handbook on Dispensational Thought* (Wheaton: Bridgepoint, 1993). Cf. the analysis in Russell D. Moore, *The Kingdom of Christ: The New Evangelical Perspective* (Wheaton: Crossway, 2004), esp. chap. 4.

13. Cf., e.g., R. T. France, *Matthew: Evangelist and Teacher* (Downers Grove, Ill.: InterVarsity, 1989), 206–41; Scot McKnight, "Matthew, Gospel of," in *Dictionary of Jesus and the Gospels*, ed. Joel B. Green, Scot McKnight, and I. Howard Marshall (Downers Grove, Ill.: InterVarsity, 1992), 536–38; Blomberg, *Matthew*, 25–27.

14. Besides France, *Matthew*, 206–10, see idem, *Jesus and the Old Testament* (London: Tyndale, 1971), 50–53; C. H. Dodd, *The Founder of Christianity* (London: Collins, 1970), 106–8.

15. See also the possible use of Hos. 6:2 in Matt. 16:21 (and parallels) as part of the motif of Jesus representing Israel.

16. The idea of the Messiah as the Son of God (e.g., Ps. 2; 110), which stems from the Davidic covenant (2 Sam. 7:12–14), also suggests that the Messiah represents Israel.

[of Israel]," and indicates that the messianic community that Jesus is founding is in some sense the "true" or "new" Israel. Furthermore, this community is centered in the twelve apostles, the number twelve representing a reconstitution of Israel (see, e.g., Matt. 19:28).[17] The impetus for founding this community is Jesus' rejection by unbelieving Jews.

3. *The Jewish rejection of Jesus leads to the rejection of Israel and establishment of the church.* A basic theme of Matthew's gospel is that Jesus, the King, preaches the kingdom of heaven to Israel (2:20; 10:5–6; 15:24) but is ultimately rejected by them.[18] This theme comes to a head in the narratives of the Passion Week, where Jesus enters Jerusalem as the messianic King but is confronted and eventually killed by the Jewish authorities. In a series of parables and denunciations leading up to the Olivet Discourse and the plot to kill him, Jesus condemns Jewish unbelief and announces the "disinheritance" of Israel. The parable of the vineyard in Matthew 21:33–45 is most significant. Jesus concludes the parable by announcing to the chief priests and elders of the people that, as a result of their rejection of him, "the kingdom of God will be taken away from you and given to a people who will produce its fruit" (v. 43). The fact that Jesus gives the kingdom to another "nation" (*ethnos*) and that Matthew explicitly reports the complicity of the entire nation in the rejection of Jesus (27:25) demonstrates that Jesus does not intend merely the rejection of the Jewish leadership but of Israel as a whole. Thus these denunciations lead on the one hand to the pronouncement against Jerusalem (23:37–39) and the Olivet Discourse (chaps. 24–25) and on the other to the Great Commission (28:18–20), which allows the gospel to move beyond Israel to all nations in fulfillment of the Abrahamic covenant (1:1) and of Israel's role in the Old Testament. This witness of the new messianic community will continue to the end of the age (24:14; 28:20) when Jesus returns.

4. *The purpose of the discourses in Matthew is to train the church in discipleship.* Another basic and related theme in Matthew is that the only proper response to Jesus is discipleship. To be a member of the messianic community is to be a disciple (or "student"), and to be a disciple is to

---

17. This is not to say that Matthew sees no future for Israel. Matt. 23:39; 24:30 suggest a conversion of Israel at the return of Christ (Zech. 12:10). Matthew 24:30, however, seems to distinguish the gathered elect from the repentant tribes of Israel.

18. France, *Matthew*, 213–27.

obey the teaching of Jesus (7:21–27; 28:19–20).[19] Matthew's gospel, structured as it is around five major discourses of Jesus, is designed to convey that teaching. Thus each discourse begins with the introductory formula "His disciples came to him" (5:1; 10:1; 13:10; 18:1; 24:1)[20] and concludes with variations of "when Jesus had finished these words" (7:28; 11:1; 13:53; 19:1; 26:1). This makes it highly unlikely that the teaching of the Olivet Discourse is directed to the disciples as anything but disciples, representatives of those the gospel is designed to instruct.[21]

I conclude, then, that when Jesus warns his disciples of the Danielic abomination of desolation and the great tribulation, he does so as to representatives of the messianic community, the church. And though the rapture itself is not explicitly mentioned in the Olivet Discourse (the most likely reference is the gathering of the elect at the *parousia* ["coming"] of the Son of Man in Matt. 24:31), what is important here is that if Matthew expects the church to see the abomination of desolation and the great tribulation, then the rapture must occur after the middle of Daniel's seventieth week. This point is confirmed in Paul's teaching on the rapture and the return of Christ in the Thessalonian epistles, which is itself a reflection of the tradition underlying the Olivet Discourse. In particular, in 2 Thessalonians 2:3–4, Paul also identifies the abomination of desolation as the major sign by which the approach of the rapture could be known, thus placing the rapture after the middle of Daniel's seventieth week.

2 Thessalonians 2

1 Thessalonians 4:15–16 Places the Rapture at Matthew 24:31

The letters to the Thessalonians are unique among the letters of Paul for containing such concentrated and detailed instruction on the parousia.[22] Much of this instruction was related orally to the Thessalonians prior to the writing of the letters, when Paul first founded the Thessalonian church (1 Thess. 1:9–10; 2 Thess. 2:15; cf. 3:6).

---

19. Thus Matthew characteristically refers to the twelve apostles as the "disciples."
20. Matthew 10:1 has "he called his twelve disciples to him."
21. So, e.g., Michael J. Wilkins, *Matthew*, NIVAC (Grand Rapids: Zondervan, 2004), 32, 770.
22. Cf. 1 Thess. 1:10; 2:19; 3:13; 4:13–18; 5:1–11, 23; 2 Thess. 1:6–10; 2:1–15.

This teaching included the certainty of tribulation (1 Thess. 3:4), the uncertainty of the timing of the day of the Lord (1 Thess. 5:1–2), and the fact that certain events must precede the day of the Lord (2 Thess. 2:1–5). Paul refers to this teaching as "traditions" (ESV; *paradoseis*) passed on to the Thessalonians by himself and his coworkers, Silas and Timothy (2 Thess. 2:15), and many have noted the probable dependence of at least some of these traditions on those underlying the Olivet Discourse, as indicated by the extensive correspondence between Matthew 24 (and parallels) and the Thessalonian epistles.[23] Thus, in response to a concern raised by the Thessalonians regarding "those who fall asleep" (v. 13), Paul reassures his readers that

> we who are still alive, who are left till the coming of the Lord, will certainly not precede those who have fallen asleep. For the Lord himself will come down from heaven, with a loud command, with the voice of the archangel and with the trumpet call of God, and the dead in Christ will rise first. After that, we who are still alive and are left will be caught up together with them in the clouds to meet the Lord in the air. And so we will be with the Lord forever. (1 Thess. 4:15–17)

The parallels between this passage and Matthew 24:30–31 are noteworthy. In both, there are references to the parousia of Jesus in the clouds to gather his saints, accompanied by a trumpet blast and angels. Some of these elements feature into other parousia passages in the Thessalonian epistles as well; for example, Jesus' coming with angels (2 Thess. 1:7 and perhaps 1 Thess. 3:13) and his gathering the saints (2 Thess. 2:1 and perhaps 1 Thess. 1:10; 3:13; 5:9; 2 Thess. 1:7; 2:13). An especially interesting parallel is 2 Thessalonians 1:6–10, in which there is an emphasis on Jesus' powerful vengeance on his enemies and glorification

---

23. See esp. Lars Hartman, *Prophecy Interpreted: The Formation of Some Jewish Apocalyptic Texts and of the Eschatological Discourse in Mark 13 Par.* (Lund: CWK Gleerup, 1966), 178–79; G. Henry Waterman, "The Sources of Paul's Teaching on the 2nd Coming of Christ in 1 and 2 Thessalonians," *JETS* 18 (1975); 105–13; David Wenham, "Paul and the Synoptic Apocalypse," in *Gospel Perspectives: Studies of History and Tradition in the Four Gospels*, vol. 11, ed. R. T. France and David Wenham (Sheffield: JSOT, 1981), 345–75, and most modern commentators (e.g., Charles A. Wanamaker, *Commentary on 1 and 2 Thessalonians*, NIGTC [Grand Rapids: Eerdmans, 1990], 170–71, 179–81, 184, and F. F. Bruce, *1 and 2 Thessalonians*, WBC 45 [Waco: Word, 1982], 95, 108).

in his saints when he "is revealed from heaven with his mighty angels in flaming fire" (ESV; cf. Matt. 24:30–31). This evidence indicates that, though no "rapture" is explicitly mentioned in Matthew 24:31, it is precisely there in the tradition that Paul places the rapture. He states in 1 Thessalonians 4:15 that at least this expansion on the tradition is due to a "word from the Lord" (ESV), whether an *agraphon* or a prophetic utterance,[24] undermining any force to the argument that points to differences between the two texts to deny a connection between them.[25] Thus 1 Thessalonians 4:15–16 confirms my reading of Matthew 24 and suggests that Paul, like Matthew, expects the church to experience the events of the last half of Daniel's seventieth "week."

1 Thessalonians 2:3 Says That the Rapture Is Preceded by the Abomination of Desolation

The dependence of Paul on the Jesus tradition underlying the Olivet Discourse continues in 2 Thessalonians 2:1–12 (cf. Matt. 24:13–15, 24).[26] Like Matthew 24:15, Paul points the Thessalonian church to certain signs related to the appearance of the Danielic Antichrist that must precede the coming of Christ to reassure them that "the day of the Lord" has not arrived. He writes:

> Concerning the coming of our Lord Jesus Christ and our being gathered to him, we ask you, brothers, not to become easily unsettled or alarmed by some prophecy, report or letter supposed to have come from us, saying that the day of the Lord has already come. Don't let anyone deceive you in any way, for that day will not come until the rebellion occurs and the man of lawlessness is revealed, the man doomed to destruction. He will oppose and will exalt himself

---

24. If the "word of the Lord" upon which Paul based his rapture teaching was a post-Easter prophetic utterance, this may account for the "mystery" of 1 Cor. 15:51–52.

25. See, e.g., Showers, *Pre-wrath Rapture View*, whose list of fourteen differences between Matt. 24:31 and 1 Thess. 4:16 is largely based on silence.

26. Cf. Wenham, "Paul and Apocalypse," 349–52. Note the concurrence of language regarding gathering (2 Thess. 2:1; Matt. 24:31), disturbance about the parousia (2 Thess. 2:2; Matt. 24:6), apostasy/falling away (2 Thess. 2:3; Matt. 24:10), lawlessness (2 Thess. 2:3, 7, 8; Matt. 24:12), deceptive signs and wonders (2 Thess. 2:10–11; Matt. 24:20), and the injunction not to let anyone deceive you (2 Thess. 2:3; Matt. 24:4). Though the correspondence between 2 Thess. 2:1–12 and the Olivet Discourse is not as obvious as that in 1 Thessalonians, the combined evidence of the two related Pauline eschatological texts makes it virtually certain that Paul is dependent on the Jesus tradition in both.

over everything that is called God or is worshiped, so that he sets himself up in God's temple, proclaiming himself to be God. Don't you remember that when I was with you I used to tell you these things? (2 Thess. 2:1–5)

Let's note a few things about this passage. First, Paul refers to the parousia of the Lord Jesus and our "gathering to him" (cf. Matt. 24:31) as "the day of the Lord." The former is language that connects 2 Thessalonians 2:1–12 to 1 Thessalonians 4:13–5:12 and the underlying Jesus tradition. It suggests that when Paul refers to signs prior to the day of the Lord in 2 Thessalonians 2:3–4, he means to include the rapture as being preceded by those signs.[27] This is also implied in 1 Thessalonians 5:1–11. There Paul continues the discussion regarding the parousia begun in 4:13–18.[28] Whereas 4:13–18 was concerned with the relationship of the resurrection to the rapture at the parousia, 5:1–11 is addressing the timing of these events[29] and the need for watchfulness on the part of the Thessalonians in light of that timing. Note that Paul refers to the parousia/rapture as the day of the Lord (5:1–2).[30] In the Old Testament, the day of the Lord is that time when God enters history to judge his enemies and, sometimes, to vindicate his people.[31] In particular, the eschatological day of the Lord is when God will gather the nations for judgment and Israel for salvation and blessing (e.g., Isa.

---

27. All sides agree that the unexpressed protasis of 2 Thess. 2:3 ("for [something will or will not be true], unless ...") is "the day of the Lord will not come." The use of "Let no one deceive you in any way" recalls the similar phrase in Matt. 24:4, where the same thought is in mind: let no one deceive you into thinking that the day of the Lord has come.

28. So, e.g., Wanamaker, *1 and 2 Thessalonians*, 176; John F. Walvoord, *The Rapture Question*, rev. (Grand Rapids: Zondervan, 1979), 211–12. Though *peri de* ("now concerning") introduces a new topic (as in 1 Thess. 4:9 and perhaps 4:13; cf. 1 Cor. 7:1, 25; 8:1; 12:1; 16:1, 12), it does not necessarily signal a radical departure from what precedes (cf. 1 Cor. 7:1–24, 25–40). First Thessalonians 5:9–11 clearly shows that Paul is continuing the discussion begun in 4:13.

29. "Times and dates," or sometimes just "the time," was stock language for eschatological events in Judaism and early Christianity, perhaps stemming from Dan. 2:21. Cf. Acts 1:7; 3:19–21; Mark 13:33; Rev. 1:3; 2 Bar. 14:1–2 (which, like Rev. 1:1, alludes to Dan. 2:29, 45); 4 Ezra 7:75.

30. All pretribulationists, as far as I know, agree with this. Most would understand that Paul uses the expression "the day of the Lord" in its broadest sense here, that is for the entire complex of eschatological events from the rapture to the millennium.

31. See, e.g., Richard H. Hiers, "Day of the Lord," in *ABD*, 2:82–83, and his bibliography. In general I concur with Walvoord, *Rapture Question*, 218, that "based on the Old Testament ... the Day of the Lord is a time of judgment, culminating in the second coming of Christ, and followed by a time of special divine blessing to be fulfilled in the millennial kingdom."

2:12–21; 13:6–16; Ezek. 30:3; Obad. 15; Zeph. 1:14–2:3). When Paul uses the phrase here, he undoubtedly has such passages in mind, for one of the primary features he emphasizes about the day of the Lord (Jesus) is the "sudden destruction" that will fall upon the unbelievers (v. 3) and the wrath in that day from which believers will be spared (v. 9; cf. 1:10). Thus, Paul can also say in 2 Thessalonians 1:6–8 (cf. 2:8) that Jesus will give rest to his church and deal out retribution to the church's enemies on the day he is revealed. But more important, it is critical to note that in this passage Paul explicitly states that the day of the Lord will overtake believers. This confirms that the rapture, associated with the parousia in 4:15–17, is in fact considered by him as part of the day.

Paul's basic response to the question about the timing of the parousia is that the Thessalonians already know that the day will come like a thief in the night (1 Thess. 5:2). Here the emphasis is on the unanticipated arrival of the parousia. Paul elaborates this concept for unbelievers in verse 3; the day will come on them both unexpectedly and destructively. In verses 4 and 5, by contrast, the day will not come upon believers as a thief, because they are not in darkness, being children of the light and of the day. Walvoord argues that Paul means in verse 4 that the day will not overtake believers at all,[32] but this interpretation is unlikely. First, this interpretation does account well for the inclusion of the comparative "as a thief."[33] If Paul meant to say that the day will not overtake believers, period, why add "as a thief"? Walvoord understands Paul to mean that the day will not overtake believers as a thief because they do not belong to the same time period (night) to which unbelievers belong. But this does not really solve the problem, since Walvoord is only accounting for the causal clauses, not the comparative. In effect it merely has Paul saying, "But that day will not overtake you as a thief, because it has nothing to do with you." The question then remains, why the comparative? On Walvoord's reading, Paul did not need to include it. Second, this reading cannot account well for the specific parenesis

---

32. Walvoord, *Rapture Question*, 221.

33. Cf. Douglas Moo, "Posttribulation Rapture," in Richard Reiter, Paul D. Feinberg, Gleason L. Archer, and Douglas Moo, *The Rapture: Pre-, Mid-, or Post-Tribulational* (Grand Rapids: Zondervan, 1984), 185. On the strong preference for the singular *kleptēs* over the plural *kleptas* found in a few manuscripts, see Bruce M. Metzger, *A Textual Commentary on the Greek New Testament*, 2nd ed. (New York: UBS, 1994), 565. Cf. Leon Morris, *The First and Second Epistles to the Thessalonians*, NICNT, 2nd ed. (Grand Rapids: Eerdmans, 1991), 155.

to watch and be sober in verses 6–8. Walvoord makes them general exhortations to the kind of behavior befitting Christians: because we are "day people," let us be sober and alert like day people.[34] But this begs the question: alert for what? The context would seem to indicate the day of the Lord. But why should Christians be alert for the day of the Lord if it will not overtake them?[35] Finally, understanding Paul to say that believers will not be overtaken by the day of the Lord overlooks the connection to the dominical traditions recorded in Luke 21:34–36 and Matthew 24:42–51.[36] In these passages the disciples are warned to remain sober and alert so that the day will not come on them suddenly like a trap or a thief. Rather, they are to look up when they see the signs of the parousia, for their redemption is drawing near (Luke 21:28). Thus 1 Thessalonians 5:4 does not seem to mean that believers will not experience the day of the Lord.

It is much more probable that this verse means that, in contrast to the day of the Lord coming on unbelievers unexpectedly and destructively, the day will not come *this way* for believers.[37] This is because believers are neither morally liable to its destructiveness nor ignorant of its approach (1 Thess. 5:4–5).[38] They are thus to watch for its coming and avoid moral slippage (vv. 6–8). Verse 9 sums up the discussion by reiterating that though the day overtakes unbelievers by wrath, it will bring believers salvation from wrath.[39] This is similar to 2 Thes-

---

34. John F. Walvoord, The *Thessalonian Epistles*, (Findlay, Ohio: Dunham, n.d.), 84. See also John MacArthur Jr., *First and Second Thessalonians*, MNTC (Chicago: Moody, 2002), 161; Morris, *Epistles to the Thessalonians*, 154–56. Cf. Moo, "Posttribulation Rapture," 186.

35. Walvoord clearly feels the force of this point, because he is forced to conclude his discussion with a subtle shift, distinguishing the *wrath* of the day of the Lord, which wrath will not overtake believers, from the day of the Lord itself, which will overtake believers, since it begins with the rapture. "In effect, Paul was saying that the time of the Rapture cannot be determined any more than the time of the beginning of the day of the Lord; but this is of no concern to believers because our appointment is not the wrath of the day of the Lord but rather the salvation that is ours in Christ" (*Rapture Question*, 222). Morris, *Epistles to the Thessalonians*, 156–57, notes the probable connection of the injunctions to watch to the context but lets the matter drop.

36. Cf. Moo, "Posttribulation Rapture," 185.

37. So most commentators. See, e.g., Wanamaker, *1 and 2 Thessalonians*, 181; Earl J. Richard, *First and Second Thessalonians*, SP 11 (Collegeville, Minn.: Glazier, 1995), 252.

38. Though Wanamaker, *1 and 2 Thessalonians*, sees unexpectedness as primarily in view, he admits the context allows both a moral and cognitive sense to being "in darkness." The parenetic focus on both sobriety and watchfulness argues for a balance between the two (so most commentators).

39. Richard, *First and SecondThessalonians*, 262.

salonians 1:7–8, a passage we noted earlier as related to the Olivet Discourse tradition, where Paul says that the revelation of Jesus from heaven will bring retribution on unbelievers and rest to believers. First Thessalonians 4:15–16, part of the larger context of 5:1–12, suggests that the salvation to be brought to believers at the parousia is in fact the rapture. We conclude then from 1 Thessalonians 4:13–5:12 that Paul understands two events to occur in relation to the parousia. Jesus will pour out his wrath on unbelievers, and he will rapture his church to allow them to escape that wrath. This complex of events Paul refers to as the day of the Lord.

The foregoing makes it extremely probable that when Paul writes in 2 Thessalonians 2 "concerning the parousia of our Lord Jesus Christ and our being gathered to him" he has one basic event in mind, the same event he spoke about in 1 Thessalonians 4:13–5:12,[40] the coming of Jesus to rapture the church and to mete out judgment on his enemies. Like 1 Thessalonians 5:1, Paul refers to this event as the day of the Lord. Pretribulationists often see a broader meaning to "the day of the Lord" here than in 1 Thessalonians 5:2,[41] namely, the seventieth week of Daniel. They thus hope to separate the signs of the day of the Lord from the rapture in order to avoid the conclusion that verse 3 gives signs that precede the rapture. Two arguments are given. The first rests on a negative understanding of the phrase "quickly shaken from mind or stirred up" (*tacheōs saleuthēnai hymas apo tou noos mēde throeisthai*).[42] This phrase is taken to mean that, due to the tribulation they were experiencing, the Thessalonians were afraid they had missed the rapture (and thus should not be in the day of the Lord). But the phrase is neutral; it can be used negatively or positively.[43] Thus posttribulationists argue that the Thessalonians are excited because they believe the rapture to be on the near horizon. The latter is better because it explains much more easily why Paul answers their misconception as he does in 2 Thessalonians

40. Cf. Bruce, *1 and 2 Thessalonians*, 163.

41. See, e.g., Walvoord, *Rapture Question*, 239; Showers, *Pre-wrath Rapture View*, 175. But cf. MacArthur, *1 and 2 Thessalonians*, 271.

42. Walvoord, *Rapture Question*, 238–39.

43. The exact phrase does not occur elsewhere in the New Testament or LXX (though cf. Acts 17:13), but the term "agitated" or "stirred" (*throeō*) can be used both ways (cf. LXX Song of Sol. 5:4; the reading of P^{75}, B, 1241 at Luke 24:37). See BDAG, 460, 911. Cf. the use of *throeō* in Matt. 24:6.

2:3–4. If Paul had taught that the day of the Lord begins at the beginning of the seventieth week and is preceded by the rapture, it is hard to conceive of why he points to signs of the *second half* of the seventieth week as reassurance.[44] In fact, Paul says the signs must happen "first," before the day of the Lord. Beyond that, if Paul had taught that the day of the Lord began with the tribulation, it would mean that he taught it begins essentially simultaneously with the abomination of desolation. But this would make the teaching about its anticipated but unknown nature in 1 Thessalonians 4 meaningless. A sign is required to make it anticipated, but an indeterminate space of time after the sign is required to make it unknown. Thus Paul probably had taught the Thessalonians that they were subject to the Danielic tribulation (1 Thess. 3:3–4) and that they would be raptured at some unknown point from the midst of the tribulation at the outset of the day of the Lord (1 Thess. 5:4–5). The Thessalonians presumably had been misled to believe they had been experiencing the Danielic tribulation and that the day of the Lord had now arrived. They thus assumed they were soon to be raptured. Paul argues that the day of the Lord had not arrived, citing as evidence to the contrary the nonoccurrence of signs that must precede that day (and not only the day of the Lord but the Danielic tribulation as well).[45]

The second argument given to support a pretribulational reading refers to the syntax of 2 Thessalonians 2:3. Robert Thomas understands 2 Thessalonians 2:3 not to give signs that precede the day of the Lord but events that occur at the beginning of, that is, within, the day of the Lord.[46] He argues on the basis of Matthew 12:29; Mark 3:27; John 7:51; and Romans 15:24 that *ean mē . . . prōton* ("unless . . . first") indicates the event in the apodosis (the "then" clause in an "if . . . then . . ." construction) is simultaneous with or included in the event in the protasis (the "if" clause in the construction). But this evidence hardly

---

44. Cf. Moo, "Posttribulation Rapture," 188–89.

45. Richard, *Thessalonians*, 345–46, suggests that 2 Thess. 2:6 serves to distinguish current Thessalonian suffering from the final period of tribulation; that is, that Paul wishes to reduce his readers' apocalyptic fervor by positing a period of eschaton-like affliction that precedes the actual end and placing his readers in that period. This pastoral strategy, if in fact it is true, corresponds to the function of vv. 3–14 in Matthew's version of the Olivet Discourse.

46. Robert L. Thomas, "2 Thessalonians," in EBC, ed. Frank E. Gaebelein, 12 vols. (Grand Rapids: Zondervan, 1978), 11:320. See also his unpublished 1975 "Exegetical Digest of the Epistle of II Thessalonians," 65, which forms the basis of his exposition in the former.

carries the weight Thomas wants it to. Romans 15:24 is not a parallel construction to 2 Thessalonians 2:3, and the other three examples (the only parallels in the New Testament, LXX, and Josephus) can easily be understood as presenting the action in the apodosis as preceding the action in the protasis. So in Matthew 12:29 and Mark 3:27, the robber gains access to the house and its goods by first binding the homeowner, and in John 7:51 judgment is not meted out unless the case is first heard. In other words, Thomas's reading of the evidence is too fine, if not also totally unnecessary and unnatural.[47] We thus conclude that when Paul gives signs in 2 Thessalonians 2:3 that will precede the day of the Lord, he means these signs to precede the rapture as well.

The second thing we want to note about 2 Thessalonians 2:1–15 is that the primary sign that must precede the day of the Lord is the abomination of desolation. That this is the case is not immediately clear; however, the connection to the Jesus tradition again suggests as much. Paul mentions two events in 2 Thessalonians 2:3 that must precede the day of the Lord, the apostasy and the revelation of the Man of Lawlessness. Neither is explicitly explained in the context. Verses 9–12 offer the most obvious contextual possibility for identifying the apostasy—a satanically inspired departure from the truth associated with the coming of the Man of Lawlessness.[48] The close connection between the

---

47. He is thus not followed by any commentators, as far as I know. What the parallels do show, however, is that *prōton* relates "the apostasy" to the day of the Lord in 2 Thess. 2:3 and not to the revelation of the Man of Lawlessness, as has occasionally been argued. Cf. Wanamaker, *1 and 2 Thessalonians*, 343.

48. Although "the apostasy" (*hē apostasia*) was something known to Paul's readers (signified by the article and the mention of Paul's oral teaching in v. 5), modern scholars disagree as to its exact referent. The term itself means "defiance or abandonment of an established authority" and thus "rebellion, abandonment, breach of faith" (BDAG, 120; cf. Heinrich Schlier, "ἀφίστημι, ἀποστασία, δικοστασία," in *TDNT* 1:512–14; W. Bauder, "ἀφίστημι," in *NIDNTT* 1:606–8). It and its cognates are used in the LXX especially in the sense of religious apostasy, though it can refer to a political rebellion. *Apostasia* itself is used only four times in the LXX (Josh. 22:22; 2 Chron. 29:19; Jer. 2:19; 1 Macc. 2:15), each in the sense of religious apostasy. Jeremiah and 1 Maccabees use the term in a virtually technical sense. Jewish apocalyptic texts speak of an apostasy of Israel in the last days, though some may envision a general worldwide religious rebellion against God (2 Bar. 41:3; 42:4; Jub. 23:14–21; 1QpHab. 2:1–10; cf. *b. Sanh.* 97. It is not clear whether 1 Enoch 91:3–10; 93:9; 4 Ezra 5:1–13 refer only to Jews or to all peoples). The New Testament foresees an apostasy of professing Christians (Matt. 24:11–12; 1 Tim. 4:1; 2 Tim. 3:1–5; 2 Peter 3:3–6). Most pretribulationists understand Paul to speak of this apostasy. The difficulty with this view is that apostasy was occurring in the church already in the first century, so that its function as a sign of the day of the Lord would seem ineffective. Thus Walvoord, *Thessalonian Epistles*, 120, and Thomas, "2 Thessalonians," 322, understand the present apostasy to become so universal as to be unprecedented. Walvoord

apostasy and the revelation of the Man of Lawlessness in verse 3 gives considerable force to this identification.[49] But more, the language and concepts of verses 9–12 closely parallel Matthew 24:24 (and parallels), forming part of the complex of passages in 1 Thessalonians 4–5 and 2 Thessalonians 2 that relate Paul's eschatology to the Jesus tradition. Both posit a period of extremely deceptive "signs and wonders" associated with a figure or figures representing a false christ. In Matthew this period is during the "great tribulation" (vv. 21, 23–24) that follows "the abomination of desolation spoken of by the prophet Daniel, *standing in*

---

associates this greater apostasy with the revelation of the Man of Lawlessness. Though Walvoord does not point to the text, 2 Thess. 2:8 may support his view. (Contra, see MacArthur, *1 and 2 Thessalonians*, 272.) Most scholars believe Paul has some such eschatological religious apostasy in mind, especially given the mention of the temple and the connection of this tradition to the Olive Discourse (cf. Matt. 24:24; 2 Thess. 2:9–12). It is worth noting the proposal by Eberhard Nestle, "2 Thess. 2.iii," *ExpTim* 16 (1904–05): 472–73, that *hē apostasia* is to be taken as "the Belial," citing Codex A of LXX 3 Kings 20:13 (ET 1 Kings 21:13); Aquila of Deut. 15:9; Judg. 19:22; 1 Sam. 2:12; 10:27; 25:17; 30:22; Prov. 16:27; Nah. 1:11. In this case, "unless the apostasy comes" means "unless Satan comes." As such, the "man of lawlessness" is the "man of Belial" (*'tš bᵉlia'al*; cf. MT 2 Sam 20:1), presumably accounting for Paul's reference to his coming in accord with the activity of Satan (2 Thess. 2:9). Interestingly, some of the church fathers identified *hē apostasia* as the Antichrist, though ultimately that would not make good sense of the following clause ("and the man of lawlessness is revealed"). E. Schuyler English's (*Re-thinking the Rapture* [Traveler's Rest, S.C.: Southern Bible Book House, 1954]) theory that *hē apostasia* refers to the rapture does not seem to be held by any modern scholars. See Robert H. Gundry, *The Church and the Tribulation: A Biblical Examination of Posttribulationism* (Grand Rapids: Zondervan, 1973), 115–18.

49. So Wanamaker, *1 and 2 Thessalonians*, 244; Richard, *Thessalonians*, 326, 348–49. Morris, *Epistles to the Thessalonians*, 219n20, notes the close connection but is unsure of the temporal connection between the apostasy and the revelation. One may wonder why Paul lists the apostasy first if it is instigated by the revelation. On the other hand, one may also wonder why Paul mentions the apostasy with the revelation of the Antichrist in 2 Thess. 2:3 but does not elaborate on it and yet elaborates on a kind of apostasy associated with the coming of Antichrist in vv. 8–12 not otherwise necessary to his argument. Richard, *Thessalonians*, 351–52, suggests that Paul begins and ends his discussion with apostasy, at least in terms of moral failure, because that is the primary danger in the Thessalonian church when Paul writes. But absent any reference associating the Thessalonians with actual apostasy, this explanation has little merit. MacArthur, *Thessalonians*, 272–74, suggests that the apostasy *is* the revelation and that both concepts signify the abomination of desolation. But it is hard to see how the *kai* functions epexegetically in v. 3, and MacArthur must downplay the force of v. 9. Marvin J. Rosenthal, *The Pre-wrath Rapture of the Church: A New Understanding of the Rapture, the Tribulation, and the Second Coming* (Nashville: Nelson, 1990), 199–206, has argued on the force of the allusion to Dan. 11:36 that the apostasy is the covenant the prince to come makes with the Jews (Dan. 9:27) that begins the seventieth "week." The revelation is then identified with the abomination of desolation that is part of the breaking of the covenant in the middle of the week. This proposal has some cogency but is somewhat speculative. It also has against it that Daniel 9 does not refer to this covenant as an apostasy, though "many" (9:27) may signal apostate Israel over against the remnant (cf. 11:39). Rosenthal offers that the contextually related capitulation to the religious domination of Antiochus IV (Dan. 11:30–32) is referred to in 1 Macc. 2:15 as *hē apostasia*.

the holy place" (v. 15 ESV, emphasis added; cf. the masculine participle in Mark 13:14, "standing where he does not belong").[50] This language corresponds to Paul's when he speaks of the Man of Lawlessness taking his seat in the temple of God, displaying himself as being God (2 Thess. 2:4). For this reason, and due to the allusion to Daniel 11:36 in 2 Thessalonians 2:4, most scholars are agreed that Paul is thinking of the abomination of desolation when he mentions the session of the Man of Lawlessness.[51] But the connection to this tradition also strongly suggests that the session of the Man of Lawlessness in the temple is in fact what Paul means by the sign of the Lawless One being "revealed," since, as we noted above, the abomination of desolation is singled out in Matthew 24:3–15 as the primary sign of the nearness of the final events.[52]

That Paul intends the session of the Man of Lawlessness in the temple to clarify what he means by that person's significant revelation is also suggested by the rest of 2 Thessalonians 2:6–12. First, there is no other likely candidate for the revelation in the context. Though Paul mentions the revelation of the Man of Lawlessness three times (vv. 4, 6, 8) in 2 Thessalonians 2:4–12 and refers to the coming of the Lawless One once (v. 9), he never explicitly says how it is that the Man of Lawlessness is revealed. Verses 6 and 8 tell us he cannot be revealed until the restrainer is removed, but the identification of the restrainer is so uncertain that the information is hardly helpful to modern exegetes not privy to Paul's oral teaching (v. 5).[53] Verses 9–12 state that the "coming"

---

50. Cf. R. T. France, *The Gospel of Mark: A Commentary on the Greek Text*, NIGTC (Grand Rapids: Eerdmans, 2002), 523.

51. Daniel's seventieth week is initiated by a covenant that the final king makes with the Jews, and that covenant is apparently broken when, in the middle of the week, the king causes sacrifices to cease in the Jerusalem temple in association with an abomination of desolation (Dan. 9:27). Daniel 12:11 mentions these same events, this time in association with a king who "exalts and magnifies himself above every god" (Dan. 11:36), the passage Paul alludes to here. So when Paul identifies this Danielic king with the one who proclaims himself in a session in the Jerusalem temple to be God, he is apparently identifying a known Danielic event. The only such event even remotely related to Paul's session is the nebulous abomination of desolation.

52. Cf. Wenham, *Rediscovery*, 177–79.

53. See the commentators for the various proposals. It is doubtful that, if the restrainer is the Holy Spirit, his removal involves the rapture of the church as many pretribulationists contend. First, Paul has already stated that the church is around in the day of the Lord, which comes after the restrainer is removed. Second, Paul would hardly offer to the troubled Thessalonians the nonrevelation of the Lawless One as evidence that the day of the Lord had not arrived if the very thing that allows the revelation of the Lawless One is the rapture. Why not just tell them that it cannot be the day of the Lord because it is impossible for the day of

(*parousia*) of the Lawless One[54] is accompanied by a vast satanic deception (endorsed by God), but the vast deception by itself cannot be the revealing of the Lawless One, especially if it is the apostasy mentioned in verse 3. Thus verse 4, which mentions a kind of manifestation of the Man of Lawlessness, his session in the temple of God wherein he displays himself as being God, is the only option left.

Second, the syntax of 2 Thessalonians 2:3–4 intimately ties the session to the revelation. Verses 3 and 4 are one sentence in Greek (contra NIV), so that when Paul follows the mention of the revelation of the Man of Lawlessness with a description of features that primarily identify him, the close connection of these clauses, and especially the forcefully concluding result clause, strongly suggests that Paul intends the session, an act of "displaying himself" (*apodeiknunta heauton*), to be an explanation of the revelation. In other words, Paul identifies the Man of Lawlessness precisely by pointing to the unique act of God-defiance by which he is manifested to the world. If Paul does not do so here, we have no good explanation for the inclusion of these clauses, especially when Paul does not otherwise explain the revelation.

One might argue that Paul mentions the session in the temple merely because that is a major action of the Antichrist. But that would beg the question. If the session is a major action by which the Antichrist can be identified, why does Paul mention *that* action in close connection with the revelation and not some other? It is possible that Paul did not need to mention what the revelation is because the readers were already well aware of it and that he just happened also to mention the session of the Man of Lawlessness. But the explanatory value of the alternative, that Paul mentioned the session because it is the act by which the Man of Lawlessness is revealed, is much greater. Second Thessalonians 2:5, far from indicating that Paul did not explain the revelation because the

---

the Lord to occur without the rapture first occurring? (The prewrath view does not have this problem, because it does not make the rapture a necessary condition for the day of the Lord.) Third, if the Holy Spirit were removed from the world after the rapture, there could be no repentance after the rapture, but the Scriptures indicate otherwise. The restrainer may be the Spirit, but if so, Paul is speaking of the removal of his restraining influence and not his complete removal from the world.

54. *Parousia* here is probably (though not certainly) parallel to the revelation (*apokalupsis*, though Paul uses the verb form), since Paul can use both terms for the coming of Christ as well (2 Thess. 1:7; 2:8).

readers already knew what it was, actually indicates that Paul is repeating here what he had taught them earlier.

Showers argues that the passive voice used to refer to the revelation of the Antichrist ("is revealed"; 2 Thess. 2:3, 6, 8) disallows its identification with the session, which is actively undertaken by the Antichrist.[55] Certainly the passive voice of the references to the revelation point to the action of God in the revealing of the Antichrist (v. 6 in particular), but unless one wants to argue that creaturely actions cannot fall under the sovereignty of God, there is no problem. Verse 10 indicates that the satanic deception at the coming of Antichrist is under the control of God. Showers further argues, based on Revelation 6:1–2, that the revelation of Antichrist will be his diplomatic or military victories by which he becomes "the next great world ruler."[56] But apart from the difficulty of conceiving how great diplomatic or military victories are sufficiently unique to constitute a sign (whether for Paul's audience, used to Roman imperial might ruling for the most part their known world, or any other audience), the context of 2 Thessalonians 2:1–12 associates the coming of the Antichrist not with political victory but with religious deception.[57] No doubt the Antichrist will be an imperial figure, but that does not seem to be what Paul has in mind in 2 Thessalonians 2.

Thus the best reading of 2 Thessalonians 2:3–5 is that Paul understands the parousia of Christ, in which he raptures the church and pours his wrath on his enemies, to be preceded by the abomination of desolation.[58] This obviously implies that the church will enter the second half of Daniel's seventieth "week." Further, 2 Thessalonians 2 as a whole is found to fit with the apocalyptic tradition represented by Matthew 24.

---

55. Showers, *Pre-wrath Rapture View*, 185–87.

56. Ibid., 187–89.

57. Cf. Matt. 24:6–7, 15: "You will hear of wars and rumors of wars ... these are [merely] the beginning of birth pains. But, when you see the abomination of desolation...."

58. Thomas, "2 Thessalonians," 321, makes much of the fact that Paul nowhere says the church will actually see the apostasy or the revelation, but this makes Paul use an odd argument to get his point across. If Paul believed that the Thessalonians would not experience the day of the Lord, why not just say so? In fact, he doesn't just say to the Thessalonians, "You can't be in the day because the events preceding or signaling the beginning of the Day haven't happened yet." Rather, he goes on to elaborate on, *for no apparent reason*, many more things they won't see. Further, the fact that Paul speaks in 2 Thess. 1:6 of the coming of Christ as dealing retribution on the Thessalonians' persecutors means he believes that the coming of Christ to destroy the Antichrist in 2:8 can conceivably be experienced by them. Cf. "we who are still alive and are left" in 1 Thess. 4:17.

Most significantly, in both places the major sign of the final events *is* the abomination of desolation. The two passages serve to confirm one another; Matthew 24 confirms that Paul teaches the rapture to follow the abomination of desolation, and 2 Thessalonians 2 serves to confirm that Matthew 24 addresses the church.

This Reading Does Not Affect the "Imminence" of 1 Thessalonians 5:1–12

Scholars have long noted the apparent inconsistency of the imminent expectation of the parousia in 1 Thessalonians 5:1–11 and the teaching that certain signs must precede that event in 2 Thessalonians 2:1–4. This has been taken by some as evidence that Paul did not write 2 Thessalonians. Pretribulationists sometimes take this as evidence that two different aspects of the parousia are in view in these two passages, an unexpected rapture in 1 Thessalonians and the wrath of God in 2 Thessalonians. But it is not necessary to see any inconsistency.[59] First, according to our exegesis, Paul expressly stated in 1 Thessalonians 5:4 that the parousia will not be unexpected for believers. Presumably this is at least because of the signs mentioned in 2 Thessalonians 2:3 (note that in both passages Paul refers to his earlier oral teaching on the issue; 1 Thess. 5:1; 2 Thess. 2:5).[60] This does not mean that believers will know "the day and hour," but it does mean that they will be aware of the general time period. Second, Jesus also mixed "imminence" with signs, not least the abomination of desolation, in the Olivet Discourse (Matt. 24:32–33, 42–44, and parallels).[61] Thus both Paul and Jesus enjoin their audiences to watch for the parousia.

More generally, the injunctions to watch and the unknowability of the time of the parousia do not logically entail an "any moment" rapture, as pretribulationists often argue, as long as the number of inter-

---

59. See esp. Bruce, *Thessalonians*, xlii–xliv. Cf. Donald Guthrie, *New Testament Introduction* (Downers Grove, Ill.: InterVarsity, 1970), 570–72; D. A. Carson, Douglas Moo, and Leon Morris, *An Introduction to the New Testament* (Grand Rapids: Zondervan, 1992), 345; Paul J. Achtemeier, Joel B. Green, and Marianne Meye Thompson, *Introducing the New Testament: Its Literature and Theology* (Grand Rapids: Eerdmans, 2001), 443–44; Wanamaker, *1 and 2 Thessalonians*, 178.

60. So Bruce, *Thessalonians*, xliii.

61. Ibid. Matthew 24:45–51; 25:5, 19; Luke 12:41–48; 19:11–27 also argue for a delay in the coming of Christ that goes against a strict imminence.

vening events or the duration between the events and the rapture are unknown.[62] This creates a problem for posttribulationism if it maintains a strict period of three and one-half years between the abomination of desolation and the rapture, but it creates no problem for the prewrath view, because the prewrath view does not specify the exact timing between the two events.[63]

Revelation

The timing of the rapture after the middle of Daniel's seventieth week is also presented in Revelation. Two passages in particular demonstrate this—Revelation 7:9–17 and 13:1–18. In the one, the church is pictured as having come out of "the great tribulation" (that is, the Danielic tribulation), and in the other the church is pictured in the Danielic tribulation. We begin with Revelation 7.

Revelation 7 Places the Church in the Tribulation

In Revelation 5, the messianic Lamb received a seven-sealed scroll from God. He began to open the scroll, breaking the first six seals sequentially, in Revelation 6. With the opening of the sixth seal, the arrival of the wrath of God and of the Lamb was recognized. The allusions to Isaiah 2:12–22; 13:6–16; 34:1–15; Joel 2:1–11, 30–32; 3:9–17; Zephaniah 1:14–18; Malachi 3:2 make clear that "the day of God's wrath" is John's language for the day of the Lord. When the seventh seal is opened, there is silence in heaven, an allusion to Zephaniah 1:7 and Zechariah 2:13, signaling the ominous calm before the storm of God's wrath. The trumpets that will effect God's wrath are then given to seven angels, and fire from the altar, mixed with the prayers of the

---

62. Cf. Millard J. Erickson, *Contemporary Options in Eschatology* (Grand Rapids: Baker, 1977), 141. Tacit, and ironic, approval of this fact is the constant search of the newspaper for signs of the near coming of Christ by some who argue for an "any-moment" rapture. On the evidence against an any-moment rapture being demanded by the New Testament language of expectancy, see Gundry, *Church and Tribulation*, 30–37.

63. Thus posttribulationists usually argue that the period between the two events is not precisely three and one-half years, either because the abomination of desolation (and all other events in the Olivet Discourse besides the parousia) occurred in the first century (so Craig L. Blomberg, *Matthew*, NAC 22 [Nashville: Broadman, 1992]; Carson, "Matthew") or because of a shortening of the seventieth week (Matt. 24:22; so Gundry, *Church and Tribulation*, 42, a position similar to Rosenthal's, *Pre-wrath Rapture*, 108–9). Moo, "Posttribulation Rapture," 209, also offers without commitment that the unknowable quality of the parousia may apply to all generations but the last.

saints (cf. 6:9–10) is cast to earth. Thereafter the trumpets are blown and supernatural cataclysms embroil the earth. Between the opening of the sixth seal in Revelation 6:12–17 and the seventh seal in 8:1–5, however, comes an interlude in the action. The process of opening the seals is halted in Revelation 7 in order to allow for the protection of God's servants before God's wrath is poured out (Rev. 7:1–3). In this interlude, John sees (or is made aware of) two groups. The first is a group of 144,000 Israelites, whose "sealing" (being given a distinguishing mark) is recorded in Revelation 7:4–8. After this, in Revelation 7:9–10, John sees an innumerable multitude from every nation standing before the throne of God in heaven, clothed in white robes, holding palm branches, and crying out with a loud voice, "Salvation belongs to our God ... and to the Lamb." When questioned regarding the identity of this group, John is told that it is comprised of those who have come out of the great tribulation. They have washed their robes in the blood of the Lamb and will experience eschatological blessings. The best way to understand this second group is as a picture of the church.

That this group is the church is clear from the language used to describe it.[64] In Revelation 7:9 the innumerable multitude is said to come from "every nation, tribe, people and language"[65] and in 7:14 to have washed their robes "in the blood of the Lamb." This is language that John already applied to the church in Revelation 5:9. There the Lamb is said to have "purchased with [his] blood ... men for God from every tribe and language and people and nation." John clearly intends to describe the church there, because 5:10 repeats the description of the church as a kingdom and priests (cf. Ex 19:6) that was used in a similar context in 1:5–6: "To him

---

64. Cf. Robert H. Mounce, *The Book of Revelation*, NICNT, rev. ed. (Grand Rapids: Eerdmans, 1998), 139; David E. Aune, *Revelation 6–16*, WBC 52B (Nashville: Nelson, 1998), 447; Henry Barclay Swete, *Commentary on Revelation* (Grand Rapids: Kregel, 1977), 100; G. K. Beale, *The Book of Revelation: A Commentary on the Greek Text*, NIGTC (Grand Rapids: Eerdmans, 1999), 433; Grant R. Osborne, *Revelation*, BECNT (Grand Rapids: Baker, 2002), 303. Showers, *Pre-wrath Rapture View*, 150, argues that the multitude cannot be the church or John surely would have recognized someone! Such an approach treats the genre far more literally than it should.

65. The phrase "every nation, tribe, people and language" comes from Daniel (3:4, 7, 29; 4:1; 5:19; 6:25; 7:14), where it describes the inhabitants of the empires generally and those who serve the one like a son of man in the eschaton particularly. It carries that same weight in Revelation (5:9; 7:9; 10:11; 11:9; 13:7; 14:6; 17:15), describing both humanity in general (ruled over by the empires) and those who belong to the Son of Man. The latter are distinguished from the former by other descriptions in context. See Alan Hultberg, "Messianic Exegesis in the Apocalypse: The Significance of the Old Testament for the Christology of Revelation" (PhD diss., Trinity Evangelical Divinity School, 2001), 277–82.

who loves us and has freed us from our sins by his blood, and has made us to be a kingdom and priests to serve his God and Father." Though it could be that the description of the innumerable multitude is intended by John to cover a larger group than the church, so that the multitude includes both the church and others, the point is moot without other compelling evidence.[66] John certainly intends to describe the church.

Some have suggested that the innumerable multitude represents a subset of the church, namely martyrs, either of all time or of the final tribulation.[67] Proponents offer that the mention of white robes (Rev. 7:9, 13, 14), the washing of the robes in the blood of the Lamb (v. 14), and the fact that the multitude comes out of the great tribulation all signal martyrdom. So it is pointed out that the martyrs under the altar were given white robes after the opening of the fifth seal (Rev. 6:11) and those victorious over the dragon in Revelation 12:11 were said to be so "by the blood of the Lamb and by the word of their testimony; they did not love their lives so much as to shrink from death." So also the whitening of the robes is said to be an allusion to Daniel 11:35, where "Some of the wise [during the Antiochene persecution] will stumble,[68] so that they may be refined, purified and made spotless [*lalbēn*, 'to whiten']" (cf. Dan. 12:10).[69] Thus, that the multitude "comes out of the great tribulation" must mean that they have been martyred.[70]

---

66. It is true that the wearing of white robes (Rev. 4:4; though cf. 3:5, 18; 19:8, 14) and the enjoyment of eschatological blessings (Rev. 21:4, 6) may apply to a larger group than the church. But this is not evidence that John is necessarily here describing a larger group than the church, since the church is clearly to be included in the group and John may only be applying the language to the church as a subset of the larger group. More telling is the lack of evidence that John intends to describe some subset of this supposed larger group other than the church.

67. R. H. Charles, *The Critical and Exegetical Commentary on the Revelation of St. John*, ICC (Edinburgh: T & T Clark, 1920), 1:189; Martin Kiddle, *The Revelation of St. John*, MNTC (New York: Harper and Bros., 1940), 133–37; G. B. Caird, *The Revelation of St. John*, BNTC (Peabody, Mass.: Hendrickson, 1966), 96.

68. Though *kāšlû* means "stumble," the verb is being used here for being killed, as Dan. 11:33 makes clear.

69. See esp. Richard Bauckham, *The Climax of Prophecy: Studies in the Book of Revelation* (Edinburgh: T & T Clark, 1993), 227–29.

70. Some also see the innumerable multitude as martyrs on the supposition that they are the same group as the 144,000 (Kiddle, *Revelation*, 138; Caird, *Revelation*, 100). Since the 144,000 are taken from the fuller number of "every tribe of the sons of Israel" (Rev. 7:4), and since the sons of Israel can only mean the whole church, the 144,000 are a subset of the whole church. But we then have the curious proposition that it is only the martyrs, those who will specifically die for their faith, who are protected from the wrath of God, while the rest of the church, who will specifically not die for their faith, are exposed to the wrath of God. For a further critique of the identification of these two groups, see below.

Most commentators, however, do not see any martyrological language here.[71] On the one hand, the church itself is often viewed as
consisting entirely of "martyrs" in the book of Revelation.[72] To be a
"witness" in Revelation is not necessarily to die for one's faith but to be
faithful throughout one's life, however one dies. Thus, even if it could
be shown that the language in 7:9–17 is undoubtedly martyrological
language, it would not show that the whole church is not in view. On
the other hand, and more important, none of this language is confined
to martyrs in Revelation. There is nothing in "These are they who have
come out of the great tribulation" that necessarily implies martyrdom,
or even death for that matter. And, though white robes are given to the
martyrs under the altar after the opening of the fifth seal (Rev. 6:11),
the wearing of white robes is common of all Christians in Revelation
(3:5, 18; 19:8, 14). Similarly, though Revelation 12:11 certainly has a
martyrological context, it is doubtful that conquering "by the blood of
the Lamb" means "being killed for the faith like he was," thus making
"by the word of their testimony [and did not love their lives so much
as to shrink from death]" synonymous with "because of the blood of
the Lamb." First, conquering by the blood of the Lamb is meant to
recall Revelation 5:5, 9, where the messianic victory was the *redemption*
wrought on the cross. The "brethren" in 12:11 are victorious over the
serpent because of the Lamb's redemptive death. Second, the syntax of
12:11, where John repeats the prepositional phrase (*dia* + accusative),
shows that John gives two reasons for the victory, not one. Thus the
brethren conquer because of the Lamb's redemptive death and because
of their own faithfulness to the gospel till death, whether by martyrdom or not (cf. Rev. 2:10). And while the whitening of the robes may
allude to Daniel 11:35 (on the strength of the clear allusion to Dan.
12:1 in the phrase "the great tribulation"), it may also allude to Isaiah
1:8 (cf. Ps. 51:7). The other evidence that "washed in the blood of the

71. See, e.g., Aune, *Revelation 6–16*, 447; Swete, *Revelation*, 100; Mounce, *Revelation*,
154; Beale, *Revelation*, 433; Osborne, *Revelation*, 318.

72. Beale, *Revelation*, 171–72, 269–72; Osborne, *Revelation*, 285–86. Cf. Caird, *Revelation*, 293, 296–298; Bauckham, *Climax of Prophecy*, 233–35. Revelation 12:11 is an instance
of the church viewed as "martyrs." Cf. 2:10, 13; 13:10; 20:4 (and 11:7, if one understands
the witnesses to represent the church). The "one who overcomes" in each of the letters to the
churches is that one who is faithful to Jesus until death of whatever sort.

Lamb" is a redemptive theme and not a martyrological one argues for the latter.[73]

It is also argued that the context requires the innumerable multitude to be martyrs. In Revelation 6:9–10, after the fifth seal was broken, John saw martyrs under the altar crying out for vengeance. In verse 11, they are told they must wait until the full number of martyrs is completed. Since God's wrath begins with the sounding of the trumpets, the innumerable multitude must be the completed set of martyrs. There is a certain cogency to this argument. But despite the reasonableness of anticipating a scene completing the martyrs before God's wrath is poured out, it seems doubtful that Revelation 7 functions that way, or, if it does, that the martyrs are to be identified with the innumerable multitude. First, as we have seen, nothing in the description of the multitude necessitates they are martyrs. Second, one wonders why, if 7:9–17 is about the completion of the set of martyrs, this scene appears after the sixth seal and not before. Though God's wrath will not be administered until the blowing of the trumpets, it is with the opening of the sixth seal that God's wrath is said to arrive, immediately upon the directive to the martyrs to wait. The implication is that by the time the sixth seal is opened, the full complement of martyrs has been achieved.[74] A better solution is to understand the appearance of the innumerable multitude in heaven to be a picture of the rapture of the church. This is confirmed by a set of scenes in Revelation 14–16 very similar to Revelation 6–8.

Revelation 12–16 forms a literary unit in the book. It is set off by the mention of three heavenly "signs" John sees (Rev. 12:1, 3; 15:1). The

---

73. Both John Walvoord (*The Revelation of Jesus Christ* [Chicago: Moody, 1966], 144–47) and Robert L. Thomas (*Revelation 1–7: An Exegetical Commentary* [Chicago: Moody, 1992], 485) understand the innumerable multitude to represent those who have believed during the tribulation era, that is, after the rapture of the church. Walvoord takes them to be martyrs, but Thomas sees no reason to view them as such; rather, he understands them to be those who have died in any way during the first six seals. But the thesis that these are "tribulation saints" runs afoul of the clearly ecclesial language of 7:9–17 and the lack of any good evidence that John means to signify a group other than the church. Walvoord offers that the twenty-four elders represent the church and that therefore the innumerable multitude must be a different group. But this is to make the obscure interpret the clear. There is no plain indication that the twenty-four elders represent the actual church (raptured and present in heaven), whereas there is clear evidence that the innumerable multitude do. Without the presupposition of a pretribulation rapture, one would hardly conclude that this is a group other than the church, whether the full body or only part.

74. Cf. Beale, *Revelation*, 396.

first two signs establish the cosmic context of the eschatological events depicted in Revelation 13–14. The war of the Danielic Beast against the saints (Rev. 13:7; cf. Dan. 7:21; 12:1; Rev. 12:11–17) is part of the larger war of the diabolical serpent against God's people that began in the garden (Rev. 12:9).[75] The war with the Beast will be concluded in the winepress of God's wrath (Rev. 14:17–20), and the third sign elaborates on that wrath (Rev. 15:1; 16:1–21). In the midst of this description, after the portrayal of the Beast's satanic domination of the world and persecution of the saints (Rev. 13:7–10; cf. Dan. 7:21), the 144,000 reappear, standing on Mount Zion with the Lamb. They seem to form the counterpoint to the Beast and his followers in chapter 13, as if John depicts two teams, poised at opposite ends of the arena awaiting a contest. In 14:6–12, three angels announce the stakes of the contest. The first angel urges repentance upon those who dwell on earth, because the hour of God's judgment has arrived (14:7). The second and third angels announce the dire consequences of those who side with the Beast: they will drink the wine of the wrath of God (14:10). But before the harvest of the grapes of wrath, John sees another harvest, when "one like a son of man" reaps the earth (14:14–16).[76] This harvest apparently completes the "redemption" begun with the 144,000, who are its firstfruits (14:4). Thereafter, in the third sign, which elaborates on the outpouring of God's wrath in 14:17–20, John sees "those who had been victorious over the beast" (Rev. 15:2; cf. 7:14) standing before the throne of God (15:2; cf. 4:5–6; 7:9) and singing of their salvation (15:3; cf. 7:10).[77]

---

75. The woman in Revelation 12 seems to be a symbol of the messianic community. Her war with the dragon extends from the garden of Eden (12:9) to the final period of history (12:14 and the rest of the book, which is dependent on this episode). Thus, as Eve, she gives birth to a messianic child whose life is sought by the ancient serpent (12:4; Gen. 3:15). As Israel, she bears the attributes of Joseph's dream (12:1; Gen. 37:9) and brings forth the Messiah (12:5; Ps. 2:9). Though she herself is protected by God, the rest of her children are exposed to the wrath of the dragon in the work of the Beast (12:17; 13:7). Cf. Osborne, *Revelation*, 456.

76. Aune, *Revelation 6–16*, among others, understands the harvest in 14:14–16 merely as an angel judgment parallel to the grape harvest that follows. This thesis is highly unlikely. See esp. the decisive argument by Bauckham, 290–96. Besides the parallelism of chaps. 14–16 to 6–8, that John can allude to Dan. 7:13 and not mean to identify Jesus is virtually impossible given the thematic centrality of Rev. 1:7, 13. Furthermore, it is hard to imagine the point of the two harvests if both are judgment, especially if the first is distinguished from the second by its agent and the second from the first by its being explicitly related to God's wrath.

77. The salvific character of the song in Rev. 15:3–4 is indicated by its being called "the song of Moses" (cf. Ex. 15:1–21). Cf. Bauckham, *Climax of Prophecy*, 296–307.

The implication is that these are those harvested by the Son of Man in 14:14–16, since the bowls of God's wrath are poured out after this group appears in heaven, just as the harvest of wrath occurs immediately after the harvest of the earth by the Son of Man.[78]

Thus Revelation 14–16 parallels Revelation 7–8 quite closely. In both we find the sequence of the 144,000 on earth with God's seal (name) on their foreheads, followed by the appearance of a victorious group in heaven that had come from the tribulation, followed by the outpouring of God's wrath.[79] This suggests that the group in Revelation 15:2 is the same as the innumerable multitude in 7:9. But the group in heaven in Revelation 15:2 arrives there not by death but by being harvested from the earth by one like a son of man coming on a cloud. This is a clear picture of the parousia, and thus the appearance of this group in heaven is probably John's version of the rapture.[80] This implies that the innumerable multitude in Revelation 7:9–17 also appear in heaven via the rapture.

----

78. Cf. Beale's elaborate analysis of the relation of the victors in 15:2–4 to the harvest in 14:14–20 (*Revelation*, 784–85). He does not tie 15:2–4 to 14:14–16 as the ones harvested due to his understanding of 14:14–16 as solely judgmental.

79. The literary connections among the three "judgment" series in Revelation indicate that the seventh seal encompasses the seven trumpets and the seventh trumpet encompasses the seven bowls. Thus the trumpets are given upon the opening of the seventh seal (8:1–2), and the trumpets end and bowls begin with the opening of the temple in heaven (11:19; 15:5). Each series then ends with the same theophanic phenomena, indicating the coming of God and his kingdom (11:15–18; cf. 16:17). Seals 1–6 bring us to the arrival of the day of God's wrath, and seal 7 (incorporating the trumpets and bowls) is the outpouring of God's wrath. The seven bowls represent a final, intense period of judgment against the Beast and his worshipers during which repentance is impossible.

80. See Traugott Holtz, *Die Christologie der Apokalypse des Johannes*, TUGAL 85 (Berlin: Akademie, 1971), 134; Pierre Prigent, *L'Apocalypse de Saint Jean*, CNT 14, 2nd ser. (Lausanne: Delachaux & Niestlé, 1981), 232–33. Both Bauckham, *Climax of Prophecy*, 293–95, and Swete, *Revelation*, 189–90, while acknowledging the harvest is the eschatological ingathering of the faithful effected by the coming Son of Man, understand this ingathering in terms of evangelism. Bauckham offers in support that the lack of judgment imagery in both Rev. 14:14–16 (in particular threshing) and Dan. 7:13–14 indicates that the reaping by the Son of Man does not lead to judgment. However, it certainly does lead to the grape harvest and the treading of the winepress, which is an image of Christ judging the nations (Rev. 19:15); and in Dan. 7:9–14 the arrival of the one like a son of man is concurrent with the judgment of the fourth beast. It is better to see a multifaceted parousia in Revelation: grain harvest/rapture, grape harvest/wrath, glorious return to consummate the wrath and initiate the kingdom. Beale, *Revelation*, 770–73, though he recognizes both the connection to Matt. 24:30 and the theme in the synoptic tradition and Revelation of the parousia as bringing salvation and judgment (a theme also present in Paul), nevertheless understands the harvest by the Son of Man in 14:14–16 as a judgment, based solely on the parallel harvest in verses 17–20. But as we have noted, the juxtaposition and distinctive descriptions of the two harvests makes their identity hard to accept.

That Revelation 7:9 is the parousia, and thus the rapture, is further suggested by the use of the Olivet Discourse tradition in Revelation 6:1–17. Many have noted the parallels between the first six seals and the events enumerated in Matthew 24:5–31.[81] Thus the first seal (Rev. 6:1–2) is probably representative of the rise of false christs, if not the Antichrist, corresponding to Matthew 24:5 (cf. 24:24). The second seal, war (Rev. 6:3–4), corresponds to the "wars and rumors of war" in Matthew 24:6–7. The third seal, famine (Rev. 6:5–6), corresponds to the famines of Matthew 24:7. The fifth seal, martyrdom (Rev. 6:9–11), corresponds to the martyrdom of Matthew 24:9. And the sixth seal, cosmic disturbances (Rev. 6:12–14), corresponds to the cosmic disturbances of Matthew 24:31.[82] In Matthew, the cosmic disturbances occur at the parousia when the Son of Man comes on the clouds and gathers the elect, a scene that surely is represented in Revelation 14:14–16 and the corresponding appearance of a group of victors in heaven. Thus it is virtually certain that Revelation 7:9–17, introduced by the cosmic disturbances of the sixth seal and parallel to the scene of the victors harvested by the Son of Man in 14:14–16, is a picture of the raptured church. The fact that in Matthew 24:29 the parousia is said to follow "the great tribulation" (Matt. 24:21) explains, then, why the innumerable multitude is said in Revelation 7:14 to have come out of "the great tribulation."

Some have argued against a rapture in Revelation 7:9–17 by noting the present participle *erchomenoi* ("coming") in 7:14,[83] which is taken to have durative force ("these are those *coming* out of the great tribulation"). Thus the arrival of the innumerable multitude in heaven is not all at once, as would be expected of a depiction of the rapture, but continuous, as would be expected of the individual dead arriving in heaven upon their deaths. But this makes the participle bear far more weight

---

81. E.g., Charles, *Revelation*, 1:158–60; Mounce, *Revelation*, 140; Walvoord, *Revelation*, 123; Thomas, *Revelation 1–7*, 416; Beale, *Revelation*, 373–74; Osborne, *Revelation*, 270. Cf. the somewhat more cautious judgment of Aune, *Revelation 6–16*, 424; Swete, *Revelation*, 92.

82. The fourth seal, death (Rev. 6:7–8), has no particular correspondence to the Olivet Discourse. Thomas, *Revelation 1–7*, 452, has argued that the cosmic disturbances of the sixth seal are like those of Matt. 24:29 but are not the same, since in Matthew they come after the tribulation, at the very end, but not in Revelation. Cf. Osborne, *Revelation*, 291. But this presupposes that the parousia is a single, unified event and that John cannot expand what Matthew has portrayed as unified.

83. See esp. Showers, *Pre-wrath Rapture View*, 147–50. Cf. Charles, *Revelation*, 1:209.

than it is able. On the one hand, the preceding evidence of a rapture in 7:9–17 argues strongly against it, and on the other hand, the other verbs in Revelation 7:9–17 make a durative understanding of the participle unlikely. So, in verse 9 John sees the multitude standing (*hestōtes*) before the throne, the perfect participle depicting them in a particular state. But one would expect a verb like "arriving" or "gathering" if John were intending to convey the continual arrival of new persons in the crowd. Thus also the elder asks John in verse 13, "From where have they come (*ēlthon*)?" (ESV), using an aorist. Though not decisive, one would expect a present or imperfect form here if John were intending to convey constant arrival. More important, a substantival participle, as is *hoi erchomenoi* ("those who come"), generally loses specific aspect in *koinē* Greek, so that there is no necessary reason for *hoi erchomenoi* to have durative force, let alone present time reference.[84] So compare the use of the present tense substantive participle in Revelation 20:10: "The devil, who deceived (*ho planōn*) them, was thrown into the lake of burning sulfur." Here the present participle refers to the past work of deception recorded in the immediately preceding verses. For this reason, most commentators understand *hoi erchomenoi* to mean merely "those who come" or "who have come" and not "those who are [continually] coming."[85]

So the best understanding of the innumerable multitude is as the raptured church. And when John says that the church has come out of the great tribulation, the most obvious implication is that the church will experience at least part of the Danielic tribulation. This also accords with the warnings to the church about the upcoming tribulation in Revelation 2:10, 22.

Revelation 13 Places the Church in the Tribulation

Though the seven churches of Asia to which John writes the book of Revelation (Rev. 1:4, 11) are seven literal, first-century churches, they are

---

84. Daniel Wallace, *Greek Grammar beyond the Basics* (Grand Rapids: Zondervan, 1996), 625–26, who notes that present participles denote time contemporaneous with the main verb or can even refer to the past, especially when articular. Cf. BDF, § 339.

85. See, e.g., Aune, *Revelation 6–16*, 430n14d-d, 473; Mounce, *Revelation*, 164; Osborne, *Revelation*, 324; Swete, *Revelation*, 102; Ernst Lohmeyer, *Die Offenbarung des Johannes*, HKNT 16 (Tübingen: J. C. B. Mohr, 1926), 69.

probably intended to represent the entire church.[86] John indicates this in several ways. First, the number seven itself is a highly significant number in Revelation (note the seven Spirits of God, seven lampstands, seven stars, seven seals, seven eyes, seven horns, seven trumpets, seven thunders, and seven bowls). It undoubtedly stands for fullness or a complete set. Thus, that John writes to seven churches suggests he intends these seven to represent all churches, especially since other churches existed in Roman Asia in the first century (Acts 20:4; Col. 1:2; 4:13). Second, though each oracle in Revelation 2–3 is addressed to an individual church, its warnings and promises are addressed to all churches, as indicated by the plural "churches" in the stereotypical call to hear (2:7, 11, 17, 29; 3:6, 13, 22; cf. 2:23). Third, the eschatological promises to individual churches in the oracles are fulfilled for all Christians in the final state (cf., e.g., Rev. 2:7; 22:2, 14). So Revelation is a book to seven first-century churches intended to instruct all churches. This makes the book of Revelation somewhat complicated in its temporal perspective.[87] On the one hand, there are clear indications of a first-century perspective, an expectation that the events prophesied in the book will be fulfilled in the lives of John and his near contemporaries (e.g., the numerous assertions of the nearness of the events and the application of the book to the seven churches of Asia). On the other hand, there are clear indications of a future perspective, so that at least some of the events await the eschaton for fulfillment (e.g., the parousia and defeat of the Beast, the resurrection, and the final judgment). This makes dealing with the symbolism of Revelation difficult, because it is not always apparent whether John is talking about the near perspective or the far or both simultaneously.

This complication is perhaps felt most acutely in the oracles to the seven churches, given that the seven churches are both real churches and representative of the entire church. Clearly first-century issues are addressed in these oracles, but they are related to eschatological events elaborated in the rest of the book. A case in point involves the oracles to the churches of Smyrna (Rev. 2:8–11) and Thyatira (2:18–29), in which the resurrected Christ warns of an upcoming period of tribulation. The Smyrnans are warned that "the devil is about to throw some

---

86. See Beale, *Revelation*, 186–87, 226–27.
87. See Marvin C. Pate, ed., *Four Views on the Book of Revelation* (Grand Rapids: Zondervan, 1998).

of you into prison, that you may be tested, and for ten days you will have tribulation" (Rev. 2:10 ESV). The Thyatirans are told that a certain false prophetess and her followers will be cast "into great tribulation, unless they repent of her works" (2:22 ESV).[88] Though the tribulation to which these churches will be exposed seems imminent, the representative nature of the churches and the portrayal of the tribulation as obviously eschatological later in the book argues that John is also warning future churches of the great Danielic tribulation.[89]

In Revelation 13 John portrays the career of a beast called forth from the sea by Satan and inspired by him to dominate the world. Features of the portrayal allude to the fourth beast of Daniel 7 and its blasphemous little horn (cf. Dan. 7:8, 20, 21, 25; Rev. 13:5–7). In Daniel the fourth beast is both a historical and an eschatological image. It represents the fourth kingdom to dominate Israel, the kingdom that supplants Greece, namely Rome, but its little horn is its final king, whose "war against the saints" constitutes the great eschatological tribulation (Dan. 7:21, 25; 12:1, 7). The Beast in Revelation has similar historical and eschatological connections. Thus, in Revelation 17:10 the Beast represents a Roman emperor. In Revelation 17 John sees the Beast being ridden by a harlot, and this harlot is interpreted for John as "the great city that rules over the kings of the earth" (v. 18) and is described as sitting on seven hills (17:9). For John's readers, the harlot can only be Rome.[90] The Beast itself is interpreted as the eighth of a series of kings and a "reincarnation" of one of the prior seven kings (17:10–11). The fact that the beast-king is ridden by a woman

---

88. On "the hour of testing" in Rev. 3:10, see below.

89. In my opinion, the best way to deal with the phenomena of Revelation is to understand them from a dualist perspective—that John portrays soon-to-be increased pressure to capitulate to Roman imperial demands through the lens of the eschatological imperial demands of the Antichrist and the final victory of Christ. A coming Roman emperor (Domitian) will be an antichrist to John's churches, a type of the final Antichrist (cf. 1 John 2:18; 4:3; 2 Thess. 2:7–8). This is similar to the perspective of the Olivet Discourse on the first-century destruction of Jerusalem as a type of the eschatological tribulation and owes itself to a similar reliance on the eschatology of Daniel, which relates the Antichrist to the first-century Roman destruction of Jerusalem and typifies him by Antiochus IV Epiphanes. Cf. C. Marvin Pate "A Progressive Dispensationalist View of Revelation," in idem, *Four Views*, 95–175; Osborne, *Revelation*, 1, 21–22. Rev. 1:19 may indicate this dualist perspective. In this case it should be read, "Write therefore about what you see (*eides*), both (or, perhaps, "namely," *kai*) what is and (*kai*) what must happen after these things." Cf. Beale, *Revelation*, 163.

90. The description of the harlot follows known iconography of the *Dea Roma*. See esp. Aune, *Revelation 17–22*, 920–22, 944–45.

representing Rome probably indicates the Beast is a Roman emperor, most likely Domitian, the eighth emperor from Augustus, who is predicted to "reincarnate" Nero as an antichrist.[91] Thus the Beast's "war against the saints" in Revelation 13:7 is primarily that historical tribulation referred to in Revelation 2:10, 22, and its worship has to do with the imperial cult.[92] And yet the Beast represents more than merely a first-century Roman emperor, because both it and the harlot who ride it are described in language that link them to broader Danielic imperial themes[93] and because they are involved in clearly eschatological events.[94] Not the least of these eschatological connections are the deceptive signs performed by the Beast's false prophet (Rev. 13:13 – 14), which should probably be taken as another reference to the apocalyptic Jesus tradition as found in the seals vision (cf. Matt. 24:24; 2 Thess. 2:9 – 10).[95] This seems to confirm that John has two perspectives in mind when he warns his churches about an upcoming tribulation. The "war against the saints" prosecuted by the Beast in Revelation 13:7 is both the historical tribulation expected to engulf the seven churches and the eschatological tribulation awaiting the future church.[96] This explains, then, why John can see the church in Revelation 7:9 – 19 as

---

91. See Swete, *Revelation*, 220 – 21; Stephen S. Smalley, *The Revelation to John: A Commentary on the Greek Text of the Apocalypse* (Downers Grove, Ill.: InterVarsity, 2005), 436. Cf. Charles, *Revelation*, 2:69 – 70. Thus many scholars understand the number of the Beast's name, 666 (or 616), to be a gematria of Hebrew transliterations of Greek and Latin versions of Nero Caesar.

92. See, e.g., Aune, *Revelation 6 – 16*, 756. The opposition of the imperial cult to the churches was alluded to in the letter to Pergamum. "Satan's throne" was said to be in that city, a reference to Pergamum's distinction as the official head of the imperial cult in Asia.

93. So, e.g., the Beast is a composite of all four of the imperial beasts of Daniel 7 (cf. Dan. 7:4 – 7; Rev. 13:1 – 2), and the harlot is identified with "Babylon the great, the mother of prostitutes and of the abominations of the earth" (Rev. 17:5; Dan. 4:30). "Babylon the great" is the expression of human imperial hubris to which God is opposed in Daniel, hubris that Daniel links to the tower of Babel in 1:2.

94. So, e.g., the Beast forms a ten-nation confederacy in opposition to the Lamb (Rev. 17:14; 19:19 – 21), and the harlot is destroyed by these kings immediately prior to the return of Christ (Rev. 14:8 – 20; 17:16; 18:1 – 19:21).

95. Thus the worship of the Beast's image may conform to the session of the Man of Lawlessness in 2 Thess. 2:4.

96. This suggests further that the details about the Beast in chapter 13 that cannot easily be given a first-century referent probably refer to realities pertaining to the future Antichrist. Though the worship of the Beast in general can refer to the imperial cult, the worship of the Beast in response to its recovery from a fatal wound, the deceptive signs of the false prophet, the talking image, and the economic control go far beyond Roman imperial efforts and are somewhat related to Paul's idea of the Man of Lawlessness in 2 Thessalonians 2.

coming out of the great tribulation. The tribulation of Revelation 13 is concluded in Revelation 14 by the harvest of the earth by the Son of Man and the subsequent outpouring of the bowls of wrath on the kingdom of the Beast and destruction of the harlot, Babylon, who rides the Beast.

Conclusion

We conclude, then, that Matthew, Paul, and John all agree that the rapture of the church will occur after the middle of Daniel's seventieth "week." All three expect the church to see the eschatological Antichrist, Matthew and Paul explicitly anticipating the church's witness of the abomination of desolation, and Matthew and John explicitly anticipating the church's experience of the eschatological tribulation. And all three are best understood as placing the rapture of the church after these events. Furthermore, all three seem to depend on the same Jesus tradition for their view. The best reading of the exegetical evidence, then, is against a pretribulation rapture. But the best reading of the exegetical evidence also undermines a posttribulation rapture, because, though the church will be raptured after the middle of Daniel's seventieth week, the evidence also demands that it will be raptured before the end of the week.

The Way the Church Avoids God's Wrath at the End of the Age Is by the Rapture

That the church will not experience God's wrath is clear first in Paul's letters. Three times in his letters, Paul mentions that Christians are not destined for God's wrath (Rom. 5:9; 1 Thess. 1:10; 5:9). Certainly Paul can mean by these statements that believers will not be exposed to the wrath of God in the final judgment because of the atonement wrought by Christ. This is probably the case for Romans 5:9. But Paul can also speak of an outpouring of God's wrath on the day that Jesus is revealed, that is, at the parousia (1 Thess. 5:2–3; 2 Thess. 1:6–10; 2 Thess. 2:8).[97] It is in this context that we find the other two promises of protection from divine wrath. Thus in 1 Thessalonians 1:10, the Thessalonians await the arrival of God's Son from heaven,

---

97. Cf. Rom. 1:18; 2:5; Eph. 5:6; Col. 3:6. These texts share language with the former that implies they are speaking about this parousia wrath, but the conclusion is not certain.

who "rescues [them] from the coming wrath." This wrath and the Thessalonians' rescue from it are referred to in 1 Thessalonians 5:2–4, when the day of the Lord overtakes unbelievers destructively but believers benignly, prompting Paul to conclude in 1 Thessalonians 5:9–10 that "God did not appoint us to suffer wrath but to receive salvation through our Lord Jesus Christ. He died for us so that, whether we are awake or asleep, we may live together with him." This latter statement refers back to the discussion of the rapture in 1 Thessalonians 4:13–18 and implies that the salvation obtained by believers on the day of the Lord is effected by the rapture. This, then, is what Paul probably refers to in 1:10. When Jesus is revealed from heaven, Christians will be rescued by the rapture from the wrath to come. The same idea is found in 2 Thessalonians 1:6–11, where the parousia brings affliction and retribution to those opposed to God and his people but relief to oppressed Christians. That Paul has the rapture in mind here is suggested by the overarching concept to the discussion of the judgment of the Antichrist and his dupes in 2 Thessalonians 2:3–12; namely, "the coming of our Lord Jesus Christ and our being gathered to him" (2:1). Like 1 Thessalonians 5:9, the discussion here concludes with an announcement of salvation to the church: "But we ought always to thank God for you, brothers [and sisters] loved by the Lord, because from the beginning[98] God chose you to be saved" (2:13). Though this may refer generally to salvation from divine judgment, the context (both 2 Thessalonians 2 and the broader Thessalonian correspondence) suggests it includes the divine wrath to be brought at the parousia.[99] Thus it is most likely that when Paul promises protection to the church from divine wrath, he means to include the rapture as protection from the wrath Jesus metes out at his coming.

This implies that Paul has a complex of events in mind when he speaks of the parousia. The parousia involves first the rapture, then divine wrath, then a return to earth. Paul does not give any indica-

---

98. The witnesses to 2 Thess. 2:13 are evenly divided as to whether Paul wrote "firstfruits" (*aparchēn*) or "from the beginning" (*ap archēs*). Though Paul's style favors "firstfruits," its lack of sense in the context leads me to accept "from the beginning" as the better reading. So also Wanamaker, *1 and 2 Thessalonians*, 265; contra TNIV, Metzger, *Textual Commentary*, 568. The text-critical problem does not materially affect my argument.

99. Cf. Richard, *Thessalonians*, 262.

tion as to the duration of this complex of events, but that he requires a complex of events is evident.[100] Thus, arguments that Paul's second-coming language suggests a unified rapture/return are of no import. For example, Paul's use of *apantēsis* ("meeting") in 1 Thessalonians 4:17 is frequently offered as evidence of a posttribulation rapture. It is argued that the word has a semitechnical meaning of local officials leaving a city to meet an approaching dignitary who is making his *parousia* there and then accompanying him back into the city.[101] Even granting Paul's use of the term here in that sense (it can also merely mean a meeting of any sort),[102] the metaphor says nothing as to the duration of the meeting and subsequent return.[103] Thus the word could still be used for a two-stage parousia, as long as the rapture and return to earth are viewed as a single event. Similarly, that Paul uses the terms *parousia* ("coming" or "presence"), *epiphaneia* ("appearance" or "manifestation"), and *apokalypsis* ("revelation") interchangeably for the rapture and return of Christ (as do the other New Testament writers) is no argument against the second coming as a complex of events.[104] In any instance, larger or narrower events may be in view. Moo admits as much but argues that the thesis "cannot be accepted unless there is clear evidence for such a division."[105] That evidence is found in Revelation.[106]

---

100. Even the posttribulationist must agree that Paul taught the day of the Lord/parousia as a complex of events, for otherwise it is impossible to explain the situation of 2 Thessalonians 2. If Paul had not taught that the day of the Lord was a complex of events, why would the Thessalonians have assumed the day of the Lord had come despite the lack of the glorious appearing of Jesus (2 Thess. 2:2), or why would Paul argue for signs to precede the day of the Lord rather than point to the obvious fact that Jesus had not returned yet? Cf. Thomas, "2 Thessalonians," 318.

101. See Bruce, *Thessalonians*, 102–3, for evidence.

102. BDAG, 97.

103. Cf. Moo, "Posttribulation Rapture," 181.

104. This is true as well for Gundry's evidence concerning the timing of the resurrection (*Church and Tribulation*, 146–51).

105. Moo, "Posttribulation Rapture," 177.

106. A similar case to this is the argument of amillennialists against a literal millennium. Certain New Testament texts are most simply understood to posit the resurrection and final judgment to occur at the second coming of Christ. Therefore the millennium must not be literal. Premillennialists respond that what seems a single event elsewhere must be a complex of events given the literalness of the millennium. Or again, Jewish theologians argue that Jesus cannot be the Messiah, since all messianic events reported of him in certain Old Testament passages did not occur during his life. Christians respond that what appears as a single event in the Old Testament is shown in the New Testament to be a complex of events separated in time.

Revelation Shows a Complex Parousia Involving the Rapture, an Outpouring of Wrath, and the Return of Christ to Earth

What could appear as nearly simultaneous in Paul is extended in Revelation. We have seen above that Revelation 6–8 and 14–16 present the rapture immediately prior to the outpouring of God's wrath. Thus in Revelation 14:14–20, following an announcement of the arrival of the hour of God's judgment (14:7) and yet prior to the grape harvest (14:17–20) in which all who worship the Beast will be forced to "drink of the wine of the wrath of God, which is mixed in full strength in the cup of His anger" (14:10, 18–20 NASB), John sees Christ harvest the earth at his parousia. Once the victorious church is in heaven (15:2–4), the seven bowls full of the wrath of God (15:1, 7; 16:1) are poured onto the kingdom of the Beast (16:1–21). At the end of this period of wrath, Jesus returns to earth to establish his kingdom (Rev. 19:11–21; cf. 16:13–18; 17:14). Similarly, in Revelation 6:17, with the opening of the sixth seal, it is recognized that the great day of the wrath of God has arrived. But prior to the outpouring of God's wrath in the trumpet judgments (8:1–11:19), the 144,000 are sealed for protection from it (7:1–3; cf. 9:4) and the church is raptured to heaven. Only after this are the trumpets blown, the last of which brings the arrival of God's kingdom (11:15–18).

A few objections to this view can be made. First, on the supposition that the 144,000 are identical to the innumerable multitude, the scene in 7:9–17 is said to be proleptic of the end. That is, John is said to see the church under two perspectives in the interlude of chapter 7: as the church militant on earth, protected by God from his coming wrath but still exposed to martyrdom at the hands of the Beast, and as the church triumphant in heaven, having completed its course of tribulation in faithfulness.[107] But, on the one hand, this reading runs afoul of the parallel passage in Revelation 14–16. There the parousia harvest *precedes* the wrath harvest. The only way to deny this is to affirm that the harvest of the one like a Son of Man sitting on a white cloud is identical to the following grape harvest. But as I have argued above, this is exceedingly unlikely. On the other hand, it is also unlikely that John

---

107. See, e.g., Beale, *Revelation*, 395–96, 405–6. Cf. Charles, *Revelation*, 1:195, who notes that in 7:9–17 "there is an actual breach in the unity of time which has been so carefully observed in iv–vii.4–8, ... looking to the close of the great tribulation."

means to convey the identity of the 144,000 and the innumerable multitude, since he almost goes out of his way to describe them in opposing terms.[108] Thus (1) the 144,000 are explicitly numbered, while the great host is explicitly called innumerable. (2) The 144,000 are explicitly listed as coming from the various tribes of Israel, whereas the innumerable multitude comes from every nation, tribe, people, and tongue. (3) The 144,000 appear on earth, while the multitude appears in heaven. (4) The 144,000 are sealed as protection against the perilous time they are about to enter (Rev. 9:4), while the innumerable multitude have come out of the great tribulation. Similarly, in chapter 14 the 144,000 are firstfruits of the harvest (14:4), while the heavenly crowd are the fullness of the harvest (14:14–16). At the very least, if the 144,000 are understood to represent members of the church, they do not represent the whole church but some subset.

Richard Bauckham has argued that the striking contrasts between the two groups are rhetorical, their juxtaposition serving to jar the reader from Jewish militaristic categories to more universal and martyrological ones.[109] The innumerable multitude is thus identical to and used to reinterpret the 144,000. He bases his reading on the analogous reinterpretation of the Lion by the Lamb in Revelation 5:5–6, where John is told of the victory of the Lion of the tribe of Judah but sees a lamb standing as though slain. Here John hears the number of those sealed as 12,000 from each of twelve tribes of Israel but sees an innumerable multitude from every tribe, nation, people, and tongue. But Bauckham's position cannot be maintained for two reasons. First, it is clear in Revelation 5 that John intends the Lamb to represent the Lion, because the Lion is a mere title mentioned before the actual appearance of the Lamb. In chapter 7, however, there is an elaborate process of directing the actual sealing of a group of God's servants (vv. 1–3) followed by an accounting of those sealed (*tōn esphragismenōn*), the perfect participle implying that the sealing had taken place. It is only after this group has actually been sealed that John sees the innumerable multitude. Second, the relevant

---

108. See Aune, *Revelation 6–16*, 440–47. Cf. A. Feuillet, "Les 144.000 Israélites Marqués d'un sceau," *Nov Test* 9 (1967): 191–224; Heinrich Kraft, *Die Offenbarung des Johannes*, HNT 16a (Tübingen: J. C. B. Mohr, 1974), 126. What follows reproduces essentially verbatim parts of my "Messianic Exegesis," 302n109, and 315.

109. Bauckham, *Climax of Prophecy*, 215–29.

language is significantly different in chapter 7 than in chapter 5. In Revelation 5:5 an elder tells John that the Lion has overcome; then John says, "And I saw ... a Lamb" (*kai eidon ... arnion*) — that is, the scene begun in 5:1 regarding the search for one worthy to open the scroll is continued. In 7:9, however, the transition statement is "After this I looked, and behold" (ESV; *meta tauta eidon, kai idou*), indicating a new stage in the action (cf. 4:1; 7:1; 15:5; 18:1; 19:1).

Thus the idea that 7:9–17, the appearance of the innumerable multitude in heaven, is proleptic of the end cannot be maintained. It neither accounts for the two harvests of chapter 14 nor for the distinction of the innumerable multitude from the 144,000.

A second objection to understanding that Revelation 7:9–17 portrays the rapture of the church is that God's wrath has already been present in the first five seals. In support of this idea, some argue that because the Lamb opens the seals, the effects of opening the seals must be considered God's wrath.[110] But granted that God is in control not just of the opening of the seals but of all events in Revelation, by expressly noting the arrival of God's wrath in the sixth seal, John clearly intends to differentiate the effects of the sixth and seventh seals from the first five. It is only the latter that encompass God's wrath in the sense that John intends.[111] This is patent also from the qualitative difference between the "normal" catastrophes of the first five seals (corresponding to the nonsign "beginning of birth pains" in Matt. 24:3–13) and the supernatural catastrophes of the last two, which include the trumpets (corresponding to the parousia of Matt. 24:29–31). Furthermore, the cosmic disturbances of the sixth seal are signs of the day of the Lord, the great day when God comes to judge his enemies, as the allusions to Isaiah 2:12–22; 13:6–16; 34:1–15; Joel 2:1–11, 30–32; 3:9–17; Zephaniah 1:14–18; and Mala-

---

110. See, e.g., Showers, *Pre-wrath Rapture View*, 52–58.

111. Thus, while I agree with Showers, ibid., 68–72, that Rev. 6:7–8 probably alludes to Ezek. 5:17; 14:21, and that in Ezekiel these represent God's judgment, for the above stated reason I do not agree that this demonstrates that the wrath of God referred to in 6:17 began in seal 4. These are still part of the "normal" catastrophes of the first five seals and not the clearly distinct catastrophes of seals 6 and 7. Showers's attempt to show that the phenomena of seal 4 signify "Day-of-the-Lord wrath" fails because it relies on the assumption that the phenomena are unique to the eschatological day of the Lord, which is hardly the case (let alone the lack of evidence that they signified as much in Jewish apocalyptic tradition), and that the use of the Hebrew words *'ap* ("anger") and *ḥēmâ* ("fury") are also uniquely associated with the eschatological day of the Lord.

chi 3:2 make clear. Hence the next events in the narrative are the sealing of the 144,000 expressly to protect from them God's wrath (7:1–3; cf. 9:4), the rapture of the church, and the opening of the seventh seal.[112] The breaking of this seal has a fourfold effect: silence in heaven for half an hour, noted in Zechariah 2:13 and Zephaniah 1:7 as attending the coming of God in judgment,[113] the deliverance of seven trumpets to seven angels, the casting of fire to the earth (mixed with the prayers of the saints, apparently for vindication; Rev. 6:9–11),[114] and phenomena indicating a theophany (Rev. 8:1–5).[115] In other words, the opening of the seventh seal initiates the wrath of the day of the Lord, taking us to the very end, when God comes to earth to vindicate his own. The seven trumpets then recapitulate the seventh seal, focusing on the extended judgments that accompany the day of the Lord but ending with the same theophanic phenomena as the seventh seal (Rev. 11:19), indicating the arrival of the kingdom of God. Thus the wrath of God that John has in mind is clearly the wrath of the day of the Lord displayed in the seven trumpets (thus 11:18, "your wrath has come"). In the sixth seal, then, the ungodly are responding to the cosmic disturbances as portents of the arrival of the day of wrath, not of its earlier presence.

Thomas argues that the aorist "has come" (*ēlthen*) in the cry of the ungodly upon seeing the cosmic disturbances of the sixth seal ("the great day of [God's] wrath has come," Rev. 6:17) is to be understood as constative, summarizing the phenomena of the first six seals.[116] But this is clearly not the case. In the first place, that the aorist indicates the arrival of the day of the Lord is manifest from what has just been said. But, second, John uses the same construction in Revelation 14:7, when an angel announces before the two harvests that the hour of God's judgment "has come" (*ēlthen*). Here *ēlthen* can only mean "has arrived." Given the parallelism of Revelation 6:12–11:18 and 14:1–16:21, the verb is to be taken in the same sense in Revelation 6:17.[117]

---

112. What follows in this paragraph is taken largely verbatim from my "Messianic Exegesis," 299–300.

113. Cf. Zeph. 1:7; Zech. 2:13, the first of which deals with the coming of God to judge the apostate among them, the second with the coming of God to vindicate his people.

114. Probably an allusion to Ezek. 10:2.

115. See esp. Ex. 19:16–20. Cf. Beale, *Revelation*, 458–59.

116. Thomas, *Revelation 1–7*, 458, 460.

117. See also Rev. 14:15; 19:7.

In support of the contention that the tribulation from which the innumerable multitude have come is equivalent to the day of wrath, pretribulationists note that some Old Testament passages dealing with a future period of distress for Israel and that are associated with the day of the Lord use Hebrew words that can be translated "tribulation" (e.g., Deut. 4:30; Zeph. 1:14–15).[118] Against this view, we note first that whatever else may be said about a period of distress for Israel in the Old Testament, John is talking specifically about the Danielic tribulation, which is the final three-and-one-half-year period when the Antichrist "wars against the saints" (Dan. 7:21, 25; 12:1, 7; Rev. 13:7).[119] This is evident from the general Danielic background to Revelation and the use of the tribulation motif in Revelation 13. Once again, though it is true that both Daniel's and John's perspectives (indeed, by nature, the perspective of all Jewish apocalyptic literature) is that God is ultimately in control of history and its outcome, neither Daniel nor John indicate that the persecution of the saints by the Antichrist is an expression of the wrath of God.[120] Second, even if it can be shown that the Jews will experience God's wrath during at least part of the tribulation period, John is talking about the church avoiding the wrath of God, not the Jews. In fact, that seems to be the point of the sealing of the 144,000 in chapter 7. This group probably represents the remnant of Israel[121] sealed

---

118. See, e.g., Walvoord, *Rapture Question*, 42–44; Showers, *Pre-wrath Rapture View*, 33.

119. Cf. Moo, "Posttribulation Rapture," 172–73.

120. Moo (ibid., 173–74) asserts that the use of *za'am* ("indignation," "curse") in Dan. 11:36 attests to divine wrath in the tribulation (cf. 8:19). But *za'am* is not always an indicator of God's wrath in the Old Testament (Bertil Wiklander, "Māʿîz," *TDOT*, 4:106–8), and in Dan. 11:36 it surely refers to the indignation of the Antichrist against the covenant (so cf. 11:30). Cf. John J. Collins, *A Commentary on the Book of Daniel*, Hermeneia (Minneapolis: Fortress, 1993), 338–39.

121. Cf. Kraft, *Offenbarung*, 126; J. A. Draper, "The Heavenly Feast of Tabernacles: Rev. 7:1–17," *JSNT* 19 (1983): 136; Feuillet, "Les 144.000," 221. Though John can speak frequently of the church in terms that relate it to Israel (e.g., as a kingdom of priests, Rev. 1:6; 5:10), he also seems to keep Israel and the church somewhat distinct (e.g., the description of the New Jerusalem incorporating elements of both, Rev. 21:12–17; cf. 4:4). The indications that the 144,000 are the remnant of Israel include the allusion to the sealing of the remnant in Ezek. 9:4 and the fact that they are taken "from every tribe of the sons of Israel" (Rev. 7:4 ESV); they are a portion of the entire nation. In Rev. 14:1–5, the detail that "no lie was found in [the] mouths" of the 144,000 (v. 5) alludes to the prophecy in Zeph. 3 of the coming of God in anger to judge the nations and restore Israel (Zeph. 3:8; cf. Ps. 2:12). The result of God's judgment will be the gathering of the nations to "my holy mountain" (3:11 ESV). In the meantime, however, God promises to leave among the nations a humble people who "will take refuge in the name of YHWH" (Zeph 3:12; cf. Rev. 14:1, where the protective seal on the foreheads of the 144,000 is the divine name), namely, "the remnant of Israel, [who] will do no wrong; they will speak no lies, nor will deceit be found in their mouths" (Zeph. 3:13).

to go through the day of wrath on earth (Rev. 9:4), while the innumerable multitude is raptured to heaven for protection from God's wrath. Presumably the 144,000 either become Christ-followers simultaneously with the rapture or are marked to become Christ-followers prior to the rapture and become such afterward.[122] They then stand with Christ as the primary witnesses during the period of wrath.[123]

If this is the case, it may explain the statements by Jesus in Matthew 24:22 (Mark 13:20) that the days of the tribulation would be "cut short" (*ekolobōsen*) for the sake of the elect and in 24:29 (Mark 13:24) that the parousia would immediately follow the tribulation.[124] It is doubtful that, as Rosenthal argues,[125] Jesus means that the originally three-and-one-half-year tribulation will be shortened to something less. Rather, Jesus is speaking in relation to the church. Though Israel will fully experience the three-and-one-half-year tribulation as Daniel predicted (and the partly overlapping day of the Lord), the church will experience only the first part of that tribulation (and not the day of the Lord). After the church has undergone its tribulation, it will be "raptured."

This understanding also renders the debate over Revelation 3:10 moot. In Revelation 3:10, the church at Philadelphia is promised that "since you have kept my command to endure patiently, I will also keep you from the hour of trial that is going to come upon the whole world to test those who live on the earth." If we understand the hour of testing to be the tribulation, then, as posttribulationists argue, "protect [you] from" (*tēreō ek*) would mean something like "preserve you in the midst

---

122. In Rev. 11:13, at the "rapture" of the two witnesses, a great earthquake destroys a tenth of Jerusalem, killing seven thousand people and causing the conversion of the rest. The number seven thousand is probably used ironically here in contrast to the number of the remnant in 1 Kings 19:18. There, seven thousand were faithful; here, all but seven thousand turn to God. The interpretation of Rev. 11 is notoriously difficult, especially with regard to the timing of the events depicted. Note that Joel 2–3 and Zeph. 1 depict the day of the Lord as a time for judgment and salvation for Israel.

123. Thus they are also described in ways that imply they are the eschatological messianic army. See Bauckham, *Climax of Prophecy*, 217–23.

124. These are hard verses for anyone to deal with, because either Jesus means that God's original determination, communicated to Daniel, that the tribulation will be three and one-half years will be altered, or he means that God in eternity past had first considered making the tribulation longer than three and one-half years but finally decided to make it precisely that length. The first seems unlikely on the face of it as well as on the emphasis of a three-and-one-half-year period in Revelation (11:2, 3; 12:6, 14; 13:5). The second makes virtual nonsense of the term "cut short."

125. Rosenthal, *Pre-wrath Rapture*, 108–13.

of and bring you safely out of" (cf. Rev. 7:14).[126] On the other hand, if the hour of testing is the period of extraordinary divine wrath, then *tēreō ek* would mean, as pretribulationists argue, "keep [you] out [entirely]." Both meanings for the phrase are possible.[127] Because Revelation emphasizes the encounter with the Beast and the decision to worship him or the Lamb as the basis for judgment or reward (Rev. 12:9; 13:3, 8, 12, 14; 14:9–10; 15:2; 20:4), it seems best to understand "the hour of trial that is going to come upon the whole world to test those who live on the earth" to focus on that particular issue rather than on the wrath of God, which is less for testing than for judgment (or perhaps to prompt those on earth to make the right choice).[128] The nature of the protection is probably more spiritual than physical, since in Revelation victory over the Beast is not in avoiding martyrdom but in remaining faithful to Jesus to the point of death (12:11). Still, if as 7:14 suggests, the rapture is in view, physical protection may be involved as well. At any rate, the evidence of the actual visions in Revelation is clear: the church will experience persecution by the Antichrist and be raptured prior to an extended period of divine wrath, a period that ends with the return of Christ to earth.

Some Objections

Revelation 20

Moo makes the point that, since the first resurrection occurs in Revelation 20:4, the rapture must also occur there, since the rapture and the resurrection are simultaneous events.[129] The point is well taken,

---

126. Gundry, *Church and Tribulation*, 57–58. The *ek* ("out of") does not need to mean "all the way through and out the other side"; it could merely mean preserve you within until such time as I take you out. If the former is accepted, then John may have only in mind the "churchly" tribulation of Matt. 24:22. But nothing in Revelation would indicate this. Rather, John seems to think of the tribulation in its entirety and the protected church being taken out of the midst of it.

127. John 17:15, the only other use of *tēreō ek* in the New Testament, does not strike me as helping to decide the case. Merely because there Jesus contrasts protection from Satan with being taken out of the world does not mean that the phrase *tēreō ek* always means protection from something while remaining within its sphere of influence, let alone in the world. This is to import the context of a single passage into the basic semantics of the phrase. The phrase means simply "protect from." Cf. Feinberg, "Case for the Pretribulational Rapture," 63–72.

128. See Smalley, *Revelation*, 92. Nevertheless, it is not impossible that the hour of testing is the period of wrath. See, e.g., Osborne, *Revelation*, 193.

129. "Posttribulation Rapture," 200–201.

but it goes against a posttribulation rapture as well, since Revelation 20:4 makes the rapture not only posttribulational but postparousia, a virtual nonrapture. According to Paul, the rapture is the meeting of the coming Lord Jesus in the air by both living and dead Christians. Post-tribulationists understand this to mean that as Jesus is descending to earth at his second coming, the dead in Christ will be resurrected and together with the living will be caught up to meet Jesus and immediately accompany him back to earth. But this is manifestly what we do not have in Revelation 20:4. If Revelation 20:4 included the rapture, John would have Jesus descend to earth, defeat the Beast, bind Satan, and then rapture the saints. What sort of rapture could that possibly be? Or does Jesus return to heaven and come a second time between 19:21 and 20:4? Surely not! In this case, either John has no doctrine of the rapture, or the resurrection of 20:4 is not a resurrection of the church, or the resurrection of 20:4 is "misplaced" for thematic reasons. The latter two options are patently better than the first for theological and exegetical reasons. Theologically, they avoid a contradiction between Paul and John. Exegetically, they conform to the other evidence in Revelation that the rapture occurs before the outpouring of God's wrath and that the parousia is a complex of events. Thus the return of Christ to earth in Revelation 19:11–21 with no rapturelike event is due to the fact that the rapture already occurred with the initial harvest in Revelation 14:14–16. The parousia is not concluded until Christ returns at the end of the second, judgment harvest, made clear by the allusions to Isaiah 63:3 and Joel 3:13 in Revelation 14:19–20; 19:15.

The fact that Jesus is accompanied in his descent by the armies of heaven gives additional credence to this interpretation.[130] In Revelation 17:14, those who accompany the Lamb, the Lord of Lords and King of Kings, in his defeat of the Beast and the kings of the earth "are the called, chosen and faithful"—almost certainly human believers. In Revelation 19:14 the armies of heaven who accompany the descending Christ, the King of Kings and Lord of Lords, are "dressed in fine linen, white and clean." This phrase was used just six verses earlier to refer to the garments of the bride of the Lamb and interpreted as "the righteous

---

130. See, e.g., Mounce, *Revelation*, 354–55; Beale, *Revelation*, 960. Cf. Hultberg, "Messianic Exegesis," 341–44.

acts of the saints." There can be little doubt that the armies of heaven are or include the church, and this suggests that the church had been raptured earlier, in line with 7:9–17 and 14:14–16.

It is granted that there is no mention of resurrection in Revelation 7:9–17 or 14:14–16 and 15:2–4. But even though a resurrection is reported in 20:4, it seems to me likelier given the preceding that either it is reported at this point because of the association with the reign of Christ (that is, that John reserves mention of the resurrection until its main significance for him, coregency, is in view) or because this is the resurrection of tribulation saints (Dan. 12:1). The latter is possible on the supposition that the 144,000 are the remnant of Israel during the last period of the tribulation.

1 Corinthians 15:52

Finally, some argue against a prewrath rapture by reading the seventh trumpet of Revelation 11:15–19 in light of 1 Corinthians 15:52. If Paul says that the rapture occurs at the "last" trumpet, and the last trumpet in Revelation occurs at the end of God's wrath, then the rapture is not prewrath.[131] Most scholars, however, see no relationship between the schematic trumpet series in Revelation and Paul's mention of the last trumpet, not least because all evidence points to Revelation having been written after the lifetime of Paul. Rather, Paul is probably referring to the frequent mention of a trumpet call announcing the day of the Lord and the gathering of Israel (Isa. 27:13; Joel 2:1; Zeph. 1:16; Zech. 9:14; cf. *ApocAb* 31:1–2; Pss. Sol. 11:1–3; Matt. 24:31; 1 Thess. 4:16).[132] It is the "last" trumpet not because Paul is thinking of a series of trumpets but because it is the trumpet that signals the final day. The image in Revelation that corresponds to this is not the seventh trumpet in Revelation 11:15–19 but the cosmic disturbances of the sixth seal and subsequent interlude before the wrath in Revelation 6:12–7:17. So, once again, John portrays both the rapture of the church in heaven, like Paul, and the sealing of the remnant of Israel on earth in anticipation

---

131. See, e.g., Gundry, *Church and Tribulation*, 148–51.

132. So most commentators. See, e.g., C. K. Barrett, *A Commentary on the First Epistle to the Corinthians*, HNTC (Peabody, Mass.: Hendrickson, 1987), 381; Gordon D. Fee, *The First Epistle to the Corinthians*, NICNT (Grand Rapids: Eerdmans, 1987), 801–2. Cf. Moo, "Posttribulation Rapture," 179.

of Israel's regathering, like the Old Testament, in association with the arrival of the day of the Lord.[133]

Conclusion

In the foregoing, I have attempted to show the following:

1. That the warnings presented in at least Matthew's version of the Olivet Discourse about the Danielic abomination of desolation and the tribulation that follows were directed to Jesus' disciples as representatives of the church, since that is how Matthew regularly views the disciples and how he regularly aims his teaching material in his gospel.

2. That Paul associates the rapture with the outpouring of Christ's wrath on the nations at the parousia, a complex of events he refers to as the day of the Lord, and that those events will be preceded by the Danielic abomination of desolation. Paul is dependent on the tradition behind the Olivet Discourse for this. Though Paul is not explicit, it is best to read him as positing the rapture as the thing that spares the church from experiencing the parousia wrath.

3. That John in Revelation also anticipates the church experiencing the Danielic tribulation, and that he makes explicit what Paul implies: the church will be raptured immediately prior to the outpouring of God's wrath in the day of the Lord, some time before the end of the tribulation period, and will return with Christ to earth at the end of that extended period of wrath. The parousia, then, is a complex of events that begins with the rapture after the middle of Daniel's seventieth "week," proceeds through a period of wrath on the nations, and concludes with the return of Christ to establish his kingdom.

---

133. This also allows mortals to enter the millennium and thus fulfill such passages as Isa. 65:17–25. I have not argued against posttribulationism on the basis of its not allowing mortals to enter the millennium, because I am not convinced that unbelievers cannot be present in the millennium. Both the sheep and goats parable (Matt. 25:31–46) and Zech. 14:16–19 can allow for it, while Rev. 19:21 does not necessarily disallow it (cf., e.g., Gundry, *Church and Tribulation*, 166–67). If mortal *saints* must be present in the millennium, then posttribulationists have a real problem. That the millennium fulfills kingdom promises to Israel would seem to argue that, in fact, some mortal Israelites must be in the millennium. Isaiah 65 and other Jewish kingdom promises appear to take this for granted.

Neither pretribulationism nor posttribulationism can account for this complex of events and its timing. The only position that can is the prewrath rapture position.

Though I believe the three propositions above represent by far the best way to interpret the evidence I have presented in this essay, I also acknowledge that the evidence is not finally conclusive. If it were, the colleagues with whom I interact in this book, who are both keen exegetes and proven scholars, would not differ with me. Nevertheless, I am fairly certain that Dr. Moo will find my evidence that the church will enter the tribulation compelling and that Dr. Blaising will find my evidence that the church will be raptured before the return of Christ to earth compelling, and I find in that some confirmation that perhaps the prewrath position integrates the evidence best.

A PRETRIBULATION RESPONSE

CRAIG BLAISING

Let me begin by expressing my appreciation to Alan Hultberg for doing double duty in this volume. Not only has he presented an argument for the prewrath position, but he has served as editor as well. He has been fair and gracious in both tasks, and it is a delight to interact with him in this work.

The argument that Hultberg presents for the prewrath rapture is clearly stated, resting, as he says, on "two major theses," which, he argues, rule out both pre- and posttribulational views. His essay is structured as an exposition of these two theses with a conclusion at the end. My response will follow the order that he has set forth.

Hultberg spends the majority of his essay developing his first thesis, which posits that the church will enter the second half of the tribulation. The argument here is aimed first of all against pretribulationism, the point being that if biblical descriptions portray the church as being *present in* the tribulation, then it could not have been raptured *prior to* the tribulation. On this basis, the argument then suggests a location for the rapture. Since the church enters the second half of the tribulation, the rapture presumably must take place sometime after the midpoint of the tribulation period.

However, the presence of the church in the tribulation does not logically preclude a pretribulational rapture. Pretribulationists have always acknowledged that biblical descriptions of the tribulation show believing Jews and Gentiles to be present. This is consistent with the counter-theme of repentance and grace found in day of the Lord passages along with the major theme of wrath and judgment. It is certainly true that a majority of pretribulationists, being also classical or revised dispensationalists, have argued that these tribulational Jewish and Gentile believers do not belong to the church. Progressive dispensationalists, on the other hand, do not make this claim, and the argument I have presented for pretribulationalism is not dependent on it. A pretribulational rapture rests upon its logical relationship to the onset of the day of the Lord, understood synthetically in relation to Daniel's time of the end. Consequently, I find the ecclesial status of these tribulational believers to be irrelevant to the timing of the rapture.

The fact that Hultberg thinks it is a relevant factor — one that precludes a rapture preceding the presence of such a group — raises a problem for his own view. For he himself identifies the 144,000 in Revelation 7 and 14 as a group of Jewish believers who will be present on earth between the supposed prewrath rapture and the end of the tribulation. If he is truly a progressive dispensationalist, as he claims, then he would acknowledge that these believers also are part of the body of Christ, the church. But if the church is present on earth right before the end of the tribulation, how could there have been a prewrath rapture before this? However, if the presence of the church at the end of the tribulation does not preclude the possibility of a prewrath rapture, neither would the presence of the church in the first half of the tribulation preclude the possibility of a pretribulational rapture. The timing of the rapture will have to be decided on other grounds.

In the process of developing his first thesis, Hultberg makes a number of points that need to be addressed. As much as possible, I will attempt to follow the order in which they are presented.

Matthew 24

I believe Hultberg is correct when he says that the pattern of events outlined in the Olivet Discourse, except for the coming of the Son of Man, received a proleptic fulfillment in the first century AD. However, if this is the case, the abomination of desolation cannot of itself be the "primary sign of the end." The fact that it is capable of proleptic fulfillment certainly prevents it from being a "primary" indicator of the descent of Christ. In the Olivet Discourse, only the appearing of the Son of Man in the sky is designated by the term "sign" in answer to the disciples' question, "What will be the sign of your coming and of the end of the age?" (Matt. 24:3).

I was somewhat surprised by Hultberg's claim that "for Matthew the church is viewed as in some sense the inheritor of the Jewish kingdom." Once again, this is inconsistent with Hultberg's self-identification as a "progressive dispensationalist." Progressive dispensationalists typically see the church as a phase of kingdom fulfillment—an intermediate phase of the kingdom—but would not see the church as the fulfillment of or replacement of Israel. Hultberg offers three lines of evidence for his supersessionist reading of Matthew. First is Matthew's portrayal of Jesus in the type and pattern of Israel. Rather than indicating Israel's replacement, I would argue that such description serves to underscore both his messiahship (as Messiah of Israel) and the surety of the hopes of Israel. Hultberg notes that Jesus is presented in Matthew as the Servant of God. But the Servant was expected to bring Israel back to God as well as extend salvation to the Gentiles. This is consistent with the Old Testament understanding of the eschatological kingdom as inclusive of both Israel and gentile nations.

Second, Hultberg argues that Jesus' use of the word *ekklēsia* for the future messianic community indicates that Jesus is founding "the 'true' or 'new' Israel." However, there is nothing in either Matthew 16 or 18 that indicates that national Israel is being displaced by another entity. Again, one needs to remember that the theme of Jesus' teaching is the kingdom of God. Israel is central to that kingdom, but the kingdom extends its dominion over Gentile nations as well. This does not mean that Gentiles become Israel or that Israel disappears. The kingdom functions as a multinational empire with subordinate states, Israel being in the primary position. The congregation of the kingdom to be set up in the interim between the ascension and the parousia would certainly include both Jews and Gentiles. When it is revealed that Gentiles will be included with equal participation in the Holy Spirit, this is not seen to be inconsistent with the prophetic pattern of a multinational kingdom. There is simply nothing here about a replacement of Israel by what is not Israel.

Third and finally, Hultberg draws his primary evidence from two texts that have been classic for supersessionists: Matthew 27:25 ("Let his blood be on us and on our children!") and Matthew 21:43 ("The kingdom of God will be taken away from you and given to a people who will produce its fruit"). Turner's recent comments on these texts are helpful. Clearly, the "you" in 21:43 refers to the religious leaders rather than to Israel per se, and the use of the word "nation" here is consistent with prophetic expectation of a future righteousness for Israel.[134] Rather

---

134. David L. Turner, *Matthew*, BECNT (Grand Rapids: Baker, 2008), 517–19.

than seeing Matthew 27:25 as "complicity of the entire nation," which forms the basis for "the rejection . . . of Israel as a whole," one should note the interchange of "all the people" with "crowd" in the context (27:15, 20), a crowd whipped up by "the chief priests and elders" (27:20).[135] While judgment falls upon a nation misled by rebellious leaders, as had happened before in Israel's history, the promise of national blessing remains and becomes the focus of hopes of restoration, as had also happened before in Israel's history. Contrary to Hultberg and supersessionists generally, Matthew actually underscores the hope of the future restoration in the parable of the tenant farmers, and also in the promise of regathering taught by Jesus in the Olivet Discourse (Matthew 24:31) just a few days before the whipped-up cries of the crowd.

2 Thessalonians 2

In order to formulate his argument from 2 Thessalonians 2, Hultberg has to relate that text to 1 Thessalonians 4–5 and to the Olivet Discourse, primarily Matthew 24–25. It seems to me that the primary theme interrelating these texts is the day of the Lord, as that theme has itself been combined with Daniel's time of the end. Key to the issue of timing is Paul's reiteration of a tradition in 1 Thessalonians 5 going back to the Olivet Discourse as seen in Matthew 24:36–44., that the day of the Lord will come *unexpectedly*. Hultberg, however, does not focus his exposition on this point. Rather, he assumes that the unexpected nature of the day of the Lord's onset has to do with the "uncertainty of [its] timing" within an *expected* sequence of prophetic events. This, of course, serves the position he is presenting in his essay, but it creates numerous exegetical problems within this complex of texts.

The Rapture at Matthew 24:31?

Hultberg argues, like Moo, that the rapture should be located at the end of the narrative structure of the Olivet Discourse. The rationale that he gives is the similarity between the descriptions of the rapture descent in 1 Thessalonians 4 and the appearing of the Son of Man in Matthew 24. That the descriptions have similarities is not debated. Both texts speak of a theophany. Consequently, both share features descriptive

---

135. Ibid., 655–56.

of theophanies elsewhere in Scripture—the accompaniment of angels, cloud(s), glory, the divine trumpet. However, to conclude on this basis that the two are simultaneous within the chronology of the tribulation begs the question. Placement with respect to other tribulation events depends on other factors—such as the explicit mention of a rapture. Actually, Hultberg does not believe that the rapture and the final descent are simultaneous. Rather, he sees the appearing in Matthew 24:30–31 as an extended parousia with the rapture as an initial subevent separated by some interval of time from the final descent. In actual fact, both Hultberg and I agree that the parousia in these texts is an extended event so that the rapture and the final descent are not simultaneous, but are subevents of the parousia, separated by an interval of time. The difference between us is that Hultberg wants to interpret Matthew 24:30–31 alone as this extended parousia. I, however, would see the parousia in the Olivet Discourse as extending from the beginning of birth pains to the appearing of the Son of Man.[136] This whole "labor process" is his coming, as I have argued in my essay, drawing particularly on the way the second part of the Olivet Discourse (24:36–25:46) relates the term *parousia* to the first part. If, as I have argued, the entire Olivet Discourse "labor narrative" is the parousia, then one has to consider the entire narrative, not just 24:30–31, when determining the location of the rapture.

Hultberg acknowledges that Matthew 24:30–31 does not mention the rapture. Neither is it mentioned in 24:4–5, the beginning of the labor narrative. To relate the rapture to the Olivet Discourse, one needs to look, as Hultberg does, for intertextual connections between the Thessalonian correspondence and the Olivet Discourse. However, Hultberg's approach is too limited and inconclusive, relying as he does only on appearance descriptions. Where one needs to look, as I have argued, is at the temporal relationship of the rapture in 1 Thessalonians 4 to the day of the Lord in 1 Thessalonians 5 and then at the intertextual descriptions linking the day of the Lord in 1 Thessalonians 5 to the parousia treated holistically in the second part of the Olivet Discourse. Hultberg, however, entirely ignores the intertextual links between 1 Thessalonians 5 and the Olivet Discourse.

---

136. This does not preclude the pattern from earlier occurrence as a type that would prefigure the actual coming at a later time, as I have argued.

Before going on to Hultberg's argument from 2 Thessalonians 2, I simply note that he has also repeated a standard posttribulational argument in his claim that the gathering spoken of in Matthew 24:31 is the rapture. Certainly, the rapture in 1 Thessalonians 4:16–17 is a "gathering" of sorts, and as I have argued, 2 Thessalonians 2:1 most likely has the rapture in view when it speaks of "our gathering to him." However, the "gathering" spoken of in Matthew 24:31 is the eschatological regathering of Israel repeated throughout the prophets and presented here in the language of Zechariah 2:10 [LXX] and Deuteronomy 30. That gathering is never presented in prophecy as a rapture (a catching up of resurrected and living ones to meet the Lord in the air). Nor does it ever include Gentile believers as the rapture of 1 Thessalonians 4 would. It is specifically about the fulfillment of the promise to Israel, and it is fitting that the Lord mentions it in this discourse about Jerusalem. It is also consistent with Daniel's prophecy that the seventy weeks have to do with the city and the people (Dan. 9:24). Hultberg himself distinguishes a gathering of believing Israel from the rapture of the church in his interpretation of Revelation. The distinction needs to be observed in the language and contextual concerns of Matthew 24 rather than forcing a harmonization with 2 Thessalonians 2:1.

The Rapture Preceded by the Abomination of Desolation?

As Hultberg proceeds to focus on his primary concern with 2 Thessalonians 2, he makes a number of connections that are not entirely objectionable. The rapture is related to the theme of the day of the Lord in 1 Thessalonians 4–5 and in 2 Thessalonians 2. I have argued that the rapture is positioned by Paul at the onset of the day of the Lord in 1 Thessalonians 5. Paul does not say, as Hultberg claims, "that the day of the Lord will overtake believers," but rather that it "will not overtake" them "as a thief." However, it is not necessary to dwell on this point. I simply note that Hultberg coordinates the rapture with the beginning of the day of the Lord.

2 Thessalonians 2

Having related the rapture (1 Thess. 4) to the onset of the day of the Lord (1 Thess. 5), Hultberg turns to 2 Thessalonians 2 to argue that the day of the Lord (and by association, the rapture with it) occurs after the midpoint of the seventieth week of Daniel, that is, after the abomination of desolation. The weakness of his argument here is his assumption regarding the missing protasis in 2 Thessalonians 2:3f. In note 27 he asserts that "all sides agree that the unexpressed protasis of 2 Thess. 2:3 ... is 'the day of the Lord will not come.'" This logically places the day of the Lord as occurring after at least two eschatological events iterated in 2 Thessalonians 2:3: the apostasy and the revelation of the Man of Lawlessness. Hultberg then forces the day of the Lord and the rapture further into Daniel's seventieth week by equating the *revelation* of the Man of Lawlessness with his *session*. Since the session of the Man of Lawlessness is the abomination of desolation, he arrives at a postmidpoint location for the rapture. However, it is not true that all sides agree on Hultberg's interpretation, as can be seen in my essay and in Hultberg's citation of Robert Thomas.[137] Thomas's argument from Matthew 12:29 and Mark 3:27 is too quickly dismissed by Hultberg. These texts offer a syntactical parallel with both apodosis and protasis present: "No one can enter a strong man's house and carry off his possessions unless he first ties up the strong man." Thomas argues that the construction *ean mē prōton*, used in these passages, denotes an apodosis that is logically included in rather than wholly preceding its protasis. To dismiss this argument, Hultberg would have to assume that the binding of the strong man entirely precedes entering the house. The syntax of *ean mē prōton* does not require the strong man to be outside of his house when he is bound. It is entirely conceivable that the strong man is inside the house and the binding takes place as a first act upon entry. In this case, the *ean mē prōton* clause iterates an element coordinate with the action even as it is necessary for the successful completion of the action. Applying that to 2 Thessalonians 2:3 indicates at least the possibility that Paul is iterating elements that belong to the day of the Lord rather than elements that precede it. And this possibility becomes the more probable interpretation when one considers (1) the integration of the day of the Lord pattern with Daniel's time of the end in the Olivet Discourse and (2) the signless onset of the day of the Lord

---

137. Robert L. Thomas, "2 Thessalonians," in EBC, ed. Frank E. Gaebelein, 12 vols. (Grand Rapids: Zondervan, 1978), 11:323.

in 1 Thessalonians 5. Daniel 9:27 indicates that the seventieth week begins with the Antichrist present and making a covenant. In the Olivet Discourse, Jesus began the tribulational pattern with the appearance of false christs (Matt. 24:4–5), a key feature of the onset of "labor pains." It is highly likely that Paul is identifying this early element of the time of the end / day of the Lord pattern when he mentions the revelation of the Man of Lawlessness. And it is most likely that the apostasy is connected to it, perhaps referencing the covenant that "the many" make with the Antichrist at the beginning of the tribulation period.

Hultberg, however, wishes to identify the revelation of the Man of Lawlessness and the apostasy with the abomination of desolation—the Man of Lawlessness's self-deification in the temple, or, as he puts it, the revelation of the Man of Lawlessness is his session. First, Hultberg is correct in identifying the session of the Man of Lawlessness (2 Thess. 2:4) with the abomination of desolation (Matt. 24:15). He is also correct when he links the revelation in 2:3 to the coming of the Lawless One with false signs described in 2:9. However, when relating this to the Olivet Discourse, he misses the fact that the false christs with deceptive signs appear at the beginning of the sequence (Matt. 24:4–5). The reference to deceptive false christs at the middle of the sequence, in association with the abomination of desolation, is a unifying feature of this integrated pattern. Consequently, it is not true that Paul's descriptive language relates only to the middle or second half of the tribulation described by Jesus.

Hultberg tries to force an identity between the revelation and the session in the syntax of 2 Thessalonians 2:3–12. He argues that since Paul's description of the session follows the mention of the revelation in 2:3–4, they should be presumed to be identical. However, compare this to 2:8. There Paul mentions the Antichrist's revelation and then follows it up with the event of his destruction by the Lord at the end of the tribulation. Should we then presume that the revelation of the Man of Lawlessness only takes place at the time of the Lord's descent? Hultberg also misses the logical force of *hōste* in 2:4 that relates the character and activity pattern of the Man of Lawlessness in the first half of the verse to the session in the temple in the second half. Logically, the former leads to, accounts for, or results in the latter. This may very well be a temporal as much as it is a logical sequence, indicating a period of character revealing activity that leads to the session in the temple. Hultberg's insistence that since Paul does not elaborate more fully on the revelation that therefore it should be presumed to be identical to the session cannot be taken seriously. Clearly, Paul does not intend to elaborate on all the details of this tribulation sequence since he refers his readers to their remembrance of his oral teaching (2:5–6). In actual fact, Paul's brief survey of tribulation events fits very well the basic three-part outline that we have from Daniel and that is reiterated by the Lord in the Olivet Discourse: a revelation of the Man of Lawlessness at the beginning of the tribulational pattern, the abomination of his session in the temple beginning at the midpoint, and his destruction by the Lord when the Lord appears at the end of the tribulation. It is simply not true that Paul speaks only of "signs" in the second half of the seventieth week.

Hultberg concludes his discussion of 2 Thessalonians 2 by insisting that his reading of the passage—a day of the Lord preceded by the sign of the abomination of desolation—is not in conflict with Paul's description of its signless coming in 1 Thessalonians 5. He postulates that because the second half of the tribulation is shortened (according to his reading) and the exact occurrence of the rapture unknown during that period, the imminency language of 1 Thessalonians 5 is thereby accounted for. But what about Paul's description in 1 Thessalonians 5 of the conditions that precede the day of the Lord? Paul describes this pre-day of the Lord, pre-rapture period as one of "peace and security." From everything we know about the second half of the tribulation, it certainly is not one of "peace and security." Hultberg confuses the conditions of nearness, such as we have in Matthew 24:32–35, with the conditions of imminency, such as we have in Matthew 24:36ff. Careful attention to the structure of the Olivet Discourse, as I have tried to show, avoids this confusion. And it clarifies Paul's reference in 1 Thessalonians 5 to the beginning of the day of the Lord as the beginning of the entire tribulation pattern presented by Jesus. No one knows when the day of the Lord will commence. Its beginning is truly imminent. Once it begins, a pattern unfolds that indicates the nearness of the Lord's appearing. Imminence and nearness in this sense are not the same thing.

Revelation

In concluding support for his first major thesis, Hultberg calls upon the book of Revelation for evidence that the church is in the tribulation. In actuality, he attempts more than that, arguing that Revelation shows the church to be present in the tribulation up to the point of the beginning of a time of divine wrath that he takes to be the day of the Lord, positioned in Revelation's sequence of judgments at the point of the sixth seal. Accordingly, he argues that a rapture takes place between the sixth and seventh seals, testified to by the vision of the innumerable multitude in heaven in Revelation 7 and the harvest of the Son of Man in Revelation 14.

The primary difficulty for Hultberg is that the distinctive features of the rapture are simply not present in Revelation 7 or 14. There is no mention of a resurrection, no mention of a transformation of living believers from mortality to immortality, no word of any "catching up" of resurrected and transformed saints to meet the Lord in the air. After envisioning 144,000 sealed from Israel, Revelation 7:9–17 portrays a great multitude of the saved from every nation. They come out of the great tribulation and are before the throne. But are we sure that the scene is heaven? One might think so on the basis of the location of the throne in Revelation 5 and 6. But Revelation 7:15–17 offers a description that sounds very much like conditions found in 21:1ff. when the throne is on the new earth. Could Revelation 7:9–17 be a prolepsis of new-earth conditions? Throughout the book of Revelation comparisons are drawn between tribulation suffering and millennial or new-earth blessing. It is quite possible that John is doing that here. Note also that a similar description is given of the 144,000 in Revelation 14:1–5. In that passage they are pictured as before the throne (14:3). But Hultberg thinks that in that passage they are neither in heaven nor on the new earth. In spite of their location before the throne, he believes that they are on the old earth in the midst of tribulation about to enter the day of the Lord. Why then does Hultberg think that the innumerable multitude in Revelation 7 is in heaven, and that as a result of a rapture? Presumably, it is because in Revelation 14, after the mention of the 144,000, there is a harvest by "one like a son of man." But nothing is said in that passage about what the harvest is or what is done with it, which is undoubtedly why many interpreters prefer to conflate it with the more specific grape harvest—a judgment scene—in Revelation 14:17–20. Nothing is said about the harvest being an innumerable company of the saved, such that we should connect the event to Revelation 7:9–17, nor is anything said about such a group being taken to heaven by way of resurrection or translation. Furthermore, although Hultberg has a point about the Son of Man imagery as normally indicating Christ, this particular "one like a son of man" in Revelation 14 receives instructions from "another angel." Christ does not receive instructions from angels; rather, he is worshiped by them.

Much more could be said, but the point is that Hultberg's claim that "Revelation 6–8 and 14–16 present the rapture" is simply a matter of what might be called "possibility exegesis." It can hardly be said to have been established as the probable reading of the text.

I will comment on Hultberg's second thesis more briefly since this is the shorter portion of his essay. His thesis here is that "the way the church avoids God's wrath at the end of the age is by the rapture." He defends this claim by appealing first to Paul and then to the book of Revelation.

Paul

The reader should not be surprised that I agree with most everything Hultberg says in the two-paragraph argument based on 1–2 Thessalonians, which he presents in this part of his essay. The crucial difference between us is the definition and extent of the wrath from which the church is delivered. However, in this two-paragraph summary, he has stated the case well for a complex parousia coextensive with the day of the Lord involving a rapture at its outset and concluding with the descent culminating the judgment. He notes well the significance of 1 Thessalonians 1:10 for the pre–day of the Lord, preparousia rapture and rightly notes that the (rapture) "meeting" may well be extended contrary to the typical posttribulational view. He correctly notes that the parousia / day of the Lord arrives differently for believers and unbelievers, linking the salvation experienced by believers to the rapture. This, in my opinion, is the central Pauline teaching one must grasp in order to understand the rapture and its place in New Testament eschatology.

Hultberg's weakness, it seems to me, comes when he moves out from 1 Thessalonians to the larger biblical context. First, in spite of its importance to his position and its prominence in the Thessalonian correspondence, he fails to explore the literary richness and complexity of the day of the Lord as a biblical theological theme. He treats it in summary fashion as a relatively brief display of divine wrath, missing its more extended nature in biblical theology. Second, as I have already pointed out, while he acknowledges literary links between the Olivet Discourse and 1 Thessalonians 4–5, he focuses primarily on a comparison of appearance descriptions in 1 Thessalonians 4:16–17 and Matthew 24:30 (and not giving sufficient notice, in my opinion, to the differences in these descriptions). He does not note the more important link between 1 Thessalonians 5:1–5 and the second half of the Olivet Discourse, beginning in Matthew 24:36. This is the most important link for determining the timing of the rapture, for timing is precisely the issue in both of these texts. The literary link to the second half of the Olivet Discourse has necessary implications for how the rapture is related to the tribulation sequence sketched by Jesus in Matthew 24:4–35 (and parallels). If the second half of the Olivet Discourse is speaking of the whole first-half sequence as the coming of the day of the Lord, then of course the rapture precedes the sequence. Further confirmation that the entire first-half sequence constitutes the day of the Lord comes from a literary study of day of the Lord features. My contention is that the tribulation sequence presented by Jesus synthesizes the day of the Lord typology with Daniel's time of the end. This in turn has implications for the apostolic tradition following Jesus, including 2 Thessalonians 2 and the book of Revelation.

Back to Revelation

I have already argued that Hultberg has failed to establish the existence of a rapture in Revelation 7 and 14. What about his restriction of the day of the Lord, and with it, the manifestation of divine wrath, to a period within the tribulation envisioned by John? Hultberg relies heavily on an interpretation of Revelation 6:17 in which the day of wrath is seen as arriving with the sixth seal judgment, not before. He argues that *ēlthen* in 6:17 can only mean "has arrived" because of the citation of the day of the Lord imagery in the overall description of the sixth seal in 6:12–17 and because of the parallel use of *ēlthen* in 14:7. However, he misses the predication of *ēlthen* to divine wrath in 11:18 where it cannot mean that God's wrath has only just arrived. Revelation 11:15–18 is speaking of the seventh trumpet, which Hultberg acknowledges is at the end of a serial outpouring of divine wrath. The verb here has to be taken as a constative aorist, meaning not "has [just] arrived" but simply "arrived." By comparison, it raises the possibility that the verb in 6:17

should be understood similarly. In both cases, John is making a cumulative assessment of the entire series of divine judgments. This becomes the more probable interpretation when one notes that the judgments of the earlier seals are phenomena belonging to the day of the Lord. Furthermore, the use of *erchomai* through the series is typical of the day of the Lord literary type and naturally connects to *ēlthen* in 6:17 such that the latter has a summary force at the end of this construct. Both of these points are developed in more detail in my essay.

The foremost problem with the prewrath rapture view, as it seems to me, is its reductionist view of the day of the Lord. And associated with this is a relatively simplistic view of divine wrath. I have addressed both of these issues in my essay and in my response to Moo. Due to the limitation of space in this response, let me direct the reader to those comments. By way of summary, I can only say that what Hultberg misses, which is also what Moo misses, is the development of the day of the Lord theme in Old Testament theology into a twofold complex event similar to the structure of Daniel's time of the end pattern, the pattern we refer to as the tribulation. But in the teaching of Jesus, Paul, and John, the day of the Lord theme is integrated with the whole of the Danielic tribulational pattern. Consequently, it is a mistake to try to isolate a portion of the tribulational pattern as the day of the Lord. The whole of the future tribulation is the day of the Lord. Furthermore, the whole of the tribulation in Daniel is the time of wrath. The term "wrath" is used to refer to the whole of the day of the Lord / tribulation complex, as well as to individual judgments within that complex. With respect to the whole, it is similar to the way wrath is presently manifested in the giving up of people to the depravation of their minds and passions (Romans 1:18–32). This "giving up" creates conditions of suffering for the saints. That doesn't mean that the suffering and persecution experienced by the saints are God's wrath upon them, but the suffering and persecution take place nevertheless in a time of and under the conditions of wrath. In the wrath to come, there will be persecution and suffering for those who turn to Christ along with numerous general and specific manifestations of that wrath. The promise to the church on this side of the day of the Lord / tribulation era is that it will be delivered. And that deliverance occurs not somewhere deep into that day, but at its very beginning.

DOUGLAS MOO

The time between the publication of the first edition of this book and the second has witnessed the appearance of a new option in relating the rapture to the final tribulation: the "prewrath" position. This option has been argued in several semipopular books, and it is now probably more widespread than the traditional "midtribulational" view—hence its inclusion in this volume. Alan Hultberg's defense of the "prewrath" position, because of its careful exegetical work and interaction with a wide range of literature, makes a very important contribution to the development of this option. Indeed, I find myself hard-pressed to argue convincingly against his presentation—especially since he bases so much of his argument on the book of the Revelation, which he knows a lot more about than I do! Nevertheless (you all knew this adversative was coming), I will do my best to suggest some problems with his interpretation and why, finally, I still think the traditional posttribulational position is a preferable option.

Hultberg makes his case by arguing two basic points: that the church will enter into Daniel's seventieth week and that the church will be raptured before the coming of God's wrath at the end of Daniel's seventieth week. The first argument is directed against pretribulationism, the second against posttribulationism. As one might guess, then, I find myself basically in agreement with the points that Hultberg makes in the first part of his essay—indeed, I make many of the same points myself. Hultberg does make several points in the course of this argument with which I disagree. But it will be more convenient to deal with them in the context of my response to his second main argument. However, before turning to that argument, I want to make a preliminary point about Hultberg's general approach to these issues.

I take issue here again (as I did in my response to Blaising) with the assumption that the seventieth week of Daniel refers to a seven-year period at the end of history. This view is widespread among North American evangelicals and basic to eschatological interpretation within certain forms of this evangelical tradition. I can therefore understand why both Blaising and Hultberg would basically assume this interpretation in their essays. But I must remind us again that this text is very difficult and that many good interpreters (including, of course, evangelical interpreters) take issue with this "end-of-history" interpretation. As I indicate in my main essay, I myself think that it is unlikely that Daniel's seventieth week refers to the end of history only. I raise the issue here for two reasons.

First, the assumption that Daniel's seventieth week refers only to the end of history can lead to the assumption that any language in the New Testament that alludes to that prophecy, or related Danielic prophecies, must refer to the end of history. Our interpretation of certain New Testament texts can then be influenced too strongly by an assumption about the meaning of a very uncertain passage. Second, I raise a "perspectival" matter closely related to this first point. Understanding Daniel's seventieth week to refer only to the end of history seems to me to be part of a broader perspective that tends to confine "eschatological" prophecies in the Old Testament and "eschatological" language in the New Testament to the future. As I argue in my main essay, this tendency inappropriately restricts the scope of New Testament eschatology, which describes the entire period of time from Christ's first coming to his second. Hultberg at times seems to fall prey to the typical "narrow" view of eschatology by contrasting "historical" and "eschatological" in the book of Revelation. In fact, I would want to argue, "historical" events (that is, events from the time period of John's Revelation) may be "eschatological" as well. Hultberg rightly argues that Revelation mixes near history and far history in a way that we cannot easily untangle. As I have argued in my essay, the fact that John cannot know the timing of the events he predicts means, necessarily, that his perspective is both "historical" and "eschatological" *at the same time*. It is not as if he thought the events of one particular vision would be fulfilled in his lifetime while he thought the events depicted in another vision would find fulfillment in "far future." To make this kind of distinction, John would have had to know more than Jesus knows: the time when the Son would return in glory to bring in the final form of the kingdom. The relevance of this perspective to the issue we are discussing is this: the "tribulation," or time of suffering, that John makes reference to throughout the Revelation cannot be identified as a "future" period of suffering separate from the tribulation Christians in his own day were experiencing.

The Parousia as a Complex of Events

The prewrath view that Hultberg argues differs from posttribulationism, as he notes, in one key point in particular. Whereas the posttribulational view that I defend holds that believers will be on earth during the outpouring of divine wrath at the end of the final tribulation, the prewrath view holds that believers are raptured before the outpouring of that wrath. This means that the parousia takes place in stages: first the rapture, then a period of wrath, then Christ's descent to judge his enemies. As Hultberg notes, I also think that the parousia is a complex of events. The question that divides us is whether the New Testament gives us reason to think that the events of the parousia will take place over a period of time (Hultberg's view) or at roughly the same time (as I argue). Hultberg's basic evidence for viewing the parousia as extended over time comes from the Revelation. But before I turn to Revelation, I want to touch briefly on the meaning of the deliverance from wrath that 1 Thessalonians predicts.

Hultberg argues that the New Testament distinguishes between the wrath of God that is revealed at the time of Christ's return and the wrath of God that occurs during the last stages of the final tribulation. This basic distinction may be granted, since the New Testament does, indeed, appear to refer to both. But Hultberg takes a further step that is essential to his view: the New Testament teaches that the rapture is the means by which believers are rescued from the wrath of the final tribulation. He appeals especially to 1 Thessalonians 4–5 for this view of the rapture. Although he dates the onset of the wrath/day of the Lord earlier, Blaising makes the same point. To be sure, Paul never explicitly associates God's wrath with the day of the Lord in the Thessalonian letters. But the reference to the "destruction" brought by the day of the Lord against unbelievers (1 Thess. 5:3) may suggest the idea. Nevertheless, I do not think that Paul in this context presents the rapture as the means of escape from this wrath. Paul refers specifically to an escape from wrath in 1 Thessalonians 5:9: "For God did not appoint us to suffer wrath but to receive salvation through our Lord Jesus Christ." Both Hultberg and Blaising think that this text, along with the reference to rescue from "the coming wrath" in 1 Thessalonians 1:10, refers to God saving his people from the wrath of the day of the Lord by means of the rapture. Both point to the parallels between 4:13–17 and 5:1–10. The ultimate point in both passages is that believers will be "with the Lord" (4:17b; 5:10b; though not necessarily "in heaven," as Blaising asserts). Therefore, it is likely that believers "receive salvation" (5:9) through the rapture (4:17). But this interpretation narrows the reference to both salvation and wrath in a way that does not fit the context well. As the "for" at the beginning of verse 9 indicates, this verse grounds what Paul has said in the previous verses: that the day of the Lord will not "surprise" believers like "a thief in the night" because believers already belong to the "day"—that is, by virtue of their regeneration, they have already entered into God's eschatological "day." Believers, then, have a solid hope of being saved in the day of the Lord (5:8b). But the critical point to note is that "believers" here refers not just to believers who are alive at the time of Christ's return: it must include all believers. This is because Paul throughout this context has dead as well as living believers in view. It is the fate of believers who have already died that sparks this whole discussion (4:13). When Paul then concludes this paragraph with the assurance that "we will be with the Lord forever," the "we" specifically includes living and dead believers (4:17b). Similarly, in 1 Thessalonians 5:10 the "we" who "live together with him" includes all believers—"whether we are awake or asleep." The close relationship between verses 9 and 10 makes it unlikely that the "we" in verse 9 has a narrower reference—living believers—than verse 10—all believers. This means, however, that the rapture cannot be the means of salvation in verse 9, since, of course, dead believers will not be raptured. In fact, both 1 Thessalonians 1:10 and 5:9 probably summarize the rather standard New Testament teaching on "rescue" from God's wrath: Christ's death, because it satisfies God's wrath (Rom. 3:25), is the means—the "once-for-all" means—by which those who belong to Christ are forever saved from God's wrath. When Paul says that we will "be saved from God's wrath through him" (Rom. 5:9), the "through him" refers to Christ's atoning death (v. 9a and vv. 6–8). The focus in these passages, then, is not on a particular "historical" expression of God's wrath (during the final tribulation) but on the wrath of God broadly conceived. That this is the case in 1 Thessalonians, I note again, is because Paul is referring to a wrath that could potentially affect all believers, living and dead — the wrath of the final judgment.

The Rapture in Revelation

Most interpreters, whatever their view on the timing of the rapture, agree that the Revelation never *clearly* describes the rapture.[138] At the same time, many scholars find hints of the rapture in Revelation, either directly, in veiled or allusive language, or indirectly, in visions of Christians enjoying the fruits of their rapture. Hultberg finds one passage of each kind in the Revelation, and he argues that their placement in the book teaches a rapture that precedes the wrath of the final tribulation.

The first of these passages is the vision of the "great multitude" in 7:9–17. The people in this vision, who come from "every nation, tribe, people and language," are worshiping around the throne of God. They wear white robes (vv. 9, 13, 14), symbolizing their ultimate salvation (3:4, 5, 18; 6:11; perhaps also 4:4; 19:14). Most important for our purposes, they have "come out of the great tribulation" (7:14). Hultberg sometimes suggests that this passage "is" the rapture, but what I think he really means is that this passage describes a group of people who have been raptured. I think he is probably right in this interpretation. I am not so sure, however, that "great tribulation" must be confined to the final tribulation. As I noted in my main essay, the New Testament consistently uses the language of tribulation for the sufferings that God's people undergo throughout the period of Christian history. This period, according to the New Testament, is the "time of the end" Daniel predicted and thus is also the "time of distress," a distress "such as has not happened from the beginning of nations until then" (Dan. 12:1). I have argued that the "great distress" of Matthew 24:21 has the same referent.

I also am not sure of another part of Hultberg's interpretation of this passage. He argues that the "great multitude" is a different group than

---

138. Blaising admits that this is the case, arguing that it was simply not part of John's purpose to refer to the rapture in Revelation. But this admission sits oddly with his contention that the rapture is the means of deliverance from the impending wrath in 1 Thessalonians 5. Surely it would have been terribly relevant to the suffering Christians in Asia Minor to be assured that God would deliver them from the coming wrath by means of the rapture.

the 144,000 people who have been "sealed" by God in 7:1–8. Commentators differ quite significantly on this point, but I think it a bit likelier that both groups in chapter 7 describe the church in general.[139] The former vision pictures the church as the "new Israel," in keeping with standard imagery in both Revelation and throughout the New Testament. The "sealing" language connotes God's providential protection of his people throughout the trials and sufferings of this life. It is the means by which God carries out his promise to "keep you from the hour of trial that is going to come on the whole world to test those who live on the earth" (3:10).[140] The second vision focuses on the *result* of the sealing. Those whom God has protected and who themselves display faithfulness and courage under trial are vindicated in the end. Hultberg, by contrast, thinks that the 144,000 describes the "remnant of Israel" that is left on the earth to go through the wrath of the final tribulation. One implication of his view on this matter should be noted: apparently the "remnant of Israel" are not granted the protection from divine wrath that is promised to the church. This means that these Jewish believers are not a part of the church (does Hultberg hint at this by calling them "Christ-followers"?). More seriously, Hultberg's interpretation assumes that Jewish believers in Christ during the final tribulation are not granted the immunity from God's wrath that the New Testament elsewhere appears to suggest is integral to Christ's atoning death. But I question whether this is theologically possible.

Hultberg thinks that Revelation 7:9–17 is an "indirect" reference to the rapture, in that it describes the immediate effect of the rapture. In Revelation 14:14–16, however, he thinks that we have a direct reference to the rapture. This text contains a vision of the Son of Man, who swings a sickle over the earth and therefore harvests the earth. As I point out in my main essay, interpreters differ fundamentally over the significance of this vision, some thinking, with Hultberg, that it describes the redemption of the saints, others that it describes judgment, still others that it may combine these ideas. A reference to redemption here is certainly possible, but it is important to note that this interpreta-

---

139. In favor of the identification are, among others, Grant R. Osborne, *Revelation*, BECNT (Grand Rapids: Baker, 2002), 303; G. K. Beale, *Revelation: A Commentary on the Greek Text*, NIGTC (Grand Rapids: Eerdmans, 1999), 424–25.

140. Osborne, *Revelation*, 301.

tion is far from certain.[141] To build very much on this very precarious identification of the rapture would not be wise. Yet, as we shall see, this is the critical link in Hultberg's argument for a prewrath rapture in the book of Revelation (and in the New Testament generally).

Before leaving this general point, I would like to point out two passages that I think may describe the rapture but which Hultberg does not. I will not repeat the arguments that lead me in my main essay to suggest that Revelation 11:11–12 may describe the rapture. If it does, the rapture would be posttribulational. The same is true if we find an allusion to the rapture in Revelation 20:4. This text describes the "coming to life" of people at the time of Christ's return in glory. I argue in my main essay that, since rapture is always temporally and conceptually linked to resurrection, the rapture is probably also to be located here. Hultberg disagrees. His main point is chronological: if the rapture occurs in 20:4, he claims, it would *follow* Christ's return, the defeat of the Beast (19:11–21), and the binding of Satan (20:1–3). It would be, he suggests, a "nonrapture." But what in the text leads us to think that these events must occur in chronological sequence? The text makes no such claim. I think it far likelier, in fact, that John reports in this context various aspects of Christ's return in chapter 19: it involves the defeat of the Beast and Satan and the vindication of the saints. Hultberg himself suggests, as one possible interpretation, that the reference to resurrection in 20:4 is chronologically displaced. Indeed! That is just the point. He suggests, as an alternate (and it seems, preferable) view, that the text refers to the resurrection of tribulation saints. And, of course, the objects of resurrection in this verse ("they") appear to be closely related, perhaps even coextensive, with "those who had been beheaded because of their testimony about Jesus and because of the word of God." Yet to restrict the subjects of resurrection in this verse to anything less than the entire body of the redeemed faces two very difficult contextual problems. First, those who "come to life" are the same ones who "reign with Christ for a thousand years." Limiting those who are resurrected here to the martyrs of the tribulation appears to require the saints who rule during the millennium to also be restricted to the martyrs.[142] Second,

---

141. In my main essay, I claim that a reference to the rapture in 14:14–16 is "probable"; after further study, I am happier with the word *possible*.

142. Some interpreters, of course, argue that this is indeed the case.

John refers to the "coming to life" in verse 4 as the "first resurrection" and contrasts it with a second resurrection, when "the rest of the dead" come to life (v. 5). This language suggests that the first resurrection includes all the righteous. If this is, indeed, the general resurrection, and the rapture takes place at the same time, the rapture appears to be posttribulational. Hultberg's attempt to avoid this conclusion seems to me to be less than persuasive.

The Rapture and the Wrath of God in Revelation

I noted above that Hultberg's interpretation of 14:14–16 as a reference to the rapture is crucial to his argument. The reason this is so is because he finds in Revelation 14–16 evidence of the chronological relationship between the rapture and pouring out of wrath at the end of the final tribulation. Revelation 14:14–16, he argues, depicts the rapture of the group pictured as rejoicing in heaven in 15:2–4. Only after this does John describe the pouring out of "the seven bowls of God's wrath on the earth" (16:1). So we have here, Hultberg argues, a sequence of rapture–wrath of the final tribulation. Hultberg uses the sequence he finds here to argue for a similar sequence in Revelation 6–8. The sixth seal of Revelation 6:12–17 brings us up to the brink of the day of the Lord. John then sees a vision of the "remnant of Israel" sealed under God's protection during the wrath of the tribulation (7:1–8) and a second vision of the church raptured out of the great tribulation (7:9–17). We then encounter the "silence in heaven" of the seventh seal (8:1–2), a silence that, as in Zephaniah 1:7 and Zechariah 2:13, prepares us for the outpouring of God's wrath. The seven trumpet judgments of 8:6–9:21, 11:15–19 then depict this wrath. Again, then, we have the sequence of rapture (chap. 7)–tribulation wrath (chaps. 8–11).

My problem with this argument is a simple one: I am not convinced that the material in either of these parts of Revelation describes a chronological progression. As I note in my main essay, the relationship between the sequence of visions in Revelation and the chronology of events in history is quite debated. But it is, I think, clearly the case that the majority of commentators on Revelation do not think that John follows a straightforward chronological scheme in his ordering of material. Most scholars think that John's "narrative" visions involve some degree of recapitulation, as he describes the same events more than once. And they also think that he intersperses in his "narrative" account visions that take us "behind the scenes" and that cannot be clearly fit into any kind of chronological scheme. The visions crucial to Hultberg's interpretation — 7:9–17 and 14:14–16 — both fit into this latter category. Of course, these general observations do not mean that these visions may not have a chronological relationship to their context. But that chronological relationship must be demonstrated, not assumed. What evidence do we have that the vision of the rapture (14:14–16) or of raptured saints (7:9–17) chronologically precedes tribulation wrath?

I begin with chapter 14, since Hultberg admits that this is a critical text for his view. As we have seen, he thinks the victorious saints of 15:2–4 refer to the group raptured in 14:14–16; and this vision comes before the preparation for, and pouring out of, the bowls of wrath (15:5–16:21). But John does not indicate that this group is in heaven before the pouring out of the bowls of wrath. He only claims that he "saw" the vision about wrath after he saw the vision of the victorious saints (15:5). Yet the sequence in which John receives his visions is not the same thing as the sequence in which the content of those visions occurs on earth. This is quite clear in our context from the fact that the vision of 14:17–20 plainly describes the last judgment, which occurs after the bowls of wrath are poured out. Moreover, John hints that this victorious group has, in fact, been on earth throughout the final tribulation. They are described as people who have "been victorious over the beast and his image and over the number of his name" (15:2). Yet the Beast's activities apparently take place throughout the second half of the final tribulation; his defeat comes only with the final victory of God in Christ (see 19:19–20). On two grounds, then, Hultberg's argument for a prewrath rapture in chapter 14 is suspect: it is not clear that 14:14–16 describes the rapture; and, if it does, its chronological relationship to the wrath of the final tribulation is not clear.

The situation in chapters 6–8 is much the same. Indeed, Hultberg as much as admits that the sequence in these chapters is not as clear by arguing that the sequence of chapters 14–16 must be brought over into these chapters as well. His claim that the series of visions in these two sections are roughly parallel has some merit. The vision of the 144,000 sealed people in 7:1–8 parallels the vision of what is apparently the same 144,000 in 14:1–5. The vision of the "great multitude" worshiping

God around the throne in 7:9–17 is roughly parallel to the victorious saints praising God in 15:2–5. And both of these texts are followed by a series of judgments (trumpets in chaps. 8–9; bowls in chap. 16). Hultberg argues for another parallel, however, that I am not sure is as clear. The bowl judgments of chapter 16 are explicitly said to be an expression of God's wrath. But, contrary to Hultberg's repeated claim, the trumpet judgments are never so described. To be sure, some of the trumpet judgments are initiated directly by God (see 9:13–16) and may be expressions of God's wrath. Moreover, the breaking of the sixth seal climaxes with the proclamation that "the great day of their wrath [that is, the wrath of God upon them] has come" (6:17). And Hultberg views the trumpet judgments as an elaboration of the seventh seal. It is certainly possible, then, that the trumpet judgments carry out the wrath anticipated with the sixth seal. Nevertheless, this is not certain. At least it must be said that John does not explicitly draw attention to a sequence of rapture–wrath in this context. But the more important point is that there seems to me no reason to insist that John implies any kind of chronological sequence between chap. 7—the great multitude raptured out of the great tribulation—and chaps. 8–9—the trumpet judgments. Chapter 7, by breaking up the sequence of seal judgments, is clearly an interpolation of some kind. There is much to be said for viewing this chapter as providing the reader with a broader theological perspective on the events of these seals and trumpets: God acts providentially to protect his people during these calamities (7:1–8), and he will bring his people victorious out of them (7:9–17). Indeed, that the vision of 7:9–17 is a proleptic view of the ultimate victory of God's people is suggested by the fact that they have "come out of the great tribulation." For the "great tribulation" most naturally encompasses the entirety of the judgments and disasters depicted in Revelation 6–16.

ALAN HULTBERG

I would like to thank Drs. Blaising and Moo for their thoughtful interaction with my argument for a prewrath rapture. As they note, I sought to defend two primary theses: that the church would be raptured sometime during the second half of Daniel's seventieth week, and that between the rapture and the return of Christ to earth will be an extended period of extraordinary divine wrath. Corollary to the second thesis was the idea that the parousia is a complex event of significant duration consisting of rapture, wrath, and return. My argument consisted especially of demonstrations that Jesus (Matthew), Paul, and John all anticipated the church's experience of the abomination of desolation and following tribulation, and that John in Revelation clarifies what Paul implies, that the rapture is that which spares the church from the parousia wrath. Blaising especially takes exception with the evidence for my first thesis, and Moo with the evidence for my second. Both find my reading of Revelation wanting. I do not find most of their critiques substantive, and I have dealt with many of their counterarguments in my initial essay and in my responses to their main essays. Nevertheless, some rejoinder is necessary. In what follows, then, I will concisely restate my own argument and then examine whether the various critiques by Blaising and Moo are warranted.

I make three main arguments that the church will experience the abomination of desolation and following tribulation. First, I argue that the structure of the Olivet Discourse and the ecclesiology of Matthew lead to the conclusion that Jesus spoke to his disciples as representatives of both the first-century generation of the church that would see a proleptic fulfillment of eschatological events in the Roman destruction of Jerusalem and the final generation of the church that would experience the ultimate fulfillment, including especially the abomination of desolation and tribulation.

Blaising takes issue with this argument in three ways. First, he finds it irrelevant that the church will experience events of the second half of Daniel's seventieth "week," since, according to progressive dispensationalism, the church will continue on earth after the rapture. I assume, then, that he admits my basic point has been made. Still, I find this an interesting admission, because Blaising himself wants to distinguish between the prerapture church and the postrapture church, only the first of which is promised deliverance from parousia wrath and will not see the abomination of desolation. His own pretribulational argument makes little sense otherwise. But why is it that only the prerapture church is given the promise? In this instance, posttribulationism makes far better sense. Without working out the details here, I only suggest that absolute ecclesiological continuity between the pre- and postrapture "church" should not be maintained. Second, and conversely, Blaising claims I argue Matthew is supersessionist (teaching that the church forever replaces Israel), a perspective he maintains is wrong. However, I make no such claim. I merely show that Matthew views the church as "in some sense" the inheritor of the messianic kingdom. The church is the messianic community founded by Jesus, the present phase of the kingdom. One would be hard-pressed to find a Matthean scholar who would disagree with this, including David Turner, whom Blaising cites against me. My only point is that one cannot argue that in Matthew 24 Jesus speaks to his disciples as representatives of Israel and not the church. Third, Blaising suggests that if the abomination of desolation had a proleptic fulfillment in the first century, it could not function as the determinative eschatological sign. But I do not maintain that the abomination of desolation happened in the first century, at least not in the significant sense anticipated by Jesus and Paul (and apparently John). The Roman destruction of the temple may have been a kind of abomination of desolation, but it was far from an imperial figure taking his seat in the temple and proclaiming himself God. That will be a unique event.

For his part, Moo contends that to distinguish as I do between "historical" fulfillment and "eschatological" fulfillment is misleading and unbiblical, since the New Testament presents the "last days," including Daniel's seventieth "week," as having begun with the first coming of Christ. First, I agree that the "last days" began in the first century and that we can therefore speak of present time as "eschatological." But I also believe there will be an ultimate Antichrist, abomination of desolation, and so on at the end of the age, even if there could be typological instances of these things in previous history. To distinguish these, I used the language of "historical" and "eschatological." Second, however, as to whether there will be an ultimate Antichrist and tribulation, I only offer that the Man of Lawlessness Paul anticipated in 2 Thessalonians (following Daniel 11), who is destroyed at the second coming, and the incomparable tribulation that Jesus anticipated in Matthew 24 (following Daniel 12), which follows the abomination of desolation and "immediately" precedes the parousia, strike me as obviously future.

My second argument is that, because the eschatology of the Thessalonian letters is based at least in part on the dominical tradition behind Matthew's Olivet Discourse, the correspondence especially between 1 Thessalonians 4:15–16 and Matthew 24:30–31 means that Paul understood the rapture to occur at Matthew 24:30–31. This in turn suggests that Paul expected the church to experience the abomination of desolation, a suggestion confirmed by 2 Thessalonians 2:1–15. Blaising disagrees on three counts. First, he thinks the correspondence between Matthew 24:30–31 and 1 Thessalonians 4:15–17 is insufficient to posit they are discussing the same event, especially since Matthew does not mention the rapture. But I believe I stand with the majority on seeing sufficient correspondence between the two texts, and, as I argued in my main essay, Paul considers his teaching on the rapture an addition to the Olivet Discourse tradition. Blaising's alternative attempt to place the rapture before Matthew 24:4 is thoroughly addressed in my response to his primary essay.

His second criticism, that the conditions of the day of the Lord as "peace and safety" (1 Thess. 5:3) disallows my view, is similarly dealt with in my response to his main essay. Finally, while Blaising agrees that Paul associates the rapture with the beginning of the day of the Lord, he disagrees that 2 Thessalonians 2:1–4 indicates the day of the Lord begins after the abomination of desolation. This is because (1)

Thomas shows that the phrase *ean mē ... prōton* ("unless ... first") does not require the apostasy and revelation of the Man of Lawlessness to precede the day of the Lord; instead, the former could initiate the latter, and Thomas's reading is better because (2) the revelation of the Man of Lawlessness is likelier the making of the covenant between the Antichrist and Israel than his session in the temple (the abomination of desolation). But in my primary essay I do not argue that the syntax of 2 Thessalonians 2:3 *requires* the apostasy and session to precede the day of the Lord, only that Thomas's evidence hardly makes his (and Blaising's) point and that the idea of precedence is much more natural and contextually fitting. Thus, it is not at all clear why, if, on Blaising's reading, Paul means to tell his readers that the rapture, which begins the day of the Lord, has not yet happened, he refers them to events that occur *after* the rapture, or yet why he tells them that the other events occur *first* in the sequence that makes up the day of the Lord. Blaising's attempt to shore up his reading by arguing that the revelation of the Man of Lawlessness is not his session but his covenant-making fails due to its dependence on his questionable exegesis of the Olivet Discourse and Daniel's "time of the end," which I deal with in my response to his primary essay. Similarly, his attempt to undermine my own equation of the session with the revelation is weak. He claims that the syntax of 2 Thessalonians 2:3 − 4 no more equates the revelation with the session than the parallel syntax of 2 Thessalonians 2:8 equates it with the destruction of the Man of Lawlessness. What's more, he argues, the *hōste* ("so that") of verse 4 makes the session the result of the blasphemous claims of the revelation, not identical to it. But though the syntax of verse 8 is similar to that of verses 3 and 4, the logic is better paralleled by following the sentence through to its conclusion in verse 10. The revelation of the Lawless One is related to his satanically deceptive "coming." And that is the point of the *hōste* of verse 4. The Man of Lawlessness is revealed to be the Antichrist when his blasphemous designs culminate in his session in the temple. Thus Paul says he "displays himself" at that time as being God.

My third argument that the church will experience the abomination of desolation and tribulation is that both Revelation 7:9 − 17 and 13:1 − 18 place the church in the tribulation. I further argue, based in part on parallels between Revelation 6:12–8:5 (11:19) and 14:1–16:21 and between Matthew 24:4–31 and Revelation 6:1–17, that Revelation 7:9–14; 14:14–16; and 15:2–4 portray the rapture. This argument is also used to support my claim that Revelation presents a complex parousia of rapture, wrath, and return

Though Moo agrees that Revelation 7:9–14 probably portrays the rapture, both he and Blaising find my evidence slim for that claim and for Revelation 14:14–16; 15:2–4. Blaising is not convinced that the innumerable multitude appears in heaven nor that the one like a son of man reaping the earth from a cloud is Christ. Moo thinks that the reference to the tribulation in Revelation 7 is to the entire church age and not a special, final distress. Both also think I have not shown that the wrath of God referred to in Revelation 6:16–17; 11:18 begins with the trumpet sequence nor that Revelation 7 chronologically falls between the sixth and seventh seals. Neither, however, offers any solid exegetical reasons for these latter claims that I had not already dealt with in my essay, much less anything that undermines my own evidence. In response, then, I can only offer my original exegesis and any clarifications I made in my responses to their main essays. With regard to the former claims, only Blaising's contention that being before the throne does not necessarily place the innumerable multitude in heaven has some cogency. The problem has to do, however, not with where the throne is, as he suggests — the whole narrative from chapters 4–14 makes clear the throne is in heaven — but with where the 144,000 are in Revelation 14:1–5. John says they are on Mount Zion and that they sing before the throne. Some suggest Mount Zion is itself a metaphor for heaven. I contend that Zion is on earth (either the real place or a symbol for restored Israel or the like), since in Revelation 7:3 the 144,000 are sealed for protection from God's wrath on earth (cf. Rev. 9:4). It is their singing that ascends to the throne.

Finally, I offer two main arguments for my claim that the church avoids God's parousia wrath by being raptured. First, the context of the Thessalonian letters makes the references in them to deliverance from God's wrath references not to the final judgment but to the parousia wrath. Second, as I discussed above, Revelation evidences the sequence of rapture, wrath, return. Moo disagrees with the first argument because the "we" who are saved from wrath in 1 Thessalonians 5:9–10 refers not just to living believers but to dead believers as well. Only the former can possibly suffer the parousia wrath, but both could suffer the final judgment were it not for Christ's salvation. I grant Moo's general point but add that he misses a more contextually sensitive alternative, that Paul moves from salvation to parousia wrath specifically in 5:1–9 (the "we" of verses 5–9 can only refer to living believers) to salvation more globally considered in verse 10. Moo disagrees with my second argument especially on the basis that Revelation is not straightforwardly chronological and that I have not shown it to be so for the visionary sequences in Revelation 6–8 (or through chapter 11); 14–16. But I make no contention that Revelation is straightforwardly chronological—it is not; the visions have numerous recapitulations, interludes, and such. What I claim is that one must follow the literary details to determine the sequence of referenced events, and I have sought to show those for the relatively parallel sequences of rapture then wrath in Revelation 6:12–8:5 (or through 11:19) and Revelation 14:14–16:21, followed in 19:11–21 by the return of Christ. The details also make it difficult for the resurrection of Revelation 20:4 to be simultaneous with the descent of Christ in 19:11–21, as Moo merely asserts it is. Again, I refer the reader to my original exposition and clarifications in my responses to the other essays and allow him or her to judge whether I have made my case. I do not think Moo has demonstrated my exegesis to be faulty.

I again want to thank Drs. Blaising and Moo for their gracious and probing interaction with my argument. Though it has ultimately strengthened my conviction that I am on the right track, my own thinking can only benefit from their keen observations. More important, however, I pray the church will benefit from our discussion. Jesus is coming again! We all want to be informed and faithful followers of his as we look forward to and prepare for that blessed day.

CHAPTER
THREE

CHAPTER THREE: A CASE FOR THE POSTTRIBULATION RAPTURE

DOUGLAS MOO

Introduction: Getting Our Bearings

In this essay I present an exegetical and theological argument for the view that the church, the new covenant people of God, will be raptured at the time of Christ's return in glory (the parousia) *after* the final tribulation. I will focus on key New Testament passages about the parousia, the final tribulation, and the reward promised to God's people at the time of Christ's return. My approach to these passages will be governed by certain assumptions and general theological perspectives that are important to get on the table at the outset of my argument. And none of these is more important than my perspective on the two key terms *rapture* and *tribulation*.

The word *rapture* is, of course, not a New Testament word. The English word comes from the Latin verb *rapio* ("seize" or "carry away"), which was used in the Vulgate to translate the Greek word *harpagēsometha*, "we will be caught up [to meet the Lord in the air]" in 1 Thessalonians 4:17. In popular circles, the rapture (in accordance with its verbal sense) is often thought of in terms of physical movement: believers are physically moved off the earth into heaven by the Lord. Moreover, this physical "taking away" is also usually thought to be necessary to rescue believers from harm. But neither of these notions gets at the heart of the matter. To be sure, physical movement is pretty clearly implied in the 1 Thessalonians text—and perhaps in others. But the more important aspect of rapture in the New Testament is bodily transformation. Theologically, rapture is best seen as a parallel to resurrection. When the Lord returns, dead saints are raised from the dead; living saints are raptured. This parallelism is especially clear in 1 Corinthians 15:50–53:

> I declare to you, brothers, that flesh and blood cannot inherit the kingdom of God, nor does the perishable inherit the imperishable. Listen, I tell you a mystery: We will not all sleep, but we will all be changed—in a flash, in the twinkling of an eye, at the last trumpet. For the trumpet will sound, the dead will be raised imperishable, and we will be changed. For the perishable must clothe itself with the imperishable, and the mortal with immortality.

The completed form of the kingdom that God will bring into existence at the time of Christ's return cannot be lived in by people in normal "mortal" bodies. So all of us must be "changed." Christians who have already died will be "raised imperishable," but the rest of us, those who are still alive when Christ returns, must also be "changed"—that is, "raptured." Second, the physical movement that is involved in the rapture is not a movement to escape something but a movement to be joined to something. This is clear from the 1 Thessalonians text I cited earlier: believers are "caught up" in order to "meet the Lord." Rapture is not the means by which we are taken away from something on earth so much as it is the means by which we are brought into the presence of Christ. In fact, there is only one text in the New Testament that might suggest that God will physically remove his people from the final tribulation (or tribulation of any kind)—Revelation 3:10—and I will argue below that even this text does not mean this.

If popular usage has shifted the theological idea of "rapture" away from the biblical perspective a bit, it is even more the case with respect to "tribulation." I assume in this essay that the Scriptures predict a period of unparalleled distress for the people of God that will immediately precede the second advent. We will call this period the "final tribulation" in this essay. But it is very important to keep this future period of intense suffering in perspective. For many Christians, "tribulation" is something confined to this period of future time. But a quick look at the occurrence of this word in the New Testament shows how wrong this perspective is. The word *tribulation* (*thlipsis*) occurs forty-five times in the New Testament. Once it refers to the wrath of God (Rom. 2:5). The rest of the occurrences of this word refer to suffering experienced by believers. But note that thirty-seven of these occurrences indisputably refer to the "tribulation" that believers experience throughout this age. Paul and Barnabas warned the new converts in southern Asia Minor, "We must go through many hardships (*thlipseōn*) to enter the kingdom of God" (Acts 14:22). Jesus neatly summarizes the basic New Testament perspective: "In this world you will have trouble [*thlipsin*]. But take heart! I have overcome the world" (John 16:33). The word *tribulation* refers to a period of intense suffering at the end of history in, at most, seven texts (Matt. 24:9, 21, 29; Mark 13:19, 24; Rev. 2:10; 7:14). And I will argue below that it is quite possible that *none* of these refers to the final tribulation.

This point about "tribulation" is one facet of a much larger and very important New Testament perspective on "eschatology." When we focus on the culminating events of this age, it is all too easy to lose perspective by setting them apart from the events of this age as a whole. The New Testament proclaims that the prophecies about the "last days" have begun to be fulfilled. Christ's death, his glorious resurrection, and the pouring out of the Spirit on "all flesh" mark the inauguration of the "last days" (see, e.g., Acts 2:14–21; 1 Cor. 10:11; Heb. 1:1–2; 1 John 2:18). Because, then, the age between the advents belongs to the "last things" (*eschata*), the entire period is "eschatological." The decisive, foundational eschatological events have taken place—but, to the surprise of many in Jesus' day, without the culminating judgment of the wicked and definitive rescue of the righteous. It is this "surprise" that Jesus seeks to explain in his parable of the weeds: Jesus sows the seed of the kingdom, producing children of the new age; but these righteous ones will live together with the wicked until the climactic judgment to come (Matt. 13:24–43). "Imminency" refers to the New Testament teaching that these culminating events could occur "at any time." James encourages his readers by reminding them that "the Lord's coming is near" (5:8). Peter announces that "the end of all things is near" (1 Peter 4:7). The New Testament Christians expected the events of the end— Jesus' return in glory, final rescue of the saints, final judgment of the wicked—to occur at any time. In contrast to the claims of many New Testament scholars, I do not think that they were certain that Jesus' return would occur within a set number of years. But they held an open-ended view of the future, sharing with their Lord uncertainty about the time of the final events (see Matt. 24:36) even as they hoped they would happen soon.

What is especially important for our purposes, then, is the realization that the New Testament writers did not view their own history and experience as fundamentally separate from the events of the end of the age. We often refer to the "last days" or "the end times" as something that is still future and reserve the language of "eschatology" for that future. We therefore tend to separate these future events from our present experience in a way that is foreign to the New Testament. Many discussions of the topic we are looking at make a fundamental error at precisely this point, assuming without argument that if a passage refers to "eschatological events" or to "the last days" that it must be speaking about the very end of history as we know it. This is simply not the case.

Do not misunderstand. I am not suggesting that the end of the age will be exactly like our present time. The New Testament clearly refers to an especially intense and worldwide time of suffering for God's people that will come at the end of history, to a climactic person of evil—the Antichrist—who will challenge God and persecute his people, and to a climactic experience of God's wrath. But my point here is to insist that Jesus and the writers of the New Testament see these events not as belonging to a new period in salvation history but as the climax to an era already begun. And they envisage this climax not as some distant series of events but as something that could emerge very quickly out of their own situation.[1]

With these preliminary, but very important, points established, I can turn now to my basic argument. Since the rapture is clearly revealed only in the New Testament, the decisive evidence for its timing with respect to the tribulation must come from the New Testament also. Furthermore, it is sound hermeneutical procedure to establish a doc-

---

1. For a good survey of this approach to eschatology, see G. K. Beale, "The Eschatological Conception of New Testament Theology," in *The Reader Must Understand: Eschatology in Bible and Theology* (ed. K. E. Brower and M. W. Elliott; Leicester: Inter-Varsity, 1997), 11–52.

trine on the basis of the texts that speak most directly to the issue. Thus the major part of the paper will be devoted to an exegesis of these texts. However, some foundational issues must be addressed before this important task is begun.

The Tribulation and the Second Coming
The Nature of the Tribulation

While "tribulation," as we have seen, is the common lot of God's people in this age, an especially intense and universal time of tribulation is predicted for the very end of history in both the Old and New Testaments. It is the nature of this "final tribulation" that I want to analyze in this section. Most scholars think that the final tribulation will involve both unprecedented worldwide persecution of God's people by anti-Christian forces as well as the pouring out of God's wrath on an increasingly wicked world. It is especially important to analyze the place of God's wrath in this period. When we turn to the Old Testament, the situation is complicated by the fact that it is often difficult to discern whether a particular description of "tribulation" relates to the exile, the final judgment, or the final tribulation as such. The distinction between the latter two is not always recognized, but it is a very important one in discussing Old Testament texts. Passages that describe the horror of the end itself, which, in any eschatological scenario, *follows* the final tribulation, cannot be used as evidence for the nature of the final tribulation, which *precedes* the end. Since many of the relevant prophetic texts involve descriptions of the "day of the LORD" and do not indicate clearly whether the final tribulation or the end itself is envisaged, the problem is a real one. Caution is called for, then, in applying these descriptions to the final tribulation.[2]

When this distinction is kept in mind, I conclude that Old Testament texts that might with some degree of probability be describing the final tribulation are confined to Daniel 7–12 (7:7–8, 23–25; 8:9–12, 23–25; 9:26–27; 11:36–12:1). It is certainly possible that other Old

---

2. The doctrine of the final tribulation formulated by, e.g., J. Dwight Pentecost, *Things to Come: A Study in Biblical Eschatology* (Grand Rapids: Zondervan, 1964), 233–35, is largely dependent on texts having to do with the day of the Lord. Even if the final tribulation is a part of the day, it is illegitimate to apply to the final tribulation any imagery associated with the day.

Testament passages *may* describe the final tribulation—Deuteronomy 4:29–30; Isaiah 26:20–21; Jeremiah 30:4–9; Joel 2:30–31; and Zephaniah 1–2, to name a few. But none of the depictions of distress in these passages is clearly distinguished from the final outpouring of God's judgmental wrath *after* the tribulation. In the interests of accuracy, then, it is important to use the texts in Daniel primarily in constructing the Old Testament concept of the tribulation and employ the other texts only as they corroborate the picture in Daniel. These chapters in Daniel undoubtedly have the greatest bearing of any Old Testament passages on New Testament eschatology. Unfortunately, they are also very difficult to interpret, and we cannot here even begin to enter into the exegetical and theological difficulties they present. Suffice it to say that I think they contain prophecies from the sixth-century Daniel in which, in typical Old Testament fashion, predictions about the Maccabean period are mixed up with predictions about the ultimate establishment of God's kingdom. I take it, for instance, that the seventy "sevens" of Daniel 9:24–27 describe the process by which this kingdom will be established, with the seventieth "seven" referring to the entire package of events spanning the time from Christ's first coming to his second coming in glory.[3]

Two points of relevance for our topic emerge from the texts in Daniel. First, the sufferings of the saints during this period are uniformly attributed to an ultimate usurper of God (7:7–8, 20–25; 11:35–48). It is "the little horn" who "was waging war against the saints and defeating them" (7:21; cf. 8:25). These passages may refer, first of all, to Antiochus Epiphanes, the pagan enemy of Israel in the second century BC. But they ultimately refer to the end-time Antichrist. Second, Daniel 11:36 and (probably) 8:19 attest to the existence of divine wrath (*za'am*)

---

3. Daniel 9:25–27 is one of the most difficult passages in the entire Old Testament. The "seventy sevens," or "weeks," and their division into units of seven, sixty-two, and one, have generated countless and mutually contradictory chronological schemes. The identity of the "anointed one" is very uncertain, as is the antecedent of the pronouns in v. 27. For a discussion of the passage along the lines I am suggesting, see, e.g., Thomas Edward McComiskey, "Seventy 'Weeks' of Daniel against the Background of Ancient Near Eastern Literature," *WTJ* 47 (1985): 18–45; Joyce G. Baldwin, *Daniel: An Introduction and Commentary*, TOTC (Downers Grove, Ill.: InterVarsity, 1978), 168–78. One of the basic problems in Robert van Kampen's presentation of the "prewrath" position is his assumption that Daniel's seventieth week refers only to the end of history (Robert van Kampen, *The Sign*, exp. ed. [Wheaton: Crossway, 1993], cf. 87–95).

during this period of intense persecution. But nothing is said about the extent or duration of this wrath, nor is it stated that the wrath falls upon the "saints," or holy people. But while Daniel is silent about the extent and objects of this tribulation wrath, it is significant that a related text, Isaiah 26:20–21, specifically depicts the selective nature of God's wrath: "Go, my people, enter your rooms and shut the doors behind you; hide yourselves for a little while until his wrath (*za'am*) has passed by. See, the LORD is coming out of his dwelling to punish the people of the earth for their sins." If this passage refers to the final tribulation, we possess clear evidence that God's people on earth are protected from the divine wrath. Even if one argues that the wrath of Isaiah 26 affects only Israel, it is still important to recognize that God's people can remain on earth while escaping the wrath. On the other hand, this text may not relate to the final tribulation at all—in which case the principle of selectivity in the exercise of God's wrath remains. At the least, then, Isaiah 26:20–21 establishes the possibility that God's people can escape divine wrath though present during its outpouring.

We conclude that the depiction of the final tribulation in the Old Testament includes severe persecution of saints at the instigation of a powerful leader along with a revelation of divine wrath, undetermined in its extent and objects.

As we have seen, the word "tribulation" as such refers to what we are calling the final tribulation at most only seven times in the New Testament (Matt. 24:9, 21, 29; Mark 13:19, 24; Rev. 2:10; 7:14; of course, the final tribulation is referred to in other language as well). All seven come within the so-called Olivet Discourse or the book of Revelation. And it has been traditional to look to these two blocks of text, along with 2 Thessalonians 2:3–8, for the most extensive New Testament data about the final tribulation. Though I doubt that Mark 13:14–23 and Revelation 6–16 describe the final tribulation per se, I do think that both texts include reference to the final tribulation in their depiction of the sufferings of God's people throughout the church age. In examining what these texts say about the nature of the final tribulation, two questions are especially significant.

First, do these texts, or others similar to them, suggest that the tribulations of the final tribulation are qualitatively different from the tribulation experienced by God's people throughout history? Only if the answer to this question is yes does it make sense to think that the last generation of believers will be exempted from tribulation. For, as I have noted, the New Testament consistently predicts that believers will suffer tribulation. Nothing in these texts suggests that the suffering of the final tribulation will be any greater in degree than what many believers throughout the age must suffer. True, the extreme sufferings of the final period may be greater in extent, afflicting many more Christians than it does now, but this does not constitute a reason to exempt Christians from it. Moreover, history affords many examples of believers suffering horrendous tribulations because of their unshakable commitment to Christ. Indeed, it is difficult to imagine suffering that could be any more intense than some believers have already experienced and that other believers continue to experience. Why should a future generation of Christians be exempt from what Christians have already been experiencing? The degree of suffering in the final tribulation provides no grounds for a pretribulational rapture.

The second question to ask of these texts is whether their references to the wrath of God require that believers be physically absent during the final tribulation. The New Testament clearly teaches that believers are forever exempt from God's wrath (Rom. 5:9; 1 Thess. 1:10; 5:9). If, then, the final tribulation includes the infliction of God's wrath, must not believers be absent during it? It is only in the Revelation that there are references to God's wrath that may be associated with the final tribulation (6:16, 17; 11:18; 14:10, 19; 15:1, 7; 16:1, 19; 19:15). Two aspects of the presentation in Revelation merit our attention.

First, the references to God's wrath in the Revelation refer mainly, if not exclusively, to the very end of history and not to the final tribulation per se. This is pretty clear in several of the references (14:10, 19; 16:19; 19:15). I think several others also refer to the climactic scene of judgment based on my reading of the structure of Revelation. As I will argue below, Revelation 6–16 appears to follow a "recapitulative" structure. John portrays the events leading up to the parousia several times, with the result that the end itself is referred to several times in the course of these chapters. The parousia and associated final judgment on sinners appears therefore to be in view in Revelation 6:16–17, which describes cosmic disasters elsewhere associated with the parousia (Mark 13:24). And the same is true of 11:18. This leaves only the references to the "bowl" judgments in 15:1, 7 and 16:1. Significantly, John introduces the bowl judgments by claiming that "with them God's wrath is completed" (*etelesthē*; 15:1). This language strongly suggests that the bowl judgments are not simply one episode or series of events within the final tribulation but that they in some fashion describe the culmination of God's judgments in history.

The second aspect of God's wrath in Revelation that we must note is the selective nature of God's judgments and wrath. The demonic locusts of the fifth trumpet are ordered to harm "only those people who did not have the seal of God on their foreheads" (9:4). The first bowl, while it is poured out on the "earth," nevertheless brings "ugly, festering sores" only on "the people who had the mark of the beast and worshiped his image" (16:2). And the recipients of a number of the plagues are said to refuse to repent (9:20–21; 16:9, 11)—an indication that only unbelievers are affected by them. In other words, there is no place in which the judgment or the wrath of God is presented as afflicting saints, and there are indications on the contrary that God is purposefully exempting the saints from their force.

The New Testament thus paints a picture similar to that of the Old Testament. The final tribulation is presented as a period of severe persecution of saints then on earth. But (1) it is not clear to what extent (if any) the final tribulation itself involves the infliction of God's wrath, and (2) there are indications that God protects his own people from his wrath. To be sure, it may be asked how God can protect his people from the universal judgments associated with his wrath—for instance, the death of every sea creature (16:3). In response two points can be made. First, this constitutes a problem for *all* interpreters. Everyone agrees that saints of some sort will be divinely protected and preserved alive until the parousia—whether they be part of the church or the Jewish remnant saved during the final tribulation. Second, the history of Old Testament Israel would suggest that, although God's judgments are never directed toward those who truly belong to him, the judgments can indirectly affect them. Thus Noah and his family were, to say the least, inconvenienced by the flood. And did not Jeremiah and other true servants of God experience suffering, even death, as a result of God's wrathful judgment upon Judah through the Babylonians? Romans 1:18 affirms that "the wrath of God is being revealed from heaven against all the godlessness and wickedness of human beings who suppress the truth by their wickedness." Yet the present infliction of God's wrath is clearly not incompatible with God's protection of believers from his wrath during this same time.

An important conclusion emerges from this discussion of the nature of the final tribulation: there is nothing inherent in it that makes it impossible for the church to be present during it. All agree that no true believer will experience the wrath of God, but no description of the tribulation presents it as a time of wrath upon God's people. All agree that the church experiences tribulation—at times severe tribulation—throughout its existence; but no description of the tribulation indicates that it will involve greater suffering than many believers have already experienced.

The Vocabulary of the Second Advent

Three words are frequently used in the New Testament to describe the return of Christ: *apokalypsis* ("revelation"), *epiphaneia* ("manifestation"), and *parousia* ("coming" or "presence"). The word *parousia*, which occurs most frequently (fifteen times), should probably be translated "coming," but its associations with the concept of "presence" should not be ignored. Its appropriateness as a characterization of the Lord's return is evident from the fact that it is used in the papyri to designate the special visits of kings. The word *epiphaneia* (five times with reference to the second coming) connotes a decisive divine appearance for the benefit of God's people, while an allusion to the completion of God's purposes is suggested by the term *apokalypsis* (five times).[4]

What is important to note about these terms is, first, that each is clearly used to describe the posttribulational return of Christ and, second, that all three also designate the believer's hope and expectation. Parousia is indisputably posttribulational in Matthew 24:3, 27, 37, 39 and in 2 Thessalonians 2:8; *apokalypsis* has the same time frame in 2 Thessalonians 1:7, as does *epiphaneia* in 2 Thessalonians 2:8. On the other hand, the parousia of Christ is explicitly stated to be an object of

---

4. On the background and meaning of these terms, see B. Rigaux, *Saint Paul: Les Epitres aux Thessaloniciens*, Etudes Bibliques (Paris: Gabalda, 1956), 196–206; George Milligan, *St. Paul's Epistles to the Thessalonians* (Old Tappan, N.J.: Revell, n.d.), 145–51.

the believer's expectation in 1 Thessalonians 2:19; 3:13; James 5:7–8; and 1 John 2:28. The word *apokalypsis* is used to describe the believer's hope in 1 Corinthians 1:7; 1 Peter 1:7, 13; 4:13, while all four references to *epiphaneia* in the Pastoral Epistles (1 Tim. 6:14; 2 Tim. 4:1; 4:8; Titus 2:13) bear this significance. If, then, believers are exhorted to look forward to this coming of Christ, and this coming is presented as posttribulational, it is natural to conclude that believers will be present through the tribulation.[5]

However, this would be to proceed too quickly. It may be that the second coming must be divided into two stages: a "coming" of Christ *for* his church before or sometime during the tribulation and a "coming" *with* his church after it. Such a two-stage coming cannot be ruled out a priori. On the other hand, it cannot be accepted unless there is clear evidence for such a division. We have seen that such evidence is not available in the terms used to depict the second advent—each of them includes both the rapture and the posttribulational descent of Christ from heaven. The analogy of the Old Testament hope of the coming of the Messiah, which in the light of fulfillment can be seen to have two stages, is often brought into the argument at this point. Of course, the two-stage nature of the establishment of the kingdom cannot be used in itself to argue for a two-stage parousia. But even as an analogy it is of limited value, because we recognize the two stages of the establishment of the kingdom of God only in retrospect. Some argue that the New Testament suggests these two stages by speaking of Christ coming "for" his saints (before the final coming) and "with" his saints (at the final coming; see 1 Thess. 3:13; 4:14; Rev. 17:14; 19:14). Not all these texts are clearly relevant, since some of them may refer not to believers but to angels. Zechariah 14:5 predicts that "the LORD my God will come, and all the holy ones with him," and this text has influenced New Testament presentations of Christ's return (see Matt. 13:41; 16:27; 25:31; 2 Thess. 1:7; Jude 14). This being the case, 1 Thessalonians 3:13 probably refers

5. On this point, see: Alexander Reese, *The Approaching Advent of Christ: An Examination of the Teaching of J. N. Darby and His Followers* (London and Edinburgh: Marshall, Morgan and Scott, 1937), 125–38; Henry W. Frost, *Matthew Twenty-four and the Revelation* (New York: Oxford University Press, 1924), 146–47; J. Barton Payne, *The Imminent Appearing of Christ* (Grand Rapids: Eerdmans, 1962), 47–48; George Eldon Ladd, *The Blessed Hope* (Grand Rapids: Eerdmans, 1956), 63–68.

to angels who accompany Christ; and Revelation 19:14 may.[6] But more to the point is the fact that 1 Thessalonians 4:14 uses the "with" language to describe believers and the Lord *at the time of the rapture*.

Therefore, a study of the vocabulary employed in describing the return of Christ paints a uniform picture: believers are exhorted to look for and to live in the light of this glorious event. And, while some texts obviously place this coming *after* the final tribulation, there are *none* that equally obviously place it before the final tribulation. However, it may be that a closer look at the contexts in which these terms occur will reveal that there is, in fact, a pretribulational aspect to the second coming. It is to these texts that we now turn.

The Rapture – Three Basic Passages

I turn now to those texts that are claimed to be "the three principal Scriptures revealing the rapture—John 14:3; 1 Corinthians 15:51, 52; and 1 Thessalonians 4:13–18."[7] Since our study of the nature of the final tribulation has revealed nothing that would necessitate the removal of the church during that period, and the important terms used to describe the second advent give no indication that anything other than a posttribulational event is envisaged, we would expect to find in these texts clear indications of a pretribulational aspect of the advent if such an aspect exists.

In the Farewell Discourse of John's gospel (chaps. 14–17), Jesus seeks to prepare his disciples for the time of his physical absence from them. In 14:1–4 Jesus encourages them by asserting that his "going" to the Father is for the purpose of preparing a "place" for them in the

---

6. Most Thessalonians commentators prefer a reference to angels (e.g., Ernest Best, *The First and Second Epistles to the Thessalonians*, HNTC [New York: Harper and Row, 1972], 152–53; Charles A. Wanamaker, *The Epistles to the Thessalonians*, NIGTC [Grand Rapids: Eerdmans, 1990], 145; Gene L. Green, *The Letters to the Thessalonians*, PNTC [Grand Rapids: Eerdmans, 2002], 181; and see also Geerhardus Vos, *The Pauline Eschatology* [Grand Rapids: Eerdmans, 1953], 137; Payne, *Imminent Appearing*, 75–76). For the opposite view, see Milligan (*Thessalonians*, 45) and Leon Morris (*The First and Second Epistles to the Thessalonians*, NICNT [Grand Rapids: Eerdmans, 1959], 114–15). Commentators on Revelation are more evenly divided about 19:14 (in favor of a reference to angels: George Eldon Ladd, *A Commentary on the Revelation of St. John* [Grand Rapids: Eerdmans, 1972], 255; in favor of a reference to believers: G. K. Beale, *The Book of Revelation: A Commentary on the Greek Text*, NIGTC [Grand Rapids: Eerdmans, 1999], 960; in favor of reference to both: Grant R. Osborne, *Revelation*, BECNT [Grand Rapids: Baker, 2002], 684).

7. John F. Walvoord, *The Blessed Hope and the Tribulation: Study of Posttribulationism* (Grand Rapids: Zondervan, 1976), 50.

Father's "house" (v. 2), and that he will come again and receive them to himself, "that you also may be where I am" (v. 3). While some think that John 14:2–3 refers to Jesus' provision of a spiritual "resting place" with the Father, the passage likely does refer to the second advent and rapture.[8] But there is no indication in the text that any "coming" other than the posttribulational one described elsewhere in the New Testament is in Jesus' mind. The fact that believers at a posttribulational rapture would rise to meet the Lord in the air only to return immediately to earth with him creates no difficulty, for the text does *not* state that believers will go directly to heaven,[9] but only that they will always be with the Lord. If it be argued that this is the inference of the text, it is hard to see how any other view can offer a more reasonable scenario. As Robert Gundry says, "The pretribulational interpretation would require us to believe that the church will occupy heavenly mansions for a short period of seven years, only to vacate them for a thousand years."[10] Neither is it true that a promise of deliverance only after the severe distress of the final tribulation could not be a "comfort" to the disciples. The "blessed hope" of being reunited with the risen Lord is surely a comfort, no matter what believers have previously experienced. Thus John 14:1–4 offers no indication at all about the time of the rapture.

In 1 Corinthians 15:51–52, it is Paul's purpose to indicate how living saints can enter the kingdom at the last day even though "flesh and blood cannot inherit the kingdom of God" (v. 50). To do so, he affirms that, while "we" (believers in general) will not all die, we will all be "changed"—whether living or dead. That Paul calls this transformation a "mystery" indicates nothing about *who* will participate in it, only that it was not clearly revealed previously.[11] And in quoting an

---

8. See, e.g., D. A. Carson, *The Gospel according to John*, PNTC (Grand Rapids: Eerdmans, 1991), 488–90; contra, e.g., Craig S. Keener, *The Gospel of John: A Commentary* (Peabody, Mass.: Hendrickson, 2003), 937–38.

9. While Gundry has argued that the *monai* ("dwelling places") are to be regarded as "spiritual abodes in [Jesus'] own person" (Robert H. Gundry, *The Church and the Tribulation: A Biblical Examination of Posttribulationism* (Grand Rapids: Zondervan, 1973), 154–55; and in more detail in "'In My Father's House Are Many *Monai*' (John 14:2)" (*ZAW* 58 [1967]: 68–72), the close connection with "my father's house," which almost certainly represents heaven, favors the traditional interpretation.

10. Gundry, *Church and Tribulation*, 153. For the pretribulational interpretation, see Walvoord, *The Return of the Lord* (Grand Rapids: Dunham, 1955), 55.

11. Contra John F. Walvoord, *The Rapture Question* (rev. ed.; Grand Rapids: Zondervan, 1979), 34–35.

Old Testament verse (Isa. 25:8) with reference to the resurrection of *church* saints in this context (vv. 54–55), Paul may be indicating his belief that Old Testament saints participate in this "change."[12] Further indication that this transformation involves Old Testament saints (and cannot thereby be limited to a separate event for *church* saints) is found in the reference to "the last trumpet." As the commentators note, this does not refer to the last in a series, but to the trumpet that ushers in the "last day."[13] And this trumpet is a feature of the Old Testament day of the Lord at which time the Jewish nation experiences final salvation and judgment (cf. Isa. 27:13; Joel 2:1; Zeph. 1:16; Zech. 9:14). The Isaianic reference is particularly suggestive since the sounding of the "great trumpet" is associated with the gathering up of the Israelites "one by one" (Isa. 27:12). This is probably a description of the gathering of Israel in preparation for entrance into the millennial kingdom—an event that is always posttribulational. Furthermore, it is probable that the trumpet in 1 Corinthians 15:52 is the same as the one mentioned in Matthew 24:31. For when one finds only one reference throughout Jesus' teaching to a trumpet, and it is associated with the gathering of the elect into the kingdom, and further finds Paul making reference to the transformation of saints in preparation for the kingdom when he mentions a trumpet, the parallel can hardly be ignored. But the trumpet sound in Matthew 24:31 is manifestly posttribulational. Thus, while dogmatism is unwarranted, the reference to "the last trumpet" in 1 Corinthians 15:52 would suggest that the "transformation" Paul describes takes place at the time when the Jewish nation experiences its eschatological salvation (Isa. 27:12–13) after the final tribulation (Matt. 24:31).

The third principal text relating to the rapture is 1 Thessalonians 4:13–18. Clearly, Paul is here seeking to comfort the Thessalonian believers over the death of believers. Why were they concerned? It is possible that Paul's forced and sudden departure from Thessalonica had prevented him from teaching the Christians there about the future

---

12. Reese, *Approaching Advent*, 63.

13. G. Kittel and G. Friedrich, eds., *Theological Dictionary of the New Testament*, 10 vols. (Grand Rapids: Eerdmans, 1964–76), 7:87, s.v. "σάλπιγξ"; Anthony C. Thiselton, *The First Epistle to the Corinthians*, NIGTC (Grand Rapids: Eerdmans, 2000), 1296; David E. Garland, *1 Corinthians*, BECNT (Grand Rapids: Baker, 2003), 744.

resurrection of dead believers.[14] However, it is perhaps likelier that the Thessalonians were worried that their deceased brothers and sisters would miss out on the benefits of being "taken up" to be with the Lord at the time of his coming.[15] It is important to note that the comfort Paul offers does not have to do primarily with the position of living believers; nor does he suggest that exemption from the final tribulation is a source of this comfort.[16] His encouragement lies solely in the fact that *all* believers, living or dead, will participate in the glorious events of the parousia and that they will as a result "always be with the Lord."[17] That such a hope, if it included a previous experience in the final tribulation, would not be a comfort to believers is manifestly untrue. For, in fact, these Thessalonians had already experienced very difficult times — they had been converted "in ... severe suffering" (1 Thess. 1:6) and were still undergoing such tribulation (3:3, 7). Nowhere does Paul seek to comfort Christians by promising them exemption from tribulation.

Are there any indications in this description of the rapture and accompanying resurrection as to when it takes place with reference to the final tribulation? The failure of Paul to mention preliminary signs is hardly relevant, for there is no reason for him to include them here — in the light of the extreme suffering that the Thessalonians were already experiencing, he hardly needed to warn them of this. He focuses exclusively on the great hope lying at the end of all earthly distresses. On the other hand, there are four indications that favor a posttribulational setting. First, while little can be definitely concluded from Paul's reference

---

14. See, e.g., Colin R. Nicholl, *From Hope to Despair in Thessalonica: Situating 1 and 2 Thessalonians*, SNTSMS 126 (Cambridge: Cambridge University Press, 2004), 35–38; Vos, *Pauline Eschatology*, 247–51.

15. James Everett Frame, *A Critical and Exegetical Commentary on the Epistle of St. Paul to the Thessalonians*, ICC (Edinburgh: T & T Clark, 1912), 164; A. L. Moore, *1 and 2 Thessalonians*, NCB (London: Nelson, 1969), 108–9; Wanamaker, *Epistles to the Thessalonians*, 166; Abraham J. Malherbe, *The Letters to the Thessalonians: A New Translation with Introduction and Commentary*, AB 32B (New York: Doubleday, 2000), 283–84. Gundry's suggestion that the Thessalonians thought that the dead would have to wait until the end of the millennium to be raised (*Church and Tribulation*, 101) moves in the same direction but with a specificity that is probably not warranted.

16. This seems to be assumed by Walvoord, *Blessed Hope*, 96. The notion that the Thessalonians would have rejoiced in the death of loved ones if they knew that they would thereby escape the final tribulation (D. Edmond Hiebert, *The Thessalonian Epistles: A Call to Readiness* [Chicago: Moody, 1971], 205) is self-refuting. Do all today who hold a posttribulational view rejoice when loved ones die?

17. Reese, *Approaching Advent*, 142.

to "a word of the Lord" in verse 15,[18] there are suggestive parallels between the parousia of 1 Thessalonians 4 and the parousia described by Jesus in the Olivet Discourse. Both refer to a heavenly event with angels (archangel in 1 Thessalonians 4), clouds, a trumpet, and the gathering of believers.[19] And while each of these mentions details not found in the other, none of the details are contradictory. However, the parousia of the Olivet Discourse is posttribulational.

A second indication that the rapture of 1 Thessalonians 4 may be posttribulational is found in the reference to the trumpet, which, as we saw in discussing 1 Corinthians 15, is an established symbol for the ushering in of the time of Israel's salvation and judgment. (And, in keeping with Paul's allusion to the trumpet of God, it should be noted that Zech. 9:14 specifically says that the Lord will sound the trumpet.)

Third, 1 Thessalonians 4:13–16 features a number of elements closely parallel to Daniel 12:1–2: the description of the dead as "sleepers"; the presence of Michael, the archangel (cf. Jude 9); and, of course, a resurrection and deliverance of God's people.[20] But the Daniel passage definitely places the resurrection *after* the final tribulation.

Fourth, the word used by Paul to describe the "meeting" between the living saints and their Lord in the air (*apantēsis*) occurs in references to the visit of dignitaries and generally implies that the "delegation" accompanies the dignitary *back to* the delegation's point of origin.[21] The two other occurrences of this term in the New Testament seem to bear this meaning (Matt. 25:6; Acts 28:15). This would suggest that the

---

18. This could indicate that Paul thinks of a specific word of Christ found in the Gospels (such as Matt. 24:31 or John 11:25–26 [for the latter, see Gundry, *Church and Tribulation*, 102–3]); of the tradition of Jesus' teaching on the parousia (David Wenham, "Paul and the Synoptic Apocalypse" [paper read at the July 1980 meeting of the Tyndale House Gospels Research Project, Cambridge], 6n1; Wanamaker, *Epistles to the Thessalonians*, 170–71); of an unknown saying of Jesus (Morris, *Thessalonians*, 141; Nicholl, *From Hope to Despair*, 38–41); or of a revelation received by Paul (Malherbe, *Letters to the Thessalonians*, 267–68; Milligan, *Thessalonians*, 58; Hiebert, *Thessalonian Epistles*, 195).

19. For these parallels, see especially J. B. Orchard, "Thessalonians and the Synoptic Gospels," *Biblica* 19 (1938): 19–42; Lars Hartman, *Prophecy Interpreted: The Formation of Some Jewish Apocalyptic Texts and of the Eschatological Discourse Mark 13 Par.*, ConBNT 1 (Lund: Gleerup, 1966), 188–89; Wenham, "Synoptic Apocalypse," 4–5; idem, *Paul: Follower of Jesus or Founder of Christianity?* (Grand Rapids: Eerdmans, 1995), 305–16.

20. Hartman, *Prophecy Interpreted*, 188–89.

21. See esp. Green, *Letters to the Thessalonians*, 226–28; N. T. Wright, *The Resurrection of the Son of God*, Christian Origins and the Question of God 3 (Minneapolis: Fortress, 2003), 217–18; Nicholl, *From Hope to Despair*, 43–45.

saints, after meeting the Lord in the air, accompany him back to earth instead of going with him to heaven. To be sure, the word does not have to bear this technical meaning, nor is it certain that a return to the point of origin must be immediate.[22] But the point is still suggestive.

It may be concluded that the details of the description of the parousia and rapture in 1 Thessalonians 4:13–18 do not allow a certain conclusion as to when these take place with reference to the final tribulation. Such indications as there are, however, favor a posttribulational setting. This we have found to be the case also in 1 Corinthians 15:51–52, while John 14:1–4 sheds no light on the question either way. The implications of this must not be overlooked. We have discovered that the terms used to describe the second advent are all applied to a posttribulational coming and that believers are exhorted to look forward to that coming. Any indication that this coming is to be a two-stage event, in which the rapture is separated from the final manifestation, would have to come from passages describing that event. *We can now conclude that no evidence for such a separation is found in any of the three principal texts on the rapture.* On the contrary, such evidence as exists is in favor of locating the rapture after the final tribulation, at the same time as the final parousia. But there are other important passages related to the parousia yet to be examined before final conclusions can be drawn.

1 Thessalonians 5:1 – 11

After the depiction of the rapture and parousia in 1 Thessalonians 4, Paul turns to the subject of the "day of the Lord" in chapter 5. He introduces this topic with the phrase: "Now (*de*), brothers and sisters, about times and dates we do not need to write to you" (v. 1 TNIV). Since this "day" includes the destruction of unbelievers (v. 3), it is clear that a posttribulational event is described. The question to be asked, then, is this: does Paul intimate that the Thessalonian Christians to whom he writes may still be on earth when the day comes? Three considerations are relevant: the relationship between chapters 4 and 5, the meaning of "day of the Lord," and the nature and basis of Paul's exhortations in 5:1–11.

It is sometimes claimed that the *de* introducing chapter 5 demonstrates a transition to a wholly new topic and that it is therefore

---

22. Henry C. Thiessen, *Will the Church Pass through the Tribulation?* 2nd ed. (New York: Loizeaux Brothers, 1941), 42; Hiebert, *Thessalonian Epistles*, 202.

inappropriate to include the rapture (4:13–18) as part of the "day" in 5:1–11. Three considerations cast doubt on this conclusion. First, while *de* generally denotes a mild contrast, it also occurs frequently "as a transitional particle pure and simple, without any contrast intended"[23] (note the TNIV translation quoted above). Second, even if a contrast is intended by Paul, one must determine the *nature* of that contrast. Rather than distinguishing two separate events, Paul may be contrasting the effect of the same event on two different groups — believers and unbelievers. Third, observe how Paul speaks of "times and dates" in verse 1 without specifying the time or date of *what*. The omission of any specific event here could indicate that the previous topic is in mind.

Next, then, we must seek to determine what Paul includes in the "day of the Lord." Can the rapture be part of that day? In the Old Testament, the day of the Lord (also "that day," etc.) denotes a decisive intervention of God for judgment and deliverance.[24] It can refer to a relatively *near* event or to the *final* climactic event — it is not always clear that the prophets distinguished the two. Although the day is frequently described as one of judgment, deliverance for the people of God is often involved also (cf. Isa. 27; Jer. 30:8–9; Joel 2:32; 3:18; Obad. 15–17; et al.). In the New Testament, the term is almost universally related to the end. From the great variety of expressions that are used in the New Testament, it is clear that there is no fixed terminology[25] and that distinctions on that basis cannot be drawn.[26]

---

23. BDAG; cf. also Margaret E. Thrall, *Greek Particles in the New Testament: Linguistic and Exegetical Studies*, NTTS 3 (Grand Rapids: Eerdmans, 1962), 51–52.

24. Cf. H. H. Rowley, *The Faith of Israel: Aspects of Old Testament Thought* (London: SCM, 1956), 178–200.

25. It is probable that at least eighteen different expressions refer to this concept: (1) "The day": Rom. 13:12, 13 (?); Heb. 10:25; "This day": 1 Thess. 5:4; (2) "The great Day": Jude 6; (3) "That day": Matt. 7:22; 24:36; 25:13; Luke 17:31; 21:34; 2 Thess. 1:10; 2 Tim. 1:12, 18; 4:8; (4) "The last day": John 6:39, 40, 44, 54; 11:24; 12:48; (5) "The day of judgment": Matt. 10:15; 11:22, 24; 12:36; 2 Peter 2:9; 3:7; 1 John 4:17; (6) "The day of visitation": 1 Peter 2:12 (?); (7) "The day of wrath": Rom. 2:5; (8) "The day when God judges": Rom. 2:16; (9) "The day of evil": Eph. 6:13; (10) "The day of redemption": Eph. 4:30; (11) "The day of God": 2 Peter 3:12; (12) "The day of God Almighty": Rev. 16:14; (13) "The day of the Lord": Acts 2:20; 1 Cor. 5:5; 1 Thess. 5:2; 2 Thess. 2:2; 2 Peter 3:10; (14) "The day of Christ": Phil. 1:10; 2:16; (15) "The day of the Lord Jesus": 2 Cor. 1:14; (16) "The day of Jesus Christ": Phil. 1:6; (17) "The day of our Lord Jesus Christ": 1 Cor. 1:8; (18) "The day of the Son of Man": Luke 17:30.

26. Note particularly the way Paul, when referring to the day, can combine "Lord" and "Christ" in one expression (1 Cor. 1:8); similarly "Lord" and "Jesus" (2 Cor. 1:14). Surely this suggests that since for Paul Jesus Christ *is* the Lord, he uses terms such as "day of the Lord" and "day of Christ" interchangeably. Walvoord makes an interesting admission in his argu-

All agree that the final judgment is included, but is the final tribulation also part of the day of the Lord? Several factors suggest that it is not. First, no reference to the eschatological "day" in the New Testament clearly includes a description of the final tribulation. In fact, it is interesting that the only two occurrences in Revelation (6:17; 16:14) refer to the final judgment brought through the parousia. Second, Malachi 4:5 (the coming of Elijah) and Joel 2:3 (cosmic portents) place what are generally agreed to be tribulational events *before* the Day (cf. Acts 2:20). Third, Paul seems to suggest in 2 Thessalonians 2 that the day cannot come until certain, clearly tribulational, events transpire. There is good basis, then, for thinking that Paul uses "day (of the Lord)" language as generally interchangeable with the parousia.[27]

This being the case, it is not surprising to find that the New Testament associates the final resurrection of the saints with the day of the Lord. Five times in John's gospel we find claims that Jesus will raise those who believe in him on "the last day" (6:39, 40, 44, 54; 11:24). And since the rapture occurs at the same time as the resurrection of believers, the rapture, too, must be part of that day. That this is so finds confirmation in the fact that Paul frequently describes the day as an event to which believers in this life look forward (1 Cor. 1:8; Phil. 1:6, 10; 2:16; 2 Tim. 4:8; cf. also Heb. 10:25)—it is a "day of redemption" (Eph. 4:30).

Thus, in the New Testament, the day includes the destruction of the ungodly at the parousia of Christ, along with the rapture and the resurrection of the righteous dead. That is, for Paul as for the other New Testament writers, the "day" is "a general denotation of the great future that dawns with Christ's coming."[28] The fact that the final tribulation seems not to be part of that day suggests that it precedes all these events, but this is not certain. What is certain is that believers cannot

ment for distinguishing "day of Christ" from "day of the Lord": "If the pretribulational rapture is established on other grounds, these references seem to refer specifically to the rapture rather than to the time of judgment on the world" (*Blessed Hope*, 119). In other words, the terms by themselves offer no basis for such a distinction.

27. Note how Paul parallels "day" language with the parousia in his prayers that believers might be "blameless" (1 Cor. 1:8; Phil. 1:10; 1 Thess. 3:13; 5:23) in his boasting about his churches (Phil. 2:16; 1 Thess. 2:19) and in his hope for salvation (1 Cor. 5:5; 15:23). See on this point Nicholl, *From Hope to Despair*, 51; J. L. Kreitzer, *Jesus and God in Paul's Eschatology*, JSNTSS (Sheffield: JSOT, 1987), 112–29.

28. Herman Ridderbos, *Paul: An Outline of His Theology* (Grand Rapids: Eerdmans, 1975), 530–31. Cf. also George Eldon Ladd, *A Theology of the New Testament* (Grand Rapids: Eerdmans, 1974), 555.

be excluded from involvement in the events of 1 Thessalonians 5 simply because the day of the Lord is the topic.

In 1 Thessalonians 5 Paul's emphasis is undoubtedly on judgment, which comes suddenly and certainly on those not expecting it (v. 3). At the very time that people are proclaiming "peace and safety," judgment comes upon them. Paul is probably dependent here on passages such as Jeremiah 6:14, which depicts Israelites who keep saying, "Peace, peace," when the Lord claims there is no peace. As in Jeremiah's day, people are finding false security in the face of imminent judgment.[29] Does Paul suggest that the Thessalonian believers may have a relationship to this judgment? If so, this would constitute strong support for the posttribulational position, because either (1) believers will be alive during the final tribulation (if this is the judgment Paul thinks of), or (2) believers will be on earth when the posttribulational parousia occurs (if the judgment occurs then).

That Christians *are* associated with the day is the clear inference of 1 Thessalonians 5:4. Here Paul tells the Thessalonian believers, "But you, brothers and sisters, are not in darkness so that this day should surprise you like a thief" (TNIV). Why, if believers are raptured *before* the final tribulation, would Paul have qualified his assertion with "as a thief"? Much more appropriate would have been the simple statement "that the day not overtake you." If you had a friend visiting from another country who was worried about becoming involved in a war you both knew would soon break out, and if you knew that he would, in fact, be safely out of the country before it started, you would assure him by telling him, "Don't worry—this war will not affect you." Only if you knew that he would be present during it would you say, "Don't worry—this war will not affect you as the kind of disaster it will be for citizens of this country." In other words, what Paul rather clearly suggests is that the day overtakes both believers and unbelievers, but only for the latter does it come "as a thief"—unexpected and harmful.[30]

---

29. See esp. Nicholl, *From Hope to Despair*, 54. The Jeremiah parallel also makes clear that people could very well be claiming such peace and security in the midst of the final tribulation (see E. Michael Rusten, "A Critical Evaluation of Dispensational Interpretation of the Book of Revelation" [PhD diss., New York University, 1977], 488–89; Norman F. Douty, *Has Christ's Return Two Stages?* [New York: Pageant, 1956], 76–77).

30. Nicholl, *From Hope to Despair*, 52–53; W. J. Grier, *The Momentous Event: A Discussion of Scripture Teaching on the Second Advent* (London: Banner of Truth Trust, 1941), 71; Payne, *Imminent Appearing*, 68–69.

A second reason for thinking that believers will be present for the day of the Lord (after the final tribulation) is the close relationship between this text and two gospel passages that encourage watchfulness in view of the *posttribulational* parousia—Matthew 24:42–44 and Luke 21:34–36. The parallels between the latter text and 1 Thessalonians 5:2–6 are particularly compelling—both have as their subject the day, which, it is warned, will come upon those unprepared suddenly and unexpectedly ("like a trap," Luke 21:34); both emphasize that there will be no escape (cf. Luke 21:35); both encourage believers to watch in light of that coming "day"; and both use the same verb (*epistēmi*, "come upon") and the same adjective (*aiphnidios*, "suddenly") about the day (the latter word occurs only in these two passages in biblical Greek).[31] There is every reason for thinking that the same event is depicted in both and, in fact, strong indications that one is dependent on the other. But if Luke 21:34–36 encourages watchfulness in light of the posttribulational coming (as both, e.g., J. Dwight Pentecost and John Walvoord argue[32]), there is every reason to think that 1 Thessalonians 5:2–6 does also.

Finally, the logical connection between Paul's assertion in 1 Thessalonians 5:4–5 and the following exhortations is also better explained if the Thessalonians are to experience the day. It is not Paul's point to encourage the believers to "watch" for the day so that they might escape it. The verbs Paul employs in his commands (vv. 6, 8) do not connote watching for something, but faithfulness to Christ, as incumbent upon those who belong to the "light" and to the day.[33] Nor can 1 Thessalonians 5:9 be used to argue that Paul promises believers such an escape. Paul never uses "wrath" without qualifiers to denote a period of time, and in view of its contrast with "salvation," it must indicate the condemning judgment of God associated with the day, not the day itself.[34]

---

31. For these parallels, see especially Wenham, "Synoptic Apocalypse," 10; idem, *Paul*, 307–11; Hartman, *Prophecy Interpreted*, 192.

32. *Things to Come*, 161–62; *Rapture Question*, 111–13.

33. On this meaning of the terms *grēgoreō* ("watch") and *nephō* ("be sober"), see esp. Evald Lövestam, *Spiritual Wakefulness in the New Testament* (Lunds Universitets Årsskrift, n.s., 55; Lund: Gleerup, 1963). The phrase "sons of the day" (v. 5) also probably associates believers with the "day of the Lord," since the eschatological dimensions of the term are to be included here (Lövestam, *Spiritual Wakefulness*, 49–51; Best, *Thessalonians*, 210; Morris, *Thessalonians*, 156). D. E. H. Whiteley, however (*Thessalonians in the Revised Standard Version*, New Clarendon Bible [Oxford: Oxford University Press, 1979], 78), takes the view that no such eschatological overtones are to be seen in the term.

34. Cf., e.g., Frame, *Thessalonians*, 188; Best, *Thessalonians*, 216.

To summarize Paul's argument: the salvation to which God has destined the Thessalonians (5:9), and which they already experience (5:5), should act as a stimulus to holy living—holy living that will enable them to avoid experiencing the day in its unexpected and destructive features. In other words, Paul exhorts the Thessalonians to live godly lives in order that they might avoid the judgmental aspect of that day—not that they might avoid the day itself. Whether this day includes the final tribulation or, as is more probable, the climactic return of Christ at the end of the final tribulation, believers on earth are clearly involved in it; and only a posttribulational rapture allows for this. Finally, this interpretation provides a coherent explanation of the transition from chapter 4 to chapter 5—whereas Paul has comforted believers about the position of the dead at the parousia in chapter 4, he turns to exhort the living about their responsibilities in light of that parousia in chapter 5.

2 Thessalonians 1 - 2

Second Thessalonians was written by Paul shortly after 1 Thessalonians in order to correct some misapprehensions about eschatology, particularly with respect to the erroneous belief that the end had to occur almost immediately.[35] Thus, Paul in chapter 1 assures the Thessalonians of the certainty of the end, with the judgment it will bring on those who are now "distressing" them. Then he seeks to calm their excitement over the nearness of the end in chapter 2.[36]

In 2 Thessalonians 1:5–7 Paul appears to provide strong support for the view that believers will not be raptured until the parousia of Christ at the end of the tribulation. For there can be no doubt that in verses 7–8 Paul depicts this coming in glory, "when the Lord Jesus is revealed from heaven in blazing fire with his powerful angels." Yet it is at this time that the believers who are suffering tribulation are given "rest." In other words, it is only at the posttribulational parousia that believers experience deliverance from the sufferings of this age. Attempts to avoid this conclusion take two forms.

---

35. I assume the majority view, that 1 Thessalonians was indeed written before 2 Thessalonians (see, e.g., F. F. Bruce, *1 and 2 Thessalonians*, WBC 45 [Waco, Tex.: Word, 1982], xli–xliv; contra, e.g., Wanamaker, *Epistles to the Thessalonians*, 37–44).

36. Johannes Munck, "I Thess. I. 9–10 and the Missionary Preaching of Paul: Textual Exegesis and Hermeneutical Reflexions," *NTS* 9 (1962–63): 100.

First, it is argued that since the Thessalonians were not in fact delivered at the time of Christ's return (they died long before it) and their persecutors will likewise not be destroyed at the return (being dead, they will not experience judgment until the conclusion of the millennium), Paul must be saying that "God in His own time will destroy their persecutors."[37] But not only does this interpretation fail to explain the fact that Paul obviously links both the "rest" and the destruction to "the Revelation of the Lord Jesus" (how can this mean "in God's own time"?), it overlooks the fact that Paul consistently writes as if the generation in which he lived might be the last. In both 1 Corinthians 15:51 and 1 Thessalonians 4:15, he indicates that the participants in the rapture are "*we* who don't sleep/are alive." Does this mean that Paul cannot be describing the rapture in these texts? Moreover, the eschatological "rest" Paul describes here does come to all believers at the time of Christ's revelation—for dead saints (including the Thessalonians) through resurrection; for living saints through the rapture. And that Paul associates the destruction of unbelievers with the "revelation" of Christ is likewise no difficulty: Scripture often associates events that will, in fact, be separated by the millennium (see John 5:29).

A second way of avoiding a posttribulation interpretation of these verses is to claim that the "rest" promised to the Thessalonians need not occur at the rapture.[38] While this point must be appreciated—believers who die before the Lord's return are certainly delivered from earthly trials before the rapture—the clear temporal link between the rest and the "revelation" of Christ cannot be severed. The only satisfactory way of explaining this text is to assume that Paul addresses the Thessalonians as if they would be alive at the parousia—and he states that they experience "rest" only at the posttribulational revelation of Christ.

Second Thessalonians 2:1–12 is a minefield of exegetical difficulties. I will not have the space here to comment on them all, far less to "solve" them. Despite these problems, enough about the text is sufficiently clear to provide strong support for the posttribulational rapture position.

Paul's eschatological teaching in this section is directed against some kind of false teaching that has led the Thessalonians to become

---

37. Walvoord, *Blessed Hope*, 123–24.
38. Allen Beechick, *The Pre-Tribulation Rapture* (Denver: Accent, 1980), 122.

"unsettled" and "alarmed" (v. 2). It is not clear whether these words connote an excited, agitated state or a state of alarm and fear.[39] The latter word, however (*throeomai*), is used elsewhere in the New Testament only in the Olivet Discourse, where Jesus urges the disciples not to be "alarmed" about "wars and rumors of wars," because "such things must happen, but the end is still to come" (Matt. 24:6; Mark 13:7). Paul's point in 2 Thessalonians 2 is roughly similar: he urges the Thessalonians not to become alarmed about "the coming of our Lord Jesus Christ and our being gathered to him" (v. 1), because, he goes on to argue, certain events must take place before the end comes. Paul says that the false teaching was claiming that "the day of the Lord has already come" (v. 2). I argued earlier that "day of the Lord" is essentially equivalent in Paul to the parousia (see v. 1). But how could it be that the Thessalonians were under the impression that the parousia had already occurred? One option is to translate the verb here "is about to come" (see KJV). But this would be an unprecedented translation of this verb in this form.[40] Perhaps, then, the final tribulation *should* be included in the day, and the Thessalonians regarded their extreme sufferings as evidence that they were in it. Their "alarm" may then have been caused by the belief that they had missed the rapture, which they knew to be pretribulational.[41] But the final tribulation can hardly be a part of the "day," since Paul goes on to argue that the "day" cannot come until events usually associated with tribulation had already transpired. Another option is to think that the false teachers had adopted a "spiritualized" view of eschatological events, according to which Christ's coming, the resurrection of believers, and the rapture had all already occurred.[42] But it is perhaps like-

39. The verb translated "unsettled" is from *saleuō* and means "shake." It is usually applied in the New Testament to physical phenomena, but note Acts 17:13, where Luke says that the Jews in Thessalonica were "agitating" the crowds against Paul. The second verb, "alarmed," translates a form of *throeomai*, which means "to be aroused" or "frightened" (BDAG). Many interpreters think that the verbs together connote "a continuous state of nervous excitement and anxiety" (Best, *Thessalonians*, 275), while others think they suggest fear (Nicholl, *From Hope to Despair*, 126–32).

40. Contra the view I adopted in the first edition of this book (and see also Morris, *Thessalonians*, 216–17), the verb Paul uses here, *enistēmi*, seems always to mean "has come" when used in a past tense form (see, e.g., Wanamaker, *Epistles to the Thessalonians*, 240).

41. John F. Walvoord, *The Thessalonian Epistles* (Findlay, Ohio: Dunham, n.d.), 115; Hiebert, *Thessalonian Epistles*, 304.

42. G. K. Beale, *1–2 Thessalonians*, IVPNTC (Downers Grove, Ill.: InterVarsity, 2003), 199–203.

lier that they were being encouraged by the false teaching to think that their suffering meant that the complex of events included in the parousia had already begun (see NLT: "the day of the Lord has already begun"). However we explain this statement, one thing is clear — the Thessalonians had not experienced the rapture, yet they thought themselves to be in the day. How does Paul disabuse them of this notion?

Paul does so by citing events that must occur before that day comes.[43] According to the apostle, there are two of these: the "rebellion" and the revelation of "the man of lawlessness ... the man doomed to destruction" (2 Thess. 2:3). This "rebellion" (*apostasia*) should be understood as a religious rebellion against God, including a departure from the faith of many from within the church itself.[44] The "man of lawlessness" is probably to be identified as the eschatological Antichrist, a figure also described in Revelation 13:1–8 and based on the depiction of the usurper of God in the book of Daniel (Dan. 7:8, 20–25; 11:36–39).[45] Paul claims that this Antichrist will "oppose and will exalt himself over everything that is called God or is worshiped, so that he sets himself up in God's temple, proclaiming himself to be God." This language is very reminiscent of Daniel's prediction of an antigodly king who will "exalt

---

43. Paul never furnishes an apodosis (a "then" clause) to complete his protasis ("If first the apostasy does not come and the man of lawlessness is not revealed") in v. 3. But there is general agreement that something like "then that day has not come yet" must be supplied (cf. TNIV; NASB; ESV; NLT; and especially the excellent discussion of Best [*Thessalonians*, 280–81]. Best offers a penetrating critique of the novel theory put forth by Charles H. Giblin [*The Threat to Faith: An Exegetical and Theological Re-examination of 2 Thessalonians 2*, AnBib 31 (Rome: Pontifical Biblical Institute, 1967), 122–35]).

44. This interpretation of *apostasia* is based on the usage of the term in biblical Greek (Josh. 22:22; 2 Chron. 29:19; Jer. 2:19; Acts 21:21) and on the observation that a religious rebellion was frequently associated with the time of the end (as in Mark 13:6ff.). Cf., e.g., Gundry, *Church and Tribulation*, 115–16; Desmond Ford, *The Abomination of Desolation in Biblical Eschatology* (Washington, D.C.: University Press of America, 1979), 201–3; Beale, *1–2 Thessalonians*, 203. A few scholars argue that the word should be translated "departure" and have seen in it a reference to the rapture. See most recently, H. Wayne House, "Apostasia in 2 Thessalonians 2:3: Apostasy or Rapture?" in *When the Trumpet Sounds*, ed. Thomas Ice and Timothy Deny (Eugene, Ore.: Harvest House, 1995), 261–96; see also E. Schuyler English, *Re-thinking the Rapture* (Traveler's Rest, S.C.: Southern Bible Book House, 1954), 67–71; Kenneth S. Wuest, "The Rapture: Precisely When?" *BSac* 114 (1957): 64–66; Gordon Lewis, "Biblical Evidence for Pretribulationism," *BSac* 125 (1968): 217–18; L. J. Wood, *The Bible and Future Events* (Grand Rapids: Zondervan, 1973), 87–88; James Montgomery Boice, *The Last and Future World* (Grand Rapids: Zondervan, 1974), 42–43. But such a translation is virtually impossible. See the full discussion in Gundry, *Church and Tribulation*, 114–18; and note that pretribulational advocates Hiebert (*Thessalonian Epistles*, 305–6) and Walvoord (*Blessed Hope*, 135) also dismiss this view.

45. Ford (*Abomination*, 199–200, 207) provides a good discussion of the parallels between Daniel and the portrayal of Antichrist in the New Testament.

and magnify himself above every god" (11:36). This same king, Daniel also says, will "with flattery" "corrupt those who have violated the covenant" (11:32) — and this sounds a lot like the "rebellion" Paul alludes to. Paul's prediction here, then, appears to reflect a reading of Daniel that sees in his language a reference to an end-time antigodly leader. Paul's claim that this last and greatest "antichrist" will take his seat in the temple may suggest that this Antichrist will work from within the church, since the New Testament suggests that the presence of God that was formerly found in the temple is now found in the new covenant community, the body of Christ.[46] But it is also possible that Paul envisages the Antichrist revealing himself in a literal Jerusalem temple.

What is crucial to notice in Paul's response to the Thessalonians' unrest is that he does not say anything about the rapture as a necessary antecedent to the day. If the Thessalonians were to be raptured before the day, we would expect Paul to say something like, "You know that your present sufferings cannot represent the final tribulation, because you will be taken to heaven before then."[47] To use the illustration introduced earlier, if you knew that your foreign friend was to be safely out of the country by the time war broke out, and if he, in seeing great unrest beginning to happen, thought that he was becoming involved in it, would you calm him by telling him that certain events had to happen before the war without reminding him that he would be safely out of the country when it actually occurred? The fact the Paul points to the nonpresence of an indisputable tribulation event, the revelation of the Antichrist, as evidence that the day has not come, surely implies that believers will see it when it does occur. Furthermore, it cannot be argued in reply that Paul simply assumes the Thessalonians know that the rapture will occur before that day. The fact that the Thessalonians believe themselves to be in the day shows either that they had forgotten or were never taught that the rapture preceded it. In either case, it is difficult to see why Paul would not mention it.

Before leaving this text, one final argument brought against a posttribulational interpretation must be dealt with. It is often argued that the

---

46. See esp. Beale, *1–2 Thessalonians*, 207–10; idem, *The Temple and the Church's Mission: A Biblical Theology of the Dwelling Place of God*, NSBT 17 (Downers Grove, Ill.: InterVarsity, 2004), 269–92.

47. Although Walvoord (*Blessed Hope*, 118) gives this as essentially Paul's answer here, there is simply no evidence in the text for such a reference.

tribulational events described here by Paul cannot transpire until the church is physically removed, because it is the Holy Spirit through the church that now "restrains" the Antichrist (2 Thess. 2:6–7). Three points need to be made with reference to this argument. First, it is unlikely that the Holy Spirit is the one whom Paul describes in these verses. There seems to be no reason for using such mysterious language if the Holy Spirit is intended, and it is not probable that Paul would have spoken of the Spirit as being "taken out of the way."[48] Neither does the fact that Paul uses both a masculine participle ("he who restrains") and a neuter participle ("that which restrains"), sometimes adduced in support of this interpretation, favor it. I can find no place in Paul's writings where he uses a neuter term to designate the Holy Spirit except where it is directly dependent on the term *pneuma* ("Spirit"; the Greek word is neuter). Second, even if the Holy Spirit is intended, there is nothing in the passage that would indicate that his restraining activity must be carried out through the church.[49] Third, and most important, it is improper to base very much on a text that is so notoriously obscure— the verb that Paul uses here (*katechō*) can be translated "hold back" or "hold fast," "occupy,"[50] and has been understood as signifying, among other things, Rome/the emperor,[51] civil government,[52] God and his power,[53] Michael the archangel,[54] the preaching of the gospel/Paul,[55]

48. Morris, *Thessalonians*, 228–29. We are assuming, with most commentators, that the subject of the *heōs* clause in v. 7 is the restrainer. It is interesting to note that some of the church fathers already were refuting the view that the restrainer is the Spirit (Rigaux, *Thessaloniciens*, 261).

49. Gundry, *Church and Tribulation*, 125–26.

50. Frame, *Thessalonians*, 259–61; Best, *Thessalonians*, 301; D. W. B. Robinson, "II Thess. 2:6: 'That which restrains' or 'That which holds sway,'" *Studia Evangelica* 2, Texte und Untersuchungen 87 (Berlin: Akademie, 1964): 635–38.

51. Tertullian, *Apology* 32, and many other church fathers; Otto Betz, "Der Katechon," *NTS* 9 (1962–63): 283–85; Bruce, *1 and 2 Thessalonians*, 171–72.

52. Milligan, *Thessalonians*, 101; William Hendriksen, *New Testament Commentary: Exposition of I and II Thessalonians* (Grand Rapids: Baker, 1955), 181–82.

53. Ladd, *Blessed Hope*, 95; Ridderbos, *Paul*, 524–25.

54. See esp. Nicholl, *From Hope to Despair*, 225–49; and also Beale, *1–2 Thessalonians*, 214–17; Orchard, "Thessalonians," 40–41; Rusten, "Revelation," 449–57; F. Prat, *The Theology of Saint Paul* (Westminster, Md.: Newman, 1952), 1:80–83.

55. In the early church Theodoret and Theodore of Mopsuestia; Oscar Cullmann, *Christ and Time: The Primitive Christian Conception of Time and History* (Philadelphia: Westminster, 1950), 164–66; Johannes Munck, *Paul and the Salvation of Mankind* (Richmond, Va.: John Knox, 1959), 36–43; A. L. Moore, *The Parousia in the New Testament*, NovTSup 13 (Leiden: Brill, 1966), 112–13; J. Christian Beker, *Paul the Apostle: The Triumph of God in Life and Thought* (Philadelphia: Fortress, 1980), 161.

Satan,[56] general evil forces,[57] a combination of benevolent forces,[58] the Jewish state and James,[59] or a mythic symbol with no particular content.

The Olivet Discourse

Many scholars have claimed that the Olivet Discourse is the most difficult portion of the Gospels to interpret. In investigating this discourse, it will be necessary to confine ourselves to those questions that are of relevance for our present topic: (1) What did the disciples ask? (2) Does the "abomination of desolation" and tribulation mentioned in conjunction with it refer to end-time events? (3) Is Jesus' end-of-the-age parousia described in Matthew 24:29–31//Mark 13:24–27? (4) Does Matthew 24:31//Mark 13:27 refer to the rapture? (5) To whom is the discourse addressed?

Jesus has just shocked the disciples by predicting the complete destruction of the temple, which they have been admiring (Mark 13:1–2). In response to this, the disciples ask, "When will these things happen? And what will be the sign that they are all about to be fulfilled?" Matthew's version of the same question shows that the disciples are associating the destruction of the temple with the events of the "end of the age": "Tell us, when will this happen [the destruction of the temple], and what will be the sign of your coming and of the end of the age?" (Matt. 24:3). It is probable that the disciples, in keeping with much Jewish eschatological expectation, believed that the close of the age would include the destruction of the temple.[60] The relationship between these two events in Jesus' answer constitutes one of the great difficulties in the discourse. Traditionally, many evangelicals have viewed the whole of the Olivet Discourse as a prophecy about events that will transpire at the very end of history: Jesus describes the

56. The view of J. Coppens, according to Giblin (*Threat to Faith*, 14).

57. Wanamaker, *Epistles to the Thessalonians*, 252; Leas Sirard, "La Parousie de l'Antichrist, 2 Thess. 2, 3–9," in *Studiorum Paulinorum Congressus Internationalis Catholicus 1961*, AnBib 17–18 (Rome: Pontifical Biblical Institute, 1963), 2:94–99; Giblin, *Threat to Faith*, 164–246.

58. Ford, *Abomination*, 216–22.

59. B. B. Warfield, "The Prophecies of St. Paul," in *Biblical and Theological Studies* (Grand Rapids: Baker, 1968), 473–74.

60. C. E. B. Cranfield, "St. Mark 13," *SJT* 6 and 7 (1953, 1954): 6, 195–96; Lloyd Gaston, *No Stone on Another: Studies in the Significance of the Fall of Jerusalem in the Synoptic Gospels*, NovTSup 23 (Leiden: Brill, 1970), 12.

final tribulation, with particular reference to the manifestation of the Antichrist (the "abomination of desolation") and his climactic return in glory at the end of history. A few interpreters (growing in number) take just the opposite approach: they think that the whole discourse relates to events that took place in the first century. Most interpreters, however, think that some combination of these two approaches is necessary to explain all the data. I will argue for this general approach in what follows and then draw out the significance of my conclusions for the question of the timing of the rapture with respect to the final tribulation.

Jesus' prediction in Mark 13:14 and Matthew 24:15 that "the abomination that causes desolation" prophesied by Daniel would stand in the "holy place" (that is, the temple) is the best place to gain entry into the discussion of Jesus' reference in the discourse.[61] Is Jesus envisaging an event that transpired in AD 70, when Jerusalem and its temple were destroyed and desecrated by the armies of Rome? Or is he referring to the end-time Antichrist? Several indications could point to the latter interpretation. First, the phrase "abomination of desolation" clearly alludes to the same prophecies in Daniel that we have just seen Paul citing to describe the end-time Antichrist (in 2 Thess. 2:3–4). Second, Mark (13:14) suggests, by using a masculine participle after the neuter "abomination," that he is thinking of a person—and, again, the similarities to the Antichrist described in 2 Thessalonians 2 are clear. Third, Jesus' claim that this "abomination that causes desolation" will come in the context of "days of distress [or tribulation] unequaled from the beginning, when God created the world, until now—and never to be equaled again" (Mark 13:19) points to an end-time event. The strength of this language suggests that only the final tribulation can be in view.[62] This appears to be confirmed by the fact that Jesus goes on to

---

61. This phrase is found in similar form in Daniel 8:13; 9:27; 11:31; 12:11. Of these, Jesus' use of the term has most in common with 9:27 (Beda Rigaux, "bdelugma tes eremoseos Mc. 13, 14; Matt. 24, 15," *Biblica* 40 [1959]: 678–79; Ford, *Abomination*, 153–54). The phrase is usually taken to indicate a detestable idol that causes religious desecration (Cranfield, "Mark 13," 298–99; G. R. Beasley-Murray, *A Commentary on Mark 13* [London: Macmillan, 1957], 55), but it may be that connotations of physical destruction should not be eliminated (Rudolf Pesch, *Naherwartungen: Tradition und Redaktion in Mk 13*, KBANT [Düsseldorf: Patmos, 1968], 142; Ford, *Abomination*, 167–68).

62. John F. Walvoord, "Christ's Olivet Discourse on the End of the Age," *BSac* 128 (1971): 208. It is sometimes argued that this phraseology is proverbial and need not be taken in its literal force (Beasley-Murray, *Commentary*, 78).

claim (in Matthew's version) that this tribulation *immediately* precedes the parousia.[63]

On the other hand, several other factors suggest that Jesus associates the "abomination of desolation" with the events of AD 70, when the Romans, in putting down the Jewish rebellion, entered the sanctuary (thus desecrating it) and destroyed much of it. First, and most obviously, Jesus would have to refer to this event if he is being truthful in answering the disciples' question. They asked when the temple they were looking at would be destroyed (not when some future temple might be destroyed)—and that temple was destroyed in AD 70. Second, Luke's version of the Olivet Discourse appears to provide strong support for an AD 70 reference. In place of "the abomination of desolation," he refers to "Jerusalem being surrounded by armies" (21:20). To be sure, this could refer either to AD 70 or to the end of the age. But he goes on to record as a consequence of this event the scattering of the Jewish people among the Gentiles (21:24)—and this only makes sense if he refers to AD 70.[64] Third, the warnings that Jesus issues on the basis of the presence of the "abomination" in both Mark and Matthew seem to envisage a local situation: "Let those who are in Judea flee" (Matt. 24:16; Mark 13:14); "Pray that your flight will not take place in winter or on the Sabbath" (Matt. 24:20). And other warnings in this context do not fit with the magnitude of judgment that will come in the end time. Why would people faced with the universal disasters of the final tribulation have to worry about whether they were on the housetop or in a field when they took place (see Matt. 24:17–19; Mark 13:15–18)? Finally, a reference to AD 70 helps explain Jesus' otherwise puzzling and problematic claim in Matthew 24:34 and Mark 13:30 that "this generation will certainly not pass away until all these things have happened." Attempts to make

---

63. Contra Alfred Plummer (*An Exegetical Commentary on the Gospel according to St. Matthew* [London: Robert Scott, 1915], 335), Matthew's "immediately" (*eutheōs*, 24:29) cannot be deprived of its temporal force in light of Matthean usage. Nor can "in these days" in Mark 13:27 be taken as a general expression for eschatological time (contra Henry Barclay Swete, *Commentary on Mark* [1913; repr., Grand Rapids: Kregel, 1997], 310–11; William Lane, *The Gospel according to Mark*, NICNT [Grand Rapids: Eerdmans, 1974], 474).

64. Luke seems to distinguish carefully between AD 70 and the time of the end; many would attribute vv. 8–24 to the destruction of Jerusalem in AD 70 and vv. 25ff. to the end (cf. M. J. Lagrange, *L'Evangile selon Saint Luc*, 6th ed. [Paris: Gabalda, 1941], 521; William Hendriksen, *New Testament Commentary: Exposition of the Gospel according to Luke* [Grand Rapids: Baker, 1978], 937).

"this generation" mean something other than "those alive with me right now" are unconvincing, so Jesus must be claiming that events he has just described will take place within forty years or so of his speaking. If the first part of the discourse (Mark 13:5–23) describes events that took place before AD 70, his claim would be quite understandable.

Of course, this same point is used to argue that all of the events Jesus narrates in the discourse must have taken place before AD 70—including the parousia of Matthew 24:30//Mark 13:26. *Parousia*, it is argued, need not refer to the final "coming" of Christ in glory. It can refer to any "coming" or "appearance" of Jesus—and there are suggestions in the New Testament that the Roman destruction of Jerusalem was seen by early Christians as a "coming" of Christ in judgment on the city and on Israel.[65] But this view—the so-called "preterist" view—has some serious problems. First, the language of Jesus' "coming" with clouds (dependent on Dan. 7:13) probably always has reference to the parousia in the New Testament.[66] Second, the cosmic signs of Mark 13:24–25 are held by the author of Revelation to be future (6:14–17)—and he is probably writing *after* AD 70. Third, and perhaps most important, is the virtually technical status that the word *parousia* had attained by the time Matthew and Mark wrote their gospels. This word, used in Matthew 24:27, 37, and 39, always, when it is modified by "Christ," refers to the climactic coming of Christ in glory at the end of history in the New Testament (1 Cor. 15:23; 1 Thess. 2:19; 3:13; 4:15; 5:23; 2 Thess. 2:1, 8; James 5:7, 8; 2 Peter 1:16; 3:4, 12; 1 John 2:28).[67]

---

65. See esp. N. T. Wright, *Jesus and the Victory of God* (Christian Origins and the Question of God 2; Minneapolis: Fortress, 1996), 339–66; and also R. T. France, *The Gospel of Mark: A Commentary on the Greek Text*, NIGTC (Grand Rapids: Eerdmans, 2002), 497–503; idem, *Jesus and the Old Testament* (London: Tyndale, 1971), 228–39; Marcellus J. Kik, *The Eschatology of Victory* (Nutley, N.J.: Reformed, 1971), 60–144; R. V. G. Tasker, *The Gospel according to St. Matthew*, TNTC (Grand Rapids: Eerdmans, 1961), 223–27; A. Feuillet, "Le discours de Jesus sur la ruine du temple d'après Marc XIII et Luc XXI:5–36," *Revue Biblique* 55 (1948): 481–502; 56 (1949): 61–92.

66. I say "probably," because Mark 14:62 is debated, many interpreters thinking that it refers to Jesus' vindication before the Father. I think it probably refers to the parousia.

67. While Wright (*Jesus and the Victory of God*, 360–67) thinks that all of Matthew 24/Mark 13 has an immediate historical reference, France (*Mark*, 541) thinks that Mark 13:5–31 is about the destruction of the temple while Mark 13:32–37 is about the parousia. I agree with France, but it seems difficult to think that a change in subject of this sort takes place between vv. 31 and 32. And note that in the comparable material in Matthew, "coming" (*parousia*) is used in both parts of the discourse (24:27, 37, 39).

If, then, the end-time parousia is indeed described in Matthew 24:29–31//Mark 13:24–27, then "all these things" in Matthew 24:34// Mark 13:30 will have to refer to events in the discourse preceding the return of Christ in glory. And, in fact, this makes very good contextual sense. For "these things" and "all these things" are used in the immediately preceding verse (Mark 13:29//Matt. 24:33) to describe events that take place before the parousia: when we see "all these things," says Jesus, we will know that "it [or he] is near, right at the door." In other words, Jesus here suggests that he has described a series of events that will take place within "this generation," events that, having transpired, will indicate that the coming of Christ is "imminent."[68]

We return, then, to the issue of the "abomination of desolation." The evidence of the text appears to point in two directions: to an end-time event and to AD 70. One attractive option is to think that Jesus "telescopes" AD 70 and the end of the age in a manner reminiscent of the prophets, who frequently looked at the end of the age through more immediate historical events.[69] Others, naturally, argue that the reference here must be to the very end of history.[70] But I think the indications of an AD 70 reference (not least because of the Lukan parallel) are more compelling. I therefore suggest that Matthew 24:4–28// Mark 13:5–23 describes the entirety of the church age, which will be marked by great tribulation and by the important event of the Roman destruction of Jerusalem (= "the abomination that causes desolation") in AD 70.[71] This must take place, Jesus suggests, before his parou-

---

68. See, e.g., C. E. B. Cranfield, *The Gospel according to St. Mark*, CGTC (Cambridge: Cambridge University Press, 1966), 407–8; Craig L. Blomberg, *Matthew*, NAC 22 (Nashville: Broadman, 1992), 363–64; Donald A. Hagner, *Matthew 14–28*, WBC 33B (Dallas: Word, 1995), 715.

69. E.g., Cranfield, *Mark*, 402; Ladd, *Theology of the New Testament*, 198–99; James R. Edwards, *The Gospel according to Mark*, PNTC (Grand Rapids: Eerdmans, 2002), 399–400; William Hendriksen, *New Testament Commentary: Exposition of the Gospel according to Matthew* (Grand Rapids: Baker, 1973), 846–47.

70. E.g., Edwards, *Mark*, 395–400; Craig A. Evans, *Mark 8:27–16:20*, WBC 34B (Nashville: Thomas Nelson, 2001), 316–20.

71. D. A. Carson, "Matthew," in *Matthew, Mark, Luke*, EBC, ed. Frank E. Gaebelein, 12 vols. (Grand Rapids: Zondervan, 1984), 8:491–95; David Wenham, *The Rediscovery of Jesus' Eschatological Discourse*, Gospel Perspectives 4 (Sheffield: JSOT, 1984); Blomberg, *Matthew*, 352–60; Hagner, *Matthew 14–28*, 684–85; G. R. Beasley-Murray, *Jesus and the Last Days: The Interpretation of the Olivet Discourse* (Peabody, Mass.: Hendrickson, 1993), 377–434. For a useful survey of interpretations, see David Turner, "The Structure and Sequence of Matthew 24:1–41: Interaction with Evangelical Treatments," *GTJ* 10 (1989): 3–27.

sia; and once it has taken place, his parousia is "near." Jesus may refer to the greatest distress of all time in this context (Matt. 24:21//Mark 13:19) as a hyperbolic way of emphasizing the suffering that the Roman destruction of the city would cause. But it is perhaps likelier that he refers to the sufferings of God's people throughout the "church age." Christ's appearance to establish God's kingdom causes an intensification in the age-old conflict between good and evil. Christ's followers must be prepared to suffer severely for their allegiance to the one who was rejected by the world and its rulers. To fully appreciate the strength of this view, one must remember the important point about the New Testament eschatological perspective that I made earlier: the New Testament writers are not thinking in terms of long ages of history or of an ordinary "church age" followed by the "end time." No, for the New Testament writers, all the church age, uncertain in length, is the "end time." From this vantage point, it makes perfect sense to see Jesus warning his followers about the suffering and challenges they will face in these "last days" that his death and resurrection are initiating. I therefore slightly favor this "sequential" way of reading the Olivet Discourse. But, for our purposes, it does not matter a great deal whether we adopt this "sequential" reading or a "telescoping" reading.

In typical New Testament fashion, Jesus urges his followers to prepare for the suffering that lies ahead in view of their vindication at the time of his own parousia. He himself knows neither the day nor the hour when the parousia will take place (Matt. 24:36). He therefore addresses his followers as if they themselves might be present for all climactic eschatological events. Of course, they were not. Contrary to many New Testament scholars, this does not mean that Jesus spoke erroneously: he does not predict that they will be present for the eschatological climax but simply suggests that they might be. This way of presenting the parousia, as an event that could take place in any generation (what we have called "imminence" above), is found throughout the New Testament.

The fact that the people whom Jesus immediately addresses—the "Twelve"—were not present for all the events Jesus describes does not mean that his teaching loses its relevance. In typical gospel fashion, the disciples are addressed not only in their own persons but also as representative of others to come after them. And it is just at this point that the relevance of our discussion of the Olivet Discourse for the issue of the timing of the rapture becomes apparent. The "Twelve" in the Gospels are very commonly addressed as representative of all disciples. When Jesus speaks to them in the Olivet Discourse, we therefore naturally assume that they stand for Christians of every age. But, if this is so, the implication of the discourse is that Christians will be present during the final tribulation. And this is true on whatever view of the structure of the discourse we adopt. If Jesus is referring to the events of the end in Mark 13:14 and parallels, then he implies that disciples will be present to see the Antichrist reveal himself in the temple: Jesus says, "When *you* see 'the abomination that causes desolation' standing where it does not belong ..." (Mark. 13:14, emphasis added). This revelation of the Antichrist is usually seen to be a tribulational event; and disciples — "you" — will be present to see it. If, on the other hand, we adopt the "sequential" view (which I favor), then Jesus implies that disciples will be present throughout the "days of distress unequaled from the beginning, when God created the world, until now" (Mark 13:19). I take this to refer to the entire "church age," the "last days" when resistance to God and his people is particularly intense.[72] But the point is that the final tribulation must surely be included in this period of time — and disciples are, again, present during it.

One way of avoiding this conclusion is to argue that the disciples are addressed in the Olivet Discourse as representatives of Israel rather than as representatives of the church. And this is exactly what some pretribulational advocates claim.[73] Validation of this claim requires some very strong evidence indeed. For it is surely a legitimate assumption to think that the disciples in the Gospels are generally representative of *all* disciples — or else why do we accept Jesus' teaching as relevant for the church in general? Only if the context clearly necessitates a restriction should any narrowing of the audience be suggested. Are there clear

---

72. Brian Pitre argues that the abomination of desolation signals the shift from the preliminary messianic tribulation to the climactic "great tribulation" (a distinction found also, he argues, in Jewish sources) (*Jesus, the Tribulation, and the End of the Exile: Restoration Eschatology and the Origin of the Atonement* [Grand Rapids: Baker, 2005], 252–53, and 41–130, with summary on 129).

73. Walvoord, *Blessed Hope*, 86–87; Stanley D. Toussaint, "Are the Church and the Rapture in Matthew 24?" in *When the Trumpet Sounds*, ed. Thomas Ice and Timothy Deny (Eugene, Ore.: Harvest House, 1995), 242–43.

indications in the Olivet Discourse that Jesus did not intend his words to apply to all the people of God, including the church?

Perhaps the strongest reason for thinking that Jesus is viewing the disciples in terms of their ethnic, Jewish identity, is the local and Jewish-oriented nature of the warnings in Matthew 24:16, 20. In response to the appearance of "the abomination that causes desolation," Jesus says, "those who are in Judea" are to flee to the mountains; and he urges his followers to pray that their flight will not be on the Sabbath. (Mark includes the former warning [13:14] but not the latter one.) As I suggested above, these references do, indeed, suggest that a local situation may be in view and that it affects Jews (or early Jewish-Christians) in particular. Pretribulational advocates would presumably argue that Jesus is referring to Jews who are converted during the final tribulation. And this would possibly explain why Jesus can call them "the elect" in Matthew 24:22—for the language of "elect" is consistently applied to Christians in the New Testament. At the same time, as I also suggested above, it would seem unusual to portray the events of the final tribulation—with its cosmic scope—in such local terms. Nor does it by any means require that the disciples throughout this text are being addressed as Jews rather than as disciples in general. In my view, Jesus' focus is local and Jewish in these warnings because he is predicting a local outrage—the entrance of the pagan Romans into the Jerusalem temple—and, because of its location, it will affect Jewish Christians. It is interesting in this respect, though by no means conclusive, that the Christian historian Eusebius notes that Jewish believers in Judea did, indeed, flee to the mountains as the Romans drew near to Jerusalem.[74]

Walvoord, for instance, also argues that the nature of the question in Matthew 24 excludes a reference to the church because the disciples were asking about the coming of the millennial kingdom. There are some real difficulties with this argument, however. First, it apparently demands that Jesus answered a different question in Mark and Luke than he did in Matthew. But where is the indication in the text of such a difference? The question relating to the temple is identical—word for word—in Matthew, Mark, and Luke. Second, this view assumes that Jesus answered the question about the destruction of the temple and the

---

74. Eusebius, *Ecclesiastical History* 3.5.3.

question about the kingdom in virtually identical discourses. Doesn't this degree of resemblance indicate that it is improper to separate them in the way Walvoord suggests? Third, Walvoord claims that the disciples asked about the coming of the millennial kingdom, which has no relevance for the church. Not only is there no indication in the disciples' question or in Jesus' answer that the millennial kingdom is the topic, but Jesus in Matthew 28:20 promises the disciples that he will be with them "to the very end of the age" — and this is the same phrase used in the disciples' question in Matthew 24:3. It is difficult to see why the parousia of Christ and the consummation of the age would not matter to the church.

On the other hand, there are a number of indications that, taken together, make it clear that Jesus addressed the disciples as representative of *all* believers (we do not want to exclude Israel, but to include the church). First, the depiction of the end-time events in Matthew 24–25 is clearly parallel to the description of the parousia found in Paul's epistles, directed to the church. Some of these have already been noted, but it will be helpful to set them out in parallel columns.

Particular attention should be directed to the obvious parallels between the Olivet Discourse and both 1 Thessalonians 4:13–18 (the parousia and the rapture) and 2 Thessalonians 2:1–12 (the parousia and the judgment on the wicked) — in fact, there are closer parallels to 1 Thessalonians 4 than to 2 Thessalonians 2. Paul clearly describes in these two passages what Jesus depicts as one event[75] — showing that it is illegitimate to separate the parousia of 1 Thessalonians 4 and the parousia of 2 Thessalonians 2 in time and making it overwhelmingly probable that Jesus addresses the church in the Olivet Discourse. For surely, if Paul addresses the church in the Thessalonian epistles, it is obvious that Jesus, who says virtually the same thing, is also addressing the church.

Another reason for thinking that the church cannot be excluded from that group represented by the disciples has to do with the nature of the exhortations addressed to the disciples at the end of the discourse. Matthew 24 describes the situation that will exist at the same time of

---

75. Beechick, recognizing the impact of these parallels with Paul, suggests that Jesus describes both the pretribulational *and* posttribulational parousia in the Olivet Discourse (*Rapture*, 233–63). But this explanation does not do justice to the clear temporal indicators in the discourse — the parousia occurs only *after* the tribulation.

OLIVET DISCOURSE		
(Matthew)	EVENT	PAUL
24:5	warning about deception	2 Thess. 2:2
24:5, 11, 24	lawlessness, delusion of the nonelect, signs and wonders	2 Thess. 2:6-11
24:12	apostasy	2 Thess. 2:3
24:15	disturbance in the temple	2 Thess. 2:4
24:21-22	tribulation preceding the end	2 Thess. 1:6-10
24:30-31	parousia of Christ on clouds at the time of trumpet blast with angelic accompaniment	1 Thess. 4:14-16
24:30-31	coming of Christ in power	2 Thess. 2:8
24:31	gathering of believers	1 Thess. 4:16; 2 Thess. 2:1
24:36, 42, 44, 50	unexpected and uncertain	1 Thess. 5:1-4
25:4	exhortation to watch	1 Thess. 5:6-8

the parousia of the Son of Man (certainly the posttribulational parousia) that has just been described. Yet the same exhortations appear in other contexts in the Gospels where it seems obvious that the disciples as representatives of the church are addressed (cf. Luke 12:39–46; 19:11–27). Furthermore, the same command addressed to the disciples in Matthew 24–25, "Watch!" (*grēgoreō*), is addressed to Christians elsewhere in the New Testament.

The inclusion of the church in the end events depicted in the Olivet Discourse would be conclusively proven if a reference to the rapture were found in it. There is some reason for finding such a reference in two places. As an event that transpires at the time of the parousia, Jesus describes a gathering of the saints "from the four winds, from one end of the heavens to the other" (Matt. 24:31; cf. Mark 13:27). This "gathering" takes place at the sounding of "a great trumpet"—a feature that Paul mentions in both of his presentations of the rapture (1 Cor. 15:51–52; 1 Thess. 4:16–17). Second, the verb "gather" that is used here (*episynagō*) is employed in its noun form to depict the rapture in 2 Thessalonians 2:1. Since the verb and noun *together* occur only nine times in the New Testament and there are so many other parallels between 2 Thessalonians 2 and the Olivet Discourse, there is good reason to accord significance to this verbal contact. But it is probable that the "gathering" includes more than the rapture—inasmuch as the description seems to envision a great coming together of *all* God's saints, it is likely that the resurrection of the righteous is included also. Thus Jesus would be depicting the great, final gathering of all saints—the dead through resurrection, the living through the rapture.[76] In a manner typical of the New Testament, Jesus takes the prophetic depiction of the posttribulational regathering of Israel (cf. Deut. 30:4; Isa. 27:12–13; 43:5–7; Zech. 2:6–13) and applies it to *all* the people of God.[77]

A second text that may refer to the rapture is the reference in Matthew 24:40–41 (parallel in Luke 17:34–35) to the "taking" of one in contrast to the "leaving" of another. It may be that the one "taken" is taken in judgment while the one left is allowed to enter the kingdom.[78] But the verb for "taking" is used of the rapture in John 14:3 (although, to be sure, it is also used in other ways), and it is significant that the verb

---

76. Beasley-Murray, *Commentary*, 93. Walvoord's view, that this text refers to the gathering of peoples into the millennial kingdom ("Olivet Discourse," 326) is adequate as far as it goes but fails to account for the parallels with Paul's depiction of the rapture. Blomberg (*Matthew*, 363) doubts that there is any reference to the rapture.

77. Feuillet, "Le discours de Jésus," 75–78; Hartman, *Prophecy Interpreted*, 158; Lane, *Mark*, 416–71.

78. Walvoord, *Blessed Hope*, 89–90.

for "take" in judgment in Matthew 24:39 is different than the one used in verses 40–41. And the analogy to the flood may suggest that just as Noah was saved by being taken away from the scene of judgment, so believers at the parousia will be taken away, through the rapture, from the scene of judgment.[79]

I therefore conclude that Jesus in the Olivet Discourse is addressing his disciples as representatives of all believers. This leads necessarily to a posttribulational location of the rapture, since those addressed in the discourse are indisputably said to be on the earth until the posttribulational parousia.

Revelation

With the concentration on the events of the end found in Revelation, we would expect that here, if anywhere, we could find clear evidence for the relationship of the final tribulation to the rapture. Unfortunately, this is not the case. Many would argue, in fact, that the rapture is never even mentioned in Revelation; all would agree that it is not described in direct temporal association with the tribulation. Therefore, evidence for the topic before us comes from three sources: promises and warnings made to the seven churches, specific texts in which the rapture may be indicated, and the descriptions of the saints who experience the final tribulation.

Before tackling these specific issues, however, a general orientation to the focus of Revelation is necessary. Interpreters generally speak of four general directions in the interpretation of the book as whole: (1) the "futurist," which tends to view everything in chapters 6 and following as referring to the very end of history; (2) the "preterist," which views the material in the book as a whole as directed to the immediate first-century situation of John's readers; (3) the "historicist," which posits a kind of chronological historical summary from John's day to the parousia; and (4) the "idealist," which avoids assigning specific referents to John's visionary symbols. Most contemporary interpreters of Revelation combine two or more of these perspectives, and I (though by no means an expert on

79. Hagner, *Matthew 14–28*, 720; I. Howard Marshall, *The Gospel of Luke*, NIGTC (Grand Rapids: Eerdmans, 1978), 668; Alan Hugh McNeile, *The Gospel according to St. Matthew* (London: Macmillan, 1928), 357; Gundry, *Church and Tribulation*, 137–38.

the book) tend to agree. The idealist approach rightly stresses the hortatory purpose of the book, a point that is too easily lost in discussions of the details of the visions. John seeks to encourage and strengthen first-century persecuted believers by reminding them of God's sovereignty and by giving them, through his visions, a richly detailed picture of how God will certainly manifest that sovereignty in the events of history. Particularly important for our purposes, however, is the debate between the "preterist" and the "futurist" models. I would hesitantly suggest that this debate is to some extent misguided and perhaps not even necessary. I return to the fundamental point about New Testament eschatology that I made at the beginning of this essay. The New Testament writers were convinced that they were already living in the "last days" and that the parousia and associated events could be occurring at any time. In at least one important sense, from this perspective, the difference between "preterist" and "futurist" approaches becomes somewhat meaningless. John's visions relate both to first-century realities and to the end of the age — with John, like Jesus, not being able to distinguish clearly between the two. As we look at specific texts and issues in Revelation, then, we will work from this "both/and" perspective rather than from an "either/or" perspective.

Although attention is often given exclusively to Christ's promise to the Philadelphian church in 3:10, there are, in fact, three other texts in Revelation 2–3 in which related promises and warnings are given. In the letter to the church of Smyrna, Christ warns the believers that they can expect the tribulation (*thlipsis*) for ten days (2:10). While it is probable that this is not referring to the final tribulation, it should be noted that believers are promised persecution and possible death. Similar to this verse is 2:22, only in this case those who engage in Jezebel's sin are promised "great tribulation" (*thlipsin megalēn*; my translation). The lack of an article in this phrase suggests a reference to intense suffering in a general sense: see TNIV, "will ... suffer intensely." Third, Christ exhorts the church at Sardis to repent and warns: "But if you do not wake up, I will come like a thief, and you will not know at what time I will come to you" (3:3). The similarity between this language and 1 Thessalonians 5 and Jesus' warnings about his posttribulational coming in Matthew 24:42–44 — all three passages have "as a thief," "watch" (*grēgoreō*), and the note of uncertainty — suggests that the church at Smyrna has exactly the same need as those addressed in Jesus' parable and in Paul's letter:

to watch lest the coming of Christ in glory take them by surprise.[80] But this, of course, assumes that they will not be raptured previously.

Finally, we must consider that much-debated promise of Christ in Revelation 3:10: "Since you have kept my command to endure patiently, I will also keep you from the hour of trial that is going to come on the whole world to test those who live on the earth." It is probable that the reference is to the final tribulation,[81] and all agree that the Philadelphian church is promised protection from it. The question is how: through physical removal in a pretribulational or midtribulational rapture or through divine safekeeping during the period of distress? The crucial language is the sequence "keep ... from" (*tēreō ek*). The nearest parallel to this phraseology (and the only other place in biblical Greek where *tēreō* and *ek* are used together) is John 17:15 — "My prayer is not that you take them out of the world but that you protect them from (*tēresēs autous ek*) the evil one." Here it seems clear that Jesus prays for the disciples' preservation from the power of Satan, even though they remain *in* the "world," the sphere of Satan's activity (cf. 1 John 5:19).[82] Furthermore, it is helpful to note that in only three other verses in the New Testament does *tēreō* ("keep") have God or Christ as its subject and believers as its object — John 17:11, 12, 15. In each case, spiritual preservation is clearly intended. With these parallels in mind, it seems best to think that in Revelation 3:10 Christ promises the church at Philadelphia that it will be spiritually protected from "the hour of trial."[83]

---

80. Cf. Rusten, "Revelation," 204–5. Walvoord gives no reason for his assertion that this language should not here be applied to the parousia (John Walvoord, *The Revelation of Jesus Christ* [Chicago: Moody, 1966], 81). Nor is it legitimate to confine the warning to unbelievers only (contra Beechick, *Rapture*, 172–73).

81. Osborne, *Revelation*, 192–93; Beale, *Revelation*, 289–90. David Aune, however (*Revelation 1–5*, WBC 52 [Dallas: Word, 1997], 240), argues that the promise is for the Philadelphian church only, while Rusten ("Revelation," 216–19) thinks of the period following the parousia, and Payne of a historical period of suffering (*Imminent Appearing*, 78–79).

82. In light of Jesus' explicit assertion in the same verse that the disciples will remain in the world, it is difficult to see how John 17:15 could indicate noncontact with the "Evil One." And there is no indication that the spiritual realm of Satan is intended (contra Jeffrey L. Townsend, "The Rapture in Revelation 3:10," *BSac* 137 1980. : 258–59).

83. The objection to this general interpretation to the effect that the suffering and even death of God's people during the final tribulation is hardly compatible with this promise of "protection" (e.g., Jeffrey L. Townsend, "The Rapture in Revelation 3:10," in *When the Trumpet Sounds*, ed. Thomas Ice and Timothy Deny (Eugene, Ore.: Harvest House, 1995), 368–69) is easily met: the promise is not physical preservation but spiritual preservation. Or are we to suppose that God grants to the saints at the very end of history a protection from physical harm that he has not given to his saints throughout history?

In this interpretation, *ek*, "out of," would denote, as it seems to in John 17:15, separation. That this spiritual preservation is to be accomplished through physical removal is not indicated, and had John intended physical removal, there were other ways of saying so that would have made it more obvious.[84] It is perhaps likelier that, as in John 17:15, believers are physically in the sphere of that from which they are protected.[85] But it must be said that neither view, nor any other that has been proposed, can be conclusively established. We must conclude that Revelation 3:10 neither offers clear-cut evidence for or against a posttribulational rapture.

Turning now to texts that may indicate the time of the rapture, we can rather quickly dismiss 4:1. The command to John to "come up here" (to heaven) is manifestly intended to suggest a visionary experience that John has while still in the body on the island of Patmos. As Walvoord rightly says, "There is no authority for connecting the Rapture with this expression."[86]

Of more significance is the depiction of events in chapter 11. Although there are many details that are obscure in this chapter, it seems reasonably clear that 11:11 – 12 describes a resurrection of the two witnesses. Does this resurrection have anything to do with the rapture? The fact that the two are said to go up "in a cloud" may suggest this, for clouds are consistently mentioned in descriptions of the rapture (cf. Matt. 24:30; Acts 1:9; 1 Thess. 4:17; Rev. 14:14). And, as elsewhere when the rapture is mentioned, a trumpet is found in this text (11:15). These indications are not, however, conclusive, and a connection between this event and the rapture and final resurrection of

---

84. E.g., the combination *airō ek*, used in John 17:15, would have plainly indicated "take out of."

85. The combination of *tēreō* ("keep") and *ek* is quite rare, but similar language in the LXX and classical Greek tend to confirm this interpretation. See, e.g., Prov. 7:5: "They will keep you from [*tērēsē apo*] the adulterous woman." LSJ mentions a somewhat amusing possible parallel: *tērein apo tou pyros*, "*protect* them from the fire, i.e., cook them slowly (*Bilabel Opsart*, p. 10)." Is John saying that believers will be "cooked slowly" during the final tribulation? For this general interpretation of Rev. 3:10, see, e.g., Aune, *Revelation 1–5*, 240; Beale, *Revelation*, 290–92; Ben Witherington III, *Revelation*, NCBC (Cambridge: Cambridge University Press, 2003), 106–7; G. R. Beasley-Murray, *The Book of Revelation*, NCB (London: Marshall, Morgan and Scott, 1974), 101; Robert H. Mounce, *The Book of Revelation*, NICNT (Grand Rapids: Eerdmans, 1977), 119; Schuyler Brown, "'The Hour of Trial' (Rev. 3:10)," *JBL* 85 (1966): 310.

86. Walvoord, *Revelation*, 103.

believers remains uncertain.[87] The most we can do, then, is to note the possible significance of this episode for the timing of the rapture. In this regard, there are many indications that strongly suggest that the very end of the final tribulation is reached in 11:11–19. The "great earthquake" that is said to take place immediately after the resurrection of the witnesses (11:13) is mentioned in only two other verses in Revelation, both of which describe the end—6:12 and 16:18. No one doubts that 16:18 occurs in a posttribulational setting, but it may be necessary to point out that 6:12–17, the sixth seal, also almost certainly depicts the end. John refers here to a "great earthquake," to the sun turning "black like sackcloth," to the moon being turned "blood red," to stars falling to earth, to the sky receding "like a scroll," and to "every mountain and island" being "removed from its place." The language, of course, is standard Old Testament apocalyptic imagery, and it need not refer to literal cosmic disasters. But the application of this imagery to events of the "day of the LORD" in the Old Testament and to Jesus' parousia in the New (e.g., Matt. 24:29–30) is telling. As G. R. Beasley-Murray says, "This language permits one interpretation alone: the last day has come."[88]

In addition to the "great earthquake," two other factors also point to the time of the final tribulation. The witnesses prophesy for forty-two months (11:2) and then lie in death for "three and a half days" (11:9). If the former reference is to the first half of the final tribulation period, the second reference could indicate the second half. But it must be admitted that this is far from certain. At the blowing of the seventh trumpet, there can be little doubt that the end is reached; the kingdom of the world becomes the kingdom of Christ (11:15), the Lord begins his reign (11:17), the time for his wrath and for judging and rewarding comes (11:18), and the heavenly temple is open. If the seventh trumpet is chronologically related to the resurrection of the witnesses, then it is rather clear that the resurrection is posttribulational.

---

87. Norman B. Harrison (*The End: Re-thinking the Revelation* [Minneapolis: The Harrison Services, 1941], 116–21) argues that the rapture of the church is indicated here and that the time is the middle of Daniel's seventieth week. Among those who doubt a reference to the rapture of the church or the final resurrection of the righteous are, e.g., Osborne, *Revelation*, 432; Beale, *Revelation*, 597.

88. Beasley-Murray, *Revelation*, 30–31.

While it is therefore probable that the resurrection of the two witnesses is posttribulational, this would have decisive bearing on the question of the time of the rapture only if it could be shown that the witnesses represent the church. But this is not clear, and the most that can be said is that this verse could be suggestive if other similar indications are found.

In one of a series of visions that occurs between the depiction of the trumpets and the bowls, John sees "one like a son of man" seated on a cloud. He descends to "harvest the earth" (14:14–16). That the parousia is portrayed here is probable in light of the references to "son of man" and "clouds."[89] But can the harvesting of the earth in verses 15–16 include the rapture? This may be the case—Jesus uses the image of harvesting to describe the gathering of God's people into the kingdom (Matt. 13:30). Verses 17–20 would then be a description of the judgment of God on unbelievers. The precise reference in the imagery of the harvest is not altogether clear, however. Scholars debate whether the first harvest is solely for the righteous,[90] solely for the wicked,[91] or includes both.[92] However, it seems difficult to exclude the saints from this first harvesting, which, unlike the second, has no reference to God's wrath. Therefore, if one holds that the church is addressed in these chapters of Revelation, the rapture would almost certainly be included as an aspect of this great ingathering of the saints at the end.

A final text that may indicate the time of the rapture is Revelation 20:4, in which John describes the "first resurrection." The participants in this resurrection are not specifically named—there is no expressed subject of the third person plural verb *ezēsan* ("they come to life"). While some would want to confine the participants to the martyrs specifically mentioned in verse 4,[93] there are good reasons for

---

89. G. B. Caird, *A Commentary on the Revelation of St. John the Divine*, HNTC (New York: Harper and Row, 1966), 190; Beasley-Murray, *Revelation*, 228; Gundry, *Church and Tribulation*, 83–84.

90. Osborne, *Revelation*, 552; Henry Barclay Swete, *Commentary on Revelation* (1911; repr., Grand Rapids: Kregel, 1977), 189–90; Gundry, *Church and Tribulation*, 83–88; Rusten, "Revelation," 516–21.

91. Beale, *Revelation*, 770–72; David Aune, *Revelation 6–16*, WBC 52B (Nashville: Nelson, 1998), 801–3; Witherington, *Revelation*, 196; Walvoord, *Revelation*, 221–22.

92. Beasley-Murray, *Revelation*, 228; Mounce, *Revelation*, 279–80; Isbon T. Beckwith, *The Apocalypse of John* (1919; repr., Grand Rapids: Baker, 1967), 662.

93. Walvoord, *Revelation*, 296–97; Mounce, *Revelation*, 355–56.

including more than the martyrs in this resurrection.[94] First, in addition to the martyrs, verse 4 also describes those who sit on the thrones and to whom judgment is given—the syntax clearly suggests that this is a group different from the martyrs.[95] Second, those who come to life are "priests of God and of Christ and will reign with him" (v. 6), and Revelation 5:9–10 stresses the fact that this group will include people "from every tribe and language and people and nation." If, as is clear, the group in 5:9–10 includes the church, it is probably not legitimate to exclude the church in 20:4. Third, John describes only two resurrections in Revelation—the "first," in verse 4 and the "second," in which the wicked take part. The first resurrection in verse 4 must certainly have a temporal force, since it is used in conjunction with "second,"[96] and it is not easy to think that John's language allows for any resurrection preceding this one. Observe also that those who do not participate in the first resurrection are labeled "the rest of the dead"—indication that John includes in his two resurrections *all* the dead. Finally, it is inherently unlikely that John, writing to churches (1:4; 22:16) would omit in his grand portrait of the end one of the most blessed and anticipated aspects of that period—the resurrection of believers.

For these reasons, it is probable that Revelation 20:4 depicts the resurrection of all the righteous dead—including church saints. Since the rapture occurs at the same time as this resurrection, and the first resurrection is clearly posttribulational, the rapture must also be posttribulational.

The third main line of investigation to be pursued in Revelation relates to the identity of the saints whom John sees experiencing the sufferings he describes in chapters 6–16. I do not think that these sufferings refer only to the final tribulation, since, as I have indicated above, it is likely that John is depicting the events of the entire church age, beginning with his own time and culminating in the parousia. But for our purposes, the point is that the final tribulation is certainly included in these sufferings. So our question is this: are believers of this

---

94. Beale, *Revelation*, 999–1000. Osborne thinks the reference is specifically to the martyrs but, by synecdoche, includes all the saints (*Revelation*, 704–5).

95. Since *tas psychas* ("the souls") is accusative, it is best taken as a second object after *eidon* (Swete, *Revelation*, 262).

96. Contra Roy L. Aldrich, "Divisions of the First Resurrection," *BSac* 128 (1971): 117–19.

dispensation, church saints, included in this group? A negative answer to this question is often given because the word *ekklēsia* ("church") does not occur in Revelation 4–19. But this is hardly conclusive—John plainly has in mind the worldwide body of saints in these chapters, and *ekklēsia* is only rarely used in the New Testament to indicate such a universal group. John himself never uses *ekklēsia* other than as a designation of a local body of believers.[97] Moreover, it is important to note that John never in chapters 4–19 calls any group in heaven the church.[98] Thus the lack of reference to *ekklēsia* as such cannot decide this issue.

Nor does the structure of Revelation shed light on the question. It has been customary to think that Revelation 1:19 suggests a division of Revelation into three basic parts: "the things you have seen" (= chapter 1), "the things which are" (= Rev. 2–3); and "the things which are about to happen after these things" (4–22; all my translation).[99] There is considerable doubt about whether this is the intention of this verse.[100] But we can still assume that most of the events that John sees in his visions in chapters 6–22 lie in the (indeterminate) future. But it is, to put it mildly, a stretch to suggest that these events must follow the "church age."

Therefore, it becomes necessary to ask whether we can identify any *particular* group in Revelation 4–19 with the church so as to enable us to determine its location during these events. In the heavenly throne room scene of chapter 4, a group of twenty-four "elders" is described, who surround God's throne and wear white robes and crowns of gold (v. 4). Most commentators think a superior order of angels is depicted here,[101] but there is some reason to think rather that the "elders" are glorified human beings or at least some kind of heavenly figures who represent people.[102] However, there are sound reasons for refusing to

---

97. This is probably why John in Rev. 13:9 omits "to the churches" from the familiar refrain, "He who has ears let him hear …" (in response to Walvoord, *Revelation*, 103; and Beechick, *Rapture*, 179).

98. Gundry, *Church and Tribulation*, 78.

99. E.g., Swete, *Revelation*, 21; Ladd, *Commentary on the Revelation of John*, 34.

100. See esp. Beale, *Revelation*, 152–70; also Osborne, *Revelation*, 97.

101. Osborne, *Revelation*, 228–30; Beale, *Revelation*, 322; Caird, *Revelation*, 63; Leon Morris, *The Revelation of St. John*, TNTC (Grand Rapids: Eerdmans, 1969), 88; Ladd, *Commentary on the Revelation of John*, 75; Beasley-Murray, *Revelation*, 114; Mounce, *Revelation*, 135.

102. Cf. especially André Feuillet, "The Twenty-four Elders of the Apocalypse," in *Johannine Studies* (Staten Island, N.Y.: Alba House, 1965), 185–94; J. Massyngberde Ford, *Revelation*, AB (Garden City, N.Y.: Doubleday, 1975), 72; Larry Hurtado, "Revelation 4–5 in the Light of Jewish Apocalyptic Analogies," *JSNT* 25 (1985): 105–24; Witherington, *Revelation*, 117.

confine the group to church saints alone. In Revelation 5:10 the "elders" address a group that includes the church in the third person—"them." The wearing of gold crowns is certainly not restricted to the church—in Revelation 9:7 the demonic locusts wear "something like crowns of gold." Neither do the white robes necessarily suggest a raptured church, since the Laodiceans are told to wear them on earth (3:18). If John's own symbolism is to be followed, it would seem that the reference to "twenty-four" most naturally suggests the whole people of God, Israel and the church. Thus, in Revelation 21:12–14, the New Jerusalem is pictured as having twelve gates with the names of the twelve tribes of Israel and twelve foundations with the names of "the twelve apostles of the Lamb." But since Daniel 12 clearly shows that Israel is not vindicated until after the tribulation, the presence of the "elders" in heaven in Revelation 4 cannot be used to refute a posttribulational rapture. In this respect, it is significant that the "twenty-four elders" are always portrayed in visions of heaven that bear no clear temporal relationship to any earthly event—in a sense it is asking the wrong question to enquire about when these scenes take place.

I think it very likely that the 144,000 of Revelation 7:2–8 is to be identified with the church,[103] but the identification is uncertain enough that I will not make a significant point about it here. Similarly it is likely that the "bride" of the wedding supper in Revelation 19:7–9 must include the church. But this does not indicate that the rapture must have preceded the parousia of 19:11–22, for the visions of 17:1–19:10 appear to give proleptic views of the effects of the parousia. Too many interpreters assume a chronology of events in Revelation that is simply not intended.

Finally, there are some general indications that taken together provide good reason for thinking that the church cannot be eliminated from the body of saints pictured on the earth during the tribulations described in Revelation. The promises and warnings issued to the church saints in Revelation 2–3 are repeated again and again in chapters 4–22, suggesting that the same group is in view throughout. Thus, for example, the church at Smyrna is promised that believers will be spared from "the second death" if they "overcome." But it is rescue from this "second death"

---

103. See, e.g., Beale, *Revelation*, 416–23; Osborne, *Revelation*, 310–13.

that the first resurrection of Revelation 20:4–6 provides (cf. v. 6). A continual theme in the letters to the churches is the need to "be victorious" (seven times); Revelation 15:2 pictures "those who had been victorious over the beast and his image." Four times in the letters the need for "endurance" is stressed; the same quality is demanded of the tribulation saints (13:10; 14:12). Other such parallels could be mentioned,[104] and whereas they cannot be considered decisive evidence (the same characteristics can be ascribed to two different groups), they do seem suggestive.

The reference to the parousia in 1:7 is also suggestive. If the church is not to take part in the events of Revelation 4–19, it seems incongruous that John should highlight this parousia, the great climax of these chapters, in the address to the churches (cf. 1:4). In 22:16 Jesus claims that he has sent his angel "to give you [plural!] this testimony for the churches." It is difficult to see how the chapters about suffering could be a "testimony for the churches" if they are not involved in it.[105] Finally, it simply appears improbable that the event described at greatest length in Revelation (the sufferings of the righteous in chaps. 6–16) would have no direct relevance for those to whom the book is addressed.

I conclude my discussion of the Revelation by attempting to indicate how my understanding of particular events in the Revelation fits into the overall structure of the book. It seems clear that the seventh in each series of seals, trumpets, and bowls brings us to the time of parousia. Interspersed among these series are visions of the heavenly warfare that is manifested in the tribulational distress (chap. 12), of the satanic power of that time (chap. 13), and of the protection and ultimate vindication of God's people (chaps. 7, 14). Immediately before the parousia we are given a proleptic vision of the judgment and salvation that the heavenly intervention brings (17:1–19:10). Following the parousia are portrayed the events that flow from it. In other words, it is the parousia of Christ that is the focal point of Revelation 6–20—all other events lead up to or follow from it, while periodic visions reveal different aspects of these events. Experts on Revelation disagree quite fundamentally about how to structure all the visions and events in the book. But I think it is tolerably clear, as I have argued above, that the events depicted in chapters 6–16

---

104. See Rusten, "Revelation," 231–53.
105. Ibid., 133–34.

are not in chronological order.[106] There is simply too much repetition as the visions unfold and too many places where the language seems clearly to be describing parousia events to think that the progression is chronological. John therefore recapitulates the sequence of events to take place during the time of the church's tribulation. The important point for our purposes, then, are the several places where John possibly describes the parousia and associated events: especially 6:12–17; 7:9–17; 11:11–19; 14:1–5, 14–20; 17:1–19:10; 19:11–20:6. These passages describe several different events that occur at Christ's parousia: the deliverance of the saints (7:9–17); the resurrection of the faithful witnesses (11:11–12); the inauguration of the day of God's judgment and his eternal kingdom (11:15–19); the deliverance of the 144,000 (14:1–5); the final gathering of believers and the judgment (14:14–20); the condemnation of the evil world system (chaps. 17–18); the union of God and his saints (19:8–9); the binding of Satan (20:1–3); the first resurrection (20:4–6). All these events occur after the series of tribulations (including, though not limited to the final tribulation) that John describes in such great detail. The rapture must, then, also be posttribulational.

Conclusion

As a result of this study of key biblical texts, I conclude that the parousia of Christ is a fundamentally single event at which time both living and dead saints of all dispensations go to be with the Lord and the wrath of God falls on unbelievers. The reconstruction of end events based on this hypothesis demonstrates a remarkable degree of consistency as we examine every important New Testament depiction of the end. I set out these events in chart form at the end of this chapter. Not every event is included in every text, of course, for the different authors chose to mention only those events that were appropriate for their particular argument.[107] The fact that this reconstruction, founded upon

106. Contra, e.g., John McLean, "Chronology and Sequential Structure of John's Revelation," in *When the Trumpet Sounds*, 313–51. Van Kampen's assumption, without argument, that Revelation is basically chronological is another major flaw in his eschatological scenario (*The Sign*).

107. Most of the differences cited as requiring a distinction between the pretribulational rapture and the posttribulational coming (cf. Pentecost, *Things to Come*, 206–7; Walvoord, *Rapture Question*, 101–2) are easily explained once this selectivity is recognized. Only if clear contradictions are involved do such differences establish a need to separate in time the parousia events.

a posttribulational rapture, fits every passage so naturally is a potent argument in favor of this position.

Israel and the Church

Advocates of the pretribulational rapture have often been influenced in their preference for this position by a theological concern that they think is deeply rooted in Scripture: the strict distinction between Israel and the church. "Progressive" dispensationalism has weakened this concern somewhat, but it is still a matter of importance. For if a disjunction between Israel and the church is assumed, a certain presumption against the posttribulational position exists. It would be inconsistent for the church to be involved in a period of time that, according to the Old Testament, has to do with Israel. However, it is important at the outset to note that a posttribulation rapture is not necessarily excluded by a view that keeps Israel and the church separate. Thus, if Scripture indicates that both Israel and the church are to experience the final tribulation, each could remain on earth during that time as separate entities. Even if it be concluded that the final tribulation is for Israel only, it is not a priori impossible to think that the church will remain on earth during that period without undergoing this climactic affliction.[108] In other words, a total and consistent separation of Israel and the church does not necessarily entail any specific view of the time of the rapture. Since this is the case, even a theological approach that continues to insist on a separation of church and Israel does not necessarily settle the matter of the timing of the rapture.

However, in our survey of this issue, we have encountered a number of texts in which language and prophecies that have reference to Israel in the Old Testament are applied to the church (e.g., the eschatological trumpet, the Antichrist, and most obviously, the tribulation itself). And, I would argue, this fits with the typical way the New Testament writers appropriate the Old Testament. Again and again, language and specific prophecies originally applied to Israel are applied to new covenant believers in general. To be sure, this does not necessarily mean that we can simply merge Israel into the church entirely. For instance, I interpret Romans 11 to teach that the nation of Israel still has its own

---

108. Cf. Gundry, *Church and Tribulation*, 25–28.

role to play in the events of salvation history.[109] What is important, I would suggest, is that we distinguish carefully between prophecies directed to Israel *as a nation* (and which must be fulfilled in a national Israel) and prophecies directed to Israel as *the people of God* (which can be fulfilled in the people of God—a people that includes the church!). It should be noted that such an approach is not allegorical or nonliteral; it simply calls upon the interpreter to recognize the intended scope of any specific prophecy. It is our contention, then, that the final tribulation predicted for Israel by, for example, Daniel, is directed to Israel as the people of God. It can therefore be fulfilled in the people of God, which includes church as well as Israel.

Imminency

I want finally to revisit a matter that has surfaced several times in my essay: "imminency." Since a posttribulational view requires that certain events must transpire before the parousia, it is often claimed that posttribulationism necessarily involves the denial of imminency.[110] In order to avoid this conclusion, J. B. Payne seeks to explain most events predicted to take place during the final tribulation in such a way that they could be present (or past) even now.[111] This attempt must, however, be deemed unsuccessful—the nature of some of these events, which are asserted to be recognizable by the saints when they occur (cf. e.g., 2 Thess. 2), precludes the possibility that they are "potentially present."[112] On the other hand, Robert Gundry, convinced of the posttribulational rapture position, wants to do away with imminency altogether.[113]

However, one very important fact must be recognized: Gundry and Payne both appear to assume that *imminent* must mean "any moment." This is simply not the case. The *Oxford English Dictionary* gives as its definition of *imminent*, "impending threateningly, hanging over one's head; ready to befall or overtake one, close at hand at its incidence;

---

109. See Douglas Moo, *The Epistle to the Romans*, NICNT (Grand Rapids: Eerdmans, 1996), 710–32.
110. Pentecost, *Things to Come*, 168; Walvoord, *Rapture Question*, 82.
111. Payne, *Imminent Appearing*.
112. See the excellent refutation by Gundry (*Church and Tribulation*, 193–200).
113. Ibid., 29–43.

coming on shortly." Clearly this meaning does not require that there be no intervening events before something said to be imminent transpires. It is quite appropriate to speak of the adjournment of Congress, for instance, as being "imminent" even if some event(s) (such as a crucial roll-call vote) must elapse before it can occur. In this sense, the term can be applied to an event that is near and cannot at this point be accurately dated, but that will not occur until some necessary preliminary events transpire. Defined in this way, the "imminence" of our Lord's return is a doctrine that should not be jettisoned. It expresses the supremely important conviction that the glorious return of Christ could take place within any limited period of time—that the next few years could witness this grand climax to God's dealing with the world. Granted that imminence can be defined in this way, is this in fact the manner in which the hope of Christ's return is viewed in the New Testament?

The first point to be made is that none of the many words used to describe the nearness of the parousia, or the believer's expectation of it, requires an "any moment" sense of imminency. "Wait for" (*prosdechomai*) (applied to the parousia in Luke 12:36; Titus 2:13; Jude 21 [?]) is used of Paul's expectation of the resurrection of the just and the unjust (Acts 24:15)—yet the latter does not occur until after the millennium. "Eagerly wait" (*apekdechomai*) (used of the parousia in 1 Cor. 1:7), can refer to creation's longing for deliverance (Rom. 8:19), which deliverance comes only after the final tribulation. "Expect" (*ekdechomai*) is applied to the parousia by James in 5:7, but the analogy in the context is with a farmer who waits for his crops—certainly not "any moment." "Look for" (*prosdokaō*) (cf. Matt. 24:50; Luke 12:46 with reference to the second coming) is the word used by Peter to exhort believers to "look for" the new heavens and earth (2 Peter 3:12–14). "Be near" (*engizō*) and the adjectival form, "near" (*engys*), applied to the parousia in numerous texts, are used of Jewish feasts and the seasons of the year (e.g., John 2:13; Matt. 21:34)—and these, obviously, are not "any moment" events. A number of other terms (*grēgoreō*, "watch"; *agrypneō*, "be awake"; *nēphō*, "be sober"; *blepō*, "look at") are used to exhort believers to an attitude of spiritual alertness and moral uprightness in the light of the second coming but imply nothing as to its time.[114]

---

114. See particularly Gundry (*Church and Tribulation*, 30–32) for studies of these words.

By themselves, then, these terms do not require that the expectation to which they refer be capable of taking place "at any moment." The context in which they are used is crucial. The most important of these contexts have already been examined, and it will not be necessary to repeat here the evidence that leads us to believe that a posttribulation rapture is consistently indicated. But some additional remarks should perhaps be added with respect to the Olivet Discourse.

In the hortatory section following Christ's depiction of the eschatological tribulation and parousia, Jesus makes three important points: (1) the disciples do not know when the Lord will come (Matt. 24:42, 44; 25:13); (2) they must therefore watch and be prepared (Matt. 24:42, 44, 25:13); and (3) when they see tribulational events, they can know that Christ is near (Matt. 24:32–33). What is particularly crucial to note is that all three statements are made with respect to the same event—the posttribulational coming of Christ. There is no basis for any transition from the posttribulational aspect of the parousia in Matthew 24:32–35 (or –36) to its pretribulational aspect in 24:36– 25.46. Therefore all interpreters, whether they believe the discourse is addressed to the church or to Israel, face the difficulty of explaining how an event heralded by specific signs can yet be one of which it is said "no one knows the day and hour." One solution may be to understand Jesus' words about the unknown day to apply to every generation except the last—that generation who, when it "sees these things happening," knows that Christ is at the very gates (Matt. 24:33–34). Or it may be that while the exact time cannot be known, one will be able to know the general time of the advent after the tribulation has begun.[115] And in this regard, the statement about the tribulational days being "shortened" (Matt. 24:22) should be noted; it may be impossible to predict the time of the parousia even after the Antichrist has been revealed.

There are also indications that the New Testament authors could not have intended to portray the parousia as an event that could happen "at any moment." Jesus frequently suggests that there will be a delay before his return (Matt. 24:45–51; 25:5, 19; Luke 19:11–27). Second, and more important, are specific predictions that could not have

---

115. Cf. Frost, *Matthew Twenty-four*, 34–36; Gundry, *Church and Tribulation*, 42–43.

been fulfilled if Christ had returned immediately after his ascension. Most notably, in my view, is the desolation of the Jerusalem temple (Matt. 24:15; Mark 13:14). But there are others. Jesus promises his disciples that they will be his witnesses "in Jerusalem, and in all Judea and Samaria, and to the ends of the earth" (Acts 1:8). The gospel must be preached to all nations before the end comes (Matt. 24:14). Peter will die a martyr's death as an old man (John 21:18–19). Paul will preach the gospel in Rome (Acts 23:11; 27:24). It is not sufficient to say that all these could have been fulfilled in the first century and therefore represent no barrier to an "any moment" rapture now.[116] For the point is to determine what the statements about the nearness of the parousia would have meant to those who first heard them. If the original speakers did not intend and the original hearers did not understand a particular statement to require an "any-moment" interpretation, that statement can hardly have such a meaning now.[117] Therefore, it does not appear that the imminence of the return of Christ can be understood in an any-moment sense. (The apostolic fathers also believed in a posttribulational rapture and expected to participate in tribulation events.)[118] It is better to define *imminency* as the possibility of Jesus' coming for his people at any time — "time" being understood broadly as a short period of time. It is in light of that "anytime" coming that the church is called on to live out its calling. But, it is objected, doesn't the denial of the any-moment coming of Christ for his church take away the force of those exhortations to right conduct? In negative applications of the return (as when people are warned to be careful lest Christ "surprise" them), an any-moment rapture adds nothing to the associated exhortations, for it is precisely and only those who do not heed the warnings who will be surprised (cf. Luke 21:34; 1 Thess. 5:2–4). And the exhortations to "watch" because the time is not known require only that the exact moment is unknown for the force of the warning to be maintained. But the stimulus to holy living provided by the expecta-

---

116. Contra Payne, *Imminent Appearing*, 89–91; Walvoord, *Rapture Question*, 150–51.

117. Millard J. Erickson, *Contemporary Options in Eschatology: A Study of the Millennium* (Grand Rapids: Baker, 1977), 142; Gundry, *Church and Tribulation*, 37.

118. See, e.g., *Epistle of Barnabas* 4; Justin, *Dialogue with Trypho* 1:4, 1–3. I do not think that Payne (*Imminent Appearing*, 12–14) is successful in establishing an any-moment parousia in the Fathers.

tion of Christ's return is based primarily on a positive application of the return in the New Testament. Believers are to remain spiritually alert and morally sober because they recognize that they will stand before their Redeemer to answer for their conduct. And the force of this appeal surely does not depend on the any-moment possibility of such an encounter.

The imminent coming of our Lord Jesus Christ is an important and indispensable element of biblical truth. I think (although I am by no means dogmatic about the matter) that this coming will take place before the millennium (Rev. 20:1–6). I also believe that the Bible predicts a time of unprecedented tribulation for the people of God at the end of time—though I would want to insist that this tribulation is not to be separated from the tribulation that believers experience throughout this interadvent period of time, the "last days." Scripture also teaches clearly that believers can look forward to joining Christ at the time of his coming: the dead via resurrection and the living via rapture. All these are clear and important biblical truths. But the time of that rapture with respect to the final tribulation is nowhere plainly stated. No Old or New Testament author directly addresses that question or states the nature of that relationship as a point of doctrine. I have indicated in these pages what I think Scripture suggests on this matter. But because this conviction is founded upon logic, inferences, and legitimately debated points of exegesis, I cannot, indeed must not, allow this conviction to represent any kind of barrier to full relationships with others who hold differing convictions on this point. May our discussions on this point enhance, not detract from, our common expectation of "the blessed hope—the glorious appearing of our great God and Savior, Jesus Christ" (Titus 2:13).

RECONSTRUCTION OF MAJOR END-TIME EVENTS

Events	Matthew 24–25	John 14	1 Corinthians 15	1 Thessalonians 4–5
Wars	24:6–7a			
Famine	24:7b			
Apostasy	24:12			
Preaching of the Gospel	24:14			
Antichrist (in Temple)	(24:15)			
Tribulation	24:16–25			
False Signs	24:24			
Cosmic Signs	24:29			
Parousia	24:30			4:16
Trumpet	24:31		15:52	4:16
Angels	24:31			4:16
First Resurrection	24:31		15:51	
Rapture	24:31(?), 40–41(?)		15:51	4:17
Judgment	25:31–46			
"With the Lord"		14:3		4:17
"Watch"	24:36–25:13			

| | Revelation | | | | |
2 Thessalonians 2	Seals	Trumpets	12-14	Bowls	17-20
	6:3-4				
	6:5-6				
2:3			13:3-4(?)		
			14:6-7(?)		
2:3-7			13:1-8		
	6:9-11 (?)	8:6-9:21		16:1-21	
2:9			13:13-14(?)		
	6:12-17				
2:8					19:11-21
		11:15			
		11:15	14:15		
		11:11-12			20:4-6
			14:14-16		
2:8		11:18	14:17-20		17:11-19:3
	7:9-17	11:18	14:1-5		19:4-9
	Throughout Revelation				

A PRETRIBULATION RESPONSE

CRAIG BLAISING

At the outset of my response, let me express my appreciation to Doug Moo for his participation in this volume. He presented the argument for posttribulationism in the earlier Counterpoints publication, and his essay here is a slightly revised version of that earlier piece. Once again we are reminded of Moo's attention to detail and his coverage of numerous texts that may have bearing on the subject. Given the limitations in length imposed on my response, what follows will focus on our disagreements. However, the reader should know of my esteem for Professor Moo's numerous contributions to evangelical biblical scholarship.

In this response, I will generally follow the flow of Professor Moo's article. However, it is not possible in the space allotted here to address every point of his lengthy and detailed composition. Moreover, there are some key issues that affect a number of his interpretations. I will focus on these issues and point out as many related matters in his hermeneutical argument as space allows. Overall, let me say that I find Moo's tone to be cordial, and it is a delight to be engaged with him on this issue.

Right at the beginning, Moo gives his "perspective on the two key terms *rapture* and *tribulation*." Obviously, we must get our definitions right if we are to have meaningful conversation about these terms. However, right at this beginning point, we encounter problems. First, we are told that "the word *rapture* is, of course, not a New Testament word." That is true of the noun, but the verb is used in the New Testament, and we use the noun to refer to the event described by the verb.

Second, Moo downplays the notion of physical movement in the word *rapture* and says, making reference to 1 Corinthians 15:50–51, that "the more important aspect of rapture in the New Testament is bodily transformation." Certainly, bodily transformation is a key aspect of the fuller New Testament doctrine of the rapture, but it has nothing to do with the meaning of the word, which can also be correctly rendered "caught up" or "snatched up." In its contextual usage in 1 Thessalonians 4:17, it speaks precisely of physical movement from earth to heaven.

Third, Moo tells us that "rapture," now defined as bodily transformation, is what happens to living saints, whereas resurrection happens to dead saints. However, 1 Thessalonians 4:17 says that the living will be "raptured together with them [the resurrected saints]" (*hama syn autois harpagēsometha*). A resurrection happens before the rapture (4:16). And then, in the rapture, both newly resurrected saints and saints who have remained alive until that time, are "together" (*hama*) caught up into heaven.

Fourth, Moo tells us that this rapture "is not a movement to escape something." But the rapture event is presented in 1 Thessalonians precisely as an escape, a deliverance, or salvation for believers (5:9) from the "coming wrath" (1:10) in contrast to the experience of others who will surely "not escape" (5:3).

Moo defines the tribulation as "a period of unparalleled distress for the people of God that will immediately precede the second advent." I would correct this somewhat. While the tribulation does involve suffering for believers who are in it, its object is not "the people of God." It would be better to say that it comes upon the world. Furthermore, while the entire tribulation is a unique time of trouble, it is not uniformly so. Rather, it builds in intensity to reach a level of "unparalleled distress" in the second half. It is not clear in Moo's essay, however, that he holds to a seven-year tribulation since he takes the seventieth "seven" in Daniel 9:24–27 as "referring to the entire package of events spanning the time from Christ's first coming to his second coming in glory." If his use of the term does not refer to the seven-year tribulation normally held by futurists, then we would certainly differ not only on its duration but also on the nature of the event itself.[119]

The Nature of the Tribulation

Moo presents the tribulation as a period of time characterized by persecution and suffering on the one hand and manifestations of divine

---

119. John F. Walvoord provides a helpful classification scheme for different types of posttribulationism. "Futurist" posttribulationism is represented by George Eldon Ladd and is the view that the tribulation is a seven-year period in future history. Futurist posttribulationists are similar to pretribulationists on this point. See John F. Walvoord, *The Blessed Hope and the Tribulation: A Historical and Biblical Study of Posttribulationism* (Grand Rapids: Zondervan, 1976), 40–59.

wrath on the other. But he treats suffering and wrath as aggregates—mixed elements separated in identity and character.

From the standpoint of this description, he argues that there is nothing about its nature and character that would exclude the presence of the church. He asserts that sufferings experienced by believers at that time are not qualitatively different from sufferings experienced by the church throughout its history, and that the manifestation of God's wrath takes place in such a way that believers present on earth will be kept apart or protected from it. A key point is the objective distinction between the sufferings of believers and divine wrath.

I need to point out here that pretribulationists do not claim that God has promised carte blanche to protect or exclude the church from suffering. The Lord warned us that the church would experience trouble and suffering (John 16:33) until he comes to deliver us. This is taught throughout the New Testament. Paul reminded the churches of this in Acts 14:22. The entire message of 1 Peter is built around this point. Even the Thessalonians, who received Paul's teaching about the rapture, were experiencing suffering during their day (1 Thess. 2:14–16; 2 Thess. 1:5). The history of the church confirms the reality of suffering, especially the history of the martyrs.

Pretribulationists believe, however, that the church is promised exemption from a unique future time of tribulation. This tribulation is a unique, integrated, complex, structured event that can be considered as a unified whole (notwithstanding its complexity). The deliverance promised to the church is from this particular complex event considered as a whole. The issue determining this exclusion is not some difference in the experience of historical versus tribulational suffering and martyrdom. The issue is whether God has actually promised believers prior to the coming of the tribulation that they would be excluded from that specific, whole, complex event. The promise of Revelation 3:10 to the church at Philadelphia, and through them to all churches (v. 13) was that they would be kept from "the hour of trial that is going to come upon the whole world to test those who live on the earth." In spite of sufferings in their own day, they, and every generation of the church since then, have been kept from the coming tribulation. And when that unique tribulation event comes, the church at that time will also be excluded by the mystery of the rapture.

The nature of the tribulation is such that the whole of it is presented in Scripture as a time of wrath, even while at the same time some judgments within the event complex are individually designated as outpourings of that wrath. Likewise, the church as a whole is excluded from the tribulation even though within the event complex believers can be seen to be present, experiencing sufferings of various kinds. Understanding this requires a more extensive textual base for the doctrine of the tribulation than that provided by Moo.

Moo does identify Daniel 7–12 along with the Olivet Discourse, the book of Revelation, and 2 Thessalonians 2 as key sources for the doctrine of the tribulation. Daniel 7–12, of course, is foundational for understanding the other texts, but Moo treats Daniel 7–12 only briefly, being primarily concerned to note references to persecution and wrath as evidence for his aggregate model of the tribulation. He does not give us any careful exposition of the pattern that is repeated and nuanced in these chapters. He misses the fact that wrath is used as a descriptor for the whole pattern as well as individual events within it. An adversarial king and army carry out God's wrath, creating the conditions in which the saints suffer persecution.[120] At the end of the pattern, God's wrath is poured out in turn on the persecutor (note Dan. 7:11, 26; 8:25; 9:27; 11:36, 45). However, wrath is descriptive of the conditions in which the persecutor had previously appeared and was active.[121] When one looks carefully at this pattern involving (1) God's judgment on Jerusalem and the temple, followed by (2) God's deliverance of his people by judgment on the persecutor, one sees a pattern that is also revealed in the greater canonical theme of the day of the Lord.

---

120. The model for the pattern in this part of Daniel is the Babylonian destruction of Jerusalem, as indicated by Daniel's prayer. The coming of the gentile army, the destruction caused by the army, and Jerusalem's ongoing desolation are acknowledged by Daniel to be God's wrath (Dan. 9:16).

121. As such, it is designated by Daniel as a time of wrath, cf. Dan. 8:19; 11:36. Collins is basically correct when he notes that "the 'wrath' [in Dan. 8:19] is not just a day of reckoning but a period of history. The closest parallel is provided by the 'age of wrath,' *qēʾārôn*, at Qumran, which involves a pun on the *haqqēhaʾārôn* or 'last age'" (John J. Collins, *A Commentary on the Book of Daniel*, Hermeneia [Minneapolis: Fortress, 1993], 338). Again, he writes, "The 'wrath' referred to in 8:19 is the period of gentile rule, which is now in its latter stage.... The 'wrath' has become a quasi-technical term for the tribulation caused by those kingdoms, especially in its latter phase" (ibid., 339). Of course, I would disagree with Collins's critical reconstruction of Daniel's history and his limitation of the reference of the time of wrath to second century BC events, which I would take to be a near-fulfillment projecting a type for a yet future far-fulfillment.

The greatest deficit in Moo's textual base for building a doctrine of the tribulation is his scant reference to and shallow exposition of this major biblical theme, the day of the Lord. Whenever he does mention it, he presumes it to be a relatively brief event of cosmic phenomena occurring at the end of the tribulation. This presupposition radically affects his interpretation of New Testament passages that draw upon this theme as a source: the Olivet Discourse, the Thessalonian correspondence, and the book of Revelation.[122]

Other than a few brief references, Moo basically ignores the biblical evidence for the day of the Lord. Nowhere does he develop the Old Testament data that form the context for the New Testament usage of the theme. However, as one examines the Old Testament, what one sees is an event pattern that is developed in complexity through the progress of revelation. It is an extended, rather than simple, event.[123] In many passages, it is the extended event of an invasion and battle, or an invasion leading to the siege and destruction of a city. Added to this are features associated with theophany. Some day of the Lord passages have to do with judgment on Gentile nations. Some speak of judgment on Israel. Most interesting are the prophecies of Joel and Zechariah 14 in which the day of the Lord comes with judgment upon Israel and then transitions to Israel's deliverance with judgment on the Gentiles. In Joel the phrase "day of the LORD" is used separately for both aspects of this complex event, the hinge between the two being Israel's repentance. This is why day of the Lord features appear in Joel 2:30–31 "*before* the coming

---

122. Moo does list numerous brief references to the day of the Lord throughout the New Testament, the brevity of which he appears to take as evidence that the end (end of the tribulation or final judgment after the tribulation) is being referenced instead of the tribulation as a whole.

123. Meir Weiss ("The Origin of the 'Day of the Lord' — Reconsidered," *HUCA* 37 [1966]: 44) writes, "One can only approve of what has been pointed out quite often in biblical research, namely, that the DL [day of the Lord] was not conceived of as a certain specific day, but that it was rather an indefinite concept of an accommodating nature, subject to divergent interpretations and applications." He adds, "The Hebrew concept of 'time' is closely coincident with that of its content. Time is the notion of occurrence; it is the stream of events.... Thus the concept 'DL' comes to indicate occurrence rather than the time. It is a 'neutral' concept, a formal one of a changing content which adapts itself to the nature of the individual DL implied by it" (46–47). Because of this, the day of the Lord can be applied to an event of whatever extent. The important point is the interconnectedness and coherence of the event. Hoffmann, noting the parallelism of "year" and "day" in some day of the Lord texts, speaks of the "semantic development of the word *yom*" and notes that "the word [day] connotes not a day but a longer period of time"; Yair Hoffmann, "The Day of the Lord as a Concept and a Term in the Prophetic Literature," *ZAW* (1981): 48.

of the great and dreadful day of the LORD" (emphasis added). It is as if two days of the Lord are combined in one extended event complex.[124] In Zechariah 14:1 this double complex event is altogether labeled "a day … coming for the LORD" (ESV). Both aspects are present: judgment falling upon Jerusalem by means of battle siege and destruction and then deliverance of God's people through judgment on the Gentile aggressors. The second judgment is described as direct divine action, whereas the first made use of human instruments. Both are aspects of one complex event tied together by the phrase "on that day." One can readily see that this twofold complex event has basically the same structure as the pattern in Daniel.[125] This same basic pattern can be seen in the Olivet Discourse, the Thessalonian correspondence, and the book of Revelation. It is a mistake to dismiss the day of the Lord as simply an end event to some other tribulation pattern. It is the tribulation itself.

In conjunction with this, the fact that the day of the Lord is designated a "day of wrath" indicates that wrath generally describes the whole of this extended event. Distinctions between human and divine wrath dissolve in a thematic type in which human action is one means by which divine wrath is accomplished. Furthermore, the theme of repentance within the day of the Lord explains one way believers come to be present in the time of wrath and then find themselves protected from certain manifestations of that wrath — they become believers by repentance during the time of wrath. The wrath comes upon them as unbelievers and although generally speaking there is no escape — there is no escape from the presence of the day once it has come upon them — nevertheless, there are those who become repentant and do escape the finality of that wrath, becoming objects of divine deliverance as the wrath culminates. This theme of repentance in the Old Testament pattern is highlighted again in the book of Revelation. The presence of believers during the tribulation belongs to the biblical pattern of the

---

124. See James D. Nogalski, "The Day(s) of YHWH in the Book of the Twelve," in *Thematic Threads in the Book of the Twelve*, ed. Paul L. Redditt and Aaron Schart (Berlin: de Gruyter, 2003), 200–203. Also, Susan F. Mathews, "The Power to Endure and Be Transformed: Sun and Moon Imagery in Joel and Revelation 6," in *Imagery and Imagination in Biblical Literature: Essays in Honor of Aloysius Fitzgerald, F. S.C.*, ed. Lawrence Boadt and Mark S. Smith, CBQMS 32 (Washington, D.C.: Catholic Biblical Association of America, 2001), 39–40, 42, 47n25.

125. See the comments of Antti Laato, "The Seventy Yearweeks in the Book of Daniel," *ZAW* 102 (1990): 222–23.

day of the Lord and Daniel's time of the end. The question of the pre-tribulational rapture is not decided by the existence of believers in the tribulation or their protection from specific manifestations of wrath during it. The question is decided by an explicit promise given in the progress of revelation that all believers living at the time the tribulation begins would be delivered from it—from the whole extended complex event, correlating their expected deliverance from wrath with deliverance from this whole extended wrath event.

Finally, on the nature of the tribulation, I explain in my essay how in the teaching of Jesus the day of the Lord theme was integrated with the content and structure of Daniel's time of the end. The integration of these two themes becomes the New Testament teaching on the tribulation, referenced mostly by some variant of the phrase "day of the Lord." We could say that the New Testament presents us with a "Danielic enhanced" day of the Lord, and this, then, is the New Testament doctrine of the tribulation. This creates, however, major problems for Moo's overall argument, because it raises a challenge at the definitional level.

Vocabulary of the Second Advent

Two things can be noted briefly about this section of Moo's essay. First, the parousia is linked to the theme of the day of the Lord, because it is the day of the Lord's coming. Just as the day of the Lord is an extended event (the entire tribulation), parousia also carries an extended sense in at least some of its uses. I pointed this out from the way Paul references the teaching of Jesus in 1 Thessalonians 5:1–4, substituting "day of the Lord" for "parousia." Consequently, it is a mistake to say, as Moo does, that "parousia is indisputably posttribulational." Rather, it is indisputably *tribulational*, simply so stated, in that the tribulation is his coming. To be sure, he *appears* at the end of the tribulation—that is the purpose of the coming, a purpose for which the metaphor of labor pains is a suitable image. Paul, I think, specifies the posttribulational appearance of this coming more exactly by the phrase "appearance of his coming" (*tē epiphaneia tēs parousias autou*; 2 Thess. 2:8). But it is not inconsistent with this purpose or with the extended nature of the coming if the Lord were to descend at the onset of the day to rescue the church and prepare them to appear with him at its climax. Because of this, although I distinguish the rapture from the posttribulational descent, I prefer to speak of one future coming, which can be looked at as a whole or from the standpoint of either its onset or its climax.

Second, Moo's complaint that a "two-stage coming" is not perceptible in the terms used for *coming* is not objectionable per se. The argument for pretribulationism does not rest on an analysis of these terms per se, but on the New Testament teaching about those terms—specifically Paul's teaching in 1 Thessalonians 4–5 about the event of the rapture in relationship to the extended coming and day of the Lord.

The Rapture – Three Basic Passages

Though not stated this precisely, Moo's argument in this section appears to be as follows: (1) The New Testament everywhere outside the traditional rapture passages presents the future coming of Christ as a posttribulational descent; (2) these rapture passages speak of the future coming of Christ; (3) we should interpret them as referring to the posttribulational descent unless there are internal textual clues inconsistent with this; (4) there are no internal textual clues inconsistent with this, (5) therefore, these passages speak of the posttribulational descent.

Of course, I have argued that 1 Thessalonians 4:13–5:9 presents a pretribulational descent of Christ, and if that is so, then that fact alone counters Moo's argument and leads us to the following: (1) One of the passages speaking of the future coming of Christ presents a pretribulational descent; (2) this raises the possibility that other passages speaking of the coming of Christ may likewise present a pretribulational descent; (3) therefore, we should look for clues of this pretribulational descent in other passages speaking of the future coming of Christ. My response to this portion of Moo's essay is that, in fact, these traditional rapture passages contain clues that indicate at least the possibility of the same pretribulational event.

When we come to John 14:1–3, contrary to Moo's claim that "there is no indication in the text that [there is] any 'coming' other than the posttribulational one," I would assert that there is no indication whatsoever in this text of any setting other than a pretribulational one. The greater context does speak of trouble and suffering in the world prior to Jesus' coming (John 16:33), but this is not the future tribulation, as Moo himself recognizes. Pretribulationists expect general conditions of trouble and suffering prior to the rapture. The simple promise that Jesus will come again and "take you to be *with me*" (emphasis added) is quite compatible with the pretribulational event revealed in 1 Thessalonians 4:17. The Lord descends and believers are caught up to be *with him*. The last phrase of John 14:3, "that where I am you may be also" forms a fitting parallel to the last phrase of 1 Thessalonians 4:17, "and so we will always be with the Lord."

Moo does well to note that the trumpet in 1 Corinthians 15:51–52 is a feature in some day of the Lord prophecies. This, as many have pointed out, is because the trumpet is a featured image in biblical descriptions of theophany, and theophany is one of the features of the day of the Lord. The fact that it is called the "last" (*eschatē*) trumpet further justifies the association. The day of the Lord is an *eschatological* day, and any feature associated with it is properly "last," including any theophanic features. Since both the rapture descent and the concluding regal descent are related to this day, either one could be characterized by a "last" trumpet. Both the appearances of Christ at the end of the tribulation (Matt. 24:31) and the descent at the rapture (1 Thess. 4:16) are signaled by a trumpet. But only 1 Thessalonians 4:16 is a true parallel to 1 Corinthians 15:52–53 since only these two texts speak of the resurrection of the dead in relation to living believers. Accordingly, the timing of the 1 Corinthians 15:51–52 event is best determined by clues in the context of 1 Thessalonians 4:16–17.

Moo tries to present 1 Thessalonians 4:16–17 as a posttribulational event on the basis of some similar descriptions found in the descent imagery of Matthew 24:30–31 and the resurrection event of Daniel 12:1–2. However, the fact that both descent descriptions feature a trumpet, and the fact that an archangel appears in Daniel 12 along with the description of the dead as "asleep," is not sufficient in itself to locate the event. These features are simply (1) a common way of describing the dead, and (2) theophanic features that might characterize any divine descent. What does determine the eschatological location of the rapture descent is its relation to the onset of the day of the Lord in 1 Thessalonians 5 and to the promise of deliverance from wrath in 1:10 and 5:9. The problem here is that Moo's identification of the rapture "text" in 1 Thessalonians is too narrow. The "text" that needs to be interpreted here covers a larger portion of the epistle.

1 Thessalonians 5:1 - 11

I would agree with Moo on several points here: (1) This portion of text is connected with chapter 4. (2) Paul is contrasting here the effect of the same event on two different groups. (3) The day of the Lord is interchangeable with parousia in this expectation. (4) The rapture is related to the day of the Lord. (5) The emphasis in 1 Thessalonians 5:3 is on the suddenness of the judgment.

However, contrary to Moo, I would say: (1) The day of the Lord is an extended, tribulational—not a brief, posttribulational—event.[126] (2) The reference to the destruction of unbelievers does not make this a posttribulational event, but rather a tribulational event. The day of the Lord as a whole is destructive. It is comprised of many destructions and culminates in a final destruction. (3) The day does not "overtake" believers. In Paul's terms, the day "comes upon *them* [unbelievers]." But believers are delivered at the onset of the day (the contrast in 5:3–4; cf. 1:10; 5:9). (4) Moo begs the question about 1 Thessalonians 5:9 when he says, "Paul never uses 'wrath' without qualifiers to denote a period of time." I would say that the use of *wrath* here must be interpreted in relation to 1:10, "the wrath to come." The wrath in 5:9 is a wrath-event that necessarily occupies time. The relation of these two texts (1:10 and 5:9) is similar to the relation of Daniel 8:19 and 11:36. The single word for "wrath" in Daniel 11:36 designates the same wrath-event described in 8:19 as the final period of the wrath. (5) Paul is not exhorting believers to live in such a way as to avoid the judgment of the day of the Lord. A distinction is proclaimed in the text. They will be delivered, and they are exhorted to live in light of that distinction.

2 Thessalonians 1 – 2

Moo draws our attention to Paul's description of Christ's future revelation in judgment in 2 Thessalonians 1:7–10. He notes that Paul speaks of this event as giving "rest" to "you who are afflicted" (1:7 ESV). He then argues that this implies that since believers will not be relieved until this posttribulational event, they consequently cannot be raptured until then either. He tries to avoid the obvious objection that "rest" comes earlier to those who die, by suggesting that the promise is hypothetical, assuming that one were alive through the tribulation to its end, relief would not come until that moment. A better explanation, it seems to me, is that

---

126. Jeremiah 6:14, cited by Moo, is actually a helpful analogy for this point. The "peace" referred to here describes conditions prior to the Babylonian invasion, attack, siege, and destruction of the city—an extended event comparable to the tribulation itself. The prior peace condition is comparable to pretribulational conditions.

Paul speaks of this rest in relation to its basis—the final judgment of the persecutor brought by the Lord at the climax of his coming. Whether believers die two thousand years prior to the tribulation, are raptured at the onset of the tribulation, or are numbered among the repentant that emerge during the tribulation—their "rest" from affliction is ultimately grounded in the fact that the Lord will cause persecution to finally and ultimately cease when he brings persecutors to their final judgment.

My remarks on 2 Thessalonians 2 in my essay are, I think, a sufficient response to Moo's posttribulational interpretation of that chapter. I would only add that the posttribulational view creates a major contradiction between this text and 1 Thessalonians 5. Paul says in 1 Thessalonians 5 that the day of the Lord will come without warning (without signs) in a time of relative peace, while Moo interprets 2 Thessalonians 2 as saying that the day of the Lord will come only after certain signs that place the event at a point in the tribulation that Daniel and Jesus describe as extreme distress. Furthermore, it is puzzling: If (1) Paul has taught the church posttribulationism, and if (2) they are looking forward to the relief they will receive at the coming of Christ, and if (3) they truly believe Christ may come in their lifetime, then (4) why should they be "shaken" and "disturbed" at a report that the necessary prelude to Christ's coming has occurred? According to Moo, they are going to be protected when it does occur, so they have nothing to fear concerning it. Rather, they should be overjoyed and expectant—looking up, for their salvation draws nigh! They would, however, be shocked and disturbed by a report that the day of the Lord had come if they had been expecting Christ to descend and rapture them (1 Thess. 4:16–17) at or before its onset (1 Thess. 5:1–9), thereby delivering them from the wrath to come (1 Thess. 1:10).

The Olivet Discourse

Moo believes that the Olivet Discourse addresses the long history of the church, concluded by the parousia. My essay treating the Olivet Discourse critiques this view. But Moo's exposition is odd, because in spite of his earlier affirmation of the Olivet Discourse as a source for the "final tribulation," here there is no "final tribulation," only the tribulation of church history climaxed by the catastrophic but relatively brief descent of Christ. Moo had also listed Daniel 7–12 as a source for the "final tribulation." But in the Olivet Discourse, where Jesus quotes Daniel, Moo relegates the matter to an event of "local" significance only. It appears that Moo does not think that the destruction of Jerusalem and the temple, a key feature of Old Testament eschatology and one that Jesus' disciples associated with the parousia, has universal significance nor that it would have anything to do with actual eschatological events. But in day of the Lord prophecies, Jerusalem is the focal point for God's judgment of the nations. Moo misses the eschatological pattern of Daniel's time of the end and the day of the Lord that structures Jesus' remarks, as well as the way that pattern has functioned historically and typologically in Scripture.

The main point Moo wishes to make about the Olivet Discourse is that believers are present in it up to the point of the final descent. However, if in fact the history of the church is in view, there is no point to be made about believers being in the tribulation. As for the Lord's exhortations to watch for his coming, they occur, as I have argued, in the second half of the Olivet Discourse, which is looking at the coming as an extended event, consistent with a view of the extended day of the Lord as the day of his coming. The exhortation is focused on the onset of that coming, just as 1 Thessalonians 5 focuses on the onset of the day of the Lord, a focus that is consistent with pretribulationism.

I, however, do see the Olivet Discourse setting forth the pattern of the future tribulation (as well as the pattern of the AD 70 destruction—minus the Lord's appearance in the clouds, which would have led to his descent). So, what is the meaning of this reference to the disciples in the "tribulational pattern"? Pretribulationists expect "believers" to be in the tribulation because of repentance and conversion in the day of the Lord. Jesus addresses these "other" believers through his disciples. Scripture has many examples of what might be called the prophetic "you." For example, in Deuteronomy 4, Moses warns that generation of Israel against forgetting the Lord. He warns of a future exile but also promises a future return when they seek the Lord. He says, "When you are in tribulation, and all these things come upon you in the latter days, you will return to the LORD your God and obey his voice" (Deut. 4:30 ESV). The "you" here is spoken to that generation, but its fulfillment will not be found in them personally but in a much later generation. In like manner, Jesus addresses his disciples in the Olivet Discourse and speaks of "you," but the ultimate fulfillment is to a later generation—one that will return to the Lord in the midst of the tribulation.

But what about the near fulfillment of the pattern in AD 70? The near fulfillment was not the Lord's coming and consequently featured neither the rapture nor the descent. In such a situation, believers alive at the beginning of the pattern would live into the pattern and would be the believers of whom Jesus spoke—whether that would be the disciples themselves, or, given the fact that many of the disciples were already dead by that time, the next generation of believers. We need to note that Paul speaks of the rapture as a mystery (1 Cor. 15:51)—something previously unrevealed but made known at a later time. Paul declares this mystery to the church by a "word from the Lord" (1 Thess. 4:15). The Lord himself promised the church at Philadelphia that they would be kept from the hour (Rev. 3:10). In the progress of revelation, then, the Lord made known a previously unrevealed truth: that his coming, the day of the Lord, the tribulation, would not come upon *them* as a thief. Believers at the beginning of the day of the Lord would be delivered from the wrath to come. Unbelievers would not escape. But in keeping with his mercy and grace, some of those upon whom the day would come would repent and be saved. They would become the "you" of that latter day.

Revelation

Moo divides his discussion of Revelation into three parts. He discusses a number of possibilities in interpretation, but I will focus on what I think has the greatest bearing on our subject. First, his survey of the letters to the seven churches leads him to Revelation 3:10, which he finds to be inconclusive on the timing of the rapture. My only comment here has to do with the implication he wishes to draw from the use of *tēreō ek* in John 17 for its use in Revelation 3:10. The notion of *spiritual* protection comes from the contextual application of the verb in John 17. It seems illegitimate to me to conclude that because *tēreō* is also used in Revelation 3, it is consequently speaking of *spiritual* protection. As Moo notes, the use of *tēreō* with *ek* means separation. The contextual application indicates the kind of separation, and Revelation 3:10 applies it to "the hour of trial that is going to come upon the whole world to test those who live on the earth." This is a reference to the day of the Lord, the time of the tribulation. The promise is that they will be separated from that day.

Second, Moo examines several texts in Revelation 4–20 that he says might indicate the rapture. He decides that the rapture should be associated with the resurrection of the dead in Revelation 20:4 since "it is not easy to think that John's language allows for any resurrection preceding this one." However, John does acknowledge that the resurrection of Jesus precedes that of Revelation 20:4 (see 1:18; 2:8). Consequently, "first" is not an absolute chronological indicator, but relative to a *second* resurrection mentioned in context—one that takes place after the thousand years. They are contrasted not only temporally with respect to the millennium, but in quality (similar to the "better resurrection" in Heb. 11:35). This does not rule out a pretribulational rapture any more than it intentionally rules out the resurrection of Christ. But the main problem in locating the rapture at Revelation 20:4 is that this text says nothing about the transformation of mortal believers into immortality, nor does the event include the catching up of those who had remained alive together with the resurrected dead to meet the Lord in the air. In fact, the resurrection in 20:4 takes place in John's sequence after the descent of Christ. It seems rather clear that the rapture is not in view in Revelation 20:4.

The matter of the identity of the saints in Revelation does not seem to me to be a decisive issue, although it is to some pretribulationists. Moo notes that the word *ekklēsia* does not appear in chapters 4–19. Consequently, it seems irrelevant to say, as he does, that "John never in chapters 4–19 calls any group in heaven the church." In these chapters, he doesn't call any group anywhere the church. Nevertheless, pretribulationists acknowledge that there are believers in Christ in the tribulation period. The issue is whether there is a rapture of all believers before the tribulation. It seems to me that Moo's interpretation of the matter confirms what we already know—Revelation doesn't identify the rapture in any vision or visionary sequence between chapters 4 and 20.

In conclusion, Professor Moo has addressed many of the texts that must be considered in relating the rapture to the tribulation. However, a posttribulational location for the rapture creates a number of hermeneutical and exegetical problems. In addition, certain biblical themes that are key to the question—themes such as the day of the Lord and Daniel's time of the end—are not given the consideration they require. As a result, Moo's argument is unconvincing. It fails to establish posttribulationism within the complexity of New Testament eschatology.

ALAN HULTBERG

Dr. Moo has presented a well-argued case for the posttribulation rapture. For the most part, I agree with his basic exegesis of the Olivet Discourse, the Thessalonian correspondence, and Revelation that places the church in the tribulation and thus necessitates a rapture some time after the middle of Daniel's seventieth week. I agree that there is nothing inherent in the tribulation that excludes the church's presence in it and that God's promise of not subjecting the church to divine wrath does not necessitate the rapture as the means of protection. I disagree, however, that Moo has demonstrated that the parousia, with attendant rapture, wrath, and glorious appearance of Christ, is a simple event at the end of Daniel's seventieth week and that therefore the rapture is not prewrath.

Though Moo does not devote sustained individual attention to it, his argument for this latter point rests on the following theses (some of which he gives more weight to than others). (1) The vocabulary of the second advent in the New Testament does not provide evidence for a "two-stage" coming. (2) The last trumpet at which Israel is saved and the church is raptured is clearly a final event and related to the resurrection of Old Testament saints. (3) Second Thessalonians 1:6–10 and 2:1–12 make the best sense on a "single-stage" reading. (4) Various passages in Revelation, when read according to the structure of the book, argue for a rapture at the end of the tribulation. I will begin my rebuttal with this last point, since it is Revelation, in my opinion, that most clearly shows that the parousia is a complex of events, rapture-wrath-return, that occur over time, and because the evidence in Revelation touches on some of Moo's other theses. After considering Revelation, I will deal with the evidence of 2 Thessalonians.

Revelation 11:11 – 12

While recognizing that conclusions on Revelation 11:11 – 12 are far from certain, Moo nevertheless suggests that, on the assumption that the two witnesses represent the church, the language of Revelation 11:11 – 12 implies the rapture. As such, he argues that there are three contextual indications that the rapture occurs at the end of the tribulation: the great earthquake of 11:13 is the same as those of 6:12 and 16:18, both of which are posttribulational; the three and one-half days that the corpses of the witnesses lie in the street could represent the tribulation and thus that their resurrection is posttribulational; and the end is clearly reached with the blowing of the seventh trumpet, thus suggesting that the rapture of the witnesses is concurrent with that event.

To begin, I agree with Moo that the language of Revelation 11:11 – 12 implies the rapture, even though the conclusion is not certain. Furthermore, it is difficult to tell whether this is a depiction of the rapture of the church[127] or of another group or of two individuals, but presumably the rapture of any group is simultaneous with that of the church. I do not agree, however, that, if this is a rapture scene, Moo's evidence indicates a posttribulation rapture. Part of Moo's argument relies on a misappropriation of the otherwise correct observation that there is significant recapitulation in the visions of Revelation. He seems to assume from this that none of the sequences in Revelation are chronological. Thus, for example, in his opinion the rapture of the two witnesses does not precede the seventh trumpet but is simultaneous with it, and both the sixth seal and the seventh seal symbolize the end of the tribulation. Such an assumption is much too facile, however; one must consider the particular evidence in every case. So, with regard to the timing of the "rapture" of the two witnesses, we need to consider on the one hand the relation of that episode to the trumpet sequence and on the other the relation of the trumpet sequence to the seals and bowls.

Most commentators on Revelation understand chapters 10 and 11 to form an interlude in the trumpet series. That is, after the sixth

---

127. The fact that the two witnesses are killed in Jerusalem (Rev. 11:8) makes it hard to understand them to represent the global church. It is possible the two witnesses represent the local church in Jerusalem, either of the first century (cf. Rev. 11:2; Luke 21:24) or the last, though the details of the vision are hard to apply to the church in any case.

trumpet is blown, the action is halted in 10:1–11:2 while John is commissioned for a new prophetic task of divulging the contents of the unsealed scroll. The description of the witnesses in 11:3–10 is a continuation of the speech of the one who commissions John to measure the temple (with comment by John), apparently providing information significant for understanding the contents of the scroll that John will prophesy. A change appears to happen in verse 11, where the verb tenses shift to aorists, as if John is now reporting the action rather than being informed about things that will happen at some indeterminate point in the future. The fact that in verse 14 the end of the second woe (sixth trumpet) is announced may thus be significant. Though the description of the two witnesses and their ministry in 11:3–10 is part of the interlude between the sixth and seventh trumpets and may find its historical fulfillment during some unknown stretch of time in relation to the trumpet sequence, in verses 11–13 the description has melted back into the vision report regarding the sixth trumpet. Though the trumpet series gives no indication of requiring a chronological fulfillment (that is, that each trumpet effects events that are prior to those of the following trumpet), the events of the first six trumpets clearly precede those of the seventh trumpet, since that trumpet brings the reader to the very end of the age. There is thus no necessary reason that the rapture of the witnesses happens right before the end.

Moo, however, offers some evidence that this is nevertheless the case. On the one hand, he notes that the ministry of the two witnesses is said to last 1,260 days, suggesting that it takes place during the first half of Daniel's seventieth week, and that their corpses remain unburied for three and a half days, suggesting that they are dead for the second half of the week; that is, right up to the end of the tribulation. Their resurrection and rapture must therefore be concurrent with the parousia signaled in the seventh trumpet. I think that he is correct in his first suggestion but incorrect in his second. The 1,260 days do seem to refer to the first half of Daniel's "week," since it is only "when they have finished their testimony" that the Beast will "attack them, and overpower and kill them" (Rev. 11:7; cf. Dan. 7:21; 12:1–8). This phrase is used again for the Beast's persecution of the saints in Revelation 13:7, during the forty-two months of his satanic reign, a period equal to the second half of Daniel's seventieth week. The witnesses thus seem to testify inviolate (11:5) for the first three and one-half years before being killed some time during the final three and one-half years. What is striking is that their bodies lie in the street for only three and one-half "days." This seems intentional, to contrast the relatively short period of the witnesses' deaths with the longer period of their witness.[128] It is possible, of course, that they are killed at the very end of the tribulation period, but it is equally possible that they are killed shortly after their period of witness and raptured not long after that, some time during the tribulation. At any rate, the use of "three and a half days" in Revelation 11:9, 11 is weak evidence for a posttribulation rapture.

A second piece of evidence that Moo offers to argue for the rapture of the witnesses at the end of the tribulation is that an earthquake attends both events (Rev. 11:13, 19). Additionally, the earthquake that accompanies the rapture is called a "great earthquake," supposedly making it equal to the earthquakes in Revelation 6:12 (seal six) and 16:18 (bowl seven), both of which, Moo contends, happen at the very end of the age. But this latter evidence actually undermines Moo's case.

It is true that the "great earthquake" mentioned in Revelation 16:18 signals the end, the arrival of the kingdom of God. It is part of the list of theophanic phenomena that occur in the seventh element of each of the three "judgment" series (Rev. 8:5; 11:19; 16:18). Revelation 11:15−19 makes it clear that these phenomena signal the arrival of God's kingdom. But is the "great earthquake" of Revelation 6:12 of the same sort? Only an uncritical reliance on the assumption that there is no chronological relation among the seals specifically or among the seals, trumpets, and bowls generally, will allow this conclusion. The text of Revelation, however, disproves that assumption in this case. The narrative development from the sixth to the seventh seal and from the seventh seal to the seven trumpets indicates that the earthquake of Revelation 6:12 precedes that of the seventh seal, trumpet, and bowl.

Thus, when the fifth seal is opened, God's wrath is prayed for but forestalled (Rev. 6:10). When the sixth seal is opened, cosmic disturbances portend the arrival of God's wrath (6:17), but the wrath is

---

128. For John's use of contrastively short periods of time, see Rev. 8:1; 9:5, 10; 17:12; 18:10, 17, 19. Cf. G. K. Beale, *The Book of Revelation*, NIGTC (Grand Rapids: Eerdmans, 1999), 595.

explicitly withheld (7:1–3) until after the sealing of the 144,000 and, as I argue in my primary essay, the rapture of the innumerable multitude. Only after these events have been completed is the seventh seal opened and God's wrath meted out, first proleptically, when fire from God's altar mixed with the prayers of the saints (of 6:10) is thrown to the earth, then explicitly, when the seven trumpets, distributed at the opening of seventh seal, are sounded. The mention of the completion of God's wrath after the sounding of the seventh trumpet (11:18) makes this clear. So the wrath of the seven trumpets is very clearly that wrath announced as impending upon the opening of the sixth seal. Certainly, then, the "great earthquake" of the sixth seal that signals the arrival of God's wrath cannot also be the earthquake of the seventh seal/trumpet that signaled the conclusion of God's wrath! Thus the "great earthquake" that accompanies the "rapture" of the two witnesses at the sixth trumpet is not necessarily the earthquake accompanying the arrival of God's kingdom at the seventh trumpet; it could be, and probably is, the sixth seal "great earthquake."

Moo and I agree that the sixth seal (Rev. 6:12–17) initiates the day of the Lord/parousia. Thus we both anticipate the rapture at this point in the vision report. But whereas posttribulationists are forced either to admit, contrary to expectations, that no rapture is presented in this parousia scene, or to ignore the clear sequencing from the sixth seal to the seventh and so posit various disjunctions in the timing, a prewrath reading is straightforward and pays attention to the temporal signals in the text. The rapture occurs in chapter 7, while God's wrath is impending, and the innumerable multitude redeemed by the Lamb appear in heaven. It is followed by the seventh seal/seven trumpets with the outpouring of God's wrath and the arrival of Christ on earth to establish his kingdom. This same sequence is at least implied in the episode of the two witnesses. The witnesses are "raptured" when a "great earthquake" kills a tenth of the population of Jerusalem prior to the theophany of the seventh trumpet and its earthquake. That the seventh trumpet is expanded in the seven bowls of wrath adds to the likelihood. So, assuming the ascension of the witnesses is in fact a rapture scene, there is no good reason for understanding the rapture of the two witnesses to happen at the very end of the tribulation, but there is sound reason to see it as happening before the end.

Revelation 14:14 - 16

The second passage in Revelation that Moo suggests portrays a posttribulation rapture is Revelation 14:14–16. His only support for this opinion is that Revelation 14:14–16 is probably a parousia scene and that it immediately precedes a reference to the outpouring of God's wrath in verses 17–20. Since he assumes that both of these events are posttribulational, he reads a posttribulation rapture into the passage. But, as I argued in my primary essay, the flow of thought of Revelation shows that this scene presents a prewrath rapture in concert with the prewrath rapture of Revelation 7:9–17. Revelation 14:14–16 is part of a larger subunit in Revelation that runs from chapter 12 through chapter 16, a subunit where John "prophesies again," divulging the contents of the scroll he had eaten in chapter 10. This subunit begins to focus on the Danielic persecution of the saints by the Beast and God's subsequent vindication of the saints, a focus that will continue through Revelation 20. The background to the persecution, the larger satanic opposition to God's people begun in Eden, is portrayed in Revelation 12, and God's intervention on behalf of the saints is portrayed in chapters 14–16, culminating in the bowls of wrath. Revelation 14:14–20 falls in this section. Like Revelation 6:12–8:5, a sequence seems intended. First, three angels announce the impending judgment (14:6–12); then the Son of Man harvests the earth at the parousia (14:14–16); and finally the judgment falls when an angel reaps the vintage of the earth (14:17–20). This sequence is expanded in the third "sign," where John sees those who had come off victorious from the Beast standing before God in heaven (15:2–4; presumably those who had been harvested by the Son of Man), followed by the outpouring of the bowls of the final wrath of God (15:5–16:21), clearly the vintage of 14:17–20 (cf. 14:8; 16:19).

It is important to note two things about this sequence. First, regardless of how literally one understands the vision of the bowls (and earlier trumpets) to correspond to its historical referents, John is envisioning a divine judgment of humanity that takes time to have its effect. The judgments of the third, fifth, and sixth bowls do not happen instantaneously, and the fact that people are given the opportunity, or at least thought liable, to repent during the judgment series (Rev. 9:20; 16:9,

11) suggests the same for all the trumpets and bowls. Furthermore, the destruction of Babylon, an event announced in Revelation 14:8 as part of the parousia judgment (cf. 16:19; 19:2–3), is carried out not by Christ at his return but by the Beast and his allied kings sometime before the return of Christ (17:16–17). Thus the parousia and its attendant wrath is a complex event occurring over an extended period of time and not (essentially) instantaneously as posttribulationism demands.

Second, it is important to note that the parousia wrath that begins with the bowls culminates in the return of Christ with his saints. Thus, the image of the winepress of the wrath of God (Rev. 14:19–20) is picked up again in the Revelation 19:15, where Christ returns to earth accompanied by the armies of heaven (v. 14). As I argued in my primary essay, the evidence strongly suggests that the armies of heaven are or include the church (17:14). But since the wrath-effecting grape harvest of Revelation 14 was preceded by the parousia harvest (subsequently depicted as a multitude of victors in heaven prior to the pouring out of the bowls), the implication is that the churchly army that accompanies the rider on the white horse to tread the winepress of God's wrath in chapter 19 are in fact those who had been harvested, or "raptured," by the Son of Man in chapter 14. Revelation thus evidences a consistent pattern of rapture-wrath-return.

Moo seeks to mitigate this evidence in two ways. First, he notes that commentators on Revelation 19:14 are apparently evenly divided as to whether John refers there to saints or angels. But this both overstates and understates the evidence. On the one hand, commentators are not evenly divided as to whether the church is in view in Revelation 19:14 in some sense, either on its own or as part of a larger group. In fact, there are relatively few commentators who deny the church is in view to some degree. On the other hand, those commentators who accept that the church is portrayed in Revelation 19:14 offer solid contextual evidence that this is the case, whereas those who see only angels argue from the general trend of the Old Testament and New Testament rather than from the context of Revelation. That the church is in view is by far the better interpretation.

Second, Moo suggests that Revelation 19:7–9 is a proleptic vision of the effects of the return of Christ in Revelation 19:11–21, since that is how the visions of 17:1–19:10 appear to him to function. As such, the giving of white robes does not necessarily precede the parousia. Once again, however, his assumption is too facile. Revelation 17:14 is certainly a prediction of the events envisioned in 19:11–21, the war of the Beast and kings of the earth with the Lamb. It is part of an interpretation given to John by one of the bowl angels about the ten horns of the Beast. Revelation 17:15–18 is an interpretation of the harlot Babylon and contains a prediction that the Beast and the ten kings will destroy the harlot city. The chronological relationship between the destruction of Babylon and the war of the Beast with the Lamb is not stated, but the destruction of Babylon by the Beast must surely precede the destruction of the Beast by the Lamb. Revelation 18:1–19:10 is the response of various heavenly beings to the prediction in 17:16–17 of the destruction of Babylon. Revelation 19:7–9, where the impending marriage supper of the Lamb and the preparation of his bride are announced, is part of this response, and it leads directly to the resumption of the vision report in 19:11–21, the return of Christ with his bride to defeat the Beast at "the great supper of God." Thus the bride being clothed in fine linen is not proleptic of the second coming but preparatory to it. The marriage supper seems to *be* the second coming itself. John signals this relationship of 19:7–9 to 19:11–21 by his use of *ēlthen*, his typical way of announcing an immediately impending or just arriving episode, and by the repetition of the wedding garment motif (clothed and ready in 19:7–8, arriving in full array in 19:14) and the supper motif (impending in 19:7–9, arriving in 19:17–21). Again, this suggests that the rapture happened prior to the return of Christ to earth, our other evidence suggesting at the harvest by the Son of Man in chapter 14.

Thus Moo's argument that the vocabulary of the New Testament regarding the second coming is inconclusive in determining the timing of the various events is only partly true. The language of Christ coming "with" his saints at his glorious return in Revelation 17:14 and 19:14 is hardly debatable and, given the structure of Revelation, lends strong support to the idea that the parousia is a complex event occurring over an extended period of time. First Thessalonians 4:14 does not overturn this conclusion since it is not at all clear that Paul refers to the return of Christ to earth in this verse or, even if he does, that the rapture had not occurred a significant time earlier than the return.

Revelation 20:4

The third passage in Revelation that Moo argues may indicate the time of the rapture is Revelation 20:4. To begin, I agree that the resurrection in Revelation 20:4 includes that of the church. Still, as I argued in my primary essay, this is not as helpful to the posttribulationist as it might first appear. For not only is the "first resurrection" posttribulational as it stands (on a premillennial reading of Rev. 20:4–6), it is also postparousia and thus involves no meaningful rapture at all. It therefore is probably "misplaced" by John for thematic or other reasons, especially given the other evidence of a rapture associated with the parousia in Revelation. At any rate, it provides no independent evidence for the timing of the rapture.

The Resurrection of Old Testament Saints

More significantly, however, Moo suggests that a group more extensive than the church is in view in Revelation 20:4, one that includes Old Testament saints. And since, as he argues elsewhere, the resurrection of Old Testament saints is posttribulational, so must be the resurrection/rapture of the church. In my opinion, this is Moo's strongest point, though I also think that it is not ultimately decisive. Moo seeks to demonstrate the connection of the resurrection of Old Testament saints to the rapture through the use of the Old Testament in especially two New Testament rapture passages, 1 Corinthians 15:1–52 and 1 Thessalonians 4:13–18. In the first is found an allusion to Isaiah 25:8, in which God promises Judah an era without death, suggesting that that promise will be fulfilled at the rapture. In the second is found an allusion to Daniel 12:2–3, a passage that clearly establishes a posttribulational resurrection of Jewish saints. And in both are found references to the trumpet of God, which in the Old Testament signals the day of the Lord and the gathering of Israel.

The difficulties with Moo's argument are several-fold, due especially on the one hand to the ambiguity of Old Testament eschatology generally and of its relationship to Paul's thought specifically and, on the other, to the ambiguity of the relationship of both to Revelation 20:1–10. First, though it is true that a trumpet blast on the day of the Lord is associated with the regathering of Israel in the Old Testament (Isa. 27:13; Joel

2:15–16?), it is also associated with an attack on Israel (Joel 2:1) and with God's defense of Israel when they are already in the land, apparently before establishing the kingdom (Zech. 9:12–14, cf. 12:1–14; 14:1–21; cf. Zeph. 1:16). In other words, the trumpet on the day of the Lord, just like the concept of the day of the Lord itself, does not signify a single event, and when it is used for the regathering of Israel, it is not clear that this regathering is simultaneous with, rather than before, the glorious return of Christ to earth. Additionally, though the regathering of Israel is associated with the image of resurrection in the Old Testament (Ezek. 37:11–14), it is nowhere explicitly related to the actual, physical resurrection of Old Testament saints. Certainly the context of Isaiah 25:8 and 26:19 (Isa. 24–27) is associated with God's restoration of Israel, but the temporal relationship of the events is not clear, let alone the relation of the events to other "kingdom" prophecies in Isaiah, not least Isaiah 65:17–20. This latter is instructive, since, on the one hand, Isaiah posits an eschatological period when Zion will be the center of God's favor and the nations will be no longer be under the pall of death (Isa. 25:6–8), while on the other he sees a similar period when death and perhaps sin are still possible (Isa. 26:10[?]; 65:20, 22; cf. Zech. 14:16–21). Though some understand these passages as irreconcilable visions of the kingdom, others see in them two phases of the kingdom along the lines of Revelation 20:4–21:8, an initial phase under the mediation of the Messiah (cf. Isa. 11:1–10; 65:25) and a final phase in which God himself reigns and all his enemies have been vanquished (Isa. 25:6–8; cf. Rev. 20:10, 14; 21:1–8). Though Isaiah conflates these two phases, John distinguishes them.[129] It is possible, then, that the resurrection in Isaiah 26:19 is part of the latter phase, when death has been defeated, what in Revelation is the second resurrection.

Daniel 12:2–3 does not necessarily undermine these points, since, though it certainly posits a posttribulational resurrection of Old Testament saints, it does not clarify the relation of that resurrection to the coming kingdom. Admittedly, the most straightforward reading of Daniel is that the resurrection occurs essentially simultaneously with

---

129. See, e.g., John N. Oswalt, *The Book of Isaiah: Chapters 40–66* (Grand Rapids: Eerdmans, 1998), 656, apparently following Franz Delitzsch, *Isaiah*, vol. 7 of Commentary on the Old Testament in Ten Volumes, ed. C. F. Keil and F. Delitzsch, trans. James Martin (Grand Rapids: Eerdmans, 1983), 492–93.

the coming of God's kingdom. This is also the most satisfying reading in terms of the hortatory value of the resurrection promise in Daniel: those faithful who suffer the tribulation will be raised to enter the ensuing kingdom. It is therefore a real problem for the pretribulation and prewrath rapture views granted only one premillennial resurrection. But if Daniel, like Isaiah, does not distinguish the two phases of the kingdom, then the relation of the resurrection to the kingdom could be blurry; the resurrection of the saints could immediately precede the latter phase of the kingdom, even though only surviving Jews enter the first phase.[130] If Daniel posits a general resurrection and glorification of all believers at the end of the tribulation, difficulties for premillennialism arise.

This makes more sense when we consider Paul's argument in 1 Corinthians 15:20–28, 50–58. As has long been pointed out, it is quite difficult to correlate Paul's argument in 1 Corinthians 15:20–28, 50–58 to the millennial reign of Christ in Revelation. Paul seems to posit a present reign of Christ that *ends* at the second coming and that immediately precedes the "spiritual" eternal state. I will not attempt to argue a premillennial reading of this passage, but assuming that such is possible,[131] it becomes clear that we cannot too quickly conclude from Paul's use of Isaiah 25:8 in 1 Corinthians 15:54 that he simply identifies the resurrection of Old Testament saints with that of the church. According to Revelation 20:14; 21:4, the final victory over death and the arrival of the eternal state occur in conjunction with the second resurrection, following the postparousia, earthly reign of Christ. This, as

---

130. Alternatively, if the Isa. 26:19 and Dan. 12:2 resurrections are construed as part of the first resurrection of Rev. 20:4, then John may have conflated the resurrection/rapture of the church with the resurrection of Israel. In favor of such a conflation is (1) that John already presents a "misplaced" first resurrection, as I argued above. This visionary resurrection occurs where it does because it fulfills the Danielic hope; that is, the first resurrection, which begins with the rapture of the church, culminates in the resurrection of the tribulation saints and is thus portrayed at the outset of the kingdom. Note that for Paul the *one* resurrection began with Christ and will culminate with the resurrection of the church (1 Cor. 15:23); (2) that John seems to get the image of two resurrections from Dan. 12:2, relying on Daniel's distinction between the "many" who awaken after the tribulation to everlasting life and others who awaken at some indeterminate time to everlasting contempt. Against such a conflation is the fact that John explicitly names only two resurrections, so that splitting the first into two phases is inherently unsatisfying.

131. See Craig Blaising, "Premillennialism," in *Three Views on the Millennium and Beyond*, ed. Darrell L. Bock (Grand Rapids: Zondervan, 1999), 203–4. It is, of course, possible that Paul knows nothing of an interregnum, something only revealed later to John.

argued earlier, is what Isaiah seems to imply. Thus Paul in 1 Corinthians 15 may be merging (whether consciously or unconsciously is moot) the two resurrections in their aspect of prosecuting the final victory over death. Isaiah 25:8 refers specifically to the second resurrection, but because the second resurrection concludes the victory over death begun in the rapture of the church (indeed, even in Christ's resurrection thousands of years before that [1 Cor. 15:23]), Paul can quote it in conjunction with the rapture.[132]

This has interesting implications for an allusion to Daniel 12:2–3 in 1 Thessalonians 4:16–17. In this passage Paul does not introduce the doctrine of the resurrection but clarifies its timing in relation to the parousia. He reassures the Thessalonians that those Christians who are alive at the parousia will not "precede" (*phthanō*, "overtake, come before, attain to") those who are dead. Rather, the dead in Christ will rise "first." This suggests that Thessalonians had construed Paul or the Old Testament to teach a general resurrection following the postparousia reign of Christ, a reign that they thus understood was only to be enjoyed by those alive at the parousia.[133] Had Paul taught them a postreign resurrection of Old Testament saints that they identified with the resurrection of the church? While the answer to that question is unknowable, it seems clear that we do not possess all of Paul's teaching on the resurrection in this passage or in 1 Corinthians 15.

It is thus far from apparent that the resurrection of the church and the resurrection of Old Testament saints ought to be equated, especially if Revelation 20 and 1 Corinthians 15 are to be read premillennially. All other indications in Revelation are of a prewrath rapture; Revelation 20:4 should be read in light of those, and neither 1 Corinthians 15:20–28, 50–58 (Isa. 25:8) nor 1 Thessalonians 4:13–18 (Dan. 12:2–3) clearly subvert that reading.

2 Thessalonians 1:6 – 10; 2:1 – 12

We can now deal briefly with Moo's contention that 2 Thessalonians 1:6–10 and 2:1–12 argue for a posttribulation rapture. While

---

132. Cf. the similar understanding of Paul in Victorinus of Pettau, *Commentary on Revelation* 20.2.

133. So P. Hoffmann, *Die Toten in Christus: Eine religionsgeschichtliche und exegetische Untersuchung zur paulinischen Eschatologie*, NTAbh 2 (Münster: Aschendorf, 1966), 232.

I agree that 2 Thessalonians 1:6–10 appears to support a posttribulation rapture simultaneous with the outpouring of God's wrath and the return of Christ to earth, two considerations call this conclusion into question. First, as I have just argued, Revelation shows that what Paul seems to present as a single event will actually occur as a complex of events. Second, Paul himself implies a complex of events in 2 Thessalonians 2, as Moo himself admits. In 2 Thessalonians 2 Paul is arguing against the Thessalonians' mistaken notion that the day of the Lord had come. Now, if Paul understood the day of the Lord to be a simple posttribulational event, one would expect him simply to argue that the day could not have come because neither the rapture, nor the wrath of God, nor the glorious appearing of Christ had happened. That he does not do so, and instead merely argues that the day could not be present because certain necessarily preceding events had not yet happened, implies that Paul did not think of the day of the Lord as a simple posttribulational event. He must have thought of it as a complex of events occurring over time. Thus 2 Thessalonians 1:6–10, which includes God's eschatological wrath, the rapture, and the glorious return of Christ, must be taken as a conflation of the parousia complex into a single depiction. While the rapture and the glorious return to earth could still be a simultaneous event within the complex, 2 Thessalonians 1:6–7 does not unambiguously demonstrate that.

Finally, Paul's argument in 2 Thessalonians 2:1–12 fits perfectly well with a prewrath rapture. If we grant the likelier positive reading of the phrase *saleuthēnai apo tou noos [kai] throeisthai* ("to be shaken from mind and aroused," 2 Thess. 2:2, literal translation), the Thessalonians are excited, because, having been led to believe that the day of the Lord had begun and knowing the rapture to be an initial day of the Lord event, they anticipate the rapture to happen shortly. Paul does not focus his attention initially on clarifying the timing of the rapture with regard to the day of the Lord since that was not the basic issue they were concerned about. Rather, he focuses on the mistaken notion that they had fixed on, that the day of the Lord had begun. But Paul does address the issue of the rapture as salvation from the effects of the day of the Lord in verses 13–14. Admittedly, he does not tie his discussion to the timing issue, but he does imply that it was part of his original teaching from which the Thessalonians had departed and which should have convinced them that the day of the Lord had not begun. In effect his argument is that the Thessalonians should not believe that the day of the Lord had begun and that the rapture was right around the corner, because the day would not begin until after the revelation of the Man of Lawlessness, and the first event of the day would be the rapture itself. Second Thessalonians, then, gives no essential advantage to a post-tribulation rapture view.

Conclusion

The primary question that distinguishes Dr. Moo's understanding of the timing of the rapture and my own is whether the parousia is a simple, posttribulational event or a complex of events that begins with the rapture and includes a significant period of divine wrath preceding the return of Christ to earth. My response to Moo's case for the former has attempted to show that none of Moo's arguments are decisive, that some of his evidence can be better understood from a prewrath perspective, and that evidence he fails to consider argues forcefully for such a perspective. So, though Dr. Moo has presented a well-articulated argument for the posttribulation rapture, in the end, I do not think he has made his case.

DOUGLAS MOO

I express appreciation again for the opportunity to engage in dialogue with two such fair and careful scholars as Drs. Hultberg and Blaising. I have learned a lot from their essays and responses. I am especially reminded of just why so many fine Christians for so many years have come to different positions on the matter of the temporal relationships among rapture, final tribulation, and wrath—the evidence is simply not clear-cut. Both Blaising and Hultberg, like gifted surgeons of logic and argument, cut right to the heart of many of my treasured arguments and exegeses. "Almost they persuadest me!"—but not quite.

I still think that a posttribulational, postwrath rapture best satisfies the scriptural data. Nevertheless, the posttribulational view has its problems—and Blaising and Hultberg have done good service by identifying them. I encourage readers to read their arguments carefully, reread my own arguments in the main essay and responses in light of them, and then turn back to Scripture to draw your own conclusions. Many of the issues and exegetical matters that Blaising and Hultberg raise I have little more to say about: I have exhausted whatever exegetical and logical ammunition I have in what I have already written. But a few of their points require a brief final rejoinder.

As I said in my response, I hate to engage Hultberg in debate over the meaning of Revelation: he knows the book far better than I. He may well be right when he insists that Revelation teaches a consistent pattern of rapture-wrath-return. Of course, as he notes, this pattern depends on reading certain texts in Revelation chronologically. Hultberg accuses me of an "uncritical" reliance on the assumption that there is no chronological relationship within the progression of seals, trumpets, and bowls. This may be a fair criticism, although I don't think myself that I have been entirely uncritical: I do advance some arguments—however weak they may be—

that lead me not to see chronology in the visions of Revelation unless it is expressly taught. I still think, then, that Revelation 11:11–12 may describe a posttribulational *and postwrath* rapture. The "three and a half days" may have been chosen to make a point about the nature of the time period involved, but it does seem to me difficult to argue that this designation does cover the same period as that designated by the 1,260 days in 11:3.

As I think I make clear in my essay, I am very much less certain about what is going on in 14:14–16. But if the rapture of the church is included in the "reaping of the earth" in this text, I still do not see why this scene must chronologically precede the harvest judgment in verses 17–20. That such a chronological relationship is not, to say the least, clear is evident from the commentators who identify verses 14–16 and 17–20 as two parallel descriptions of *the same event*.[134] Hultberg also argues a rapture–return of Christ sequence from Revelation 17–19: the saints must be clothed in white linen (19:6–9) *before* the return in 19:11–21. I am still not convinced that such a chronological relationship exists. But if it does, the question remains how much time must intervene between the two events. In arguing that the rapture takes place "at the time of" the posttribulational return of Christ, I do not mean to imply that these events must be simultaneous. A rapture of the saints as Christ begins to descend — an event pictured in various ways, including the reward scene of 19:6–9 — and the consequent accompaniment of the saints as Christ descends to earth fits well into the scenario that I see.

My disagreement with Hultberg, then, focuses mainly on the question of chronology in Revelation. He sees a sequence of rapture-wrath-return and insists that the wrath must extend over a period of time. The rapture cannot, then, occur "at the time of" the return. I am not as convinced as Hultberg that Revelation teaches such a sequence. And it does seem to me that an argument based on the very greatly debated chronological relationship of various visionary reports in Revelation is not the strongest foundation on which to build a view of eschatology.

Blaising's response restates many of the points he makes in his primary essay, to which I respond above. So I will content myself with a few clarifications and observations. Blaising suggests that I pay insuf-

---

134. E.g., G. K. Beale, *The Book of Revelation: A Commentary on the Greek Text*, NIGTC (Grand Rapids: Eerdmans, 1999), 774.

ficient attention to the Old Testament teaching about the day of the Lord and especially to the way this general concept is developed in Daniel. He is probably right: I should have spent more time here. His claim that the "day" is presented in these texts as an extended period of time, involving both tribulation and wrath, has some merit when one looks at the Old Testament evidence. Still, I think he would agree that the New Testament data on this matter are critical: for the New Testament obviously develops Old Testament eschatological concepts in a variety of ways. Here it does not seem to me that Blaising pays enough attention to "inaugurated eschatology." The New Testament proclaims that many of the "day of the Lord" events have already come to pass in the first coming of Christ and in the subsequent life of the church. The destruction of Jerusalem in AD 70, for instance, while not exhausting the prophecies about the day of the Lord or being equivalent to the "parousia," is one part of the larger "day of the Lord" New Testament fulfillment. I repeat here again what I emphasized in my primary essay: our discussions of "eschatology" in the New Testament often get off on the wrong foot right from the start when we neglect two fundamental New Testament perspectives: (1) that the "eschatological" time, the "last days," had already begun with Christ's first coming; and (2) that Jesus and the New Testament authors did not know the time of his coming. Once these two factors are considered, many of Blaising's criticisms on this "day of the Lord" issue fall to the wayside.

However, Blaising still has a good point to make. Even with full allowance for the New Testament inaugurated eschatology perspective, the New Testament clearly and often speaks about a "day of the Lord/ Christ" to come. Must this future day of the Lord be an extended time of tribulation and wrath? Both Blaising and Hultberg insist that it is. I continue to disagree. I still think the New Testament usage of the language suggests a complex of events, including judgment on God's enemies and deliverance for God's people that will occupy a very short space of time.

I applaud Blaising's insistence that the key question must be whether the New Testament explicitly promises that the church will be "delivered from" the final period of tribulation and wrath. He is right to put the issue in these terms; and he has, in my mind, considerably strengthened the pretribulational view by jettisoning some of the more questionable dogmatic arguments used to "prove" the view in the past. Of course, we disagree about whether the New Testament promises that the church will be "delivered from" this tribulation by physical removal. He again refers to the promises in 1 Thessalonians that the church will be rescued "from the coming wrath" (1:10) and that the church is not destined to "suffer wrath" (5:9). Physical removal (1 Thess. 4:17) is the means of this rescue. Of course it is clear that believers are delivered from wrath. But I see nothing in 1 Thessalonians that suggests the wrath is a period of extended time; nor is it at all clear that rapture (1 Thess. 4:17) is the means of protection. The rapture is presented positively, as the means by which believers are joined with Christ. Nothing is said about rescue "from" something in 1 Thessalonians 4:13 – 18. And it does seem to me that the evidence of 2 Thessalonians still suggests very strongly that (1) believers are rescued at the same time as unbelievers are judged (chap. 1) and that (2) the "day of the Lord" cannot include the tribulation, because Paul claims that demonstrably tribulational events must precede the day of the Lord (chap. 2). Blaising contests the first point by suggesting that Paul is referring just to the "basis" for the believers' rest in chapter 1. But the temporal language is unambiguous:

> God is just: He will pay back trouble to those who trouble you and give relief to you who are troubled, and to us as well. This will happen *when* the Lord Jesus is revealed from heaven in blazing fire with his powerful angels. He will punish those who do not know God and do not obey the gospel of our Lord Jesus. They will be punished with everlasting destruction and shut out from the presence of the Lord and from the majesty of his power *on the day* he comes to be glorified in his holy people and to be marveled at among all those who have believed. (2 Thess. 1:6 – 10a; emphasis added)

The Thessalonian epistles, taking the whole of this "text" into account (as Blaising urges us to do) teaches a sequence of tribulation (which the Thessalonians are already suffering) — day of the Lord, the day of the Lord including judgment on unbelievers and deliverance for believers.

Another text that Blaising thinks teaches that believers will be physically rescued from the future time of tribulation/wrath is Revelation 3:10. I will not repeat here my interpretation of that text. But I would note a slight misstatement in Blaising's portrayal of my view. He claims that I view the combination *tēreō ek* (used in that text) as indicating "separation." In fact, I argue that the preposition *ek* by itself has this meaning; the combination *tēreō ek*, I argue, refers to "protection from."

Blaising faults my treatment of the Olivet Discourse for failing to see any reference to "final tribulation" here. But I think I was clear in my main essay: "the final tribulation must surely be included in this period of time [e.g., the great time of tribulation in Matt. 21]." More significantly, he seeks to blunt criticism of the pretribulational view by arguing that Jesus ultimately has in view in the discourse not the disciples of his day but a future generation of disciples. Of course, he is right to note that an immediate audience in Scripture can sometimes represent, generically, a future group of people. But this seems to be unlikely in the Olivet Discourse, since Jesus plainly warns his audience that "no one knows about that day or hour" (Matt. 24:36), with the important assumption that every generation of believers must be prepared for the events described in the discourse. Did the disciples whom Jesus addresses here at some point realize that he was not talking about them? This seems to me very unlikely.

More, of course, could be said. These debates have a way of going on ... and on ... and on. I suspect all three of us have said more than enough. I conclude with a final observation. It is a principle of logic that the "simplest" explanation of the data should be preferred (the famous "Occam's razor" principle). In this light, I note that, for Blaising's and Hultberg's views "to work," one or the other must posit two "comings," two different "three and a half" periods of time, two earthquakes at the end, two trumpet blasts, and two separate resurrections of saints at the end (Isa. 25:6–8; 66:22–24). I grant, of course, that it is necessary to posit these dual references where textual data demands it—and "simplicity" should never be preferred if it becomes "simplification." But I fear that the need to posit these dual events—especially a separate resurrection for Old Testament saints and New Testament saints—points to hypotheses that are more complicated than they need be. Posttribulationism avoids some of these complications. I would like to pretend that posttribulationism solves all our problems—textual, conceptual, theological, etc. Alas, I know that this is not the case. It has its own weaknesses. But I still think it is the best reading of the biblical data.

Whatever our view, may we join together as God's people in eager anticipation of the "blessed hope" and in devoted service to Christ, his people, and the world, as we look toward that day.

CONCLUSION

The reader has now heard all three arguments, their rebuttals, and rejoinders, and the time to take stock has come. First, we note that a key issue that distinguishes each presentation has to do with the nature of the "day of the Lord," since all presenters equate the day of the Lord with the parousia, including the rapture, and make fundamental recourse to arguments regarding the day of the Lord. More specifically, the presenters differ on their understanding of the length of the day of the Lord, the timing of its onset, and the nature of its wrath. Each presenter has marshaled several texts to make their case, many of which were appealed to by more than one presenter in quite different ways. So rather than review the use of all these texts in each author's argument here, a chart is appended to the end of this chapter that lists the major passages considered in the arguments and briefly gives each author's understanding of that passage as well as can be determined. It is hoped the reader will find this format helpful.

We conclude by noting two major and important commonalities among the three contributors to this volume. The first is the irenic spirit with which they pursued the debate. Each respected the others as scholars committed to understanding and living out God's word. It is hoped that all who read this book would engage in this debate—indeed any debate—in the same spirit. The second is that, though each is committed to their position and argue for it forcefully, they all agree that the timing of the Rapture is not absolutely clear in Scripture. They thus refuse to allow debate about the timing of the Rapture to become a wedge issue in Christian fellowship and prefer instead to focus on the undeniable fact that Jesus is coming again to consummate our salvation and that this constitutes the blessed hope of the church. This is not to say that the issue of the timing of the Rapture is irrelevant or that we should not search the Scriptures diligently to try to come to a conclusion on the issue. As we do so, however, let us recognize our common confession as Christians and discuss the future coming of our Lord and Savior as brothers and sisters in Him.

A COMPARISON OF THE AUTHORS' INTERPRETATIONS OF PASSAGES IN THE DEBATE

	BLAISING	HULTBERG	MOO
Daniel 9:25–27	The seventieth week is the future, seven-year tribulation. It is antitypical of a period called in Daniel "the time of the end," "the time of wrath," and is marked by the rise of an imperial persecutor (Antichrist) who makes a covenant with Israel, and by wars, a desolating sacrilege in the temple after three and a half years, intense persecution, and the destruction of the persecutor.	The seventieth week is the final seven years of history before the coming of Christ. The "wrath" of this period is that of the final imperial persecutor (Antichrist) and focuses on the intense persecution of the last three and a half years of the week, the period following the abomination of desolation. This period was typified by the Antiochene persecution of the Jews.	The seventieth week, including the tribulation, is probably about the inter-advent age, though there will also probably be a final Antichrist and tribulation. The time of tribulation in Daniel is the second half of the week.
Matthew 24:4–25:46	The Olivet Discourse divides into 24:4–35 and 24:36–25:46. The first part answers the "sign" question, the second part the "when" question. Verses 4–31 integrate Daniel's seventieth week structure with features of the day of the Lord as the pattern of the parousia. 24:32–35 offers a teaching point concluding the first part of the discourse. Jesus applies the typed pattern to the soon destruction of Jerusalem, but cautions that it may not be the parousia. The sign that distinguishes the pattern as the parousia is the glorious appearing of the Son of Man at its conclusion. *cont.*	The Olivet Discourse divides into 24:4–14, 15–35; and 24:36–25:46. 24:4–14 is about normal catastrophes of the church age, beginning with the destruction of Jerusalem and allied events. 24:15–31 is explicitly contrasted with 24:4–14, beginning with the significant eschatological event of the abomination of desolation (perhaps typified by the destruction of the temple by the Romans) and concluding with the parousia (day of the Lord) complex in 24:29–31. 24:36–25:46 is about watching for and living in light of the parousia of 24:30–31. "Cutting short" the tribulation (24:22) may indicate the *cont.*	The Olivet Discourse up to 24:28 is about the church age, beginning with the destruction of Jerusalem. 24:29–35 is about the parousia at the end of the age. 24:36–25:46 consists of exhortations based on the parousia of 24:30–31. The "gathering" there is not just of the church but is the regathering of Israel as well (to be resurrected and raptured with the church). The disciples represent all Christians. Matt. 24:40–41 may refer to the rapture.

	BLAISING	HULTBERG	MOO
Matthew 24:4 – 25:46 cont.	Parousia in 24:27 has a narrow reference to Jesus' glorious appearing at the end of the day of the Lord. In 24:36 it refers more broadly to the whole day of his coming. 24:31 is the regathering of Israel. The disciples represent all believers (the church), pre- and post-rapture.	24:29 – 31. 24:36 – 25:46 is about watching for and living in light of the parousia of 24:30 – 31. "Cutting short" the tribulation (24:22) may indicate the church's rescue from the midst of the tribulation by rapture. Disciples represent all Christians, including the first and final generations.	
John 14:1 – 4	Jesus will come again and rapture his saints to be with him. The parallels with 1 Thess. 4:17 favor pretribulationism.		Jesus raptures his saints at his parousia; no indication of timing.
1 Corinthians 15:20 – 28, 50 – 58	"Last" trumpet means merely the eschatological trumpet of the day of the Lord. Both the rapture descent (1 Thess. 4:16) and the regal descent (Matt. 24:31) are signaled by a trumpet but are distinct. 1 Cor. 15 parallels 1 Thess. 4:16 with resurrection, so is pretribulational. No allusion to Dan. 12:1 or Matt. 24:30 – 31.	"Last" trumpet means merely the eschatological trumpet of the day of the Lord. The relationship of the rapture to the resurrection of OT saints is not clear here. Isa. 25:8 seems concurrent with the "second" resurrection of Rev. 20:11 – 15. Paul probably doesn't distinguish the two resurrections.	"Last trumpet" (Isa. 27:12 – 13) and quote from Isa. 25:8 probably indicate resurrection of OT saints is concurrent with the rapture. Allusions to Dan. 12:1 and Matt. 24:31 make this posttribulational.
1 Thessalonians 1:10	Rapture rescues the church from God's parousia wrath mentioned in 1 Thess. 5.	Rapture rescues the church from God's parousia wrath mentioned in 1 Thess. 5.	Jesus rescues the church from God's final judgment; says nothing about the rapture.

	BLAISING	HULTBERG	MOO
1 Thessalonians 4:13–18	The Thessalonians were concerned about those who die before the parousia. Paul assures them that when the Lord comes, their dead will be raised and raptured together with living believers. Though the idea of a meeting is inherent, the language focuses more on a rescue. The timing of the rapture must be determined from the relationship of 1 Thess. 4:13–18 to 5:1–11. Differences in textual features preclude a clear parallel with Matt. 24:31.	Relies on the Olivet Discourse tradition and places the rapture at Matt. 24:31. A "delegation meeting" may be implied, but it says nothing about timing. The word of the Lord may be a post-Easter prophetic utterance teaching the rapture in conjunction with the Olivet Discourse tradition. The Thessalonians had been led to believe, perhaps by the OT, that the dead would be resurrected after the earthly reign of Christ. Paul clarifies that they would be raised at the parousia.	Thessalonians worried their dead would not be taken to be with Jesus at the parousia, not whether believers would undergo tribulation. Paul assures them that their dead would participate in the benefits of the parousia. Parallels with Olivet Discourse and Dan. 12:1–2 make this Posttribulational. A "delegation meeting" is probably implied and suggests a return to earth, not to heaven.
1 Thessalonians 5:1–11	With respect to the timing of the rapture, Paul alludes to Jesus' teaching in the second part of the Olivet Discourse (Matt. 24:36–25:46), which speaks to the coming of the entire event complex outlined in the first part (24:4–35). That event complex is the day of the Lord structured with the pattern of Daniel's seventieth week. 1 Thess. 5:1–11 speaks of believers in relation to the day of the Lord as understood in the Olivet Discourse. The day of the Lord will come suddenly during a time of calm, bringing destruction on unbelievers and rescue from destruction for believers (v. 9). A comparison *cont.*	Continues to rely on Olivet Discourse tradition underlying 4:13–18. Paul is discussing the timing of rapture/parousia. He refers to the parousia as the day of the Lord and notes that it will overtake believers with salvation and unbelievers with wrath. Unbelievers will be caught unawares, but not believers. The salvation of believers in the day of the Lord will be the rapture. "Peace and safety" alludes to Jer. 6:14 and refers to unbelievers' inability or refusal to recognize impending doom. Paul moves from salvation from parousia wrath in 5:1–9 to salvation more globally considered in 5:10.	Continues to rely on Olivet Discourse tradition underlying 4:13–18. 1 Thess. 4 gives comfort about dead believers; 1 Thess. 5 exhorts living believers. The day of the Lord is the parousia (and is probably preceded by the tribulation). Both believers and unbelievers experience the day of the Lord; the one expectedly and benignly, the other unexpectedly and destructively. Believers are to guard themselves against the day by living holy lives. The switching between pronouns in 5:9–10 indicates the salvation from wrath experienced by living believers is from God's final judgment, not parousia wrath. "Peace and safety" refers to *cont.*

	BLAISING	HULTBERG	MOO
1 Thessalonians 5:1 – 11 cont.	of 5:9 – 11 with 4:14 – 17 shows the rescue to be the rapture. Since the rapture occurs at the onset of the day of the Lord, and the day of the Lord refers to the entire tribulation, the rapture is pretribulational. 1 Thess. 5:1 – 5 and exhortations to watch link to Matt. 24:36 – 25:13. Destruction of unbelievers points to the tribulation, and allusion to Jer. 6:14 makes this an extended event. Paul exhorts believers to live in light of their salvation, not to avoid wrath.		Jer. 6:14 and indicates finding false security in the face of imminent judgment.
2 Thessalonians 1:5 – 10	All believers past, present, and future receive "rest" and vindication when Jesus brings final judgment upon their persecutors. This text gives no indication of the timing of the rapture.	Paul conflates the extended parousia of rapture and wrath into a single event. Believers are raptured when Jesus comes to pour out his judgment on their persecutors.	Rapture and wrath constitute a single, posttribulational event.
2 Thessalonians 2:1 – 15	Paul argues against rumors that the day of the Lord had arrived (without the rapture). The ellipsis in 2:3 – 4 should be "the day of the Lord would not be here, would not have come, unless" the "apostasy" and the "revelation" of the Man of Lawlessness (his appearance as an imperial figure) had occurred "first" (as beginning features of the day of the Lord). The session in the temple of the Man of Lawlessness *cont*	Paul argues against undue enthusiasm that the rapture is soon to occur. The Thessalonians have been misled to believe that the day of the Lord had begun and are thus expecting the rapture as an initial day of the Lord event. Paul disabuses them of the notion by noting that the Day cannot come until after the apostasy and the Antichrist's revelation (which is the abomination of desolation). The ellipsis should be "the day of the *cont*	Paul argues against undue enthusiasm that the rapture is soon to occur. The Thessalonians had been led to believe that their suffering indicated the complex of events culminating in the parousia (the day of the Lord) had begun. Paul disabuses them of the notion by noting that the Day cannot come until after the apostasy and the Antichrist's blasphemy. The ellipsis should be "the day of the Lord will not *cont*

	BLAISING	HULTBERG	MOO
2 Thessalonians 2:1–15 cont	is the culmination of his blasphemous claims. 2:13–17 deals with the rapture and refers explicitly to 1 Thess. 4:13–17; 5:9. "Appearance of his coming" specifies a particular event (the glorious appearing) at the end of the complex parousia.	Lord will not come." Paul establishes a sequence: "first" comes the apostasy and the revelation of the Man of Lawlessness; then the day of the Lord begins sometime later. In 2:13–17, Paul reminds the Thessalonians that he had in fact taught them in his earlier letter that the day would begin with the rapture.	come." Paul establishes a sequence: "first" comes the apostasy and the revelation of the man of lawlessness; the day of the Lord begins after this.
Revelation 3:3, 10	The "hour of trial" is the seven-year tribulation/day of the Lord. "Keep you from" the hour of trial means "keep you away from," not "keep you through."	The "hour of trial" is probably the tribulation that begins after the abomination of desolation, the pressure to worship the Beast. The protection of the church is spiritual, not physical.	Rev. 3:3 parallels 1 Thess. 5:4–6 and Matt. 24:42–44 and refers to the return of Christ in glory. Rev. 3:10 suggests spiritual protection during the final tribulation.
Rev. 6:1–17	Seals 1–6 are based on the Olivet Discourse and also integrate the day of the Lord and Daniel's "time of the end." The day of the Lord/day of God's wrath begins with the first seal. "Has come" in Rev. 6:17 has summative force for the entire series of seals, answering the calls to "come" beginning with the first seal.	Seals 1–6 are based on the Olivet Discourse. Seals 1–5 are the normal catastrophes of Matt. 24:4–14. The day of the Lord/day of God's wrath is portended in seal 6 (Matt. 24:29). "Has come" means "has now arrived." The earthquake of the sixth seal is probably that of 11:13 and certainly not that of the seventh seal, trumpet, and bowl. The wrath of the day of the Lord is summarized in seal 7 and portrayed in the seven trumpets. Though the trumpets are not necessarily sequential, they require time to have their effect and certainly precede the theophany of 8:5; 11:15–19.	The sixth seal is the parousia and bears no particular chronological relationship to scenes of Rev. 7 and the seven trumpets. The earthquake of the sixth seal is identical to that of the seventh seal, seventh trumpet, seventh bowl, and 11:13.

	BLAISING	HULTBERG	MOO
Rev. 7:1–17	Distinctive features of the rapture are not present in Revelation 7. The vision of the 144,000 refers to a remnant of Jewish believers during the tribulation. The vision of the innumerable multitude may refer to eternal blessing in the new earth rather than temporary blessing in heaven during the tribulation. The innumerable multitude are the martyred tribulation saints.	Forms not just a narrative interlude but a step in the action from the call for vengeance in seal 5 to the outpouring of wrath in seal 7 and the seven trumpets. Portrays the protection of God's people from the impending judgment: the Jewish remnant (144,000) by "sealing" and the church (innumerable multitude) by rapture. The church has been raptured out of the tribulation.	The 144,000 probably indicates the church sealed to go through God's wrath before the end of the age, while the innumerable multitude is the church raptured at the end of the tribulation. "The great tribulation" is the whole church age. John does not make the chronological relationships clear. The trumpet sequence is not clearly God's wrath.
Revelation 11:11–13	There is no clear reference to the rapture in this passage.	Not clear whether the two witnesses are symbolic of the church or are two eschatological individuals. If not the church, their "rapture" may still be concurrent with the rapture of the church. The 42-month prophetic ministry is the first half of Daniel's seventieth week. The three and a half days are a relatively shorter period after the beginning of the second half. The great earthquake is probably that of the sixth seal, which precedes that of the seventh seal, trumpet, and bowl.	The witnesses may be symbolic of the church and their "rapture" of the rapture. The 42-month prophetic ministry may be the first half of Daniel's seventieth week, while the three and a half days may be the second half. The great earthquake accompanying the "rapture" is indicative of the arrival of God's kingdom and identical with that of the sixth seal, seventh trumpet, and seventh bowl.
Revelation 13	The final tribulation prosecuted by the Antichrist.	The war of the Beast against the saints refers both to first-century Roman persecution and the eschatological tribulation under the Antichrist. It indicates that the church will experience the tribulation.	Suffering of the church age, including the final tribulation.

	BLAISING	HULTBERG	MOO
Revelation 14:14–20 (15:1–16:21)	Distinctive features of the rapture are not present in this passage. Harvest by the one like a son of man is more likely a reference to judgment. The one like a son of man is not an obvious reference to Christ.	Shows the same sequence as 6:12–8:5 (11:19) of rapture-wrath-return. Rev. 14:6–12 announces impending parousia wrath, 14:14–16 (= 15:2–4) portrays the rapture, and 14:17–20 (= 16:1–21) is the outpouring of wrath. (The seventh seal, trumpet, and bowl all bring the reader to the glorious appearing, though the seventh seal encompasses the seven trumpets, and the seventh trumpet the seven bowls.)	Rev. 14:1–5 is parousia. 14–16 is a possible reference to the rapture but not chronological. 14:17–20 is the final judgment. The bowl judgments are the culmination of God's judgments in history.
Revelation 17:14, 19:11–14	The rapture is not in view in these passages.	Jesus will come with his raptured saints to defeat the Beast at his glorious appearing. Rev. 14:14–20; 17:14; 19:7–9, 11–21 indicate a sequence of rapture-wrath-return.	May refer to angels accompanying Christ at his second advent. The bride is the church, but the scene is not chronological. All of 17:1–19:10 and 19:11–20:6 are recapitulated images of parousia and associated events.
Revelation 20:4–6	Key features of the rapture are not present here. This resurrection is only temporarily "first" in relation to a second resurrection at the end of the millennium; it is not absolutely first, since John acknowledges that Christs's resurrection precedes it (1:18; 2:28). It is the resurrection of believers martyred during the tribulation. It is also first in quality in that it does not lead to the second death.	Either the resurrection of tribulation saints or, better, resurrection of all saints "misplaced" for thematic reasons (to tie the resurrection to the reign of Christ).	The resurrection of all saints is concurrent with the rapture. Though in the visionary sequence it occurs following the return of Christ, the visionary sequence is not chronological.

ABOUT THE AUTHORS

Craig Blaising (ThD, Dallas Theological Seminary, and PhD, University of Aberdeen) is executive vice president and provost and professor of theology at Southwestern Baptist Theological Seminary. He is a past president of the Evangelical Theological Society and also holds memberships in the Society of Biblical Literature and the International Association of Patristics Studies. He writes in the areas of patristics, biblical theology, and eschatology.

Alan Hultberg (PhD, Trinity Evangelical Divinity School) is associate professor of Bible Exposition and New Testament at Talbot School of Theology. His specialization is in the area of eschatology as it relates to the Old and New Testaments. In addition, Dr. Hultberg holds academic memberships in the Society of Biblical Literature, Institute for Biblical Research, and the Evangelical Theological Society.

Douglas Moo (PhD, University of St. Andrews) is the Blanchard Professor of New Testament at Wheaton College. His work centers on understanding the text of the New Testament and its application today. He has written extensively in several commentary series, including the NIV Application Commentary, Pillar Commentary, Tyndale New Testament Commentary, and the New International Commentary on the New Testament.

SCRIPTURE INDEX

SUBJECT INDEX

Abomination of desolation, 13, 19, 21, 22, 38, 43, 55, 66, 77, 79, 80, 82, 84, 88, 99, 110, 111–12, 124, 125, 127, 128, 156, 161, 162, 178, 180, 181, 213, 214, 216, 279, 280; preceding rapture, 160; and rapture, 117–28

Agraphon, 117

Amillennialism, 12, 15, 143

Angels, 196, 282

Antichrist, 12–13, 18, 21, 55, 60, 66, 77, 79, 93, 103, 124, 127, 140, 148, 162, 180, 181, 188, 190, 209–10, 211, 213, 218, 234, 279, 281. *See also* False christs

Antiochus, 34, 77–78, 190

Any-moment rapture, 20, 129, 238

Aorism, 61, 147, 258

Apantēsis, 143, 200

Apodosis, 122–23, 161, 209

Apokalypsis, 194, 195

Apostasia, 209

Apostasy, 55, 56, 84, 123–24, 161, 162, 181, 279, 280

Apostles, 113, 114, 115, 217–18

Archangel, 250

Asia, seven churches of, 137–38

Babylon, destruction of, 262, 263

Beast, 87, 134, 135, 139, 140, 150, 151, 176, 258, 261, 263, 281; defeat of, 174, 282; worship of, 144, 280

Believers, 91, 171, 183, 223, 279; dead, 199; living, 278; and rapture, 68, 204, 205, 206; suffering of, 187, 244; and tribulation, 192

Birth pains. *See* Labor pains

Blasphemy, 55, 279

Blessing, eternal, 281

Body of Christ, 156

Bowls, 277; and end times events, 241; judgment, 177, 193; seven, 175, 260, 282; seventh, 232, 259, 280; of wrath, 87, 135, 144, 176, 261

Christ: atoning death of, 171, 173; return of, 263, 282

Church, 173; in Asia, 137–38; disciples as representatives of, 221; and Israel, 234–35; local, 257; and rapture, 121; resurrection of, 267; and the seventieth week, 110; suffering of, 281

Church age, 216, 217

Clouds, 226, 228

Community, messianic, 114–15, 134, 157, 179

Cosmic disturbances, 45, 136, 146, 152, 215, 227, 259, 280

Day of the Lord, 22, 29–32, 43, 44, 46–49, 52, 61, 74, 79, 88, 90, 91, 118–19, 120, 121, 122, 125–26, 142, 143, 152, 155, 158, 161–62, 163, 164, 165, 166, 167, 170, 175, 180–81, 189, 198, 201–6, 208, 227, 245, 246–48, 252, 268–69, 272, 275, 277, 278, 279; biblical evidence for, 246; as extended coming of Christ, 82–83; in the New Testament, 203, 246; and Old Testament, 202; and Olivet Discourse, 53, 60, 81–82, 83–84, 95–99; onset of, 156; and parousia,

NAME INDEX

Share Your Thoughts

With the Author: Your comments will be forwarded to the author when you send them to *zauthor@zondervan.com*.

With Zondervan: Submit your review of this book by writing to *zreview@zondervan.com*.

Free Online Resources at
www.zondervan.com

Zondervan AuthorTracker: Be notified whenever your favorite authors publish new books, go on tour, or post an update about what's happening in their lives at www.zondervan.com/authortracker.

Daily Bible Verses and Devotions: Enrich your life with daily Bible verses or devotions that help you start every morning focused on God. Visit www.zondervan.com/newsletters.

Free Email Publications: Sign up for newsletters on Christian living, academic resources, church ministry, fiction, children's resources, and more. Visit www.zondervan.com/newsletters.

Zondervan Bible Search: Find and compare Bible passages in a variety of translations at www.zondervanbiblesearch.com.

Other Benefits: Register yourself to receive online benefits like coupons and special offers, or to participate in research.